FOODS OF THE SUN

By the same author

CREATIVE FOOD PROCESSOR RECIPES
CUISINE OF THE AMERICAN SOUTHWEST
CREATIVE MEXICAN COOKING

FOODS OF THE SUN
NEW SOUTHWEST CUISINE

ANNE LINDSAY GREER

Illustrations by Wendy Wray

HARPER & ROW, PUBLISHERS, New York
Cambridge, Philadelphia, San Francisco, Washington
London, Mexico City, São Paulo, Singapore, Sydney

FIRST EDITION

Copy editor: Susan Derecskey
Designer: C. Linda Dingler
Index by Maro Riofrancos

Library of Congress Cataloging-in-Publication Data

Greer, Anne Lindsay.
  Foods of the sun.

  Includes index.
  1. Cookery, American.   I. Title.
TX715.G8164   1988   641.5   86-46068
ISBN 0-06-181321-4

88   89   90   91   92   MPC   10   9   8   7   6   5   4   3   2   1

To my courageous son Will and my enthusiastic son Don,
to my mother and the memory of my father
and to Kelly

CONTENTS

FOREWORD

More than any other food writer or restaurant chef, Anne Lindsay Greer can be credited with the popularity of New Southwest cooking today. It was Greer who served as the catalytic force in her adopted city of Dallas to bring national attention to this cooking movement, and such chefs as Stephan Pyles at the Routh Street Café and Dean Fearing at the Mansion on Turtle Creek drew strength from her national reputation and the credibility she imparted to all of their innovations. Greer's generous and giving personality, coupled with her creativity, turned a group of chefs sharing an interest in similar ingredients into a culinary movement, and soon Houston-based chefs Robert Del Grande and Amy Ferguson were included in the synergistic discussions.

While interviewing Greer in order to include her in *Cooking with the New American Chefs,* I was fortunate enough to be the visiting guest at the first dinner the members of this group cooked together in 1983 to share ideas on the offshoot of New American Cuisine they were forging in Texas. I still recall the crunchy salad of jícama and apples in a cilantro vinaigrette, tamales filled with shrimp mousse, and foie gras with fried cayenne pasta.

Greer explained to me that the seeds of this new style of cooking are found in *Cuisine of the American Southwest.* It was in that Tastemaker Award–winning work that she published her first recipe for cilantro pesto, now a standard of the entire region, and jalapeño pasta. However, such new dishes were few, and their presence was eclipsed by the traditional nature of the work.

I find *Foods of the Sun* to be as important to New Southwest cooking as her previous work was to documenting the classical base on which she and her contemporaries are improvising. However, unlike the chefs with whom she is associated, Greer is also a writer and teacher, and these facets of her career have led to the creation of a book of solid technique that readers can apply to many recipes.

The innovative recipes contained in this volume fall into two distinct schools: those which utilize the traditional forms of Southwestern cooking but use a far wider range of ingredients, and those which utilize the native foods of the region to form dishes more akin to classic European cookery. In the first camp are such stellar recipes as quesadillas filled with brie and mango, tamales made with shrimp, and chilies stuffed with a spicy duck hash in lieu of the traditional picadillo. Examples of the second approach are soufflés with green and red bell pepper, a grits soufflé with ham and shrimp, and entree salads.

Greer's first artistic endeavors were with paints rather than pots and pans, and her artist's eye is evident in the use of pleasing colors as well as textures in her dishes, especially the relishes that elevate simple grilled entrees to elegance. The same care is given to the exciting chapters on side dishes. There could be no more inviting way to fill a bread basket than peppered popovers or pecan muffins.

Because of both personal interest and professional obligations, I spent the fall of 1986 trekking the Southwest. In the three years since that first dinner in Greer's kitchen, the new Southwest cuisine movement has spread like a fire of aged mesquite. And now, through *Foods of the Sun,* home cooks in all regions can experience the vibrancy of this exciting food as taught by its master.

ELLEN BROWN
Washington, D.C.

ACKNOWLEDGMENTS

Many friends, both personal and professional, have helped to make this book one that is useful for both chefs and amateur cooks. The integration of Southwest ingredients and customs, whether in a creative interpretation of a taco or a butter sauce seasoned with chilies, has been close to my culinary heart since my college days in Arizona. The evolving concept of "foods of the sun" presented in this book has been supported and influenced by many.

I would like to thank my friends who are talented chefs in Texas, Stephan Pyles, Dean Fearing, Robert Del Grande, and Amy Ferguson, for their contributions to this work, as well as other chefs who share an appreciation of the ingredients: John Sedlar, Mark Miller, Brendan Walsh, Michael McCarty, Jimmy Schmidt, Bradley Ogden, Jeremiah Tower, Bruce Auden, Steve Singer, Richard Chamberlain and John Macon Brown.

I would also like to express my appreciation to enthusiastic friends Sherry Ferguson and Camille Warmington, who tested recipes and contributed ideas for the home cook; to those in food and wine who provide the ingredients: Frieda Kaplan of Frieda's Finest, JoAnn and Ben Martinez of Herb Valley, Mike Hughes of Texas Wild Game Cooperative, Susan and Ed Auler of Fall Creek Vineyards and Tor Kenward of Beringer Vineyards for the wine selections; to my editors, Susan Derecskey and Pat Brown; to Joseph Montebello for his expert sense of design; to my illustrator, Wendy Wray, and to all my friends at Harper & Row for their dedication and support of this project.

Finally, my sincere thanks go to those personal and professional friends who have given so much: Martha Casselman, Ann Bramson, Ellen Brown, Harvey Steinman, Diane Teitelbaum, Michael Bauer, John Thacker, Randy Gantenbien, Dotty Griffith, Erica Sanchez, Candy Sagon, Liz Logan, Jinx and Jeff Morgan, Karen MacNeil, Cynthia Jubera, John Mariani, Marian Burros, Babs Harrison, Jan Wiemer, Diane Worthington, Ann Criswell, Jim Nassikas, Marion Cunningham, Mary Ann Zimmerman and Kitty Crider, as well as to Billie Bledsoe, Anthony Dias Blue, Ann Clark, Betty Cook, Bert Greene, Karen Harem, Steven Poses and Carl Sontheimer.

INTRODUCTION

Cleverness comes and goes, off-beat food combinations attract temporary attention, but the best food is often the simplest, when the old and new come together harmoniously to reflect the cultural traditions of a region in an appealing, new style. That is what I have attempted to present in this book: the techniques, ingredients, and personal interpretations of a new and important style of American cooking.

For years American food has been taken for granted. While it was the soul of regional America, the important (and expensive) food that required a jacket and tie and a vintage bottle of wine was either French or Continental. The French taught us to take food seriously and to pay attention to techniques and presentation, but American cuisine today is far more than simply French technique applied to the culinary traditions of America. Those traditions are based on an abundant food supply and varied cultural influences; put together they create a vibrant, fresh, healthy cuisine that is uniquely American.

Memories of family holiday dinners when food was prepared from scratch and apple pie cooled on the windowsill can be romanticized, but remembering those home-cooked foods our mothers and grandmothers cooked and indulging our new curiosity about regional food have resulted in a real movement to codify American cuisine.

Americans today have a new appreciation for food in a cultural sense. They think about good food; they are adventurous enough to support hundreds of new restaurants where chefs express their individual philosophy in new, creative dishes. Actually, in many parts of the country that appreciation began with restaurant chefs themselves who sought out high-quality products and new ingredients which in turn created a market for such foods as radicchio, yellow bell peppers and wild mushrooms. Many young American chefs (often trained in Europe) have made sophisticated food more accessible to the average cook than ever before. A young, urban, sophisticated population with an adventure-some palate has supported these chefs, and newspapers and magazines have brought their food into the average home.

In the south, especially Louisiana, as well as the Southwest and parts of the West, the reverse is true: home cooking has influenced restaurant chefs. They may employ enlightened cooking techniques and be motivated by a determination to reinvent familiar foods in contemporary terms, but their food has deep regional roots and is prepared with an understanding of the ingredients and the simple integrity of home cooking.

Many of the foods from the Southwest have evolved into culinary clichés (chicken-fried steak, tacos, chili) that bear little resemblance to the original, authentic dishes upon which they are based. The Southwest has the oldest indigenous cuisine in this country, beginning in New Mexico with native Indians and the Spanish conquerors. Isolated areas have many ingredients and some dishes in common but wide environmental and cultural diversity results in dishes that embrace many contradictions.

The culinary influences from Mexico or so-called Tex-Mex cooking—the popular adaptation of Mexican food to the American border palate—are only a small part of the picture. In Texas, the Confederacy and ante-bellum South, Central Europeans, Louisianans, chuck-wagon cooks and conservative midwesterners have had an equal voice. So we have East Texas gumbo and Cajun dishes, cobblers and biscuits, hill-country barbecue, venison sausage and German beer. Many of the early settlers lived on wild game, native plants, and fresh fish from inland rivers and the Gulf coast. The Rio Grande valley had a wealth of fruits and vegetables. Other more isolated areas had a sparse diet, primarily of beans, corn and wild greens. Red and green chilies brought flavor to a bland diet. The Spanish enriched native food with nuts, fruits and dairy products to create a new range of earthy, intense and sometimes exotic flavors and textures. Thus a style of cooking evolved that is simple and approachable, reflecting the wide open spaces and lively colors of the Southwest and the desert. The ingredients—tomatillos, chilies, cilantro, Mexican mint marigold and epazote—vary in acid and heat intensity and have distinctive characteristics. They rely on a delicate balance to maintain crisp, clean flavors that is often baffling to those outside the region.

If the cultural diversity in cooking styles, techniques and variety of ingredients sounds complicated, putting it together on your own is not, I can assure you. You will find in the pages that follow specific information on unfamiliar ingredients, how they interact with each other or with other ingredients as well as details on traditional techniques—especially grilling—which are important to preparing food true to the region. American cuisine is still in its infancy, drawing from a wealth of ingredients and cultures. I have enjoyed and learned a lot about the foods of the West and Southwest over the past twenty years. I hope you will share that pleasure in these recipes and menus and perhaps be inspired to create some of your own.

—ALG

"We're American with a melting pot of cultures behind us and we don't have to do things the classic way. . . . Consult your own taste and style and feel free to experiment. American cooking, after all, is built on variations of old recipes from around the world."

—James Beard

INGREDIENTS

"Let the quality of your ingredients speak . . . taste every time you cook."
—James Beard

Chilies

If there is any one ingredient associated with the regional food of the Southwest, it is the chili. There are many varieties, ranging from mild to incendiary. They come in many different sizes and shapes and colors, ranging from palest yellow through every shade of green to deepest red. The chilies used in recipes in this book, whether fresh or dried, are easily found in full-service markets. Both the large cooking chilies, the poblano and Anaheim, and the smaller garnish or relish chilies, the serrano and the jalapeño, are widely, almost universally, available.

When buying fresh chilies, pick the firm-fleshed ones with bright, smooth skins and no bruises or dark areas. Dried chilies should have unbroken skins, be free from mold, dust and pests. The skin should be somewhat soft to the touch rather than dry and brittle. Store fresh chilies wrapped in paper towels. They do not keep more than several days and are very susceptible to rot in a damp environment. Dry chilies should be kept refrigerated in heavy-duty plastic bags; they will keep for up to 6 months.

It is not the purpose here to identify all possible chilies. If you want to know everything there is to know about chilies, there are some excellent books on the subject, particularly Jean Andrews' volume *Peppers: The Domesticated Capsicum* (University of Texas Press). The fresh and dried chilies discussed are those commonly used and generally available. Happily, some of the more unusual chilies are becoming easier to get, both in the stores and by mail order.

Confusion seems inevitable with chilies, as the vast numbers of varieties are compounded by different names for the same chilies and the same name for different chilies. Like *banditos,* they change their name when they cross state lines, and even your grocer may not know which is which. To be sure, take a picture or drawing with you when shopping.

Hot chilies fit into contemporary food trends and the ongoing love affair with intense flavors and highly spiced foods. Mild chilies can give rich, wonderful flavors once you know how and what chilies to use.

All chilies are high in vitamins A and C, and lose very few nutrients when frozen. Once roasted, they freeze quite well for 6 to 9 months. The benefits of chilies have been said to include everything from improving your romantic capabilities to curing the common cold. There is some evidence that chilies do promote gastric secretions so there may be some truth to the notion that they aid digestion. But whether or not you subscribe to romance or folklore, once you have used chilies it is more than likely they will earn a permanent place in your kitchen.

One of the simplest ways to use chilies and bell peppers is to cut them into strips. Wide strips are decorative and can serve as an accompaniment; narrow strips can be put in salads, *quesadillas,* egg dishes and casseroles. They can be cooked with onions, cream and cheese to make a creamy concoction to serve with French bread or warm tortillas. Roasted peppers, chilled for 4 to 6 hours before using, add bright color to sauces and soups. Chilies are easy to fit into the menu: they have an affinity for corn, cilantro, tomatillos, tomatoes, garlic and onion, and citrus fruit and berries. They work well with basil and mint. They are good with dairy products, shellfish and cheese, both soft and hard. And, of course, they are used to make chili pastes, powders and sauces.

Handling chilies. Small chilies like the serrano and jalapeño do not need to be roasted and peeled, though you certainly may do so if you want the roasted flavor. They do, however, need to be stemmed and usually deveined and seeded. Larger cooking chilies must be peeled and to do that, you

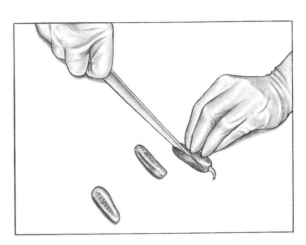

need to roast them. First some general rules for handling chilies:

- Wear rubber gloves or generously oil your hands first and wash them thoroughly afterwards as the volatile oils can burn your hands and sensitive parts of the body, like the eyes.
- Avoid wooden cutting surfaces as the oils seep into the wood and will season foods that come into contact with it later.
- Do not cut chilies under running water: the water vapor carries the burning oils and you may irritate your eyes and find yourself gasping. Snip veins with scissors (which also releases the seeds), then place in a colander and rinse quickly.
- Keep at a safe distance when blending or processing fresh chilies: the whirling blades will disperse those oils that can literally take your breath away.
- If you taste a chili relish or a chili that is too hot, take some sugar on the tongue or a drink of buttermilk or any other dairy product to help neutralize the bite. Cold water or beer just keeps the heat going.

Roasting chilies and peppers. There are several ways to roast chilies, depending on the equipment you have and the intended use for the chili or pepper. The only method I have omitted is that in which many chilies are immersed at the same time in hot oil to loosen the skins. This yields little flavor and I see no benefits. No matter which method you choose, you will have to do the following steps:

- Make a slit in all chilies prior to roasting (this is not necessary with bell peppers).
- Watch closely: it is all right if the skin gets charred or blackened but the tender flesh should never be bruised or burned.
- After roasting, put peppers or chilies in heavy-duty plastic bags, seal and place them in the freezer for up to 10 minutes. This stops the cooking process and steams the skin off. The chilies are now easy to peel and prepare. Roasted chilies should be frozen unpeeled until ready to use.
- Accumulate juices from bell peppers by peeling them (do not seed or stem) and putting them in sealed plastic bags for 4 to 6 hours, or overnight, before using. Use the juices to add wonderful

flavor to pureed peppers or in sauces and vinaigrettes that are made from or accompany the roasted peppers. Then seed and stem the peppers over a bowl to catch any additional juices. Strain to remove seeds.

To roast chilies or peppers on a **gas stove,** arrange them on the grid above a medium flame. Turn to blister and char all sides. Put in heavy-duty plastic bags and continue as in the general directions. The advantage is that flame-charred peppers have better flavor and are less likely to have burned flesh; the disadvantage, it can be messy as bell peppers exude quite a lot of juice.

To use the **electric range,** put a heatproof cake rack on top of the burners. Set the heat to medium-high. Put the peppers on the rack and turn to char on all sides. Watch the burners as they need to be hot enough to char fairly quickly but not so hot as to burn. You may need to increase and decrease the heat occasionally. Put charred peppers and chilies in plastic bags and continue as in the general directions. The advantage of this method is that it is fast; if you have several cake racks, you can manage quite a few at a time. The disadvantages are that the heat is difficult to regulate and the flesh is easily burned. Also, the bell-pepper juices can be messy.

To roast peppers in the **broiler,** place the peppers or chilies on the rack of the broiler pan. Place 4 to 6 inches from the broiling element and keep the door ajar. Turn until blistered and charred on all sides. Proceed as in the general directions. The major advantage of this method is you can do many peppers at one time quite easily. There are a couple of disadvantages: peppers can overcook and Anaheims lose their bright green color quicker. If you are planning to prepare roasted bell peppers or to stuff the chilies, choose another method. If you are pureeing them, this method is all right.

The easiest time to roast the peppers on the **grill** is after you have already used it and the fire is still hot. Otherwise, first be sure the grill surface is clean and rub it with an oil-dampened cloth. Prepare a fire and let it burn down until a white ash covers the coals. Spread out the coals, then place peppers on the grill. Turn to char all sides, without covering the grill. This takes about 15 minutes depending on the wind, fire, and kind of grill. Put in heavy-duty plastic bags and proceed with the third and fourth steps. The great advantage is that the peppers and chilies take on the smoky flavors of the grill and whatever aromatic woods you are using. This method also avoids making a mess in the kitchen.

Using a **cook's torch** is an excellent method when chilies or peppers are going to be stuffed and baked or stuffed and grilled. Spear the chili or pepper with a long-handled fork and work in the sink area. Hold the torch about ½ inch from the pepper and torch all sides. The skin will turn black and shrivel. Torch until all the skin is loosened, then place in heavy-duty plastic bags. When ready to peel, simply rinse off the skin, using a soft brush if necessary to remove it all. The great advantages of this method, though it might be uncomfortable for some, are that peppers and chilies retain their color and stay crisp; they do not get too soft when stuffed and baked or grilled. It is also easy to reach all the nooks and crannies of poblano chilies and bell peppers with the torch. On the other hand, some flavor is lost.

For a different flavor, place the chilies or peppers in the **smoker.** Smoke for 20 to 25 minutes to absorb smoke and aromatic wood flavors. Roast and peel, using your favorite method.

Descriptions of some of the more commonly found chilies, fresh, dried and ground, follow.

Fresh Anaheim

The Anaheims—and there are many, particularly in New Mexico—are sometimes called chile verde, Big Jim or simply green chili. These varieties differ somewhat in size and greatly in heat, those from New Mexico and the El Paso area being hotter. They are long, usually firm-fleshed and light green. Avoid badly twisted chilies as they are difficult to roast. Anaheims are available spring through fall, and often in the winter months as well. They should be roasted and peeled before using. Because they are large, they are particularly well suited to stuffing. (See pages 66–69 for stuffed-chili recipes.)

Canned green chilies, whole or diced, are a variety of the Anaheim, unless they are labeled jalapeño or serrano, and may be substituted for the fresh.

Fresh Poblano

The poblano, also called pasilla in California, is a dark green chili shaped like a bell pepper with collapsed sides. Twisted ones are difficult to roast and peel. The skin wrinkles as they age so look for smooth-skinned chilies when buying. Hotness varies, but all are hotter than a mild Anaheim, milder than New Mexico green chilies. Poblanos must be roasted and peeled to bring out their rich, aromatic flavor. If you find the skin has begun to wrinkle, roast but do not peel; freeze in heavy-duty plastic bags to use at a later time. Peel when ready to use.

Fresh Jalapeño

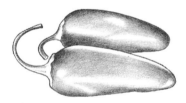

A small, fat, round-tipped chili with dark green, smooth skin, the jalapeño has become a symbol for Tex-Mex food. Dry lines or striations are supposed to be a sign of hotness, but jalapeños are all very hot. The hotness is apparent the minute the chili touches your lips. It has more of a raw taste than the serrano. It is available year round. Jalapeños must be handled with care. Cut away the stem and lay the chili on its side. Trim away a slice from one long side, avoiding veins and seeds. Turn the chili on its now flat side and repeat until all sides are removed. Discard seeds and veins. Cut off the tip and then dice. To make chilies less hot, soak in ice water for 1 hour before using.

Canned jalapeños can be substituted for the fresh. They should be rinsed before using. If pickled, they are often milder.

Use jalapeños when you want heat or their unique

flavor. They bring out great flavor in relishes, soups, stews and marinades. Used sparingly, they intensify fruit and berry flavors in ices and sorbets. They are good in jelly (see pages 249–250). Eggs and flour and salt tend to neutralize their hotness, allowing the flavor to come through.

Fresh Serrano

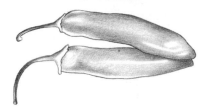

A small, thin chili, ranging in color from light to dark green, with smooth skin. Smaller than the jalapeño and just as hot, though the hotness comes through later, at the back of the throat; it is less raw than the jalapeño. Stem, seed and devein for relishes or to add spice to sauces. Cut them in half (do not stem or seed) for marinades. Small chilies must be handled with care. Cut away the stem and use a sharp knife to remove seeds and veins. To make chilies less hot, soak in ice water for 1 hour before using.

Grind serrano chilies to flavor fresh pasta or for basting pestos made with herbs. Use serranos in spicy marinades for beef, lamb, fish and poultry. They intensify the flavor of fruit and berries in chutney.

Canned substitutes are available. They are usually pickled: rinse them before using.

Dried Anaheim

The dried Anaheim has almost as many names as its fresh counterpart. It may be called New Mexico red, chile colorado, chile riestra or just red chili; all are varieties of the dried Anaheim. Color is reddish, brighter than the ancho chili and easy to distinguish because of its long pod and smooth skin. Sundried chilies have a more transparent skin and are somewhat sweeter, though many of these are from New Mexico where they are so hot, you might not notice the sweetness. Avoid split or yellowed dried chilies. Roast the dried Anaheims the same way as ancho chilies, then grind into powder or paste for sauce. Traditional red chili sauces made from Anaheim chili paste are done much the same way as ancho chili sauce, with tomatoes often added. It is customary to cook meat (usually pork) in such a sauce.

Dried Ancho

This is the dried poblano, again often called pasilla in California. Mulatto chilies look similar and are often sold as anchos (which means wide). Ancho chilies are deep red; mulattos are almost black or dark brown. The skin is wrinkled, but should not be extremely dry, bruised or dust-caked. Fresh ones have a soft, pliable feel and a deep, rich color. Anchos have an intense, smoky flavor and are medium-hot. Ancho chilies need to be toasted to bring out their flavor. Then they can be ground into powder or soaked in water and pureed.

Traditional Mexican-American sauces from ancho chilies are made by cooking the chili puree in a little oil or pork fat with garlic (and onion, if desired). Chicken or beef stock is added. The sauce is left to simmer and thicken. Sometimes tomatillos are added.

There is no substitute for pure ancho chili powder. The chilies are toasted, stemmed, seeded and deveined, then ground into a brick-red powder. Even those powders labeled ancho are often a blend of garlic, salt, cumin and other spices. Sauté unroasted or raw chili powder over medium-low heat in a small amount of oil to bring out a roasted flavor.

Ancho chili paste and powder are also used to season sauces, marinades and barbecue sauces. They can be whisked into butter sauce or cream sauce or a sauce made from natural meat juices and stock.

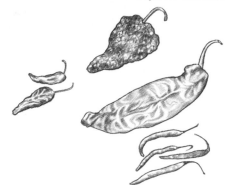

ROASTED ANCHO CHILIES

Preheat the oven to 350° F. Put the chilies on a cookie sheet and bake for 10 minutes, turning once. Remove from oven. Soak the chilies in hot water to cover for about 45 minutes to 1 hour, until the skins loosen. Pull away the skin and discard; discard the water.

For an ancho chili liquid or paste, blend the chilies in a blender, adding enough water to facilitate blending; use this to make a sauce.

Small Dried Hot Chilies

There are many small, slender, incendiary chilies, 1½ to 2 inches long, ranging in color from red to black (japonés, serrano seco, and chile de arbol), and tiny, round or pellet-shaped chilies such as chile tepin and chile pequin. They can be crushed or left whole. Store them in covered containers away from direct sunlight.

Crush chilies and use in place of chili powder. Use whole in stir-fries and marinades. Ground coarse, these little chilies can be added to relishes; ground fine, to homemade pasta along with garlic and other chili powders. Remember: they are hot!

Canned Dried Chipotle

This is the dried jalapeño, canned in an orange-red sauce that is very hot with a strong, smoky flavor. It should be ground along with the liquid for a sauce base.

Reduce the sauce by cooking slowly over medium heat and use it to make a smoky, hot homemade pasta. Add the puree to meat or cream sauces or mayonnaise. Chipotles have an affinity for eggs and lamb.

Chili Powders

All chili powders should be stored in a dark place; they will keep their flavor even longer if refrigerated or frozen. Chili powders should be toasted to enrich their flavor before using. All chili powder should have good color; if it is yellowish, it may have been ground with the seeds or be old.

True **ancho chili powder** (called pasilla on the West Coast) has a brick-red color and is not blended with other powders. Toast for 3 to 4 minutes in a 350° F. oven before using or soften over medium-hot heat in oil or butter.

There are so many chili varieties in New Mexico it is hard to tell which one you are getting. **New Mexico chili powder** is more orange than the brick-red ancho and usually much hotter. Toast before using or cook briefly in medium-hot oil or butter.

Commercial chili powder is always a mixture of several kinds of dried ground peppers (often including cayenne and paprika) and may have cumin, salt, cloves, coriander, turmeric, black pepper or garlic added. It loses character quickly. You may wish to make your own blend using paprika and other pure chili powders. Add cayenne to increase hotness if needed.

Chili powder has myriad uses. Traditionally it is used to make chile con carne and red chili sauces for enchiladas, beef and pork. It is also used to season stews, soups and chowders. It adds flavor and color to pasta. Used in small amounts, it can be added to sauces for game or vegetables, including corn. It can be sprinkled on fresh raw vegetables in combination with lime juice or stirred into vinaigrette dressings. It can be blended in dry seasoning-salt mixtures to rub on meats, poultry or fish that is to be grilled or pan-fried.

Cayenne

Cayenne pepper is made from the ground seeds and pods of dried peppers. It is very hot. Use in dry seasoning blends for grilling, to season soups, stews, sauces, pasta and breads or as an ingredient in your own chili blend.

Hungarian Paprika

This has the best flavor; other kinds are merely decorative. It comes in three strengths: sweet (mild), piquant, and hot. Use it in dry seasoning blends for grilling.

CHILI PASTE

3 to 4 cups

Making your own chili paste is quite easy and it gives you some control over the heat level. This recipe uses both mild and hot chilies; it is not so intense as one made with all small japonés chilies but it still qualifies as hot.

1 cup, tightly packed, small hot chilies (dried japonés or serranos)
¼ cup petin chilies or any small hot chili
20 dried Anaheim chilies (about 2 cups, crushed)
5 dried New Mexico chilies (about ½ cup, tightly packed)
½ cup white wine vinegar
1 teaspoon finely ground sea salt

Stem and seed the chilies, then rinse and let dry. Preheat the oven to 350° F. Place the chilies on a cookie sheet and roast for about 10 minutes. Watch closely as chilies burn easily. Remove and let stand a few minutes until crisp. Cut large chilies in 4 pieces. Put half the chilies in a blender or food processor fitted with the metal blade. Process until finely chopped. Add the vinegar, ¾ cup water and salt and process to combine. Store the chili paste in a glass container, refrigerated, for up to three months.

Herbs

Fresh herbs play an almost indispensable role in American regional cooking. Their intense, clear flavors characterize Southwest food as they enhance indigenous ingredients. Marinades, pestos and basting mops for grilled foods, as well as finishing sauces and vinaigrettes, depend upon fresh herbs for their character. Many kinds of herb leaves and flowers are used in salads; sturdier herbs with branch-like stems are often thrown on the charcoal grill to flavor the smoke. Fresh herbs are a vital ingredient in soups and sauces and in the many chutneys and relishes that enrich the cuisine of the American Southwest.

Refrigerating herbs. Freshly cut herbs, especially cilantro and basil, can be stored in the refrigerator. Place the herbs in a tall glass of cold water. Cover with a reclosable plastic bag that fits loosely without crowding the herbs. Refrigerate for 3 to 4 hours. (This helps herbs adjust to the colder temperature.) Rinse the herbs, using as little water as possible. Stem and shake to remove excess moisture. Dry thoroughly between paper towels. Discard any spoiled or bruised leaves. Line plastic bags with paper towels and pack loosely with herb leaves. Refrigerate.

Salt Storage. Some tender herbs like dill, basil, and fennel leaves can be stored between layers of table salt. They will lose their color but retain more flavor than when preserved by other methods. Wash leaves and dry thoroughly, then place between layers of salt and store, covered, in the refrigerator, for up to 2 months.

Freezing herbs. Most fresh herbs lose a lot of flavor when frozen but at the end of the season you may want to freeze some, particularly basil, cilantro, fennel, tarragon, chives or dill. Some herbs may be frozen in sprigs, others after mincing or after mincing with oil (basil and cilantro).

Drying herbs. Fresh herbs are easy to dry. Trim away any yellowed or bruised leaves and wash the stems. Tie them at the base in bunches and hang upside down in a place that is warm, dry, clean and away from direct sunlight. (If the room is dusty, punch holes in a paper bag and place the herbs in the bag.) Hang about 2 weeks, then store leaves in airtight jars. Crush before using and sauté in butter or blanch in water to release best flavor. (Another way to dry herbs at home is to spread the washed and dried leaves on a cookie sheet and place in a 200° F. oven for one hour.) Herbs that dry with especially good results are thyme, marjoram, bay leaf, sage, rosemary, savory and oregano. Drying intensifies the flavor of dominant herbs like rosemary and sage.

Storing dried herbs. All dried herbs should be stored in airtight containers away from direct sunlight, heat and air. That rules out most places in the kitchen, except drawers or special racks that are easy to see in a pantry. Use dried herbs within 6 months if possible; they may last longer but they lose their flavor.

Substituting dried herbs for fresh. While fresh herbs are always best, you may substitute dried herbs by using about 1 teaspoon dried leaf herbs for every 1 tablespoon minced fresh herbs. If the dried herb is ground, use about ½ teaspoon ground for each 1 tablespoon fresh. Since herbs vary in intensity, your palate will always be the ultimate guide in determining final amounts.

Combining herbs. It is an old theory that dominant herbs such as rosemary, marjoram, sage or thyme should not be combined with other dominant herbs. This still holds as a general principle; however, there are some cases, such as with bread stuffings or marinades, when complementary dominant herbs can be combined. Basil, mint and cilantro are all assertive but they blend very well in a vinaigrette dressing for salads, for example, or in pesto.

Using herbs. There are so many ways to use herbs that it is impossible to name them all. They can be used in flavored butters and in compound-butters to use with grilled or sautéed meat, poultry or fish. In grilling, they are used to add flavor and color to both meat and vegetables. They may be used to flavor pasta, crêpes, bread and muffins. They turn ordinary mayonnaise into something special and they can help tie a sauce to a particular dish by intensifying or softening it. Many cheeses are delicious with herbs: mozzarella with basil or mild goat cheese with thyme or chervil, for example.

A few of the herbs and spices that are used widely in Southwestern cooking are described in more detail in the pages that follow.

BASIC PESTO SAUCE

1½ cups

Pesto can be made from almost any kind of herb, not just basil; it can contain cheese or nuts or not, depending on what it is intended for. In this book, pestos made of herbs, garlic, chilies and oil are used in marinades, combined with butter and stock to brush on grilled meats, blended with cheese and toasted nuts for stuffing meat or with cheese and tomato relish for filling *quesadillas*.

2 cloves garlic, peeled
2 tablespoons lightly toasted nuts (pine nuts, almonds, pecans or walnuts)
2 cups fresh herb leaves (basil or cilantro or a combination of both)
½ cup parsley leaves
¼ to ½ cup safflower oil or virgin olive oil
½ cup grated Parmesan or Romano cheese (optional)
2 small hot chilies, ground (optional)

Put the garlic, nuts, herbs, parsley, oil and Parmesan cheese and chilies, if using, in a blender or food processor fitted with the metal blade. Process until finely minced. Store in the refrigerator for 1 week.

For *grilling,* season the meat, fish or poultry with salt and pepper, then squeeze lime juice on both sides. Thin the pesto with stock and brush it on the meat or fish or poultry during grilling to add flavor and moisture.

For a *marinade,* brush the pesto full strength on the meat, fish or poultry. Place in a shallow layer of marinade and turn several times. Do not submerge meat. Fish and poultry require only 15 to 20 minutes marination but tough cuts of meat may be marinated overnight. The drained marinade may be used for basting during cooking.

For *seasoning,* stir 3 to 4 tablespoons (or to taste) of pesto made without cheese and nuts into cheese or creamy dips or rice or risotto. Pesto can also be used to liven up bland soups, particularly those made with pinto or black beans, lentils or other legumes.

HERB VINEGARS

To prepare herb-flavored vinegar, allow 4 ounces fresh herb sprigs to 1 quart cider vinegar. Bring herbs and vinegar to a boil, then let stand, covered with cheesecloth, for at least 1 hour or up to 3 days. Strain and pour into clean bottles. Put a fresh herb sprig in each bottle. You may vary vinegars, using malt vinegar, rice wine vinegar or wine vinegar.

Fresh Coriander (Cilantro)

Fresh coriander, called cilantro in Spanish and also known as Chinese parsley, is a parsley-like plant with thin, round, lightly fringed leaves. It goes well with Mexican or Chinese food. The smell and taste are pungent. Cilantro is one of those herbs people either love or hate. Leaves should have life when you buy it: it yellows quickly, loses flavor fast. Do not remove roots if it is sold with them. Store, roots and all, wrapped in paper towels and placed in a plastic bag or in a covered jar in refrigerator. Wash when ready to use. It does not dry well but you can chop coriander, mix it with olive oil and freeze the mixture in ice-cube trays. Leave sprigs intact for garnish, otherwise mince. A brief sautéing in oil softens the flavor and helps preserve the color. The delicate individual leaves can be used whole in cheese, for garnish or to add flavor. Cilantro is used extensively in Mexican and Southwest cooking with many vegetables and fish and in relishes, sauces and pestos. Added fresh to salsas or sauces that are made with cumin, cilantro adds a touch of lightness and freshness.

Epazote

Epazote, also called Mexican tea or wormseed, is a pungent herb with pointed, serrated leaves, native to tropical America. It is definitely an acquired taste. Store dried epazote away from direct sunlight. Fresh epazote may be stored in plastic bags, refrigerated. Epazote is used in many Mexican dishes and soups and with cheese for *quesadilla* fillings. Its main use, though, is in bean soups, for it is believed to take the wind out of beans. Add it to tortilla soup for 20 minutes; remove before serving.

Mexican Mint Marigold

Known in some areas as sweet mace, Mexican mint marigold is a beautiful, fragrant plant with abundant golden-yellow blossoms. The leaves taste a bit like tarragon but with a milder anise flavor. Store Mexican mint marigold in the refrigerator in a plastic bag, being sure leaves have no moisture on them. It will keep approximately 2 weeks. The leaves can be dried and reconstituted when the fresh herb is not available. Once the leaves are completely dry, place in airtight container and store in cool dark place. Use whole leaves for garnish, otherwise mince them. Mexican mint marigold can be substituted for tarragon if used very sparingly. It works well with meat dishes that have a robust flavor. It makes an interesting pesto sauce with pecans and garlic and it can be used in butter sauces and vinaigrettes. It goes well with bell peppers, pecans, garlic, and tomatoes. Use it with lamb and together with ancho chilies.

Cumin

Cumin seeds are straw-colored with a very distinct flavor. They are essential to curry powder and com-mercial chili powder. Store seeds away from direct light. Grind fresh for best flavor. Toast ground cumin to bring out the flavor or soften it by sautéing in oil or butter before using. Use with restraint to season soups, to make your own chili powder blend or curry powder. A pinch added to a butter sauce, along with a pinch of cayenne, is good on fish or chicken. Cumin combines well with fresh mint and cilantro. Try it with cheese, creamy cole slaw or in small amounts with cucumber and onions.

Annatto Seeds (Achiote)

Annatto seeds are deep orange and prized for their color and earthy flavor. Store them in jars away from direct sunlight. The seeds are extremely hard and have to be softened before they can be ground. To do so, cover with water, bring to a boil and let simmer for 5 minutes. Soak for 2 to 4 hours or overnight. Crush the seeds roughly with a mortar and pestle, then grind in blender as fine as possible. Use the seeds to color and flavor pasta or rice. They can also be added to barbecue sauce, marinades for seafood or chicken or butter sauces. Use annatto together with garlic, ancho chilies or hot green chilies. It is good in a pesto for brushing on grilled foods.

Edible Blossoms

Some flowers are excellent for garnishing platters of appetizers like *quesadillas* or for salads. Among them are garden-grown **carnations** (special varieties), **nasturtiums, blue borage** flowers with their cucumber-like taste, **day lilies** (for garnish or to batter-fry) and **garlic or chive blossoms. Impatiens** can be used to garnish desserts. The petals of **Gerber daisies** can be used to add color to salad.

Fruits and Vegetables

The past decade has seen an explosion of exotic fruits and vegetables, many available in specialty markets and some in supermarkets. A national interest in healthy eating has caused many supermarkets to devote more space and attention to fresh produce than ever before—and that is good news for home cooks. Starting with the best ingredients is probably the most important part of cooking. The finest meal begins with high-quality ingredients, picked at their peak, stored properly, cooked to enhance their natural flavors and presented in a simple, appetizing way.

Small baby vegetables have become big news and restaurant chefs have been quick to adopt colorful arrays of miniature squash, eggplant, carrots and beets as well as boutique vegetables in designer colors. Unfortunately, these are often more trendy than practical (at outrageous prices) and too often look better than they taste. On the brighter side, the wide availability of such fruits as mangos, papayas and persimmons as well as different kinds of lettuces and other vegetables have been an inspiration for the adventurous, creative cook.

Exotic Fruits

Among the exotic fruits that are starting to appear more and more often in the marketplace are some with tart or sour characteristics that pair well with the assertive and sweet-sour flavors of Southwestern cuisine. **Lychees** have a thin pebbly shell and a smooth texture; their flavor marries well with pineapple. **White sapote** is round, about the size of an orange, with a sweet milky pulp; it ripens quickly at room temperature. **Guava,** formerly available mainly in paste or nectar form, has a seductive, penetrating aroma and tart flesh; the wood is often used for grilling because of its intense perfume. **Gooseberries,** whether red or green, are slightly sour even when ripe; they can be used with game sauces or in a port reduction. The **feijoa,** with its thick green skin and pale yellow flesh, has a powerful scent and a subtle flavor of mint and pineapple that is good in chutney, jam or fruit sauce with pineapple.

Some other fruits and vegetables that are used often in the cooking of the American Southwest are highlighted in the pages that follow. This is by no means an exhaustive list; it is rather a guide to some of their special characteristics and uses.

Carambola

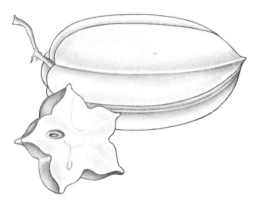

The carambola is sometimes called star fruit because when sliced it forms golden stars. There are many varieties, ranging from very tart or sour to sweet and from the size of a small plum to a large orange. The skin is thin, waxy and yellow when ripe. Refrigerate when ripe and use in 3 to 4 days. To use, trim away all dark areas; the peel is edible. The tart varieties are too sour to eat out of hand but can be used in jellies, chutneys, or as a decorative garnish for meat dishes or cheese platters. The sweet varieties are edible raw; in fact, they lose their flavor when cooked. They can be added to fruit salads and cold dishes. Combine carambola with soft sweet fruits, such as melons, peaches or persimmons for ices or in drinks.

Champagne Grapes

These are tiny sweet table grapes, not the kind used to make champagne. They are probably so named because they are so good with champagne. Add them to salads or use small bunches to garnish a butter plate, salad, entree or cheese platter.

Chayote (Mirliton)

The pear-shaped chayote ranges in color from creamy white to dark green and in length from 3 to 8 inches. It is a member of the squash family and

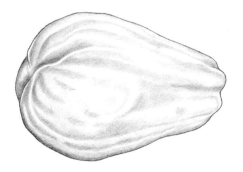

has a crisp, almost cucumber-like taste. It is available sporadically year round and can be stored, refrigerated, for up to 3 weeks.

Large chayotes need to be peeled but not small ones. Wash or peel the chayote, split and seed. The seed is considered a delicacy. Chayote can be cooked or served raw. It should be combined with flavorful ingredients, herbs and seasonings as the taste is a bit bland. Add it to vegetable soups, stir-fried vegetables or salads, combining it with other julienned vegetables (jícama, carrot, bell pepper). It is also good with seafood, spicy Creole or Mexican food.

Cherimoya

Cherimoya is a heart-shaped fruit with a thick armor-like shell and custardy soft white flesh that tastes sweet like a combination of pineapple, banana and strawberry. Store at room temperature to ripen and then refrigerate for 1 to 2 days. Cherimoya should be used as soon as possible as it deteriorates rapidly under refrigeration. To serve, cut into halves or quarters, remove seeds and eat with a spoon. Puree and strain for custards and sauces. You can add the puree to custard sauce; it is particularly good with chocolate. You can also use it in soufflés or as sauce for raspberry or chocolate soufflé. It is good combined with pineapple in a sorbet.

Citrus Fruits

All citrus fruit, whether the familiar lemon, orange, lime and grapefruit or less familiar varieties, should be moderately firm with no sign of mold or bruised, soft areas. Citrus should be stored refrigerated. For highest juice yield, bring it to room temperature; roll it back and forth before squeezing. Peel or grate the zest, if using, before extracting juice or removing sections. **Lemons** are a cook's best friend and most valuable seasoning agent. A squeeze of lemon on fresh greens, in a sauce or a soup brightens all the flavors. Use lemons with bell peppers, fruits and berries, in both sweet and savory dishes. **Limes** are available all year but their season is summer. The **Persian lime,** which is more widely marketed, is large and seedless; the **Mexican** or **Key lime** is smaller, with a light green to yellow color. Use like lemons for curd sauces, butter sauces with fish or chicken, in marinades for meat (fajitas), fish or poultry. Lime has an affinity for cilantro, other citrus and many tropical fruits like mango, papaya and melons. **Ruby red grapefruits** combine well with pomegranates or tequila and make a refreshing ice. It is not necessary to sweeten them. **Ugli fruit** is an expensive, misshapen relative of the grapefruit, sweeter and with fewer seeds. Use like grapefruit.

Tangelos can be used in butter sauces, dessert sauces or to reduce the intensity and flavor of vinaigrettes. Their flavor can be accented by serrano chilies used with discretion. They go well in garden salads with watercress, Belgian endive or radicchio and toasted nuts; use also in marmalades or with chilies in pepper jellies. **Blood oranges** have a rich red color and slightly sour flavor. Juice and use in dark meat sauces, sorbets and ices, drinks with tequila, marinades and marmalades.

Corn

Corn is a staple of Southwest cooking; it has many uses. Common varieties are white and yellow, but blue corn (Indian corn) can sometimes be had from local farmers. Rows of kernels should be even and fully developed; husks green with golden silk that is free from decay. Surprisingly perishable once picked, corn loses both sweetness and moisture rapidly. Buy from a local farmer or farmers' market and chill after purchasing. Never store at room temperature. If the corn is not used within 2 days, blanch the cob for 1 minute, then cut the kernels from the cob and store refrigerated. Do not cook corn with salt as it toughens the kernels; a pinch of sugar draws out the sweetness. Season corn with chili powder when grilling. Grilled corn may be used in corn soup. Among the infinite number of ways to use corn is succotash with lima and fava beans. It can be cooked with milk or cream with peppers or chilies; it has an affinity for bell peppers, chilies and tomatillos. Ground kernels can be mixed with cornmeal to make tamales. Whole kernels can be added to cornbread or corn muffins or used in relishes. You can even make a corn sorbet.

Dried **corn husks** from sweet or Mexican field corn are traditionally used for tamales. They are ideal for steaming and contribute a faint corn flavor. Besides tamales, they can be used for steaming vegetables, fish, fish mousse or corn pudding or to line a pie plate for tamale pie. Packages of dried husks can be found in some supermarkets and stores catering to a Latin American clientele. To prepare the husks, clean them under running water and remove all the silks. Discard any badly damaged ones. Place the rest in a large bowl of warm water and weigh down with a smaller bowl. Soak until flexible, about 2 hours. Drain and press on towels to remove excess moisture. Use imperfect husks for ties.

CORN ON THE COB

To cook corn on the cob in boiling water, bring the water to a boil, then add the husked corn, cover and return to a boil. Boil until tender, about 5–8 minutes depending on the number of ears. Drain and serve immediately.

GRILLED CORN

Soak ears for 20 to 30 minutes and grill in the husk, turning often to ensure even cooking, for 8 to 10 minutes. Or husk the corn and blanch it first; finish on the grill, basting with lime butter, for about 3 or 4 minutes.

Garlic

Garlic, the most pungent member of the onion family, is essential to Southwestern cooking. Heads should always feel firm; if the cloves seem light, the garlic may have deteriorated. Peeled whole cloves added to or steeped in vinegar, oil or sauce will give a mild flavor; minced or pressed cloves, a stronger flavor. Roasted garlic has a rich and subtle flavor; large cloves can be served with roasted or grilled meats. The longer garlic cooks, the milder it becomes. **Elephant garlic** is much larger than ordinary garlic and also much milder. It is excellent soaked in oil and charcoal-grilled or stuffed in the cavity of poultry or game birds. **Mexican red or purple garlic** has small cloves that are very pungent.

ROASTED GARLIC

Soak unpeeled garlic cloves in virgin olive oil or safflower oil for 15 minutes. Drain and bake in a preheated 350°F oven until soft, about 20 to 35 minutes. Check after 15 minutes: small cloves sometimes explode if left too long.

SAUTÉED GARLIC

Heat ½ inch oil in a sauté pan over medium-low heat. Sauté garlic cloves, turning often, until soft and golden brown. Reserve the oil for cooking purposes.

GRILLED GARLIC

Do not peel garlic but baste with oil or an herb marinade during grilling. Cloves or whole heads of garlic may be grilled this way. Shallots, unpeeled and skewered, may also be grilled; be sure to baste with oil frequently.

Jícama

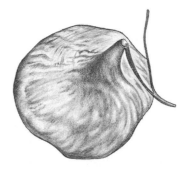

Jícama is a tuber usually twice the size of a potato or larger. Its bland taste and crisp texture are its chief merits as it tends to absorb more dominant flavors and thus blend easily with a variety of other ingredients. Choose smaller jícama as the large ones tend to be woody (like overgrown radishes). Do not wash before storing. A whole jícama will keep for several weeks in the refrigerator. Once cut, it should be wrapped in plastic wrap and used quickly. It also may be peeled, cut and kept in ice water. Jícama must be peeled deeply to remove the spotty outer coat and the fibrous inner skin as well. Add jícama to green salads for crispness or to meat salads as a foil for smoked poultry or duck. Sauté it with herbs for a quick garnish or cut in julienne strips for hash-browns. Use in relishes with fruits or vegetables.

Mango

The mango is very popular in Southwest regional cooking. It has a round to oval kidney shape and taut skin that may be green or yellow to red. Some ripe mangos are predominantly green but it is probably safer to buy reddish or yellow ones with a sweet smell. Peak season is early summer, though they often appear in the markets in the winter months as well. Ripen mangos at room temperature, then refrigerate them wrapped in plastic for 2 to 3 days. To prepare, peel, then cut away strips of flesh from around the stone. Squeeze pulp and juice from the stone if using for a sauce or puree, otherwise nibble away and consider it the cook's bonus. Mangos are excellent raw or heated with tequila or orange liqueur and served over ice cream or in crêpes. They can be combined with lime juice to make a pureed dessert sauce or sorbet spiked with a little hot serrano chili. Put them together with peaches in a cob-

bler. Combine with peaches or oranges to make marmalade or a savory chutney spiced with dried chilies. Mangos are delicious with berries. Use slices of mango with spicy sausages as an appetizer or brunch dish. Mango has an affinity for basil, especially in butter sauce or sorbet.

Wild Mushrooms

Fresh wild mushrooms have a distinct, intense flavor. They should be firm when purchased, without signs of decay or bruising; they are delicate and should be used soon after purchase. Store refrigerated, wrapped loosely in paper towels or paper bags that have holes for ventilation. Do not clean until ready to use. Then, brush loose dirt away with a soft brush and rinse briefly, if necessary, using as little water as possible. Dry immediately. Trim bruised stem ends and the spore-bearing body under the cap as it has an unpleasant texture after cooking. Wild mushrooms enhance sauces served with meat, poultry, game or wild rice. Use several varieties (including cultivated mushrooms) with sherry, cream and herbs for an appetizer. Sundried tomatoes, shallots, basil and summer savory all complement wild mushrooms.

Several varieties of wild mushrooms are available in specialty shops and supermarkets. Most common are the **Boletes** (cèpes and porcini), which are in season in the late summer and early fall; they have a reddish brown cap and a large stem. They have a very rich woodsy flavor and are also widely available dried. Use them alone or together with cultivated button mushrooms in all recipes. The **Chanterelle** is often seen from fall through winter; it is tulip shaped and yellow-orange to beige in color. Before sautéing, sprinkle with salt and put in nonstick pan over medium heat. Shake until water exudes, then sauté or braise as desired. **Horn of Plenty** mushrooms, which the French call *trompette de la mort* because of their funereal appearance, are sometimes available. They have an affinity for pecans and pomegranates. **Morels** are available in the spring; they look like little sponges and have a smoky and nutty flavor. *Do not eat raw.* **Oyster mushrooms (Pleurotte)** are very delicate with large, floppy heads and a creamy white color; they are available year round. Use in soups, stews or sauces or with pork, sausages or sweetbreads. The **Shiitake** has a large dark brown cap and a thin, tough stem that should be discarded before cooking; it is available year round. Use in sautés or combine with other mushrooms. The **Enoki,** available from early fall through spring, is long stemmed,

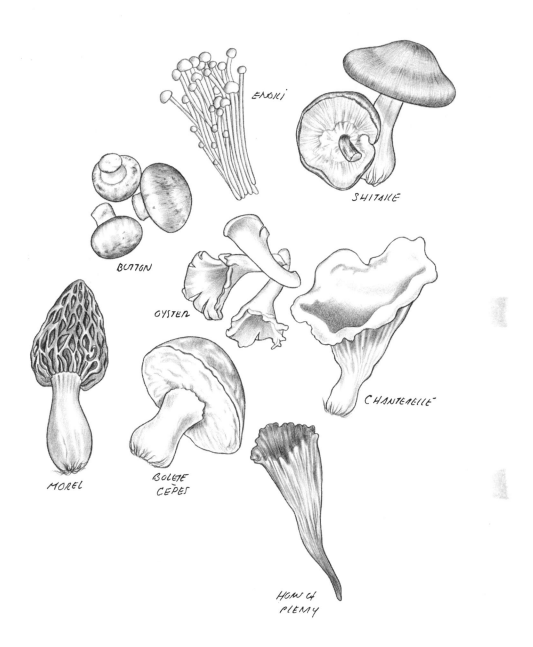

ENOKI

SHIITAKE

BUTTON

OYSTER

CHANTERELLE

MOREL

BOLETE CÈPES

HORN OF PLENTY

Oyster mushrooms (center) are surrounded by (clockwise from left) Morel, Button, Enoki, Shiitake, Chanterelle and Horn of Plenty.

thin and white with a tiny button cap. Trim ends and use raw in salads or toss into a vegetable sauté at the last minute. Enoki also makes an attractive garnish.

The popularity of wild mushrooms has encouraged a market for dried mushrooms. These can be very expensive, depending on type, but they do have a wonderful flavor when reconstituted. Soak in warm water, chicken broth or wine for about 20 minutes before using, then chop and substitute for fresh mushrooms or combine them with cultivated button mushrooms to bring more flavor to the dish. Use them to flavor sauces or grind them for making mushroom pasta.

delicious in gumbo or stewed with tomatoes, onion and garlic. It is not necessary to rinse before using. Deep-fry young pods in light batter either plain or stuffed with goat cheese and serve with a spicy tomato relish.

Nopales

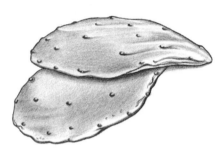

Nopales are pads from the prickly pear cactus; they are called *nopalitos* when cut up. Nopales taste like a peppery green bean similar to okra in texture. Buy young pads; they are available from late spring through early fall. Store pads refrigerated and use within 2 to 3 days while pads are firm. Cut off all the prickers with a sharp knife; some peel will come off in the process but it is not necessary to peel completely. Slice and cook until tender. Use chilled in salads or like okra in soups, stews or gumbo. Add to egg dishes with chilies and tomatoes or blanch, cut in julienne strips and toss with jícama, lemon juice and red bell peppers. Fry in tempura batter (in this case it is not necessary to cook first). Nopales have an affinity for garlic, onions, tomatoes, chilies and oregano.

Okra

Okra is green with a fuzzy texture and tapering, pod-like shape. Peak season is July and August. Buy crisp, small young pods, 3 to 4 inches long with a flexible tip, free from wilted appearance. They are very perishable and should be stored in paper-lined plastic bags, refrigerated, for about 2 days. Young okra is

Papaya

Papaya is a favorite fruit in the tropics; it is imported and also raised commercially in Hawaii and Florida for sale in the United States. Papayas have to be picked green because they are quite delicate; they do not always ripen well en route. Buy smooth-skinned fruit with a yellowish tinge. A toothpick test may help determine ripeness: insert a toothpick into the fruit; if it comes out clean, the papaya is ripe. Leave unripe fruit in a dark place or put in a paper bag with a banana. Slice the papaya to eat raw or cook in sauces. Remove the seeds and fill halves with fresh berries or seafood or poultry salad. Use the skin to add to marinade as it has enzymes that tenderize meat; or add slices, including skin, to barbecue sauces that include chilies. Papaya can be made into ices and sorbets and dessert sauces. It has an affinity for avocados, lime, strawberries and dried red chilies. Papaya seeds are edible.

Passion Fruit

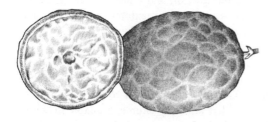

This sweet egg-shaped fruit, also called purple granadilla, is very popular in the Southwest. The fruit has a tough purple skin, wrinkled when ripe, and yellow to pale green pulp. It has many very small seeds, which are edible. Ripe passion fruit has a sweet aroma. Use in sorbets or ices, jams, jellies or drinks, or serve with fresh cream or vanilla ice cream. Strain the pulp if using for sorbets.

Persimmon

A fully ripe persimmon is very sweet and juicy; less than ripe, it will make your mouth pucker. Buy fruit that is very soft, with a rich, deep orange color and no tinge of yellow or mustard. One way to ripen persimmons is to place them in a plastic container and pour a few drops of brandy on the sepals of the crown. Close the container and allow the fumes to work until the fruit is soft, 3 to 6 days. Another is to place them in a bag with a ripe banana or apple for a few days. Store ripe persimmons in the refrigerator. Persimmons do not have to be peeled except for salads. To do so, slice the fruit first, then trim the skin from each piece, as skin and pulp can be hard to separate.

Use persimmons in sauces with game or in sweet, steamed puddings or for pastry and pie fillings. They are good to stew in chutney or stew and use in cakes.

Stew persimmons with sugar if they are not sweet enough; add small amounts of sugar syrup for an ice or sorbet.

Pomegranates

Pomegranates are widely grown in the United States. Buy richly colored, large, heavy fruits. If powdery, smokelike puffs emerge when the crown of the fruit is pressed, it is probably moldy. Freeze whole pomegranates or seed and freeze the seeds in airtight containers. To remove seeds, carefully cut out the blossom end, taking some of the white pith with it but not piercing the seeds. Lightly score the skin into quarters, break the fruit in half and then in half again. Bend back the rind to release the seeds. Use to make vinegar or to add to sauces, especially with duck, poultry and game. Use raw seeds for garnish, particularly on salads with fruits or nuts and cheese platters. Pomegranates have an affinity for pecans and walnuts.

Prickly Pear

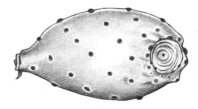

The prickly pear, also called cactus pear and barbary fig, is the fruit of the nopale cactus. It is egg shaped with a skin color that ranges from yellow to magenta, depending on the variety. Its rind is covered with spines. The deep red flesh is similar to watermelon in taste and texture; there are many small edible seeds. It is very sweet. Ripen pears at room temperature and refrigerate for up to 3 days.

To use, carefully cut off the ends of the fruit and

slit the skin down the center lengthwise. Lift out the pulp with a spoon. Use in drinks, sorbets or to make vinegar. Cactus pear can be made into marmalade. It has an affinity for red wine and can be used for red-wine granita. It will give food and drinks a deep pink shade.

Quince

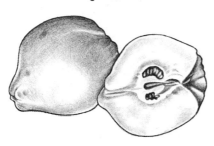

This is a very aromatic fruit that is large and varies in color from yellow to pale green. It somewhat resembles the Golden Delicious apple. Quince must be cooked, at which point it turns coral in color and develops a rich sweet aroma. Choose large smooth fruits. They are easier to peel and less wasteful. Store quince at room temperature for about a week or for 1 to 2 months refrigerated. For even longer storage, double-wrap fruits in plastic and place them in the refrigerator where they will not get bruised.

Prepare for cooking by peeling and coring; the flesh will hold its shape during cooking. Quince is often candied and used for a filling in *empanadas* (pastry turnovers). It can be used for jams, jellies, and marmalade or stewed and combined with apples or pears in a cobbler.

Summer Squash

Summer squash is best eaten young when the skin is fine and thin and the seeds barely developed. Generally speaking the flavor of summer squash decreases as the size of the squash increases. Buy firm, unblemished squash with bright skin; the squash should feel heavy to the hand. Store squash open to air. To use, wash and trim ends. Peeling is not necessary. Grill, steam or sauté squash or batter and deep-fry it. Squash can also be julienned and combined with other vegetables like carrots, jícama, chayote. Cook it with okra, eggplant and tomatoes for a Southwest ratatouille.

Among the varieties of squash commonly available are **patty pan,** 2 to 4 inches across with round scalloped edges, pale or yellow green in color; **yellow crookneck,** 6 to 8 inches long with bright yellow, slightly bumpy skin and a narrow curving neck (buy smaller ones with firm textured skin); **zucchini,** also called courgette or Italian squash, 4 to 6 inches long, in a variety of colors—pale grey to green and yellow, although the green varieties are most common at supermarkets; **scallopini,** shaped like a patty pan but green like a zucchini; **green round zucchini,** sometimes called tatum or tatume, available in southwest Texas markets and sometimes in California, with more seeds and pulp than zucchini and somewhat sweeter, good to stuff.

GRILLED SUMMER SQUASH

Slice ¼ inch thick or cut in chunks to skewer. Blanch for 30 seconds in boiling salted water; rinse under cold water immediately. Sprinkle with salt and pepper or brush with vinaigrette dressing. Grill for 5 to 6 minutes, turning once. Baste with vinaigrette, oil or clarified butter several times during grilling, taking care not to drip the basting medium on the coals and cause flames to flare up.

Golden **squash blossoms** from round zucchini or long zucchini taste like a delicate zucchini and literally melt in your mouth. They are available May through September. Pick before blossoms close, preferably choosing male blossoms (though female blossoms, attached to the squash, are also edible); include some of the stem.

Refrigerate with stems in ice water for no longer than 12 to 24 hours. When ready to use, wash flowers gently and remove green, scratchy calyx at the base. Pat dry. Soak in ice water to open blossoms. Dip in seasoned flour and sauté or stuff with mild goat cheese or a mix of several cheeses and deep-fry. Dip in ground hazelnuts, pecans or walnuts and flour and sauté; serve with lime butter. Add to squash- or turnip-based soups and puree; garnish each serving with a blossom. Garnish tortilla-based dishes like *quesadillas* or tacos with squash blossoms.

Sundried Fruits

Fruits that have been dried in the sun, like papaya, pears and pineapple, often have a sort of honey flavor that adds a special twist to salads with smoked or grilled meats. The fruit can also be cut in slivers and added to salads of julienned vegetables or to mixed salads of somewhat bitter greens or cabbage.

Sundried Tomatoes

Sundried tomatoes come both plain and packed in oil. Those not packed in oil need to be soaked in hot water or steamed before using. They have an intense, slightly salty flavor. Once reconstituted, they should be used within several days or held in olive oil with fresh herbs (basil or rosemary, for example). Drain and blot dry the tomatoes and cut them up to use in salads, sauces, relishes or with pasta. They can be pureed and added to tomato puree to make tomato pasta. They go well with mild cheeses.

Tamarillo

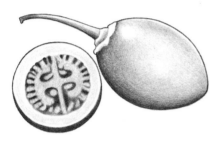

The tamarillo is an egg-shaped fruit, native to Peru, that has been grown since ancient times. The red variety is very tart; the gold and amber varieties mildly tart. The skin is tough and inedible; the flesh is soft. It is available from early summer through fall. Allow the fruit to ripen at room temperature for several days. Ripe fruit is very fragrant and yields to gentle pressure. To remove the skin, pour boiling water over the fruit and let stand for a few minutes. Peel from the stem end, being careful how you handle it as the juices stain. Tamarillos can be used in meat sauces, particularly game, and in relishes, chutney, jam and stews.

Tamarind

Tamarind, the "secret ingredient" in Worcestershire sauce, is a tropical fruit that looks like a brown lima bean. The taste is a cross between apricots and dates but more acidic. Tamarind pods can be stored in the pantry or refrigerator for a long time, up to 6 months. The pulp can be frozen and will keep indefinitely.

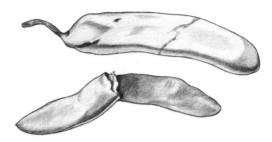

Pods need to be soaked in hot water for 1 hour, then shelled and the pulp scraped from the seeds. Tamarind pods, paste and dried pulp are available in specialty food shops, especially those catering to a Middle Eastern clientele. Directions for making your own tamarind paste and water follow.

TAMARIND PASTE

Cook the pods in water to cover for about 30 minutes, adding additional water if necessary. Remove seeds and press through a strainer. Freeze.

TAMARIND WATER

Cook pods in water, allowing 3 cups water for every 5 pods. Simmer over low heat for 45 minutes to 1 hour. Seed and press through a strainer.

Tomatillo

When their papery husks are removed, tomatillos resemble unripe cherry tomatoes. They have a slightly lemony flavor that is quite different from the tartness of a green tomato. At the peak of freshness, the husk is split, showing a firm, green skin that is slightly sticky. Yellow-green ones are riper than darker ones but they lack their crisp, fresh flavor. Buy firm fruit, wrap in paper towels to avoid bruising, and refrigerate for 3 to 4 weeks. Before using, remove husks and rinse to remove sticky residue or dirt. Save husks to fill with relish and garnish the plate. Tomatillos may be used cooked or raw. They will neutralize hot chilies; they have an affinity for cilantro, basil, other tomatoes—particularly yellow tomatoes—melons, mango, corn and garlic. Add them to guacamole instead of lemon: the bonus is that tomatillos retard browning. Cooked or raw, in sauce or salsa, tomatillos go well with poultry or fish, particularly salmon. They make a delicious cold soup or a hot soup with green chilies and fresh corn. Use tomatillo relish with creamy corn chowder.

Lettuce and Greens

Lettuce now plays a role in American cuisine going far beyond salads. There are so many new varieties to use to add color, taste and texture that a plate almost looks neglected without some greens to garnish it. They create a wonderfully inviting look with their fresh, garden appeal.

Lettuce

Among the more familiar kinds of lettuce are **romaine,** which is as good as iceberg in tacos and combines well with some of the more bitter greens; the tender and sweet butterhead lettuces, **Boston** and **Bibb;** the curly-leaved green and red-tip **leaf lettuces;** and the somewhat bitter **escarole** and **curly endive.**

Less familiar varieties of lettuce include **limestone** (from the butterhead family) with tender, delicate leaves; **arugula,** also known as roquette or rocket, with its sharp, spicy flavor; **oak leaf,** named for the appearance of its very delicate leaves; **mâche,** also called lamb's lettuce, a mild and nutty flavored green that grows in clumps of tender oval leaves; **radicchio,** a red-leaved chicory that grows in round or oval heads; and **Belgian endive,** with tight, pale yellow elongated heads.

Sometimes called "designer greens," these can support the more flavorful oils and more assertive warm dressings. A wide range of other ingredients may accompany them, such as fruits or julienned vegetables. They can be mixed with other compatible kinds of lettuce to frame grilled salmon, shellfish or lamb chops. Sometimes these greens are sautéed or used in a warm salad in which the greens are first chilled and tossed with a vinaigrette of lemon or vinegar and oil, then combined with meat, fish or poultry in a warm dressing or buttery sauce of natural juices.

Other greens that may be used in salad are **dandelion,** with its sharp, arresting flavor; crisp and tangy **watercress;** and **sprouts,** which add flavor and crunch to salads.

When buying lettuce, pick heads that are crisp and not bruised, with a good deep green color. Store it unwashed in heavy-duty plastic bags at 32° F., or as close to that as possible, in the refrigerator. Wash just before using and refrigerate in paper-towel-lined plastic bags or place in the freezer for 2 minutes to crisp the leaves. They must be dry before dressing is added or they will wilt. Some of the sturdier varieties, like escarole or radicchio, may be crisped in ice water for several hours before using. For attractive salads or garnishes, leave small leaves whole and tear large ones in half. Combine different types for maximum appeal.

Greens

Lettuce should not be confused with greens. Wilted greens, chard for example, or crisp radicchio leaves make good taco-like wrappers for such fillings as duck, papaya and jícama. Cooked greens, a Southern tradition, might be **collards, chard** or **kale, mustard, spinach** or **turnip greens.** Sometimes two or more

kinds are combined. Buy young greens with good color and store them in sealed plastic bags without rinsing. Use them within 1 or 2 days of purchase.

SOUTHERN-STYLE GREENS

To clean and prepare greens, rinse them first 2 or 3 times, until the water runs clean. Drop in boiling water with ham hocks, salt pork and onions and cook until tender. Add diced cooked turnips to the cooked greens and season to taste with salt and pepper. Greens are traditionally served with black-eyed peas; they may also be used as a bed for sliced grilled meats, barbecued pork or sliced smoked birds.

Grains and Beans

Recognition of the vital role complex carbohydrates play in our health and well-being has brought grains back to the forefront in American cuisine, but rice, corn and wheat products have always been an important part of regional cuisines.

Pasta

Pasta has become so established in America, one has to wonder if our children will know it was originally from Italy. Now you can buy fresh pasta, both plain and flavored, as well as dried pasta and hard-wheat semolina pasta flour to make your own. Inventive chefs and cooks have expanded the pasta horizon by adding various ingredients, such as chilies, for some exciting new flavors and textures. Other flavorings include dried mushrooms, peppercorns, dried ancho chilies or a combination of chili powders, smoked chilies (chipotle), fresh herbs and fresh small hot chilies (jalapeño and serrano).

When making your own pasta, feel free to experiment; just taste and adjust as you go along. To intensify color, use annatto seeds (page 26) or saffron for yellow-orange, parsley for green pasta. Strong flavorings make the most interesting pasta: add jalapeño chilies to spinach pasta, for example. If you are using flavorings with high water content (spinach, bell peppers, beets, etc.), you should grind them first, then squeeze out excess moisture. For citrus-flavored pasta, reduce the juices from about 1½ cups to 3 or 4 tablespoons by boiling them down in an uncovered skillet. (Add some zest from the fruit you are using to the finished dish.) This is especially important if you are using an extruding machine. See pages 292–293 for more details on pasta.

Corn

Corn products in nearly every form are central to Southwest regional cooking. *Masa harina,* a kind of corn flour made from corn that has been treated with lye, is used frequently as a shortcut for tamales. The tamales in this book, however, are all made with cornmeal and freshly ground corn. *Hominy* is hulled white corn; it is available dried and canned. When ground, it is called *grits.* In addition to serving grits for breakfast, you can make little pancakes (page 65) to serve with game birds or a soufflé with ham and shrimp (page 84). *White cornmeal* and *yellow cornmeal* are supposed to be interchangeable; however, I find the white somewhat sweeter. The yellow has slightly more nutrients. Use either for cornbread, in pasta or for homemade tamales. *Blue cornmeal,* which comes from blue corn, not unlike the Indian corn found in the Midwest, is a bit grainier than the yellow or white. It makes a more fragile tortilla and needs more fat when used for muffins or tortillas.

Rice

Rice is easy to store and fits into the contemporary healthy lifestyle. The most commonly used is *long-grain white rice,* which is polished and usually enriched. So-called converted long-grain rice, which is steam-processed to prevent the grains from sticking during cooking, is also available. Converted or not, long-grain rice is best for serving as an accompaniment. Italian *Arborio rice* is a short-grain white rice that is ideal for risotto, in which the rice is first sautéed and then liquid is added little by little. See page 188 for more details about risotto. *Brown rice* is unpolished rice, more beige than brown in color.

It is available plain and in converted form. It can be substituted for white rice but it takes longer to cook. **Wild rice** is a grass rather than a grain, despite its name. If cooked too long, it becomes very soft; it is better left crunchy, especially for salads.

Beans

Beans are used in virtually all cuisines and they are particularly important in the American South and Southwest. Once considered "poor man's food," they have become trendy fare. Some beans are available fresh in season. Dried beans have a long shelf life but they do begin to deteriorate after about a year. All beans, dried or fresh, require a longish cooking to be digestible; soaking dried beans shortens the cooking time but it is not necessary. All beans should be well rinsed and any broken beans discarded. Cook the beans in well seasoned stocks or together with bones from smoked ham or game birds. Salt and acid ingredients such as lemons, tomatoes and vinegar should be added only at the end as they slow the cooking time. Beans marry well with chilies and other assertive ingredients because of their characteristic blandness. They should be cooked until tender but still firm for relishes, cold or warm salads or garnishes. Cook them longer for soups, sauces or refrying or as a filling for tortillas or crêpes.

Black beans (turtle beans) have an earthy, distinctive flavor and are excellent in relishes and for garnish. **Pinto beans** are widely used in traditional Mexican cooking; they are one of the most nutritious beans. They can be combined with **pink beans,** which are smaller and have a rather nutty flavor, or with any other kind of beans. **Northern beans** are large white beans, generally available in dried form. Depending on the locality, there may be up to ten different kinds of dried beans and legumes on the shelf in the supermarket; they are all handled the same way, though they vary considerably in flavor and cooking time.

Black-eyed peas are available dried year round and fresh in the spring and summer. They are often found already shelled. If not, the peas should slip easily from their pods when mature. Cook them with flavored meat stock and use them pickled in relish, in salads or warm with bacon, ham or smoked-game sausages. **Fava beans** are also available fresh in spring and summer. They taste something like lima beans, but richer. Pods should be shiny and bright green with evenly developed beans.

Game and Exotic Meats

Game cooking has strong traditional roots in the Southwest and has filled many a creative cook's need for a "new beast to roast." Enthusiastic hunters in the Southwest and South have spent many mornings shivering in duck blinds or perched atop deer blinds to bring home their quota. Home cooks have stewed, braised, grilled and roasted everything from dove to wild boar.

They did not have the carefully raised, fed, selected and processed game that restaurant chefs have been using to bring it into the limelight of regional American cooking. Small farms that raise pheasant, quail and rabbit—as well as ranches raising big game animals—are becoming big business in Texas. The flavor of farm-raised wild birds and game is not so strong as in the wild. Many local smokehouses will smoke venison and make sausages for private customers. While game's popularity may lie in its novelty and romance, its increasing acceptance is also due to its low fat and cholesterol content and calorie count and above all to the quality and variety of game now available.

Venison

Venison has about a third the calories of beef. It dries out rapidly, so wrap it in plastic wrap, and since that may hasten the meat's deterioration, use it within a day or so. Double-wrapped in freezer wrap, venison will keep in a freezer for several months. The loin may be grilled or roasted but it needs to be barded with suet or bacon or basted frequently with an oil-based marinade. Braising, stewing, smoking or quick sautéing are more suitable methods. To barbecue venison, treat it like brisket (page 162) and serve with barbecue or dark chili sauce or sweet-sour berry-flavored sauces. Use venison in pâtés served with chutney or in chile con carne. It has special affinities for berries and chestnuts.

Antelope

Black Buck antelope is raised in south Texas and is small with fine-textured sweet meat. The Nilgai is larger, with rather coarse-textured meat. Treat antelope like venison; since it is not so dry, though, it does not require so much basting. Prepare the loin as you would beef tenderloin.

Wild Boar

Boar, leaner than pork, tastes much like the loin of pork. It is not quite as tender, and it benefits from marinades with a high acid content and enough fat to compensate for its leanness. Use like pork, with similar accompaniments, sauces and herbs. Roast, covered tightly, or grill whole over apple, hickory or mesquite, basting often. Boar has an affinity for apricots, prunes and Bourbon.

Buffalo

There is an increased popularity for buffalo, primarily that raised on private ranches. More disease-resistant than beef, it has less fat and cholesterol. Since it is not marbled like beef, it tends to absorb heat faster. It is best cooked medium to rare: treat it like beef, compensating for its leanness in cooking techniques and with marinades.

Rabbit

Rabbit is lower in cholesterol and fat than chicken, which it tastes very much like. Fryers are younger, about 2½ pounds, and may be sautéed, panfried or grilled. Roasters are about 5 pounds, and are better for stewing or making sausages or smoking. Use as you would chicken. Rabbit may be chicken-fried (dipped in seasoned flour and deep-fried). The loin is the most tender cut. It can be sliced, lightly pounded and sautéed like veal medallions. Use the leg meat for sausage patties. Rabbit has an affinity for mustard.

Game Birds and Poultry

Dove is very small with dark meat and tastes a bit like liver. Texans remove the breastbones, wrap the meat around a jalapeño chili, then wrap the bird in bacon and deep-fry it for about 8 minutes. Dove may also be grilled. **Quail** is larger and more tender with less taste of the wild. Quail may be grilled, smoked or cut in half and sautéed. **Pheasant** is larger and tastes much like small chicken. Smoke, roast or cut in half and grill. Serve with a herb- or tequila-flavored sauce of natural juices or sauces with spicy chilies. Pheasant is also good with corn, chayote and fruits like mango, papaya and orange. **Guinea hen** (also called pintelle, pintade or African pheasant) is very lean and though it weighs only 2 to 3 pounds, it can serve 4 or 5. It has dark meat that tastes faintly of game. Guinea hens are usually braised, though they can be roasted. **Squab** is young pigeon. It has moderately dark meat with a mild, sweet flavor and may be treated like Cornish game hen. The **poussin** is a young chicken; it is particularly moist and flavorful. **Wild turkey** should be treated like fresh domestic turkey; baste it frequently since it does not have much fat. It is surprisingly tender. **Free-range chickens** are those that have not been cooped up and fed grain. They have better flavor and less fat than other chickens.

Special Ingredients

The Southwest has been quick to enjoy the many specialty ingredients that have been available in California and New York, and add a few of its own regional specialties. It is fascinating to see how the same ingredients are used in different ways by different regional chefs and cooks—with different results.

Cheese

While it is not possible to buy Mexican cheeses everywhere, most Southwest restaurants do use them. Substitutes range from Longhorn Cheddar to many different types of Monterey Jack, including some speckled with jalapeño peppers. Brie and Camembert are good substitutes, alone or in combination with Monterey Jack, because they melt quickly and pair well with chilies, particularly in *quesadillas*. Mozzarella is also a good substitute. Cheese is used in many ways, often paired with chilies, savory, black beans and tomato salsas.

Smoked Sausages

Early German settlers established sausage-making in the Southwest, particularly sausages made from game. These are barbecued or grilled and included in a barbecue platter with ribs and brisket. Depending on the flavor and spice intensity, smoked sausages are sometimes simmered to warm and then finished on a grill. Sausages can be added to pasta salads, gumbo or pizza or cooked with beans. They are often served with shrimp and spicy mustard sauces or crumbled and sautéed to garnish roasted-corn soup.

Caviar

Caviar is fish roe, washed and processed with salt to preserve it. In the past, virtually all caviar came from Iran and the Soviet Union and it was prohibitively expensive. Now there is domestic American caviar on the market at far more reasonable prices. The three types most commonly found are: salmon caviar, with large red-orange eggs with full flavor; golden whitefish caviar, good, small-grained with mild flavor; and regular whitefish caviar, small and black with a distinctive flavor and delicate crunch. All caviar is highly perishable. Store it at 28° to 32° F. and use it promptly.

The salty flavor of caviar pairs well with beans, tortillas, guacamole and butter sauces. It is a colorful garnish for poached fish with a simple butter sauce or for beancakes or corncakes garnished with sour cream or crème fraîche. Along the same lines, it is a very special topping for nachos made with corn tortillas or puffy, fried flour tortillas served with black beans, guacamole and sour cream.

Fresh Foie Gras

Fresh foie gras, whether domestic or imported, is very high in fat. It needs careful, quick sautéeing in a hot skillet or on a very hot grill. It can also be breaded with jalapeño-cornbread crumbs before sautéing. Serve it from the grill on a salad of julienned jícama, apple or papaya and greens with a pistachio vinaigrette.

Honey

Honey is a favorite ingredient in Mexican-inspired and Southern cooking. It is used to glaze ham and to sweeten and balance sauces for that prized sweet-sour-hot flavor.

Maple Syrup

Maple syrup is sweeter than sugar, with a soft, distinctive flavor. It is much appreciated for its subtle sweetening power in berry and meat sauces, particularly those served with game. Used to sweeten ancho chilies and tomato or tomatillo relishes, it smooths out the bitterness or strong acids.

Oil

For general use, I prefer a light **safflower oil,** particularly in vinaigrette dressings. I use **virgin olive oil** for specific purposes. For frying, **peanut oil** seems to maintain the highest heat without smoking or adding taste to the foods. Olive oil can overwhelm a dressing, making it impossible to taste anything else but it can be very good with certain vegetables or in marinades or on pastas. I do not find most olive oils compatible with assertive-flavored chilies unless they are tempered heavily by tomatoes or citrus. Of the olive oils, *extra-virgin olive oil* is made from the first pressing and has the most intense, robust flavor. *Virgin olive oil* is from subsequent pressings and is nuttier. *Pure olive oil* has a blander taste and is pressed from olive pulp using chemical additives. It keeps for about 6 months, sealed and refrigerated. **Dark sesame oil** has the distinctive flavor of sesame seeds and adds an oriental touch. Use sparingly. **Walnut and hazelnut oil** are nuttier in flavor; both are quite strong. Use in moderation or combine with bland oils in vinaigrettes. They are good in basting vinaigrettes for poultry and certain fish. **Avocado oil** from California has a buttery, nutty flavor that is good in salad dressings, especially for tossing with greens, nuts and tropical fruits.

Vinegar

Vinegar is very important in Southwest cooking for it is the base for vinaigrettes that are used for salads and grilling and on fruits and vegetables; vinegar is also used for butter sauces. It balances relishes made with chilies and adds acidity where needed. There are many varieties of flavored vinegars available and you can also make your own (page 25). *Raspberry vinegar* gets its intense fragrance and flavor from fresh raspberries and red wine. It is used on salads and in sauces for fish, poultry and duck. *Rice wine vinegar* is a Japanese vinegar that is naturally sweet and very mild. It works extremely well in chili-based relishes or where acidity is needed but the sharpness of ordinary vinegar is undesirable. Good in vinaigrettes for basting seafood or to season vegetables and greens. *Balsamic vinegar* is a mild, full-bodied vinegar that has been aged in special wood. It is dark in color and thicker than most other vinegars. Its extremely well balanced flavors enhance vinaigrettes, sauces and many sautéed or grilled vegetables (particularly eggplant and roasted or grilled peppers). Use it also for deglazing. *Sherry vinegar* is also aged and has a rich, slightly sweet flavor. Use it as you would balsamic vinegar. Balsamic, sherry and rice wine vinegars all go well with chilies and peppers. They are also less inimical to wine than cider or wine vinegar.

Warm vinaigrettes or vinaigrettes with finely chopped nuts can be used instead of butter to dress steamed vegetables or to add moisture and flavor to grilled fish or poultry. Used on salad greens, warm dressing should not be hot, only warm; it is poured onto crisp, chilled greens and tossed.

Pepper Jellies

Commercial varieties are usually tinged bright red or green with food coloring while homemade jellies are mostly pale orange and green. It is easy to make your own (pages 249–250). Use as a jelly or melt down to a liquid and use for a sweet-hot flavor in sauces, on vegetables or in vinaigrettes.

Mustard

The array of specialty mustards available is staggering. They range from coarse-grain, herb-flavored and pepper-infused to Creole-style. Dijon and coarse-grain mustards are the most common. Dry mustard is good to add to dry seasoning mixes for grilled foods or to use to make your own mustard if you are so inclined. It is easier, however, to take a plain Dijon mustard and personalize it with honey or your own combination of seasonings. Add mustard to meat or poultry sauces or compound-butters. Mustard adds zest to mayonnaise and cream sauces and just about everything from bread to seafood.

TECHNIQUES AND EQUIPMENT

Frying

When I first came to the Southwest it seemed to me everything was dipped in batter and fried, including steak and fresh vegetables. Fried foods seem in conflict with contemporary health-conscious lifestyles; however, I would surely miss that wonderful crunch of deep-fried corn tortillas. I also like deep-fried fresh pasta, whether as a nest for salads of julienned vegetables, seafood or poultry or for sautéed seafood, or added to green salads or used to garnish mayonnaise-based salads. I also like to mound several different colors and flavors in bowls for cocktail snacks. What would I do without it!

Deep-frying

Most foods fry best at 350° to 375° F. It is not necessary to use an electric deep-fat-fryer; in fact, many do not have good heat recovery and the oil temperature can drop rapidly once the food is added. Use a heavy-duty saucepan with good heat retention. Peanut oil is best as it smokes less at high temperatures. A bread cube dropped in the hot oil turns golden brown in 60 seconds when the oil is 350° F., in 40 seconds at 375° F. Use a candy thermometer to be exact, and once within 5 degrees of desired temperature, reduce the heat source to medium until the temperature stabilizes. Always test one item.

CORN TORTILLAS

Cut tortillas into ⅛-inch strips or into triangles and let stand at room temperature for at least 3 hours or up to 8 hours to dry out. This lets the water evaporate and keeps the oil from foaming up. Preheat the oil to 350° F. Fry strips in batches until crisp; it takes just seconds. Drain on paper towels. Salt lightly, if desired, while still warm. Cool and store in an airtight container until ready to use.

PASTA

Heat oil to 350° F. Pasta must be fried while still soft; for best results it should not be made with more than 60 percent semolina flour. Allow the cut or extruded pasta to rest for 10 minutes before frying, but do not let it dry out. Fry it in sticks or baskets or knots or simply drop it in and let it take a free swirl form. It should puff slightly. Watch closely as pasta browns very quickly. Drain and salt lightly while still hot.

HERBS

Parsley, basil and other fresh herbs can be deep-fried with or without coating. Make sure the leaves are bone-dry to avoid splattering. Oil temperature should be between 350° and 365° F. For more details, see fried sage leaves (page 60).

VEGETABLES

Most vegetables can be fried using the same double-coating technique as for chicken-fried steak. For a very crisp coating, use a baking mix (like Bisquick) instead of flour or use the batter for fried sage leaves (page 60). Vegetables do not need to be blanched or parboiled before deep-frying. Heat the oil to 375° F. and fry until golden brown. Drain on paper towels.

SWEET POTATOES

Foods with high water or sugar content like sweet potatoes fry best when allowed to rest at room temperature for at least 3 hours before frying. Peel and cut sweet potatoes into matchsticks. Let stand for 3 hours. Heat oil to 375° F. and fry in batches until lightly browned, 2 to 3 minutes. Drain and salt while hot.

Chicken-frying

Almost anything can be chicken-fried and I know Texans who have chicken-fried everything from rabbit to rattlesnake. They all have their own technique; the following seems to work consistently well with veal or pork cutlets, tenderized beef cuts or game, as well as chicken or rabbit or medallions from a venison or pork loin. Marinating the meat first in buttermilk makes it very tender. Chicken-frying began as a way to cook tough cuts of meat, which were always served with cream gravy made from the pan drippings (pages 47–48).

CHICKEN-FRIED STEAKS

Pound round steak or cutlets to tenderize (about ¼ inch thick). Marinate in buttermilk for at least 1½ hours or overnight. Combine 1 beaten egg to every 2 tablespoons milk or buttermilk in a shallow dish. Put plain or seasoned flour on a plate. Lightly salt and pepper the meat to be fried, then dip in flour and shake off all excess, leaving a very thin coating. Dip the meat in the egg mixture, then again in the flour. Heat at least ½ inch oil (for beef or chicken) or ¼ inch (for veal or pork) in a large skillet. The oil temperature should be about 350° F.: use the bread cube test if the oil is not deep enough for a thermometer. Add the meat and cook quickly on both sides until golden brown. Some cooks then add a couple of tablespoons of water, cover the pan tightly and let it steam 3 to 4 minutes. Drain some fat, then make cream gravy (pages 47–48) from drippings.

Variation

- Tender cutlets of rabbit, chicken, veal, pork or beef may be marinated in buttermilk, then dipped in a combination of flour and cornbread crumbs. Sauté quickly in butter or a combination of oil and butter until crisp and golden.

Panfrying

Both fish and steaks will be succulent and moist when panfried quickly at a high temperature. Fish will not dry out and a steak sears quickly, sealing in all the flavorful juices. The method may alarm your neighbors or set off a few smoke alarms but since there is little or no fat added to the skillet, you are not likely to start a fire. Cast-iron skillets are common in Southwest kitchens and many steak lovers swear by them for cooking a steak.

PANFRIED FISH

Pat fish dry and coat lightly with flour, cornmeal, breadcrumbs or cornbread crumbs. If desired, use a seasoned flour or season the coating with cayenne pepper or chili powder. It is not necessary to dip fish in egg first; the coating will adhere. Coat the fish 15 to 20 minutes in advance, then cover and refrigerate until ready to fry. Heat oil or clarified butter to 325° F. to 350° F. (Having the oil at that high a temperature prevents the coating from getting greasy.) Add the fish and fry on both sides until golden brown, about 3 to 4 minutes, depending on thickness of fish.

PANFRIED STEAK

Trim excess fat from a well-marbled steak, ¾ to 1 inch thick. Heat a well-seasoned cast-iron skillet over high heat. Sprinkle salt on the pan as it heats. When a droplet of water dropped on the pan sizzles, it is hot enough. Put the steak in the pan and cook 5 minutes before trying to turn. As the fat melts, it helps season the pan (and prevents sticking); even so, you will have significant smoke and sizzle. Turn the steak and cook another 5 minutes on the other side. The steak will be medium rare, crisp on the outside and juicy inside. Let stand about 5 minutes before serving.

PANFRIED HAMBURGERS

Follow the method for panfried steaks. This gives a crisp outside and juicy rare center.

PANFRIED GAME OR BEEF PATTIES

Heat equal amounts of butter and oil, or clarified butter over medium-high heat to sizzling. Add the patties and cook about 5 minutes on each side. When they are done, deglaze the skillet with ½ cup wine or ¼ cup sherry or balsamic vinegar plus ½ cup beef or veal stock. Add a minced shallot, grainy mustard or blue cheese to taste. Cook, stirring constantly, until thickened. Finish the sauce with up to 3 tablespoons butter (use less with cheese). Season to taste with salt, pepper and a squeeze of lemon.

Grilling

See Pages 196–221.

Cracklings

Cracklings are what is left when the fat is rendered from pork or duck skin. Actually, they may be made from almost any poultry that has a good layer of fat beneath the skin. Crisp, seasoned cracklings add flavor and crunch to salads and pasta dishes.

CRACKLINGS

Cut the skin and fat layer, in one piece, from a cooked bird and dice it ¼ inch thick or use a piece of solid pork fat, diced ¼ inch thick. Preheat the oven to 350° F. and cook the fat or skin and fat until crisp and browned, about 30 minutes. You will need to pour off the rendered fat 2 to 3 times during this process. Reserve the fat. Drain the cooked, crisp cracklings on paper towels, then sprinkle lightly with salt and pepper, minced herbs or a seasoning combination that complements what they will garnish. If you are using both toasted nuts and cracklings to garnish a salad, sauté the nuts in a small amount of rendered fat instead of butter. Toss nuts and cracklings together.

Meat Sauces and Gravies

Simple *au jus* sauce, pan gravy and cream gravy are certainly a significant part of our American heritage, particularly in the Southwest. In its simple, traditional form *au jus* is made from the captured juices of a rib roast or leg of lamb or almost any other roast. Most of the fat is removed from the roasting pan, which is then deglazed with stock and or beef broth; the liquid is boiled down to reduce it to a thin flavorful sauce. Meat juices that seep from the roast before and after slicing are added. For traditional gravy, flour is added to the pan drippings to make a roux, broth or stock (or stock and wine) are blended in and the gravy is cooked until thickened. In cream gravy, milk or milk and cream is used instead of stock.

In the recipes that follow, the gravies are not as thick as traditional ones; if you prefer a thicker gravy, increase the amount of flour by 2 tablespoons. Thin gravy by adding more broth; strengthen the flavor by simmering it longer over low heat. The longer it cooks, the more it thickens.

AU JUS SAUCE FOR A ROAST

Choose a deglazing liquid to match the meat. Homemade stocks made from the same meat are best; if not available, use chicken and beef stock with veal, chicken or beef stock with pork, beef stock with game, or canned broth. Select herbs that complement the meat or that have been used to season the meat. Degrease the pan, then add 2 to 4 cups stock, depending on how much sauce you want to make, herbs and minced shallot or garlic. Scrape up all the pan juices and let sauce simmer to reduce for 20 to 35 minutes. Add any accumulated meat juices, strain and season to taste with salt and pepper.

AU JUS SAUCE FROM A SKILLET

Pour off most of the fat but leave any browned bits in the pan. Add minced shallot or garlic and an herb sprig; add chopped mushrooms or minced hot chilies and diced tomatoes or a grainy or flavored mustard if desired. Pour in 1 to 1½ cups stock and wine. (Amounts will vary: for 4 hamburgers, cutlets or steaks, 1 cup stock and ⅓ cup wine is about right.) Scrape up the browned bits and boil for 5 minutes or until the strong wine taste is gone. Strain into a small pan; place over medium-low heat, whisk in 2 to 3 tablespoons butter and season with salt and pepper. If homemade stock is used, the sauce will be thicker than if canned stock is used. (Balsamic or sherry vinegar can be substituted for wine: then increase the amount of butter to 3 to 4 tablespoons.)

PAN GRAVY

Remove all but 3 to 4 tablespoons fat from the pan. Stir in 3 to 4 tablespoons flour over medium heat to make a roux. Add 2½ to 3½ cups stock to deglaze; cook, stirring constantly, until thickened. Strain and season to taste with salt and pepper.

Variations

- For a lighter sauce, use 2 tablespoons flour in place of 4. Dissolve 1 teaspoon cornstarch in ¼ cup water and stir it into the sauce after deglazing.
- For a berry reduction, put 1 shallot, 1 cup cranberries and 2½ cups wine plus ½ cup chicken stock in a saucepan. Bring to a boil and continue boiling to reduce to about ½ cup liquid. Strain and add to pan gravy. (For poultry use chicken stock or broth; for meat, use beef or veal stock. For pork or lamb, add 4 to 5 tablespoons balsamic or sherry vinegar with the stock.)
- For richer flavor, add mushrooms, shallots or garlic to the pan gravy. Strain before serving.

- For a piquant gravy, add peppercorn mustard, finely diced fresh or ground chilies or whole peppercorns. Strain before serving.
- If you are serving the meat with a relish, add all the drained relish juices to the gravy. Strain before serving.

SOUTHERN CREAM GRAVY

2 cups

Cream gravy can be made from the drippings from fried chicken, breaded veal cutlets, chicken-fried steak or breakfast sausage. Flour is stirred into pan drippings to make a roux, then milk or cream is added to make a cream gravy. This is certainly not light fare, but when the dish is well seasoned and accompanied by a fresh relish and homemade biscuits, anyone from the warm states will tell you, "That's pretty darn good."

In my ultra-light, flourless version of this old classic, a homemade veal stock is essential; without that, the sauce will not thicken unless you add flour or cornstarch. Serve meat with gravy and accompany it with one of the tomato-based relishes (pages 226–227) or grilled-corn relish (page 238). The fresh relish complements a crisp-coated chicken or cutlet and cuts the richness of the cream gravy. If the gravy is spicy, do not use hot chilies in the relish.

3 tablespoons all-purpose flour
3 tablespoons fat from skillet (fried chicken, chicken-fried steak, pork chops or breakfast sausage)
3 cups milk or 1½ cups milk and 1½ cups cream
Salt
Black pepper
Cayenne pepper (optional)

Stir the flour into the hot fat and stir to make a roux. Gradually add the milk and cream or just milk, stirring constantly until thickened, about 5 to 6 minutes. Season to taste with salt, pepper, and cayenne pepper, if using.

LIGHT SOUTHERN CREAM GRAVY

2 cups

Pan drippings
3 tablespoons all-purpose flour
2 sprigs fresh thyme
1 shallot, minced
1 clove garlic, minced, or 3 tablespoons minced onion
1 cup chicken stock, preferably homemade
1½ cups milk
½ cup cream
Salt
Pepper
Cayenne pepper
Minced fresh herbs such as tarragon, Mexican mint marigold or basil (optional)

Pour off all but 3 tablespoons fat from the pan, leaving all the browned bits. Add the flour, thyme, shallot, garlic or onion, and cook, stirring constantly, until you have a light-colored roux. Gradually stir in ½ cup chicken stock, then stir in the milk and cream. Cook until thickened, about 5 to 6 minutes. If you want a thinner gravy, use as much of the remaining chicken stock as needed to reach the desired consistency. Strain the gravy, then season to taste with salt, pepper, cayenne pepper and herbs if using.

ULTRA-LIGHT SOUTHERN CREAM GRAVY

2 cups

Pan drippings from steak, veal or other cutlets, chicken or breakfast sausage
2 thyme sprigs
1 shallot, minced
1 clove garlic, minced
2½ cups homemade veal stock (page 98)
1 cup heavy cream
Salt
Pepper
Cayenne pepper

Pour off all the fat from the pan, but reserve the browned bits. Add the thyme, shallot, garlic and ½ cup stock. Stir over medium-high heat to incorporate all the drippings. Add the remaining stock and heat to a boil. Lower the heat to medium-high and simmer until reduced by more than half. Strain the sauce and pour back into the same pan. Add the cream and simmer until thickened and smooth. Season to taste with salt, pepper and cayenne pepper.

Clarified Butter, Compound-Butter and Butter Sauce

Clarified Butter

When butter is clarified, the milk solids that cause heated butter to burn are removed and discarded. The fat that is left does not burn as easily as ordinary butter and can be heated to a higher temperature. A shortcut (sometimes used in recipes in this book) is to substitute equal amounts of butter and oil, but then you lose the full buttery flavor.

CLARIFIED BUTTER

Heat unsalted butter in a medium saucepan or skillet over medium-low heat to melt. Skim the foam that rises to the surface and discard. Cool the clarified butter and store refrigerated.

Compound-Butter

Compound-butters made with unsalted butter, chilies, toasted nuts, fresh or roasted garlic, herbs and other spices and seasonings are a simple way to enhance grilled meats, poultry, fish or vegetables like corn on the cob and baked potatoes and they are easy to prepare.

COMPOUND-BUTTER

For each ¼ pound butter use about 1 tablespoon fresh dominant herbs or about 4 teaspoons less dominant herbs. Place in a blender or food processor fitted with the metal blade; blend or process until well mixed. Store in the refrigerator until ready to use. To use, allow butter to come to room temperature. Place a dollop on warm steak, poultry, fish or vegetables just before serving. Or melt the butter in a skillet over medium heat and add blanched vegetables. Sauté a few minutes, just long enough to reheat.

Some combinations
- Rosemary (2 teaspoons) and mint (1 tablespoon) —with fish, lamb or pork
- Cilantro, basil and mint (2 teaspoons *each*)— with fish, vegetables, chicken or pasta
- Lemon zest, lemon basil or lemon thyme and garlic for veal, fish or chicken
- Orange zest and rosemary for lamb, chicken or veal chops

Butter Sauces

A simple butter sauce prepared the French way makes a light base that lends itself to flavoring with fresh herbs, herb pestos, spicy chilies or smoke-flavored peppers. Butterfat softens the harshness of chilies and leaves a pleasant, intense flavor that complements simple grilled foods. The combination of butter sauce and relish is a delicious and colorful way to enhance fish and poultry.

Butter sauces can be tricky as they break easily and must be held at a controlled temperature that does not exceed 90° F. Restaurant chefs often use reduced cream to stabilize the sauce and prevent it from breaking when it is made in advance; that way it can be held at a higher temperature. The disadvantage of using cream, particularly reduced, is that the flavor intensity of the herbs or chilies is dulled and the overall taste becomes heavy or too rich. Here are some hints that will help you make a successful butter sauce every time.

- Use a blender or food processor to emulsify the sauce before straining. This helps stabilize the sauce or bring it back quickly if it threatens to break.
- If the sauce breaks during the addition of butter, whisk in 1 to 2 tablespoons of crushed ice or a few teaspoons of chilled butter.
- Hold the sauce in a hot-water bath, off the heat. Add additional hot water to keep the temperature at around 90° F.
- Butter sauces also hold well in a crock pot or thermos bottle. Put the finished sauce in the container; do not allow the crock pot to go above 90° F. or the warm setting. Sauce will keep warm in a thermos bottle for about 45 minutes.

BUTTER SAUCE

About 1 cup

1 shallot, minced
1 sprig fresh thyme or 1 white mushroom, sliced
　(optional)
¼ cup white vinegar
½ cup white wine
½ cup heavy cream (optional)
1½ to 2 sticks unsalted butter, at room
　temperature
Salt
White pepper
Lemon juice

Heat the shallot, thyme or mushroom if using, vinegar, and wine to a boil in a saucepan. Boil until reduced to 4 to 6 tablespoons, leaving more liquid if you plan to use cream. If so, add the cream and heat to a boil. Boil until reduced by about half. This is the liaison that will bind the butter into a smooth, creamy sauce.

Lift the skillet from the heat to cool and reduce the temperature to medium-low. Whisk in the butter over low heat, 2 to 3 tablespoons at a time, until all the butter is added and the sauce is smooth. Do not let the pan get too hot or the butter will separate and the sauce will break. Strain, then season to taste with salt, pepper and a couple drops of lemon juice.

Variations

- To make a citrus butter sauce with lemon, lime or orange juice, use only 1 tablespoon vinegar in place of ¼ cup and add at least ½ cup fresh fruit juice. Add several tablespoons of tequila as well if you wish.

Toasted Nuts

All nuts benefit from an initial toasting, which brings out their true character. Walnuts lose their tannic aftertaste when toasted and skinned and take on a rich, buttery flavor. Pine nuts and almonds develop a full, nutty flavor.

Nuts should be purchased as fresh as possible and stored in the freezer. Double-wrap the nuts in freezer wrap or heavy-duty plastic bags. Toasting will remove any freezer taste. Nuts are much less oily after toasting. They are easier to chop or grind for nut coatings or to combine with flour or breadcrumbs to use for sautéed fish or poultry. Nuts also benefit from sautéing with a little butter, particularly if they are to be used to garnish salads, relishes or desserts.

Toasted Nuts

Preheat the oven to 300° F. Spread the nuts out on an ungreased cookie sheet and bake them until golden brown and slightly brittle, about 20 to 30 minutes depending on the kind of nut. Cool for 5 minutes. If toasting walnuts, hazelnuts or pistachios, place the nuts in a wide-mesh sieve and gently rub with a towel to loosen the skins. When cool enough to handle, remove any remaining skin with a sharp knife.

Sautéed Nuts

For each 1½ cups nuts heat about 1 tablespoon unsalted butter in a skillet over medium heat. Add the nuts and sauté, stirring constantly, for about 1 minute. Drain the nuts on paper towels to remove excess butter. Sprinkle lightly with salt, then chop or leave whole.

Variation

- To season nuts with spices or spice combinations (cinnamon, nutmeg, cayenne pepper) or finely minced herbs, proceed as follows (unless the recipe calls for honey or maple syrup, which will make the seasonings stick). Toast and peel the nuts as directed; leave the oven turned on. Whisk together 1 egg white, 1 tablespoon water and 1 tablespoon oil. Toss the mixture with 2 cups nuts. Heat 1½ tablespoons butter in a large skillet. Add the nuts and seasonings to taste and sauté until the nuts are well coated. Spread the nuts out on a cookie sheet and put them back in the oven. Reduce the temperature to 250° F. Bake until hardened, about 15 to 20 minutes. Break apart if necessary when cool.

Roasted Chilies and Peppers
See Pages 19–23

Vegetables

Interesting combinations of steamed or grilled fresh vegetables add color, texture and interest to meals. Preparation need not be a burden for the cook as vegetables may be parboiled in advance for reheating at the last minute. Grilled vegetables may even be grilled in advance until barely tender and then reheated in a hot oven. During parboiling (or blanching), vegetables need to be timed according to their texture: carrots may need more time than turnips or green beans, for instance. When choosing vegetable combinations, keep flavor compatibility, color and texture in mind and then parboil those vegetables with different cooking times separately.

Reheated Vegetables

Several hours before you plan to assemble the meal, blanch the vegetables of choice until just barely tender. Those that cook in about the same time, like carrots and cauliflower, may be blanched together; those that need only a short time like asparagus tips are best done separately. Boil the water, then add the vegetables and cook until just barely tender. Drain and immediately rinse under very cold water. Keep the vegetables at room temperature or refrigerate until ready to reheat. Bell peppers do not need parboiling.

To reheat, you have several choices. One is to sauté all the vegetables together in butter or a compound-butter until tender-crisp and hot. Another is to heat 1 tablespoon butter with enough water to cover the vegetables; add herbs or fresh ginger if desired. Add the vegetables and cook just long enough to reheat, then drain and serve. Season to taste with salt and pepper or a small amount of vinaigrette dressing. A third way is to heat a skillet with a small amount of oil, then add zucchini, onion and peppers (or strips of eggplant and mushroom), quickly turn and add a squeeze of lime juice, *fajita* style.

Some combinations

- Cauliflower, red pepper, carrots (sliced on diagonal or baby carrots), broccoli and snow peas or Sugar Snap peas
- Diced turnips, rutabaga or cubed acorn or butternut squash with Roma tomatoes
- Sliced zucchini and yellow squash with diced red bell peppers
- Julienned carrot, green beans, yellow squash, red pepper strips and black beans cooked tender-crisp (reheat in spicy ham stock or add several slices of smoked sausage to the water)
- Grilled eggplant strips with slices of zucchini and yellow squash and diced sundried tomatoes for garnish
- Fresh green peas and baby onions in rosemary-mint butter

Steamed Vegetables

You can use a bamboo steamer which gives excellent results, a conventional steamer, or improvise with a large, deep saucepan or roasting pan. It is important that the rack for the food be at least 1 inch smaller in diameter than the pot to allow for steam circulation and that the pot have a tight-fitting lid. The advantages of steaming vegetables are that no fat is added; the vegetables do not dry out; and more vitamins and minerals are preserved than by other methods.

STEAMED VEGETABLES

Let the water come to a boil, then add the vegetables. Check and add more boiling water if necessary. Steam those vegetables that cook longer first, then add those with shorter times. For more flavor add several slices of smoked sausage or julienne strips of ginger with the vegetables. Serve with a slice of lemon or lemon wedges or if calories are not a concern, an herb butter or herb-citrus butter.

Grilled Vegetables

Some vegetables, particularly winter and summer squashes, benefit from an initial blanching or salting before grilling. Squashes seem to accept the grill flavor better when blanched, even if only briefly. Parboiling in this case is considerably less than when vegetables are to be reheated. Other vegetables take to a brief marination and basting with a mild oil, herb-scented oil or vinaigrette. Others, such as eggplant, need to be salted and weighed down before being seasoned or marinated. Bell peppers need only minimal basting with oil or clarified butter. Vegetables may be grilled until barely tender, then arranged in a single layer on a cookie sheet, covered with foil, and reheated in an oven preheated to 375° F. If vegetables have been grilled with just salt, pepper and a light oil basting, brush them with an herb butter or combination of herbs and equal amounts of butter and reduced chicken stock to retain moisture. Among the vegetables that take well to grilling are the following.

SUMMER SQUASH

See page 34.

WINTER SQUASH

Acorn or spaghetti squash may be grilled whole on a cooler portion of the grill until fork-tender. The only difference from baking in the oven is that they will take on a charcoal flavor. Most squash should be seeded and cut ¼ inch thick. It is not necessary to peel. Parboil for about 1½ minutes, then spread pieces out and season with salt and pepper, or a seasoning salt or brush with vinaigrette dressing. Baste with oil, vinaigrette or clarified butter several times during cooking being careful not to drip any on the coals and cause flare-up.

MUSHROOMS OR SMALL ONIONS

These do not need parboiling unless you are doing mixed skewered vegetables. In that case, blanch the onions, unpeeled, for about 1½ minutes, then peel and thread on skewers. Skewered or not, baste with oil, clarified butter, herb-flavored oils or vinaigrette during grilling.

LARGE ONIONS

Slice ½ inch thick. Season with salt and pepper and baste as for other vegetables. If you like the onions very soft, place slices in a hinged rack that you can turn over; a rack also allows you to grill thinner slices, which may be tossed with greens for a warm salad.

CORN

See pages 28–29.

POTATOES OR YAMS

Parboil, in skins, for 3 to 4 minutes, but not long enough to loosen or split the skins. Put small potatoes on skewers and baste as with other vegetables. For large potatoes, either boil whole potatoes until a fork meets resistance in the center, about 7 to 8 minutes, or slice lengthwise about ⅛ to ¼ inch thick and parboil for 2 minutes. Treat like winter squash or combine minced rosemary and thyme with coarse salt and coarse pepper and oil to use as a baste during grilling.

Foil-grilling

Some vegetables and vegetable combinations like peas, cauliflower and cabbage or alternating slices of potatoes, onions, and herbs can be tightly sealed in foil and grilled along with the meat or poultry. Add a little chicken stock, water or herb butter to ensure adequate moisture. The vegetables steam in these packages. Many fruits can also be cooked this way. Leave them on the grill while the coals cool down. Softer fruits take less time than hard ones. Try peaches with brown sugar and brandy to serve warm on gingerbread or with crème fraîche and raspberries. Another good combination is apples or pears with cinnamon sugar, lemon juice, applejack and raisins to serve with ice cream and caramel sauce.

Vegetable Flans

See pages 294–296.

Kitchen Equipment

I do not believe one has to have a designer kitchen filled with every modern device to be a good cook or to create the dishes of the Southwest. There are, however, some basic pieces of equipment that will ensure better results as well as make your cooking easier and more enjoyable. I have also found some unconventional uses for certain items that have been most helpful. What follows is a list of some of my favorite tools and ones you will need for some of the recipes in this book.

Cookware   There is no bargain when it comes to cookware. You need high-quality cookware with good heat conduction and retention. I prefer stainless steel with a copper-sandwich bottom. It is very useful to have a large sauté pan, a steamer and a stock pot. For warming and cooking flour tortillas you can use either a cast-iron skillet, a griddle or a nonstick pan. If *fajitas* become a favorite of yours, especially for entertaining, you will want a large griddle (usually found in hardware stores) so you can make a sizzling presentation.

Knives   A good set of knives including a paring knife, boning knife, fillet knife for fish, chef's knife and serrated bread knife is essential. Sharpen after each use and cut only on wooden surfaces.

Food Processor   A food processor is extremely useful for all kinds of mixing, grating, blending, pureeing, slicing, shredding, cutting julienne strips and controlled, uniform chopping. It can also be used to make bread and homemade sausage meat.

Blender   A blender is not necessary if you have a food processor, but it can be used for liquefying and pureeing.

Stripper   A handy tool to remove uniform strips of peel from citrus.

Zester   A small tool that removes bits of zest from citrus.

Pastry Scraper   Indispensable for quick and easy removal of sticky flour from work surfaces. It is also useful for transferring crabcakes or delicate risen rolls to the sauté pan or baking sheets.

Chinois or Fine Sieve   Indispensable for straining custards and custard sauces, dark sauces enriched with chilies or other ingredients with peel, seeds or fiber.

Scissors   Use sharp, high-quality scissors for cutting away seeds and ribs from chilies without tearing the skin, for snipping delicate herbs or cutting strips of spinach, sorrel or Belgian endive.

Kitchen or Poultry Shears   To trim small game birds.

Long-Shanked Tweezers   To pull tiny bones from small game birds.

Ice-Cream Scoops   Very useful for making uniform cookies of variable sizes or perfect scoops of seafood or poultry salads for payaya or melon halves as well as for ice cream. Get the squeeze-handle kind in 3 or 4 sizes.

Small Propane Blow Torch   To peel tomatoes and peaches effortlessly or to roast chilies when you want to ensure firm texture. Use also to caramelize crème brûlée or floating island.

Meat Grinder   To make homemade sausages or to process tomatoes for large quantities of gazpacho or finely diced relishes.

Cordless Whisk-Mixer   A convenient tool for whisking and mixing.

Kitchen Scale   Essential for baking and always very useful for measuring ingredients.

Miniature Madeleine Pans   Excellent for small cornbreads with an attractive shell shape. Cast-iron cornstick molds are also good; you will need several to prepare cornsticks for a crowd.

Squirt Bottle   Save an old plastic mustard or catsup bottle or buy a bottle from a beauty-supply house. Use for making designs with dessert sauces or with flavored creams for soups.

Parchment Paper   Use for baking cakes and cookies. Essential for delicate cookie tacos.

Grills and Grill Tools   See pages 192–193.

Spice Grinder   A coffee grinder that you use only for grinding spices.

Fat Separator   To degrease roasts.

Ladles, 2- and 4-Ounce Size   For soups and sauces.

Narrow Rolling Pin   Get one the thickness of a broom handle for flour tortillas.

Large Spatula   Try to find a restaurant-size turner for fish and other foods cooked on the grill.

Ice-Cream Maker   For homemade ice cream and sherbet.

Small Meals, Appetizers, Brunch

Tequila Grapefruit and Strawberries
Grilled Chicken Wings
Fried Sage Leaves
Mushrooms with Basil Cream
Corn Shortcakes with Spicy Oysters
Texas Tapas
Chili Crêpes
Wild Rice Crêpes
Fresh Corn Crêpes
Baked Stuffed Chilies
Grilled Stuffed Chilies
Chiles Rellenos
Gulf Shrimp Hash
Santa Fe Tortillas with Chili Sauce and Gulf Crabmeat
Quesadillas
Tortilla Pizzas
Ancho Chili Cakes with Shrimp and Corn Sauce
Fire Shrimp
Scallops in Hollandaise Sauce
Grilled Sea Scallops in Orange Juice
Dean's Seafood Tacos
Crabcakes
Crabmeat Strata
Crab and Chili Tortas
Stephan's Catfish Mousse
Grits Soufflé with Ham and Shrimp
Vegetable and Pasta Soufflé
Shrimp and Spinach Lasagne
Pasta with Seafood and Pine Nuts
Lime Pasta with Hazelnuts
Chicken in Tomatillo Sauce
Chicken and Chili Sausages
Wild Game Sausages
Lamb Sausage with Mint, Thyme and Rosemary
Poblano Chili Dip

Traditionally much of the creativity in restaurant menus could be found in the appetizer or brunch section; entrees were more conventional and accompanied by the vegetable of the day, soup or salad. The recent so-called grazing trend, that is, sampling a variety of tastes at one meal, and an adventurous spirit to try new things have resulted in what might be called small meals.

These actually can be almost anything, from miniature samples of an entree or appetizer, often with a touch of extravagance (a few strips of smoked fish, a spoonful of caviar, a succulent lobster claw), to a tiny one-dish meal of something very special and fresh. A small meal can be pizza, pasta, a soft taco or calzone with a little relish. With some fresh fruit and homemade muffins to round things out in the morning, the meal becomes brunch. A small meal need not be followed by another course, but it could be accompanied by bread, a glass of wine and perhaps a salad. Appetizer plates with a few slices of barbecued homemade sausage, fresh Gulf crab on a tortilla with a dollop of poblano chili dip and several slices of perfectly ripe mango are reminiscent of Spanish *tapas* and Italian antipasto . . . except that little comes after.

The recipes that follow are suitable for appetizers, brunch or small meals at any time of day. They might be accompanied by bread or muffins and salad. Consult the relish chapter for more mix-and-match ideas.

TEQUILA GRAPEFRUIT AND STRAWBERRIES

6 servings

Grapefruit sections and strawberries, glazed with a tequila syrup and seasoned with fresh mint, combine deliciously for either an appetizer or dessert.

3 fresh grapefruit, preferably pink, halved
½ cup water
½ cup sugar
½ cup tequila
14 large unblemished strawberries, hulled
8 leaves fresh mint, chopped
6 mint sprigs for garnish

Using a paring knife, cut around the exposed grapefruit membrane to remove the sections. Put sections in a bowl. Squeeze the shell to extract the juice and pour it in a saucepan. Cut away and discard all membrane and save the shells to serve the fruit in.

Add water and sugar to the saucepan and bring to a boil. After 3 minutes add the tequila and boil the liquids an additional 3 minutes to make a thick sugar syrup. Do not allow the syrup to caramelize. Cool for 5 minutes.

Cut the strawberries in half or thirds, and combine with the grapefruit sections in a small bowl. Stir in the chopped mint. Spoon the fruit into the reserved grapefruit shells and drizzle with tequila syrup. Garnish each serving with a sprig of fresh mint and serve immediately.

GRILLED CHICKEN WINGS

12 servings

Chicken wings are delicious whether dipped in seasoned flour and fried or rubbed with spices and grilled. Either way, serve them with a mild creamy dip or buttermilk ranch dressing (page 152).

36 chicken wings
Oil for grilling or frying (see note)

BARBECUE RUB
2 tablespoons salt
1 tablespoon black pepper
½ teaspoon cayenne pepper
1 tablespoon Hungarian paprika
1 tablespoon garlic powder
1½ tablespoons minced fresh parsley
3 tablespoons vegetable oil

MOPPING SAUCE
¼ cup vegetable oil
1 cup chicken broth
¼ cup fresh lime juice
¼ cup Worcestershire sauce
2 tablespoons bottled barbecue sauce
  (optional)

———

1½ cups all-purpose flour for frying

Remove the wingtips and skin from the wings.

If grilling, clean the grill surface and rub with a cloth dampened with oil. Preheat the grill.

Combine the dry ingredients for the barbecue rub in a small bowl. Combine ¼ cup of the vegetable oil and the remaining ingredients for the mopping sauce in another small bowl.

Rub the chicken wings with oil, then rub with the barbecue seasoning rub. Place on the grill and brush with the mopping sauce 3 or 4 times during grilling. Grill until the juices run clear, about 8 to 10 minutes. Put the chicken wings on a warm platter and brush again with the mop. Serve with mild sour cream dip or buttermilk ranch dressing.

If frying, combine the barbecue seasoning rub with flour. Dip the chicken wings in the flour mixture, coating all sides.

Heat about 1½ to 2 inches oil in a deep saucepan to 350° F. Line a cookie sheet with paper towels. Preheat the oven to just under 200° F. Deep-fry all the chicken wings, a few at a time, using tongs to turn them until they are golden brown on all sides. Put the fried chicken wings on the cookie sheet and keep them warm in the oven while frying the rest. Serve with the same dip or dressing as for grilled wings, on a large platter garnished with fresh greens or watercress.

NOTE.   Use safflower oil for grilling, peanut oil for frying.

FRIED SAGE LEAVES

10 servings

Southwesterners will fry just about anything and this recipe has become very popular among cooks with herb gardens. You can fry basil leaves the same way. Serve with a roasted-pepper catsup (page 241.)

30 sage leaves

BATTER
1¾ cups all-purpose flour
½ teaspoon salt
¼ teaspoon garlic powder
Pinch cayenne pepper
3 tablespoons safflower oil
2 eggs, separated
Pinch sugar
¾ cup beer
1 tablespoon minced fresh parsley

_____

Peanut oil for frying

Medieval cooks believed that sage improves the memory. The blue-violet flowers make an attractive garnish and the leaves add subtle seasoning to berry sauces for game. They also combine beautifully with mint for pineapple.

Rinse and carefully dry sage leaves.

Put flour, salt, garlic powder, cayenne pepper, safflower oil, egg yolks, sugar, beer, ½ cup water and parsley in a bowl and mix with an electric mixer until smooth. Let the batter stand at room temperature at least 1 hour before using.

Heat 2 inches of peanut oil to 350° F. in a large saucepan. When it reaches that temperature, reduce the heat to medium.

While the oil is heating, beat the egg whites in separate bowl until they hold stiff peaks. Fold into the batter. Dip each sage leaf in the batter, drop in the hot oil and fry until golden brown, about 2 minutes. Drain on paper towels.

FRIED SAGE LEAVES WITH CHEESE AND RED PEPPER

6 servings

30 sage leaves
Batter from main recipe
Peanut oil for frying
1 egg
15 leaf-size slivers of mozzarella or Monterey Jack cheese
¼ cup flour
1 red bell pepper, cut in julienne strips
Lemon wedges for garnish

Prepare sage leaves and batter as described in main recipe. Heat oil as described. Beat egg with 3 tablespoons water. When oil is hot, place a thin sliver of cheese between 2 sage leaves and hold together with tongs. Dip in egg, dust lightly with flour and coat with batter. Deep-fry until golden brown, about 2 minutes. Dip red bell pepper strips in the batter only and deep-fry until golden, about 2 minutes. Alternate sage leaves and pepper strips in a paper-lined basket and serve with wedges of lemon.

MUSHROOMS WITH BASIL CREAM

5 servings

The mushrooms may be served on slices of toasted French bread but they have enough sauce to be combined with buttered pasta or wild rice or used as a topping over veal or chicken.

10 slices French bread, cut from baguettes
Butter for the bread
1 pound medium-to-large white button mushrooms, rinsed and dried, or a combination of wild mushrooms such as chanterelles or morels
2 tablespoons unsalted butter
2 shallots, minced
4 sundried tomatoes, drained and diced (about 3 tablespoons), or 2 tablespoons diced pimiento, drained
10 fresh basil leaves, chopped, or 1 teaspoon dried basil
2 tablespoons white wine
½ teaspoon cornstarch
⅓ cup heavy cream
¼ teaspoon salt
Freshly ground black pepper
4 or 5 sprigs of basil for garnish

Preheat the broiler. Toast the baguette slices by placing them 4 inches from the broiling element until lightly browned. Turn and butter the other side and toast it.

Cut large mushrooms into pieces about ¼ inch thick. Heat the butter in a large skillet over medium heat. Add the shallots and mushrooms and sauté, stirring constantly, until they begin to soften, 1 to 1½ minutes.

Dissolve the cornstarch in the cream. Add to the skillet with the basil and wine and cook over medium heat, stirring gently, about 2 minutes. Season to taste with salt and pepper.

Put two pieces of toast on each plate and mound the mushrooms and sauce between them, allowing the sauce to spill onto the plate. Garnish each plate with a sprig of fresh basil.

CORN SHORTCAKES WITH SPICY OYSTERS

8 servings

The creamy, spiced butter sauce is wonderful with a moist, polenta-like cornbread. Bake the cornbread in muffin tins; it does not rise very much so the muffins will have slightly flat tops, perfect for shortcake. They do not need to be split.

Hot-water cornbread (page 310)

————

½ cup white wine
¼ cup white wine vinegar
1 shallot, minced
1 serrano chili, halved and stemmed, with seeds
1 sprig fresh thyme
¼ to ½ cup water, or as needed
32 freshly shucked oysters (3 ten-ounce jars)
½ cup heavy cream
1 cup (2 sticks) unsalted butter, at room temperature
1 tomato, preferably Roma, peeled, seeded and chopped
4 scallions, white part and about 1 inch of the green, sliced
1½ tablespoons minced fresh basil or tarragon
1 serrano chili, stemmed, seeded and minced (optional)
Salt
Freshly ground black pepper
Lemon juice
Sprigs of fresh basil or tarragon for garnish

Prepare the hot-water cornbread according to recipe directions.

Heat the wine, vinegar, shallot, chili and thyme to a boil in a large skillet. Add the oysters, including all their liquid, and enough water to moisten the oysters. Bring back to the boil, stirring to turn the oysters, then remove from the heat. Cover and let stand about 5 minutes. Remove oysters with a slotted spoon and cover to keep warm.

Strain the liquid into a smaller saucepan and heat to a boil. Add the cream and boil until reduced to about ⅓ cup. Lower the heat to medium and whisk in the butter about 2 tablespoons at a time, lifting the pan from the heat if necessary to keep the sauce from separating. When all the butter has been added, stir in the tomato, scallions, basil or tarragon and serrano chili if using. Season to taste with salt, pepper and a squeeze of lemon.

Just before serving, briefly warm the oysters in the sauce. To serve, spoon oysters and sauce around the corncake. Drizzle a little sauce over the top of each corncake and garnish with a sprig of basil or tarragon.

TEXAS TAPAS

10 servings

These skewered meats are called *anticuchos* in the Southwest where they are a Tex-Mex border specialty. Beef tenderloin is traditionally used but you can substitute chicken or rabbit or a firm-fleshed fish, such as swordfish, or shrimp. The strong basting pesto gives a wonderful flavor to the fish or meat. The lime juice is not mixed with the pesto as it would destroy the bright green color. These Texas *tapas* may be served with a homemade relish or triple-mustard sauce (page 256) or just as is.

2½ pounds beef tenderloin, chicken breast or rabbit or 2 pounds swordfish or other firm-fleshed fish or shrimp
4 cloves garlic
4 or 5 serrano chilies, stemmed
1 cup cilantro leaves, packed
⅓ cup fresh parsley leaves
2 tablespoons Worcestershire sauce
½ cup chicken broth
3 tablespoons melted butter
3 tablespoons safflower oil
⅓ cup fresh lime juice
Salt
Freshly ground black pepper

Soak 10 bamboo or wooden skewers for at least 2 hours before grilling (see note).

Cut the meat or fish into pieces about the size of a large thumbnail. Leave shrimp whole. Thread them on skewers, about 4 pieces each. Arrange in a single layer in a shallow glass dish.

Put the garlic, chilies, cilantro, parsley, Worcestershire sauce and chicken broth in a blender jar and blend on high speed until garlic, chilies and herbs are very finely minced. Pour into a small bowl and stir in the butter and oil.

Clean the grill surface and rub with an oil-dampened cloth. Preheat the grill, allowing about 30 minutes for the fire to be ready.

Brush the skewered meats or shrimp with lime juice, then with sauce on all sides. Sprinkle lightly with salt and pepper.

Grill the *anticuchos* on both sides, brushing several times with the sauce and lime juice. Use lime juice sparingly, as the meat should be well browned. Remove after about 3 minutes or when well browned, and wrap in foil.

Preheat the oven to 400° F. Let meats stand for no more than 30 minutes, then reheat in the oven for 5 to 6 minutes.

Anticuchos may also be served directly from the grill. Add about 2 minutes to the cooking time and test one to be sure they are done.

NOTE. If you do not have time to soak the skewers, wrap the ends in aluminum foil after threading. Remove foil before serving.

CHILI CRÊPES

20 crêpes

Made with jalapeño chilies, these crêpes have a bright green color and mild pepper taste. With ancho chili pods, they are reddish-brown. A soft cream cheese or goat cheese filling suits both as would one of your favorite poultry or seafood fillings.

6 to 7 jalapeño peppers, stemmed and seeded, or 2 ancho chili pods, toasted, stemmed and seeded (page 22)
3 sprigs fresh cilantro or parsley
5 tablespoons butter, melted
4 large eggs
¾ cup milk
1 teaspoon salt
1¾ cups all-purpose flour
½ teaspoon to 2 tablespoons sugar
2 to 3 tablespoons butter for cooking the crêpes

Put the peppers and cilantro in a blender jar. Blend on and off several times to mince the peppers. Add the butter, eggs, milk, ¾ cup water, flour and sugar and blend until smooth. Use the greater amount of sugar if using ancho pods. The batter should have the consistency of heavy cream. Let the batter rest at room temperature at least 1 hour before preparing the crêpes. When ready to make the crêpes, stir the batter and follow the directions given in the recipe for fresh corn crêpes (page 65).

WILD RICE CRÊPES

20 crêpes

Wild rice adds a crunchy texture and nutty flavor to ordinary crêpes. You can use a variety of fillings or sauces. Seafood is particularly good with a cheese-and-pepper sauce. Or you could serve them filled with chicken and pecan-butter sauce (page 259) or plain with a mushroom sauce.

4 tablespoons unsalted butter, melted
2 cups milk
3 large eggs
1½ cups all-purpose flour
½ teaspoon salt
1 tablespoon fresh minced parsley
2½ cups cooked wild rice
Butter for preparing the crêpes

Put the butter, milk, eggs, flour and salt in a blender jar and blend on high speed until smooth. Pour into a shallow bowl and stir in parsley and wild rice. Let the batter stand for at least 45 minutes before using. When ready to make the crêpes, stir the batter and add water if needed to achieve the consistency of heavy cream. Prepare the crêpes as directed in the recipe for fresh corn crêpes on page 65.

FRESH CORN CRÊPES

20 crêpes

Fresh corn gives these crêpes their rich color and delicate corn flavor. Fill them with seafood and a creamy sauce or with cheese and a tomatillo relish (pages 230 and 231) or roast-bell-pepper sauce (page 253). Crêpes may also be layered with refried black beans, seafood and chili fillings or Robert's game ragout (page 164).

1½ cups fresh corn kernels or thawed
    frozen kernels
⅔ cup all-purpose flour
6 tablespoons cornstarch
1 tablespoon sugar
¾ cup milk
2 tablespoons butter, melted
3 large eggs
1 teaspoon salt
Butter for preparing the crêpes

Place the corn kernels and ¾ cup water in a blender jar. Blend on high speed until liquefied, about 1 minute. Pour the mixture through a coarse strainer, then put back in the blender jar and add the flour, cornstarch, sugar, milk, butter, eggs and salt. Blend on high speed until smooth. The batter should have the consistency of heavy cream. Let it rest for at least 30 minutes, at room temperature.

Melt a dot of butter in a well seasoned crêpe pan over medium-high heat. When the butter is hot, lift the pan from the heat and pour in ¼ cup of batter. Tilt the pan so the batter covers the entire surface. Return pan to the heat and cook the crêpe until the surface looks dry and the bottom is browned. Use a spatula to turn the crêpe and cook on the opposite side about 30 seconds. Remove to a warm plate. Repeat, buttering the pan for each crêpe. Stack finished crêpes. They may be double wrapped in plastic bags and frozen; they will keep for up to 3 months.

Crêpes may be filled and rolled or folded in quarters. Serve two crêpes per person.

CORNMEAL CRÊPES

12 crêpes

5 tablespoons unsalted butter, melted
4 eggs
¾ cup milk
1 teaspoon salt
¾ cup plus 2 tablespoons all-purpose
    flour
¾ cup plus 2 tablespoons yellow or
    blue cornmeal
1 teaspoon sugar
½ teaspoon baking soda

Combine all of the ingredients in a blender jar. Blend on high until smooth. The batter should rest at room temperature for 1 hour before preparation of the crêpes. When ready to make the crêpes, stir the batter and proceed as directed in the recipe for fresh corn crêpes, above.

BAKED STUFFED CHILIES

8 servings

The flavor of walnuts in the filling enhances both the chilies and the artichokes. Poblano chilies are larger than Anaheim chilies, so you may need to adjust the amount of filling.

8 poblano or Anaheim chilies, roasted and peeled (page 20)

TOMATO SAUCE
1 tablespoon safflower oil
1 clove garlic, minced
4 fresh tomatoes, peeled, seeded and chopped, or 1 can (14½ ounces) Italian-style tomatoes, including juices, chopped
1½ tablespoons fresh minced basil or cilantro
Salt
Pepper

SAUTÉED WALNUTS
½ tablespoon unsalted butter
½ cup toasted walnuts (page 50)

CHEESE FILLING
4 ounces fresh cream cheese, at room temperature
4 ounces Monterey Jack or Asiago cheese, grated (about 1 cup)
8 ounces mozzarella cheese, grated (about 2 cups)
1 to 2 tablespoons sour cream, as needed
6 freshly cooked artichoke hearts, diced (optional)

———

Butter for baking dish

Use scissors to make a lengthwise cut down each chili. Snip the seeds from the veins to avoid tearing, and remove the seeds and stringy veiny portion. Leave tops and stems intact. Set aside while preparing the walnuts, sauce and filling.

Heat the oil in a large skillet over medium heat. Add the garlic and tomatoes and sauté in oil 1 to 2 minutes. Add basil or cilantro, season to taste with salt and pepper and remove from heat. Leave uncovered.

Heat butter in a small skillet over medium heat. Add walnuts and sauté for 1 to 2 minutes. Remove and chop coarse.

Cream together the cream cheese, Monterey Jack and mozzarella. Add just enough sour cream to bind filling. Fold in the walnuts and artichoke hearts if using. Carefully stuff each chili, leaving the slit partially open.

Preheat oven to 350°F. Butter a baking dish lightly. Place the stuffed chilies in the dish and bake until the cheese is melted and creamy, 10 to 15 minutes. Serve each chili with tomato sauce on the side.

PICADILLO DUCK FILLING FOR CHILIES

6 servings

6 poblano chilies, roasted and peeled
(page 20)

DUCK PICADILLO
1½ tablespoons duck fat or safflower
oil
1 garlic clove, minced
1 pound duck meat, ground
¼ pound pork shoulder, including
fat, ground
½ large yellow or white onion,
chopped
⅓ cup diced red potato, unpeeled
1 small Granny Smith apple, peeled,
cored and diced
1 serrano chili, stemmed, seeded and
minced
¼ cup beef broth
1 tablespoon red wine or balsamic
vinegar
1 tomato, peeled and diced
1 teaspoon chili powder
1 teaspoon salt, or to taste
1 teaspoon ground cinnamon
1 teaspoon ground cumin
½ teaspoon ground cloves
⅓ cup raisins or currants
⅓ cup chopped toasted pecans (page
50)

SAUTÉED PECANS
1 tablespoon unsalted butter
12 toasted pecan halves (page 50)

———

1 cup crème fraîche (page 112)
Seeds from 1 pomegranate, or ½ pint
fresh raspberries for garnish

Prepare the chilies as described in the recipe for baked stuffed chilies.

For the *picadillo,* heat the duck fat or oil in a large skillet over medium-high heat. Add the garlic, ground duck and pork and sauté, breaking the meat up with a fork, until well browned, about 5 to 6 minutes. Add the onion, potato, apple, serrano chili and cook 5 minutes, then stir in the beef broth, vinegar, tomato, chili powder, salt, cinnamon, cumin, cloves, raisins or currants and pecans. Cook, stirring occasionally, until thickened with nearly all the liquid incorporated, about 10 to 15 minutes. Let cool.

To sauté the pecans, heat the butter in a small skillet over medium-high heat. Add the pecan halves and sauté for about 1 minute. Drain on paper towels.

Preheat the oven to 375°F. Fill the chilies with *picadillo* and place them close together in an 8″ x 8″ baking pan. Cover with foil and bake until heated through, about 10 to 12 minutes.

To serve, place 1 chili on each plate. Put a dollop of crème fraîche on each, topped with 2 pecan halves. Garnish with pomegranate seeds or fresh raspberries.

GRILLED STUFFED CHILIES

6 servings

Cheese and chilies are a wonderful combination, particularly when you add the flavor of an outdoor grill. Poblano chilies are best for grilling because Anaheim, unless you find the thick-flesh variety, tend to hold up less well. I prefer to remove the peel with a blowtorch before grilling. The chilies may also be stuffed without peeling but you will need to remove the peel before serving as it is tough and bitter. Serve with a fresh zucchini salad (page 146), a tomato relish (pages 226–228) or goat cheese sauce (page 262) and ancho cream (page 112).

6 poblano or Anaheim chilies, peeled (page 20)

FILLING
6 ounces fresh mozzarella cheese
6 ounces Monterey Jack cheese
6 ounces bel paese cheese or another soft melting cheese

———

2 tablespoons melted butter
Oil for the grill
Sour cream for garnish (optional)

Using scissors, cut the stem top from each chili. Carefully snip away veins and seeds. Set aside while preparing the filling.

Grate the three cheeses and toss them together in a mixing bowl. Carefully stuff each chili to within ¼ inch of the top. Replace top and secure with a moistened toothpick. Brush with melted butter.

Clean the grill surface and rub it with an oil-dampened cloth. Preheat the grill. Place chilies on the coolest part of the grill. Use tongs to grill on all sides. Cover the grill after turning. Grill until the cheese is melted, about 6 to 8 minutes in all. Remove toothpicks.

If using goat cheese sauce, film the plate with sauce and place the chili on the plate. Decorate with the ancho cream.

If using the vegetable salad, arrange the greens on one half of the plate and place the chili on the other. Garnish with sour cream if desired. Use the same presentation and garnish if using relish.

CHICKEN FILLING FOR CHILIES

8 servings

8 poblano chilies
1 tablespoon vegetable oil
1 clove garlic, minced
1 yellow or white onion, halved, cored and thinly sliced
¼ to ½ cup heavy cream
¼ cup grated Parmesan cheese
2 cups freshly poached chicken, shredded
Salt
Pepper

Prepare the chilies for stuffing as described above.

Heat the oil in a medium skillet over medium heat. Add the garlic and onion and sauté until the onion softens, about 2 minutes. Stir in ¼ cup cream and simmer about 5 minutes. Add the cheese, chicken and additional cream if needed to make a moist filling. Stuff the chilies and set aside. Prepare the grill and grill as described in the recipe for grilled stuffed chilies, allowing more time if filling was made in advance and chilled. Serve with salad or relish or with sauce.

CHILES RELLENOS

8 servings

Chiles rellenos, which are stuffed chilies dipped in batter and deep-fried, can be prepared using Gulf shrimp hash or any one of the fillings for stuffed chilies. Serve with a sauce or relish, such as ranch-style tomato sauce (page 252), cilantro hollandaise sauce (page 258) or the corn sauce for tamales (page 290).

8 poblano or Anaheim chilies, roasted and peeled (page 20)
Cheese or poultry filling (page 68) or Gulf shrimp hash (page 70)

CHILE RELLENO BATTER
3 eggs, separated
1½ tablespoons all-purpose flour
½ teaspoon salt
Pinch of white pepper

Oil for frying

Leave the chili stems intact and use a sharp knife to make a slit starting ½ inch below the stem to within ½ to 1 inch of the base of the chili. Use scissors to trim away the seeds and veins. Fill the peppers with the filling of choice, leaving enough room for the edges of the chili to overlap.

Beat the egg yolks with the flour, salt and pepper until light and lemon-yellow in color. In a separate bowl, beat the egg whites to stiff peaks. Fold the yolk mixture into the whites.

Heat the oil in a deep sauté pan or saucepan to 375° F. Dip each pepper into the batter and then transfer to the oil. Cook, turning once, until the batter puffs and is golden brown. Serve immediately.

GULF SHRIMP HASH

3 cups

Typically, *picadillo,* a pork or beef hash with potatoes, is served in a flour tortilla or used to fill *chiles rellenos* (stuffed chilies that are dipped in an egg batter and fried). This *picadillo,* which is made with shrimp and pork sausage, may be used either as a filling for chilies or as an accompaniment to fried eggs or omelets. In all cases, a tomato-based relish (pages 226–228) goes well as does triple-mustard sauce (page 256).

4 tablespoons safflower oil
3 tablespoons butter
1 clove garlic, minced
1 cup yellow or red onion, minced
1 large potato, boiled and diced
¼ pound (about ½ cup) bulk pork
   sausage
2 tablespoons diced red bell pepper
3 tablespoons green chili or poblano
   chili, roasted, peeled and diced
   (page 20)
¼ cup corn niblets (optional)
2 cups (1 pound), raw Gulf shrimp
2 teaspoons minced fresh oregano or
   ½ teaspoon dried leaf oregano
Salt
Black pepper
⅓ to ½ cup heavy cream (optional)

Heat 2 tablespoons oil and 1 tablespoon butter in a large skillet over medium-high heat. Add garlic and onions and sauté 1 to 2 minutes. Add the potato and sauté, turning potatoes frequently, until crisp, about 3 minutes. Remove and set aside.

Spread the sausage in the same skillet, breaking apart with a fork. Sauté until browned. Stir in the red pepper, green pepper or chili, corn if using, and shrimp and sauté until the shrimp turns pink. Stir in oregano and season to taste with salt and pepper. Cool.

When ready to serve, mix in the cream if using. Shape the hash into patties and sauté until crisp in the remaining butter and oil or bake the hash in a buttered pan and serve with fried eggs. It may also be used to stuff bell peppers or roasted poblano chilies.

SANTA FE TORTILLAS WITH CHILI SAUCE AND GULF CRABMEAT

6 servings

The combination of crisp tortillas, a rich green chili-flavored sauce and slightly spicy crabmeat makes an elegant appetizer that looks as exciting as it tastes. You may vary the dish by using one or more colorful bell pepper sauces (page 253) or substituting a fried chili pasta (pages 292–293) for the tortilla strips.

4 corn or flour tortillas (page 300), cut into very thin (1/16 inch) strips
Peanut oil for frying
Salt
3 poblano chilies or 4 green or Anaheim chilies, roasted and peeled (page 20)
2 green bell peppers, roasted and peeled (page 20)
2 cups chicken stock, preferably homemade (page 97)
2 tablespoons all-purpose flour
1 clove garlic, chopped
½ cup heavy cream
Salt
Pepper
2 tablespoons unsalted butter
2 shallots, minced
2 serrano chilies, stemmed, seeded and minced
1 pound Gulf crabmeat, rinsed and cartilage removed, or 1 pound frozen crabmeat, thawed
2 tomatoes, seeded and cut in ¼-inch dice
1½ tablespoons minced fresh cilantro
3 tablespoons vermouth

Let the tortilla strips stand, uncovered, at room temperature for at least 1½ hours to dry out before frying. In a large saucepan over medium-high heat heat enough peanut oil to deep-fry the tortillas to 375° F. Fry the tortillas in batches until crisp. Drain on paper towels. Sprinkle lightly with salt.

Cut the poblano, green or Anaheim chilies and bell peppers up and place them in a blender jar. Be sure to add any juices that have accumulated after roasting the peppers. Add 1 cup chicken stock, flour, garlic and blend on high speed until smooth. Pour the pureed peppers into a medium saucepan over medium heat. Add the remaining chicken stock and cream and cook, stirring constantly, until the sauce is thickened, about 5 minutes. Season to taste with salt and pepper. Strain the sauce through a fine sieve and then put it back in the same saucepan over low heat to keep warm until ready to use.

Heat the butter to a sizzle in a large skillet. Add the shallots and serrano chilies and sauté for 1 minute. Stir in the crabmeat, tomatoes, cilantro and vermouth and cook, tossing to combine the ingredients, until the crab is hot, about 3 to 4 minutes. Season to taste with salt and pepper.

Spoon some of the sauce on each serving plate and tilt the plate to cover it with sauce. Arrange the tortilla strips on the plate at random. Mound the crab in the center.

QUESADILLAS

30 quesadilla pieces

Quesadillas are like turnovers made from flour or corn tortillas. This is one of the simplest ways to make them. Flour tortillas are softened, filled with chilies, cheese and fruit, then sautéed quickly on both sides. They may also be grilled for a smoky flavor. Be careful not to let the fire flare up or your *quesadillas* may go up in flames.

½ yellow onion, halved and cut in thin slices
10 flour tortillas (page 300)
1 pound soft cheese that melts easily, like Brie or Camembert, cut in ¼-inch strips
2 poblano chilies, roasted, peeled and diced (page 20)
1 mango, stoned, peeled and diced, or 1 papaya, pitted, peeled and diced
4 tablespoons butter
4 tablespoons oil

Heat ½ cup water to a boil in a medium skillet. Add the onions, cover and remove from heat. Let stand until onions wilt, about 12 minutes. Drain completely.

Heat a nonstick or well seasoned skillet over medium heat. When it is hot, heat each tortilla about 15 seconds on both sides to soften.

To fill, place 2 strips of cheese, several onion strips and 1 tablespoon each diced chilies and fruit on half of each tortilla. Fold the tortilla over and brush with melted butter.

Heat 1 teaspoon butter and 1 teaspoon oil in a skillet over medium heat. Cook each *quesadilla* on both sides for 1 minute, until it is golden brown and the cheese melts. Continue until all are done. Cut each *quesadilla* into three.

CRAB QUESADILLAS

48 quesadilla pieces

You might think of this as a Southwestern crabcake. It makes a great appetizer to pass on trays as well as an attractive individual portion garnished with tomato and green chili relish (page 227), avocado relish (page 229) or tomatillo relish (page 230).

⅓ cup butter, melted
¼ cup safflower oil
1 clove garlic, minced
½ medium onion, chopped
1 poblano chili, roasted, peeled and diced (page 20), or 2 jalapeño chilies, stemmed, seeded and finely diced
1 pound lump crabmeat, cartilage removed
¼ cup mayonnaise or 3 ounces fresh cream cheese and 2 tablespoons mayonnaise
1 teaspoon salt
1 tablespoon minced fresh cilantro
16 flour tortillas (page 300)
4 ounces Monterey Jack or Pepper-Jack cheese

Heat the butter and oil in a medium saucepan to melt and combine. Pour off all but 2 tablespoons into a small cup and set aside. Add the garlic and onion to the remaining butter and oil and sauté over medium-high heat until translucent, about 2 minutes. Remove from the heat and stir in the chilies, crab, mayonnaise, salt and cilantro. Mix well.

To soften the tortillas heat a nonstick skillet over medium-high heat for about 3 minutes. Put tortillas in the skillet one by one, turning each once, until soft. Spread some crab mixture over half of each tortilla, top with cheese, then fold over. Brush liberally with melted butter and oil and repeat with the remaining tortillas. This may be done early in the day. Cover the tortillas and refrigerate until ready to sauté.

Heat a nonstick skillet over medium-high heat. Sauté the *quesadillas* 2 or 3 at a time until golden brown on both sides, about 3 to 4 minutes. Cut each into 3 triangles. Pass on trays or arrange on appetizer plates and garnish with relish.

GRILLED QUESADILLAS

30 quesadilla *pieces*

10 corn or flour tortillas (page 300)
1 pound Mexican cheese (Oaxaca, Chihuahua or asadero) or whole-milk mozzarella, thinly sliced
1 tablespoon diced mild green chilies or poblano chilies, roasted and peeled (page 20)
5 tablespoons snipped fresh cilantro, basil or chervil
1 to 2 tablespoons melted butter

Soften the tortillas as described above. Place some cheese on half of each tortilla, leaving a 1-inch border. Top with chilies and cilantro or other herb and fold over. Brush both sides liberally with melted butter, using more butter for corn than for flour tortillas.

Prepare an outdoor grill, positioning the rack at least 8 inches from the coals. When they form a white-hot ash, spread them out. If grilling indoors, preheat grill to highest setting. Place the tortilla on the rack. After about 30 seconds, or when marked, turn and grill on the opposite side, until the cheese is melted, about 1 to 2 minutes. Cut into thirds and serve immediately. Accompany with a tomato relish if desired.

Quesadilla Variations
- Spread the tortillas with herb pesto (page 211), then add goat cheese. Omit the fresh herbs.
- Add sliced scallions and finely diced seeded tomatoes.
- Use roasted and peeled bell peppers together with or instead of chilies. Combine red bell peppers with chopped toasted walnuts.
- Use a puree of black beans, Brie cheese and tomato relish (page 226).

TORTILLA PIZZAS

10 pizzas

Flour tortillas, lightly toasted, make a great base for a Southwest-style pizza. The choice of fillings and toppings is endless, limited only by your personal taste and imagination. You can use packaged flour tortillas but the results do taste better with homemade. You may also substitute prepared spaghetti sauce or *salsa* for homemade spaghetti sauce to make the recipe a very quick and easy one.

10 flour tortillas (page 300)
1½ cups homemade spaghetti sauce
   or 1½ cups tomato-based relish
   (pages 226–228)
4 cooked chicken breasts, preferably
   grilled, cut in julienne strips
1 moderately firm avocado, peeled,
   pitted and cut in julienne strips
1 red bell pepper, cut in julienne
   strips
2 tablespoons virgin olive oil or
   avocado oil
2 tablespoons minced fresh thyme,
   basil or oregano
8 ounces bel paese cheese, thinly
   sliced
8 ounces mozzarella cheese, thinly
   sliced or another soft, white
   melting cheese

Preheat the oven to 400° F. Spread the tortillas out on an ungreased cookie sheet and bake until lightly toasted, about 5 to 8 minutes. Remove from oven, turn over and spread each with about 2 tablespoons sauce. Put the chicken strips on top of the sauce. Add the avocado and red bell pepper, then sprinkle with several drops of olive or avocado oil. Sprinkle with fresh herbs and top with 2 to 3 slices of each cheese.

Increase the oven temperature to 450° F. Bake the pizzas until the cheese is melted and the tops are lightly browned, about 10 to 12 minutes. Serve immediately.

Variations

- Top toasted tortillas with thinly sliced goat cheese, Brie or other melting cheese. Warm and serve with a tomato or tomatillo relish.
- Spread toasted tortillas with pesto and top with slices of ripe tomato. Cover with thin slices of mozzarella, bel paese or havarti cheese. Bake until cheese is melted and lightly browned, about 8 to 10 minutes.
- Spread the toasted tortillas with bulk sausage, cooked and crumbled, or diced smoked sausage. Top with a mild goat cheese and strips of red, yellow and green bell pepper. Sprinkle with rosemary and virgin olive oil. Bake until the cheese is warm, about 5 or 6 minutes ·
- Spread toasted tortillas with a basil or herb pesto instead of sausage. Continue with goat cheese and pepper strips. Sprinkle with olive oil. Bake 5 or 6 minutes, just long enough to warm the cheese.

ANCHO CHILI CAKES WITH SHRIMP AND CORN SAUCE

6 servings

This is a beautiful and colorful dish for a festive Southwest brunch. The crushed chili pods give a subtle roasted flavor to these delicate pancakes. Shrimp powder also adds a unique, slightly salty flavor, but it is not essential.

SAUCE
3 ears fresh corn
3 tablespoons butter
1½ pounds medium shrimp, peeled and deveined
½ teaspoon salt
¼ teaspoon white pepper
1 tablespoon minced fresh parsley
5 scallions, white part only, sliced
2½ cups heavy cream

PANCAKES
3 ancho chili pods, toasted, stemmed and seeded (page 22) or 1½ tablespoons chili powder
1 cup light cream or half and half
¼ cup yellow cornmeal
¼ cup all-purpose bleached flour
1 teaspoon sugar
2 teaspoons baking powder
1 teaspoon salt
¼ cup (½ stick) unsalted butter, melted
2 teaspoons shrimp powder, if available (see note)
3 large eggs, separated
Clarified butter

———

Fresh snipped chives or minced parsley for garnish

Cut the corn kernels from the cob, cutting close to the cob to obtain all the starch, and set aside.

Heat 2 tablespoons butter in a large skillet over medium-high heat. Add the shrimp, salt, pepper and parsley and sauté for a total of 2 minutes. Remove shrimp.

Reduce heat to medium and add the remaining butter to the skillet. Add the corn and scallions and sauté for 3 minutes. Add the cream and simmer until the sauce thickens to the consistency of heavy cream, 5 to 8 minutes. Then add the reserved shrimp and cook over medium-low heat for 5 minutes. Season to taste with salt and pepper.

Put the chili pods on a cutting board and chop coarse with a chef's knife. Gently mix the chilies or chili powder, cornmeal, flour, sugar, baking powder, salt, butter, shrimp powder if using and egg yolks in a mixing bowl. Beat the egg whites in a separate bowl with an electric mixer until stiff. Gently fold the batter into the whites.

Heat a seasoned griddle over medium-high heat. Brush lightly with clarified butter and drop 2 to 3 tablespoonfuls of batter on the griddle for each pancake. Cook pancakes until the edges are light brown, then turn and cook on the other side for about 1 minute. Keep them warm in the oven until all are done.

Arrange 3 overlapping pancakes on each serving plate. Using a slotted spoon, mound the shrimp on top. Spoon the sauce around the outer edges of the plates, reserving 2 to 3 tablespoons to drizzle over the shrimp. Sprinkle with fresh chives or parsley for garnish. Serve with seasonal sliced melons and berries.

NOTE.   Shrimp powder is available in food specialty shops catering to an Oriental clientele.

Variations
- Blue cornmeal may be used instead of yellow cornmeal for the pancakes.
- Corn crêpes (page 65) or chili crêpes (page 64) are also good served with the shrimp and corn sauce.

FIRE SHRIMP

6 servings

Present these spicy grilled shrimp as an appetizer, either on the skewers, or removed from the skewers, and serve with guacamole on tortilla chips. They could also be served as an entree accompanied by the corn and pepper flan (page 295) and tomatillo relish (page 230). Use large shrimp for entrees, small ones for appetizers.

2 pounds shrimp

MARINADE
2 cloves garlic, finely minced
2 serrano chilies, stemmed, seeded
 and finely minced
1 teaspoon cayenne pepper
⅓ cup clarified butter or vegetable oil
⅓ cup lime juice
Salt
Pepper
2 tablespoons minced fresh parsley

GUACAMOLE
1 tablespoon finely minced onion
2 tomatillo, minced, or lime juice to
 taste
2 medium ripe avocados, peeled and
 pitted
1 tomato, finely diced
Salt
Pepper

---

1 cup sour cream for garnish

Soak 6 bamboo or wooden skewers for at least 2 hours while the shrimp is marinating.

Peel and devein the shrimp. Leave the tails intact if you plan to serve them as an entree, otherwise remove them. Make a deep enough cut when deveining so that the shrimp can be stood upright.

For the marinade, combine the garlic, chilies, cayenne pepper, clarified butter or oil and lime juice. Lay the shrimp on plastic wrap and brush both sides with the marinade. Wrap up to seal and refrigerate for 2 hours.

Clean the grill surface and wipe with an oil-dampened cloth. Preheat the grill. Remove the shrimp from the marinade and sprinkle with salt and pepper. Thread the shrimp on skewers, 2 or 3 per skewer. Stir the parsley into the marinade.

For the guacamole, put the onion, tomatillo or lime juice and avocados in a small bowl, mash with a fork and combine, then stir in the tomato. Season to taste with salt and pepper.

Grill the shrimp on both sides, allowing about 2 to 3 minutes per side. Brush several times with the marinade during grilling. Remove shrimp to a hot platter and brush again with marinade.

If serving the shrimp on tortilla chips, spread each tortilla chip with guacamole and place a shrimp on top. Garnish with a dollop of sour cream.

If serving the shrimp as an entree, remove skewers and stand shrimp up in the center of a plate and serve with corn and pepper flans and guacamole. Garnish with sour cream.

SCALLOPS IN HOLLANDAISE SAUCE

8 servings

The methods used for poaching the scallops and toasting the muffins make for moist, tender scallops and crisp muffin shells. The hollandaise sauce is lightened by the orange juice and tomato.

1 cup hollandaise sauce (page 258)
4 English muffins, split with a fork
6 tablespoons butter
3 tomatoes, peeled, seeded and cut in
   ¼-inch dice
1 large shallot, minced
3 tablespoons fresh orange juice
1 cup white wine
1½ pounds sea or bay scallops
1 teaspoon minced fresh cilantro or
   basil
Salt
Pepper

Prepare the hollandaise sauce according to recipe directions and keep warm.

Preheat the broiler. Pull away the doughy center from the muffins to hollow them out and spread each half lightly with butter. Place on a cookie sheet 4 to 6 inches below the broiling element. Toast with the door ajar until lightly browned.

Heat 2 tablespoons butter in a medium skillet over medium-high heat. Add the tomatoes and shallot and cook to warm for 1 to 2 minutes. Put the tomatoes in a sieve to drain excess juices.

Heat the remaining butter, orange juice and wine in a saucepan to a boil. Add the scallops, tossing to coat them with the liquid. Cover the skillet and remove from heat. Let the scallops poach, undisturbed, for 8 minutes. Remove the scallops from the liquid with a slotted spoon and cover with foil to keep warm.

To prepare the sauce, heat the liquid to a boil and boil for 5 minutes. Remove from the heat and cool 2 minutes. Gradually whisk in the hollandaise sauce until smooth and creamy. Add the basil or cilantro and drained tomatoes and cook over low heat until the tomatoes are warm. Season to taste with salt and pepper.

Mound the scallops in each muffin shell. Spoon the sauce over the top and serve immediately.

GRILLED SEA SCALLOPS IN ORANGE JUICE

6 servings

This is a lively combination of flavors that complements the delicate scallops. If you are not using a grill, you can poach the scallops in a skillet instead (see page 102).

12 thin slices baguette-size French bread
Butter for the bread
1 shallot, minced
½ cup white wine
Juice from 1 orange (about ⅓ to ½ cup)
1 tablespoon light soy sauce
4 tablespoons unsalted butter, at room temperature
3 sundried tomatoes, diced and drained (about 2½ tablespoons)
1 pound large sea scallops of uniform size
1½ tablespoons fresh minced chives or green scallion tops

Soak 6 bamboo or wooden skewers for at least 2 hours before grilling (see note).

Preheat the broiler. Place the bread on a cookie sheet and toast under the broiler on one side. Turn and butter the opposite side. Place 4 inches from the broiling element and toast until golden brown.

Prepare a charcoal or gas grill or set an electric grill to the highest temperature. Dampen a cloth with oil and rub the grill surface.

To make the sauce, heat the shallot, wine, and orange juice in a small saucepan to a boil. Boil 5 minutes, then strain and pour back into the same pan. Add the soy sauce and butter and whisk to make a smooth sauce. Stir in tomatoes and heat just to warm.

When the fire is ready, thread the scallops on skewers and grill 2 minutes on each side.

Arrange 2 pieces of toast on each serving plate. Slice the scallops in thirds and arrange on top. Drizzle with the sauce and sprinkle with chopped chives or scallion tops.

NOTE. If you do not have time to soak the skewers, wrap the ends in aluminum foil after threading them. Remove before serving.

Variation
- Substitute 3 tablespoons peeled, seeded and diced tomato (1 medium-large tomato) for sundried tomatoes.

DEAN'S SEAFOOD TACOS

6 servings

Dean Fearing makes these tacos with lobster, though any shellfish may be used. The success of the dish depends on using homemade flour tortillas. You could serve the Veracruz butter sauce (page 261) or cheese and pepper sauce (page 263) with the tacos instead of tomato relish. In that case, sprinkle the white sauce with a tablespoonful of minced chives or cilantro for looks.

12 flour tortillas (page 300)

FILLING
2 tablespoons safflower oil
2 tablespoons butter
2 pounds raw lobster or a
  combination of bay scallops,
  shrimp and lump crabmeat
2 tablespoons fresh orange juice
¼ cup heavy cream
Salt
White pepper
2 cups spinach leaves cut in strips
2 cups grated Monterey Jack or
  Pepper-Jack cheese

GARNISH
Pico de gallo (page 159) or grilled-
  tomato relish (page 227)

Prepare tortillas according to recipe directions. They may be made in advance.

Heat the oil and butter in a large skillet. Cut the lobster or other seafood into bite-size pieces and add to the skillet. Sauté, stirring frequently, until pink and tender, about 3 to 5 minutes. Stir in the orange juice and cream and heat to a simmer. Cook for 3 to 4 minutes, then season to taste with salt and pepper.

If tortillas were made in advance, warm and soften them by heating in a nonstick skillet over medium-high heat. Place the tortillas in the skillet one at a time and turn frequently until warm and soft, about 2 minutes.

Lay warmed tortillas on a flat surface. Put a dessertspoonful of seafood down the middle and then top with spinach and cheese. Roll up into a cone shape. Serve two tacos per person and put several generous spoonfuls of relish on each plate.

CRABCAKES

10 crabcakes

These plump, moist cakes have lots of crab and no fillers and are lightly spiced with herbs and cayenne pepper. Crabcakes can be served many different ways and they are always a hit.

⅓ cup butter, melted
½ cup chopped onion
1 serrano chili, stemmed, seeded and minced, or ¼ teaspoon cayenne pepper
2 eggs
1 pound lump crabmeat, all cartilage removed
⅓ cup mayonnaise
1 tablespoon coarse-grain mustard
1 teaspoon salt
1 tablespoon minced fresh thyme or ¼ teaspoon dried thyme
1 tablespoon minced fresh parsley
⅓ cup safflower oil
1 cup fine cornbread crumbs
1 cup fine, dry breadcrumbs
1 tablespoon minced fresh parsley

For a very professional-looking poached egg, add 1 teaspoon vinegar or lemon juice to each quart of water used for poaching eggs. Never allow the water to boil once the eggs have been slipped in. Trim off ragged ends before serving.

Heat 1 tablespoon butter in a medium skillet over medium-high heat. Add the onion and chili and sauté about 1½ minutes.

Beat 1 egg in a mixing bowl and add the onion and chili mixture, crab, mayonnaise, mustard, salt, thyme and parsley and toss to combine. Shape the crab mixture in cakes 2½ to 3 inches in diameter.

Put the other egg in a mixing bowl and beat together with 2 tablespoons of the oil. Combine the crumbs and parsley on a shallow plate. Brush each cake with the egg mixture, then dip in the breadcrumbs, coating all sides, and place on a cookie sheet. Cover and refrigerate for at least 2 hours or up to 12 hours, until firm.

Heat the remaining oil and butter in a large skillet over medium-high heat. Use a spatula to transfer the crabcakes carefully to the skillet. Sauté on both sides until golden, about 2 minutes per side. Crabcakes may be cooked 30 minutes ahead of time and kept warm in a 200° F oven.

If using as an entree, serve with colorful seasonal vegetables.

Garnishes
Serve one or more of the following as garnish:
- Grilled-corn and pepper relish (page 238)
- Grilled-tomato relish (page 227)
- Pico de gallo (page 159)
- Roasted-pepper catsup (page 241)
- Triple mustard sauce (page 256)
- Sweet corn sauce (page 254)

Variation
- Another version of these crabcakes that is particularly well suited for brunch can be made by replacing the mustard with 2 to 3 tablespoons of tomato and green chili relish (page 227), well drained. Serve with poached eggs, if desired.

CRABMEAT STRATA

6 servings

A strata is a casserole-type dish of layered bread, meat, fish or poultry and vegetables, baked in an egg custard. It puffs when baked and has the consistency of a light quiche. Since it may be prepared a day in advance and refrigerated overnight, it is an ideal dish to serve weekend guests.

3 large eggs
1½ cups whole milk
1 teaspoon dry mustard
Pinch of white pepper
½ teaspoon salt
1 tablespoon butter
½ small yellow onion, peeled and
  chopped
8 slices French-style bread, crusts
  removed and cut in 1-inch cubes
  (about 4½ cups)
3 poblano chilies, roasted, peeled,
  and cut in ¼-inch dice (page 20),
  or 1 can (4 ounces) diced mild
  green chilies, drained
4 ounces Monterey Jack cheese,
  grated (about 1 cup)
6 ounces lump crabmeat, all cartilage
  removed
2 tablespoons minced fresh parsley
¼ cup heavy cream

Beat the eggs, milk, mustard, pepper, and salt with an electric mixer in a small mixing bowl.

Heat the butter in a small skillet over medium heat. Add the onion and sauté until soft and translucent, 2 to 3 minutes.

Butter a deep 9-inch pie pan. Arrange ⅓ of the bread cubes in the pan. Put half the onions and chilies on top, then half the cheese and crab. Repeat, ending with bread cubes on top.

Pour the egg mixture over the strata and press the top layer down to be sure all the ingredients are moistened. Sprinkle with parsley and refrigerate, covered, until ready to bake.

Preheat the oven to 350° F. Drizzle cream over the top of the strata and bake, uncovered, until puffed and golden brown, 40 to 45 minutes. Cool for 5 minutes before serving.

Cut in wedges and serve with fresh fruits such as melon slices and seasonal berries.

CRAB AND CHILI TORTAS

6 sandwiches

This is a super-easy appetizer because you can use rolls from a bakery. The combination of poblano chilies, red peppers, seafood and cream is truly elegant.

12 round French rolls (3½ to 4 inches in diameter)
3 tablespoons unsalted butter, at room temperature
1 tablespoon safflower oil
1 onion, peeled and sliced into strips (¼ × 1½ inches)
2 cups heavy cream
2 poblano chilies, roasted, peeled and cut in strips (½ × ¼ inch)
1 pound fresh crabmeat, all cartilage removed, or 2 packages (6 ounces each) frozen crabmeat, drained
1 red bell pepper, roasted, peeled and cut in strips (½ × ¼ inch)
3 tablespoons grated Parmesan cheese
Salt
White pepper

Preheat the oven to 400° F. Slice the tops from the rolls. Pull the doughy portion from the center of the bottom portion, leaving a shell about ¼ inch thick. Save the excess for bread crumbs or discard. Butter the inside of each generously and place on a cookie sheet. Bake until the crusts are crisp and the insides lightly browned, 3 to 4 minutes.

Heat the oil in a large skillet over medium heat. Add the onion and sauté until translucent, 3 to 4 minutes. Add the cream and poblano chilies and bring to a boil. Reduce heat and cook over medium heat until the mixture thickens, about 8 to 10 minutes. Remove the skillet from the heat and add crabmeat, red bell pepper and cheese. Stir to combine. Season to taste with salt and pepper.

Spoon the crabmeat and pepper mixture into the rolls. Return to the oven and bake 10 to 12 minutes or until hot.

Variation

- For an open-face sandwich, use a larger roll and reserve the top portion. Butter and toast it. Continue as in the main recipe. When filling the rolls, allow some of the sauce to spill over onto the plate and cap each torta with the toasted top portion.

STEPHAN'S CATFISH MOUSSE

5 to 6 servings

Stephan Pyles, chef of the celebrated Routh Street Cafe in Dallas, makes a wonderfully light and delicate catfish mousse. It goes well with a bell pepper sauce (page 253), a light lime butter sauce (page 259) or, my favorite, Veracruz butter sauce (page 261).

Butter for 8 custard cups 3 inches deep (6-ounce size)
8 cilantro leaves
1 medium shallot, peeled, or 1 small garlic clove, peeled
1 pound fresh catfish, filleted, well chilled, or ¾ pound catfish fillets
1 egg white
1 large egg
2 cups heavy cream, well chilled
1 teaspoon salt
½ teaspoon white pepper
Pinch of cayenne pepper

Butter the custard cups and press a cilantro leaf into the bottom of each one.

Preheat the oven to 325° F.

Use a food processor fitted with the metal blade. Start the machine and drop the shallot or garlic through the feed tube to mince. Add the fish in four batches and process, stopping several times to scrape down the sides of the bowl, until the fish is completely smooth, about 3 to 4 minutes.

With the machine still running, add the egg white and whole egg, then gradually pour in the cream. Stop as needed to give the fish time to absorb the cream. When all the cream has been added and the mixture is completely smooth, add the salt, pepper and cayenne pepper. Spoon some mousse into each mold and smooth the top.

Put the molds in a baking dish half filled with water and bake until a knife inserted in the middle comes out clean, 20 to 25 minutes.

Run a knife around the edge of each mousse and unmold. Serve warm with the sauce of your choice.

GRITS SOUFFLÉ WITH HAM AND SHRIMP

6 servings

This soufflé may be served as an appetizer or for a brunch dish. It is very moist and requires no sauce, although if you use a soufflé dish rather than individual dishes, a sauce makes it more appealing.

Butter for a 6-to-8 cup soufflé dish or 6 individual soufflé dishes, at least 2 inches deep

1½ tablespoons grated Parmesan

3 tablespoons butter

1 large shallot, minced

1 cup chicken stock

1½ cups half and half

½ teaspoon salt

½ cup hominy grits

4 egg yolks

½ cup ham, diced

½ cup shrimp, peeled, deveined and chopped

¼ cup green chilies, chopped

2½ ounces Monterey Jack cheese, grated (about ⅔ cup)

6 egg whites

2 tablespoons grated Parmesan cheese

Minced fresh parsley for garnish

Preheat the oven to 400° F. Butter the soufflé mold or dishes. Sprinkle the sides and bottom with Parmesan cheese and set aside. Fill a baking dish half full or at least ½ inch deep with warm water.

Melt 1 tablespoon butter in a small saucepan over medium heat. Add the shallot and sauté until softened, about 1 minute. Add the chicken stock, half and half, salt and grits and heat to a boil. Reduce the heat and cook over medium heat until the grits are thick and tender, about 8 minutes. Stir in the remaining butter, egg yolks, ham, shrimp, chilies and cheese.

Beat the egg whites until stiff peaks form. Fold a third of the egg whites into the grits mixture to lighten, then fold the lightened grits into the remaining whites. Pour the soufflé mixture into the dishes or mold and sprinkle with Parmesan cheese.

Place in the water bath and bake for 20 minutes. Reduce the heat to 350° F. and continue baking until the soufflé is just set but still moist, 5 to 10 more minutes. If using a large soufflé mold, increase the initial baking time to 30 minutes, and the final time to 15 minutes.

Serve individual soufflés without unmolding. If serving from a single dish, use a large spoon to spoon out oval servings and drizzle the top with sauce. Sprinkle with minced fresh parsley for garnish.

Garnishes

You may want to serve the soufflé with a sauce or relish such as:
- Roast-bell-pepper sauce (page 253)
- Grilled-tomato relish (page 227)

VEGETABLE AND PASTA SOUFFLÉ

8 servings

This colorful combination of pasta and vegetables does double duty as a starch and a vegetable. Unmold it on seasonal greens and garnish the plate with quartered red and yellow cherry tomatoes or a tomato relish, depending on the main course.

½ pound angel's hair pasta
   (cappellini)
Butter for 8 individual (1 cup) soufflé
   dishes
2 tablespoons grated Parmesan
   cheese

SAUCE
4 tablespoons butter, melted
4 tablespoons all-purpose flour
2½ cups half and half
½ cup grated Monterey Jack or bel
   paese cheese
Pinch of coriander
¼ teaspoon white pepper
Salt to taste
3 egg yolks

VEGETABLES
4 tablespoons butter
1 clove garlic, minced
¼ cup onion, minced
¼ cup finely diced turnips
¼ cup corn niblets
¼ cup finely diced carrots
¼ cup finely diced red bell pepper
¼ cup finely diced green bell pepper
6 ounces fresh turnip, collard or
   spinach greens, ribs removed and
   cut in strips ¼ × 2 inches
6 egg whites

Cook the pasta, drain and set aside.

Butter the soufflé dishes and lightly dust with Parmesan cheese, shaking out the excess.

For the sauce, put melted butter and flour in a blender jar. Heat the half and half to scalding in a medium saucepan. Add 1½ cups of it to the blender jar and blend until smooth. Pour back into the same saucepan with the remaining half and half and cook over medium heat, stirring constantly. Add the cheese, coriander, white pepper and salt to taste. Whisk in the egg yolks and set aside to cool.

Preheat the oven to 450° F.

Heat the rest of the butter in a large skillet. Add the garlic, onion, turnips, corn niblets, carrots and bell peppers. Stir in the greens and remove from heat.

In a separate bowl beat the egg whites until stiff but not dry peaks form. Fold into the cooled sauce.

To assemble the soufflés, fold about half of the sauce into the pasta and place some in each dish. Add the vegetables, then spoon the remaining sauce on top.

Bake the soufflés for 10 minutes, then reduce the heat to 350° F. and bake an additional 20 minutes, or until they are puffed and browned.

Since this is a firm soufflé, it will unmold easily; just run a knife around the edge to loosen. Unmold the soufflés on several leaves of fresh greens and garnish with quartered cherry tomatoes or a tomato relish.

SHRIMP AND SPINACH LASAGNE

8 servings

Lasagne remains a favorite for entertaining because most of the preparation may be done in advance, leaving the cook free to be with guests. Add a color accent to this pink and green lasagne with a layer of roasted bell peppers.

SAUCE
5 tablespoons melted butter
5 tablespoons all-purpose flour
2 cloves minced garlic
1 teaspoon dry mustard
1 teaspoon salt
¼ teaspoon white pepper
3½ cups hot milk

SPINACH FILLING
10 ounces fresh spinach, finely
   chopped
About ¼ cup finely chopped fresh
   basil
16 ounces ricotta cheese
½ cup grated Parmesan or Romano
   cheese
2 beaten eggs
½ cup heavy cream
1 teaspoon salt
¼ teaspoon white pepper

LASAGNE AND SHRIMP
¾ pound spinach lasagne noodles,
   preferably homemade (see note)
1¼ pounds medium shrimp, peeled,
   deveined, and coarsely chopped
   (about 2½ cups)

TOPPING
2 tablespoons melted butter
½ cup coarse breadcrumbs
1 clove garlic, minced
2 tablespoons minced fresh basil

GARNISH
8 medium to large shrimp for garnish
   (optional)
Salt
Pepper
2 tablespoons butter

Preheat the oven to 350° F. Pour the butter, flour, garlic, mustard, 1 teaspoon salt, ¼ teaspoon pepper and 2 cups milk in a blender jar. Blend on high speed until smooth, adding the remaining milk through the top during blending. Pour the sauce in a saucepan and stir until thickened and smooth, about 2 minutes. Set aside about ¾ cup sauce to serve with the finished lasagne.

Combine the spinach, basil, ricotta and Parmesan cheese, eggs, cream and 1 teaspoon salt and ¼ teaspoon pepper in a mixing bowl.

To assemble, pour ⅓ of the sauce in an 8 × 11-inch baking dish. Layer the ingredients beginning with ⅓ of the uncooked lasagne sheets, ½ of the cheese and spinach mixture, ½ of the chopped shrimp. Repeat and top with the remaining layer of noodles and sauce. Cover with foil and bake 35 minutes.

Combine remaining butter with breadcrumbs, garlic and basil. After the lasagne has cooked for 35 minutes, spread the crumbs on top and place the dish on a rack 6 to 8 inches from the broiling element. Broil 5 minutes to brown the crumbs. Allow the cooked lasagne to rest about 8 minutes before slicing.

If you are garnishing with shrimp, sprinkle them with salt and pepper. Heat the butter in a small skillet and sauté the shrimp over medium-high heat for 2 minutes and set aside.

To serve, cut the lasagne into squares and place each in the center of a plate. Warm the reserved sauce and spoon over. Garnish each serving with one whole shrimp and serve with fresh seasonal vegetables.

NOTE: Substitute 8 ounces dry lasagne noodles for home-made noodles. Parboil according to package directions.

PASTA WITH SEAFOOD AND PINE NUTS

8 servings

Pasta is always a hit among family and friends. The combination of the delicate angel's hair pasta and lightly poached seafood in a mustard-flavored cream sauce makes both an appealing appetizer and a satisfying entree. Vary the seafood according to personal taste or what is available fresh. Choose from lobster, shrimp, clams, scallops or a combination of shellfish and firm-fleshed fish such as monkfish or swordfish.

2 shallots, minced
1½ cups white wine
¼ cup (½ stick) unsalted butter
2 cups lobster meat, cut in bite-size pieces
½ pound shrimp, shelled and deveined
1 pound bay scallops, rinsed
1½ cups heavy cream
1 clove garlic, chopped
1 tablespoon green peppercorn or wine mustard
2 tablespoons all-purpose flour
Salt
Pepper
1 pound angel's hair pasta (cappellini)
20 fresh spinach leaves, cut in narrow strips
⅓ cup pine nuts, toasted (page 50)
Freshly cracked black pepper

Heat the shallots, wine, 1½ cups water and butter in a large skillet to a boil. Add all the seafood and cover the skillet. Remove from the heat and let stand, undisturbed, for 12 minutes. Strain and reserve both the liquid and the seafood.

Heat the strained liquid in the same skillet to a boil. Boil until reduced to about ¾ cup.

Put the cream, garlic, mustard and flour in a blender jar and blend on high speed until smooth. Whisk the cream mixture into the reduced liquid and cook, stirring constantly, until thickened and smooth, about 5 minutes. Season to taste with salt and pepper.

Bring 2 quarts lightly salted water to a boil in a large saucepan. Add the pasta, stir to separate strands and cook until tender to the bite. Drain the pasta and put it back in the same saucepan. Add half the cream sauce and the spinach and heat to warm, about 2 to 3 minutes. Spoon onto serving plates.

Heat the remaining sauce and seafood in the same saucepan over medium-high heat. When warm, spoon over the pasta. Sprinkle with pine nuts and freshly cracked black pepper.

LIME PASTA WITH HAZELNUTS

4 servings

Hazelnuts and lime are a good combination in themselves and the citrus cuts the heaviness of the cream sauce as well. Add colorful slivers of red, yellow and green bell peppers. Or add smoked chicken or turkey to make this a main-dish pasta.

1 tablespoon unsalted butter
½ cup toasted hazelnuts or pistachio
   nuts (page 50)
2 cloves garlic, minced
3 tablespoons minced lemon zest
⅓ cup lime or lemon juice
1 tablespoon vinegar
1 large shallot
1½ tablespoons all-purpose flour
½ cup chicken broth
2½ cups heavy cream
Salt
Pepper
½ pound fresh pasta (fettuccine or
   spaghetti), plain or spinach, or
   about 4 ounces dry pasta
1 tablespoon vegetable oil
½ cup fresh Parmesan cheese, grated
Freshly ground black pepper

Heat the butter in a small skillet over medium heat. Add the nuts and sauté 2 minutes. Remove to paper towels, then chop coarsely.

Combine the garlic and lemon zest and set aside.

To prepare the sauce, heat the lime or lemon juice, vinegar and shallot to a boil in a medium saucepan. Boil until reduced by about a third, about 3 to 4 minutes.

Stir the flour into the chicken broth and mix until smooth. Add the broth to the saucepan, then, stirring constantly, whisk in the cream. Cook over medium-high heat until the sauce has thickened enough to coat a spoon, about 5 to 8 minutes. Season to taste with salt and pepper.

Cook the pasta in lightly salted boiling water until tender to the bite. Drain and immediately return to the same pan over medium heat. Add the sauce, garlic and lemon zest and toss to coat all the strands. Heat long enough to warm.

Divide the pasta among 6 serving plates and sprinkle with cheese and toasted nuts. Or serve the pasta on a platter lined with sorrel leaves, allowing the tips of the leaves to show. Sprinkle with freshly ground black pepper.

Variation
- Omit the nuts or cheese and add finely minced lemon basil and thyme or basil instead.

CHICKEN IN TOMATILLO SAUCE

8 servings

Chicken cooked in a savory tomatillo sauce with shallots, cilantro and fresh basil is a quick and easy appetizer. You can serve it over pasta that has been tossed with a light cream sauce or with thin corn tortillas, fried crisp, as well as with herb biscuits.

1 tablespoon vegetable oil
2 tablespoons butter
2 shallots, minced
2 garlic cloves, minced
2 tablespoons minced fresh cilantro
  or parsley
1 tablespoon minced fresh basil
8 fresh tomatillos, husks removed, cut
  in ¼-inch dice (see note)
3 red tomatoes, peeled, seeded and
  cut in ¼-inch dice
2 serrano chilies, stemmed, seeded
  and finely minced
½ cup dry white wine
1 tablespoon fresh lemon juice
4 chicken breasts, boned, skinned and
  sliced thin
Salt
Pepper

———

8 herb biscuits (page 301)
Sprigs of cilantro, parsley or basil for
  garnish

Heat the oil and butter in a large sauté pan over medium-high heat. Add the shallots and garlic and sauté until softened, about 2 minutes. Add the cilantro or parsley, basil, tomatillos, tomatoes and serrano chilies. Cook, stirring constantly until the sauce comes to a simmer, 1 to 2 minutes. Add the wine and lemon juice and heat to a boil. Stir in the chicken, cover the pan and remove from the heat. Let stand, undisturbed, for 12 minutes.

Put the pan back on medium-high heat. Remove the cover and heat to warm, about 1 to 2 minutes. Season to taste with salt and pepper.

Place a biscuit, split and toasted, on each plate. Spoon the chicken and sauce on the toasts, covering partially and letting the sauce spill onto the plate. Garnish with a fresh sprig of parsley, basil or cilantro.

NOTE.　If tomatillos are not available, substitute 2 large green tomatoes, seeded and cut in ¼-inch dice.

CHICKEN AND CHILI SAUSAGES

12 sausage patties

These little sausages are seasoned with fresh cilantro and serrano chilies. Serve them with miniature blue or yellow cornmeal muffins and relish. Or use the bulk sausage on a Southwest-style pizza (page 74). Sausages are very easy to make—no more difficult than a meatloaf. If you do not have a food processor or meat grinder, ask the butcher to grind the meat and poultry for you.

2 garlic cloves
3 serrano chilies, stemmed and cut in thirds, or 2 jalapeño chilies
3 chicken breast halves (about 9 ounces), boned and skinned and cut in 1-inch cubes
8 ounces veal shoulder, cut in cubes
5 ounces pork fatback, cut in cubes
⅓ cup fresh cilantro leaves, packed
¾ teaspoon salt
¼ teaspoon coarsely ground black pepper
2 tablespoons vegetable oil
Fresh greens for garnish (watercress, sunflower sprouts or cilantro sprigs)

Put the garlic and chilies in a food processor with the metal blade. Process until minced. Add the chicken, veal, pork, cilantro, salt and pepper and process until ground.

Shape the sausage into 1-inch-thick patties. Heat the oil in a medium sauté pan over medium-high heat. Add the patties and cook to brown on both sides, about 7 to 8 minutes.

Arrange 2 patties on a salad plate with one or two relishes and a miniature corn muffin. Garnish the plate with fresh greens.

Garnishes
Serve with yellow or blue cornmeal muffins (pages 310 and 312) and one or two of the following relishes or sauces:

- Roasted-pepper catsup (page 241)
- Pepper-spiced pears (page 246)
- Tomatillo relish (page 230)
- Ricotta ranch compote (page 255)

WILD GAME SAUSAGES

12 sausage patties

If you have a hunter in the family, this is a great way to use wild goose or duck. The sausages have a wonderful mild game flavor. Serve them with various relishes or your favorite beans. Domestic duck may also be used; the sausages will be good but they will lack that gamey taste.

2 serrano chilies or 1 jalapeño chili, stemmed and minced
2 cloves garlic, minced
½ cup cilantro leaves, minced
½ cup fresh basil leaves, minced
¼ cup fresh mint leaves, minced
8 ounces raw pork fatback, ground
9 ounces raw chicken breast meat, ground
6 ounces raw wild goose or duck breast, ground
1 teaspoon salt

Basil may be finely chopped with olive oil and refrigerated for 1 week or frozen for up to 1 year. Use only enough oil to moisten. Basil has a surprising affinity for mango sauces, many sweet custards or flans and peaches as well as tomatillos, tomatoes and bell peppers. It can also be combined with mint and cilantro for a refreshing taste.

Put the chilies, garlic, cilantro, basil and mint in a mixing bowl. Add the pork fatback, chicken, goose or duck meat and salt and mix well. Remove and shape into patties about ½ inch thick.

Sausages may be either grilled or sautéed in hot butter and oil. Cook until the juices no longer run red, about 6 minutes. Serve the sausages with a relish and sliced papaya.

Garnishes
- Serve with one of the tomato relishes (pages 226–228) or pepper jellies (pages 249–250).
- Serve with a fruit-based relish, such as the melon relish on page 232, papaya and red pepper relish (page 233) or cranberry-apricot relish (page 234).

Variation
- Substitute domestic duck for wild duck or goose, using 7 ounces each of duck and chicken breast and 6 ounces of pork fatback.

LAMB SAUSAGE WITH MINT, THYME AND ROSEMARY

16 sausage patties

The combination of lamb, veal and fresh herbs makes mild but well seasoned sausages. They go well with the tomato-mint chutney (page 243) and may also be served with sautéed lamb medallions or lamb chops as an entree.

¾ pound lamb shoulder, ground
½ pound veal shoulder, ground
8 ounces pork fatback, ground (see note)
1 shallot, minced
2 garlic cloves, minced
2 teaspoons fresh thyme, minced
1 teaspoon fresh rosemary, minced
1 tablespoon fresh mint, chopped
½ teaspoon coarse ground black pepper
¼ teaspoon cayenne pepper
1 teaspoon salt

Put the lamb, veal, pork fat, shallot, garlic, thyme, rosemary, mint, peppers and salt in a mixing bowl and mix thoroughly until combined. Shape into patties about ½ inch thick.

The sausage patties may be either grilled or sautéed in hot butter and oil. Cook until the juices no longer run red, about 6 minutes. Arrange 2 patties on each plate with a generous spoonful of the chutney. Garnish with fresh rosemary or mint sprigs.

NOTE: If the lamb is very lean, you will need to increase the amount of fatback.

POBLANO CHILI DIP

1½ cups

This spicy dip may be served with corn chips, raw vegetables or seafood. If mild green chilies are substituted for poblanos, use more serrano chilies.

3 poblano chilies, roasted, peeled, stemmed and seeded (page 20) or 1 can (4 ounces) mild green chilies
1 or 2 serrano chilies, stemmed
1 package (3 ounces) cream cheese, at room temperature
½ cup sour cream
Several sprigs fresh cilantro or parsley, minced
1 sprig fresh oregano or ¼ teaspoon dried oregano
½ teaspoon salt

Put all the chilies in a blender jar and blend on high speed for a few seconds. Add cream cheese, sour cream and herbs and blend until smooth. Season to taste with salt.

SOUPS AND CHOWDERS

Stocks

Chicken or Game-Bird Stock
Fish Stock
Beef or Veal Stock
Shortcut Beef Glaze
Dean's Spicy Ham Stock

Soups

Chilled Cucumber–Granny Smith Apple Soup
Green Gazpacho
Roasted Corn Soup
Corn and Potato Chowder
Creamy Carrot Soup with Dill
Cream of Cilantro Soup with Seafood
Roasted Pepper Soup
Roasted Red Pepper Soup with Corn
Tortilla Soup
Southwest Vegetable Soup
Winter Squash Bisque with Wild Rice
Stephan's Southwest Creams
Black Bean Soup with Cilantro-Poblano Cream
Dean's Pepper Cheese and Black Bean Soup
Black Bean Chili with Relishes
Green Chili Soup
Green Chili Gumbo

In Southwestern cooking, vegetable soups take on a whole new bright and appealing look. Economical and low in calories, they can be served refreshingly chilled as well as hot. Like sauces, the best are based on well seasoned, homemade stock. No matter how good the stock, though, the soup will only be as good as the ingredients that go into it.

Many of the soups in this book lend themselves to a dual or triple presentation, that is two or three different soups served in one bowl. Garnished with Southwestern creams, they might be likened to a painted desert. For example, you could pair two roasted-pepper soups, one red and one yellow, and decorate them with a swirl of green cilantro-poblano cream.

To combine soups, you will need rimmed soup bowls, a ladle for each soup and a squirt bottle for the cream. Ladle both soups at the same time so that they do not run into each other. Decorate with one of the flavored creams and garnish with crisp tortilla strips, relish (at room temperature) or fresh herbs minced with toasted nuts. Some felicitous combinations are described in individual recipes. Here are some other good ideas.

• Black-bean soup and red roasted-pepper soup garnished with crisp tortilla strips or ancho chili cream.

• Green-chili soup with pepper-cheese or roasted-corn soup garnished with a tomatillo or tomato relish.

• Winter-squash bisque and roasted red pepper soup garnished with wild rice or cilantro cream.

Stocks

I am often asked how to prepare sauces, salad dressings, soup or black beans that do not taste bland. The answer is always the same—use stocks—and is consistently met with resistance. Maybe people just do not want to believe it is that simple, maybe they are a little intimidated by the thought of making stock, not realizing how easy it really is. The reward of stock-making is that last-minute cooking and those finishing touches like a quick little sauce of pan juices become a breeze. All you need to do is stay in the kitchen long enough to get the stock started and come back 4 to 5 hours later to finish.

What follows are some simple techniques for making three basic stocks, clarifying them to make a clear broth to showcase colorful vegetables in a vegetable soup, and reducing them to a more concentrated glaze. Meat glaze *(demi-glace)* is made from beef or veal stock that has been strained, degreased, and then cooked down to a thick syrup like meat essence. You can also make a glaze with chicken or duck stock. Chicken stock never gets quite that syrupy consistency.

Veal stock is probably the most versatile stock, as you may use it with almost any meat, poultry or game. As a rule, the stock you use should be one made from the bones of the meat used, but veal stock blends in well without adding any intrusive character of its own.

When making stock, keep the following points in mind.

- Bones for duck stock are best when browned; reserve the fat. Chicken or poultry bones may be from grilled or smoked poultry.
- Bones for beef or veal stock may be roasted to make a darker stock with a roasted flavor. You can grill them or simply cook them in the water along with the vegetables and herbs.
- Choose bones that have gelatin, like marrow bones. They should also have some meat attached; if not, add trimmings from roasts or steaks.
- Save all meat trimmings, smoked bird carcasses, grilled bones and ham bones for stock. You can keep them in the freezer until ready to use.
- All stocks have a combination of aromatic vegetables (carrots, celery, onions or leeks), which are added after the bones have been roasted. These vegetables may be sautéed in a little butter or oil until soft if you have the time; if not, add them as is, cleaned and cut up.
- Keep the bones covered with water.
- Check the simmering rate before you go off and leave the stock. Hard boiling tends to incorporate more fat.
- Cook stocks uncovered and do not cover them until they have cooled or the taste may become distorted.
- Do not add salt; season the finished sauce, soup base or final application. Remember salt is easy to add and almost impossible to remove.
- Invest in a large stockpot, a heavy-duty strainer and a skimmer.

CHICKEN OR GAME-BIRD STOCK

3 quarts

1 chicken (3 pounds), cut up, or 2 to
 2½ pounds legs, thighs and wings
 or same amount game birds
2 garlic cloves, coarsely chopped
2 leeks, cleaned and sliced, or 2
 medium onions, quartered
2 celery stalks, cleaned and cut in 1-
 inch pieces
6 sprigs fresh parsley, including stems
2 sprigs fresh basil (optional)
2 sprigs fresh thyme or 1 teaspoon
 dried leaf thyme
2 whole cloves
6 to 8 whole peppercorns

Put all the ingredients in a large stockpot, cover with cold water and bring to a boil. Skim the foam that rises to the top, then reduce the heat to medium and cook for 2 to 2½ hours. If you used a whole chicken and plan to use the meat, remove the chicken after 45 minutes, cool and remove the meat. Return the carcass and bones (but not the skin) to the stockpot and continue to cook the stock over medium heat for another 1¼ to 1½ hours. Strain and skim to remove as much fat as possible. (The remaining fat can be removed after refrigerating.) Cool, uncovered, then refrigerate to allow the fat to harden for easier removal. Transfer to storage containers and refrigerate or freeze.

Variation
- To make duck stock, roast the bones in a preheated 475° F. oven, turning several times, for 35 to 40 minutes, then proceed as directed. Reserve fat for another use.

FISH STOCK

3 quarts

Do not use salmon, salmon trout, fresh water trout or catfish. Take care not to overcook fish stock.

2 pounds fish bones and heads and
 shells from shellfish
2 tablespoons safflower oil
2 leeks, cleaned and sliced, or 1
 medium onion, quartered
1 shallot, chopped
1 carrot, cut in 1-inch pieces
1 stalk celery, cut in 1-inch pieces
3 cups white wine
1 sprig fresh thyme
1 sprig fresh fennel weed, if available
4 sprigs parsley
Juice from 1 lemon
6 peppercorns

Break the fish bones up into smaller pieces. Heat the oil in a large stockpot over medium-high heat. Add the bones, leeks or onion, shallot, carrot and celery and sauté until the vegetables are softened, about 5 minutes. Add the wine and bring to a boil, then add the thyme, fennel weed, parsley, lemon juice, peppercorns and 2½ to 3 quarts water. Simmer over medium to medium-low heat, uncovered, for about 45 minutes. Strain and cool.

BEEF OR VEAL STOCK

3 to 3½ quarts

2 tablespoons vegetable oil
5 to 6 pounds bones and trimmings
   from beef or veal or a combination
   of both
3 garlic cloves, chopped
2 leeks, cleaned and sliced, or 2
   onions, quartered
2 carrots, cut in 1-inch pieces
1 celery stalk, cut in 1-inch pieces
2 large, ripe tomatoes, quartered, with
   cores intact
2 sprigs fresh thyme or 1 teaspoon
   dried leaf thyme
6 to 8 sprigs fresh parsley
1 bay leaf
6 to 8 peppercorns

Preheat the oven to 475° F. Put the oil in a roasting pan, add the bones and trimmings and roast, turning several times, until well browned, about 35 to 40 minutes. Transfer the bones to a large stockpot and add all the vegetables, herbs and peppercorns. Pour 2 cups water into the roasting pan and heat over medium-high heat long enough to loosen all the browned particles. Pour this liquid and 4 quarts water into the stockpot and heat to a boil. Skim the foam from the top and reduce the heat to medium. Simmer, skimming and degreasing from time to time, adding water if necessary to keep bones covered, for 5 to 6 hours. Strain and clean the stockpot. Pour the strained stock into clean pot and continue to simmer for an additional 1½ to 2 hours. Cool, degrease and store.

CLARIFIED STOCK

4 egg whites
3 quarts stock

Lightly beat the egg whites, then pour them into a clean stockpot. Add the hot stock and heat to a simmer without stirring. Do not let the stock boil at any time. The impurities will rise to the surface and after about 5 minutes a thick foam will form. Line a strainer with cheesecloth and place it over a large saucepan or another stockpot. Use a ladle (do not pour) to ladle the stock through the strainer. Use immediately or store in the refrigerator or freezer.

SHORTCUT BEEF GLAZE

1 cup

When you do not have the time to prepare a classic glaze, this is a good substitute. The reduction of the canned beef broth makes a rather salty glaze; therefore you will need to adjust the amount of salt when using this glaze for finishing and enriching sauces.

1½ to 2 cups beef and/or veal
    trimmings, including some bones
Vegetable oil
½ yellow onion, peeled and quartered
1 celery stalk, cut in 4
1 carrot, cut in 4
3 cans (14½ ounces) beef broth
1 bay leaf
3 sprigs fresh parsley
Freshly cracked black pepper
½ teaspoon thyme
1 tablespoon tomato paste

Ask the butcher to cut large bones into 2- to 2½-inch pieces.

Heat 1 tablespoon oil in a large skillet over medium-high heat. Add the bones and trimmings and cook to brown, 5 to 6 minutes. Add additional oil if necessary to prevent sticking, then add the onion, celery and carrot. Cook over medium to medium-high heat or in a preheated 425° F. oven until the vegetables are browned and caramelized, about 45 minutes.

Add the beef broth, 2 cups water, seasonings and tomato paste, scraping to loosen all the browned bits from the pan. Bring to a boil and skim the top as necessary, for at least 20 minutes or up to 35 minutes. Strain the stock, pressing to extract the flavor from the meat and bones. Put the stock back in the saucepan and heat to a boil. Skim the top and simmer over medium heat until you have a thick liquid, 20 to 25 minutes. Refrigerate the glaze for 1 week or freeze for up to 6 months.

DEAN'S SPICY HAM STOCK

2 to 2½ quarts

Black beans, pinto beans and black-eyed peas are quite bland, and need a well seasoned stock with rich ham or meat flavor, particularly when used in relishes. This is Dean Fearing's favorite stock for seasoning beans or black-eyed peas. If you have bones from a smoked turkey or game birds, save them and use them along with the ham bone. You may also use this stock for a Southern flavor when you cook vegetables like green beans.

1 ham bone, about 1 pound, including
    about 1½ to 2 cups scraps,
    preferably from a smoked ham
Bones from smoked birds (optional)
1 small onion, diced
1 stalk celery, diced
1 small carrot, diced
1 bay leaf
1 tablespoon black peppercorns
3 serrano chilies, stemmed and halved
4 cloves garlic
1 cup cilantro leaves and stems
6 cans (14½ ounces) chicken broth
Salt

Put all the ingredients and 4 cups water in a large stockpot and heat to a boil. Skim the surface and then simmer for about 2 hours. Season to taste with salt. Strain, cool and refrigerate for 1 week or freeze in 1-quart containers. Or use immediately to cook beans or black-eyed peas.

Black beans, cooked in a spicy stock until tender but still whole, make a colorful and tasty addition to salads of julienned vegetables (page 147), relishes and other cooked vegetable combinations.

Soups

CHILLED CUCUMBER–GRANNY SMITH APPLE SOUP

4 servings

This is a light refreshing soup with a hint of mint that is a perfect prelude to a summer meal from the grill.

5 medium cucumbers, peeled, seeded and cut in 1-inch sections (about 2 cups)
1 Granny Smith apple, peeled, cored and cut in 1-inch pieces (about ¾ cup)
1 small onion, diced
¼ cup white wine
½ cup chicken broth
1 cup buttermilk
½ cup crème fraîche, preferably homemade (page 112)
1 teaspoon salt or to taste
¼ teaspoon white pepper
Several sprigs fresh parsley
8 fresh mint leaves
⅓ cup sliced toasted and skinned almonds (page 50)

Granny Smith apples are bright green in color, crisp and juicy, with a slightly tart flavor. They keep well, retaining their crisp quality. Bowls or baskets filled with apples of different colors and sizes, interspersed with pine cones, make a stunning fall or Christmas table decoration.

Put half the cucumber and apple in a blender jar. Heat the onion, wine and chicken broth to a boil and boil 5 minutes. Pour into the blender jar and blend on high speed with the cucumber and apple until smooth. Pour into a bowl and set aside. Put the rest of the cucumber and apple in the blender jar. Add the buttermilk, crème fraîche, salt, pepper, parsley and mint and blend on high speed until smooth. Add to the first mixture and stir to combine, then transfer to the blender again in three batches and blend until very smooth. Chill until ready to serve.

Taste the soup before serving and adjust salt. Whisk briskly if the soup has separated. Ladle into chilled bowls and garnish with toasted almonds.

GREEN GAZPACHO

6 servings

The combination of honeydew melon, green tomatoes, mint and cucumber makes a colorful and refreshing chilled soup. You can make a golden version by using Cranshaw melon and yellow tomatoes. Chilled poached scallops may be added to the soup for an elegant appetizer or first course.

1 tablespoon vegetable or safflower oil
2 shallots, minced
½ large honeydew melon, peeled, seeded, in 1-inch pieces
1 cucumber, peeled, seeded, in 1-inch pieces
4 medium tomatillos, quartered, or 2 green tomatoes, quartered
5 ounces jícama, cut in 5 pieces
½ yellow bell pepper, stemmed and seeded (optional)
2 cups chicken stock, all fat removed
3 tablespoons fresh lime or lemon juice
1 serrano chili, stemmed and cut in half
1 teaspoon salt
¼ teaspoon white pepper
1 tablespoon minced fresh cilantro
½ tablespoon minced fresh mint

VEGETABLES
½ cup seeded cucumber, finely chopped
½ cup yellow bell pepper, finely chopped, or ½ cup papaya, finely chopped
¾ cup seeded tomato, finely chopped
1 small carrot, blanched and finely chopped

Heat the oil in a small skillet over medium heat. Add the shallots and sauté a minute or until translucent.

Place about half the melon, cucumber, tomatillos or tomatoes, jícama, yellow bell pepper and the shallots in a blender jar and blend until smooth. Divide the chicken stock and lime juice and add half to the vegetables in the blender jar; blend until smooth. Empty into a large bowl and repeat process with remaining half. Combine both batches. Add the serrano chili and let it stand in the soup for 5 minutes to add flavor. Remove and discard. Season the soup with salt, pepper, cilantro and mint to taste. Stir in chopped vegetables and refrigerate for at least 4 hours or up to 24 hours.

Variations

- For a golden gazpacho, substitute Cranshaw melon for honeydew and yellow tomatoes for tomatillos or green tomatoes and use 1 whole yellow bell pepper instead of half.
- For gazpacho with scallops, poach ¾ pound scallops as follows. Bring ¼ cup butter, 1½ cups white wine and 1½ cups water to a boil in a skillet. Add scallops, cover and remove from heat. Let poach, undisturbed, for 12 minutes. Remove scallops from liquid, cool and toss with 1 tablespoon each cilantro and mint. Slice sea scallops thin and divide among individual bowls of gazpacho. (Bay scallops do not need to be sliced.)

ROASTED CORN SOUP

8 servings

Grilling or roasting the corn in the husks gives this light corn soup its unique flavor. The green chili imparts a subtle seasoning and keeps it from being too sweet. With fresh seafood added, the soup turns into a delicious chowder. Other good variations can be made by adding seeded, diced tomatoes or by serving the soup with a fresh tomatillo relish (page 230).

8 ears fresh corn, grilled or roasted
6 scallions, white part only, sliced
1 Anaheim chili, roasted and peeled
   (page 20), or 1 canned mild green
   chili, rinsed and drained
1 cup white wine
1 celery stalk, diced
2 cups half and half
1 cup chicken stock, all fat removed
1 to 2 teaspoons minced fresh dill
1½ teaspoons salt
Pinch cayenne pepper
¼ teaspoon white pepper
Fresh chives or dill sprigs for garnish

Dill has an affinity for corn and is delicious snipped into a corn chowder. It gives a special twist to mustard sauce for beef or crabcakes. And it is superb with many of the Gulf shellfish.

Soak the ears of corn in the husk for 20 to 30 minutes. To grill, place on hot grill and cook, turning often, for 20 minutes. To oven-roast the corn, preheat the oven to 400° F. Place soaked corn directly on the oven rack and bake until tender, about 20 minutes.

Cut the kernels from the cob with a sharp knife and set 1½ cups aside. Put the rest of the corn, scallions and chili in a 3-quart saucepan over medium-high heat. Add wine and 1 cup water. Simmer, stirring occasionally, until the vegetables are soft, about 10 minutes.

Put the vegetables and liquid in a blender and blend on high speed. Strain, pressing firmly to remove all the liquid from the kernels. Put the liquid back into the saucepan over medium heat. Add reserved corn kernels, celery, half and half, chicken stock, dill, salt, cayenne pepper and white pepper. Cook for about 10 minutes. Serve the soup hot. Sprinkle with fresh chives or a sprig of dill for garnish.

NOTE.   If you make the soup a day before you serve it, it will thicken as it stands and may need to be thinned with water.

Variation
- Add 1 pound of freshly cooked shrimp, lobster, crayfish or crab to the finished soup.

CORN AND POTATO CHOWDER

6 servings

The spicy sausage in this chowder provides a nice contrast to the delicate creamy texture of the soup. It is very easy to prepare and it is a recipe my guests always request.

2 small red potatoes, about 6 ounces, scrubbed, or 1 sweet potato, about 6 ounces, scrubbed
Salt
6 ears fresh corn (about 3½ cups corn kernels)
2 cups heavy cream
3 cups chicken stock, preferably homemade (page 97)
1½ tablespoons unsalted butter
6 scallions, sliced thin
1 red bell pepper, finely diced
Pepper
1 cup smoked sausage or bulk chorizo, cooked and crumbled

Put the potatoes in a saucepan of lightly salted water and bring to a boil. Boil until tender, about 10 minutes. When cool, peel and dice into ¼-inch cubes.

Cut the corn kernels from the cobs and set ½ cup aside for finishing the soup. Heat the remaining kernels, the cream and chicken stock in a medium saucepan over medium-high heat for 5 minutes. Reduce the heat to medium-low and continue to cook, stirring occasionally, for 10 minutes.

Put the corn and cream mixture in a blender, and blend on high speed to liquefy. Strain into the same saucepan, pressing to extract all the liquid from the kernels.

Heat the butter in a skillet over medium heat. Add the scallions, reserved corn and red pepper and sauté until soft, 5 minutes. Add to the cream mixture with the potatoes and simmer, stirring occasionally, until corn is tender and the soup is hot, 10 to 12 minutes. Season to taste with salt and pepper. To serve, ladle hot soup into bowls. Top each with a spoonful of sausage.

NOTE. Corn soup tends to thicken when refrigerated, so if you prepare it in advance, you may need to thin it with water when you reheat it.

Variation
- Substitute smoked fish for the sausage. Skin and debone the fish and cut it into bite-size pieces. You should have about 1½ cups. Add the fish shortly before serving and heat for 10 minutes. Do not boil.

CREAMY CARROT SOUP WITH DILL

6 servings

This is a light but creamy soup that combines carrots, parsnips and complementary herbs. It makes a wonderful first course and may be served hot or cold. For a more elegant presentation and an unusual color and flavor combination, fill a soup bowl on one side with the carrot soup, and the other with red pepper soup (page 108). How to combine two soups in the same bowl is explained on page 95.

2 cups chicken broth
2 medium leeks, white part only,
    sliced and rinsed
5 large carrots, cut in 2-inch pieces
6 parsnips, cut in 2-inch pieces
    (about 3 cups)
1 celery stalk, cut in several pieces
3 parsley sprigs
1 cup half and half
1 cup heavy cream
2 teaspoons minced fresh thyme or 1
    teaspoon dried thyme
1½ tablespoons chopped fresh dill or
    1 teaspoon dried dillweed
1 teaspoon salt
¼ teaspoon white pepper
Pinch of cayenne pepper
⅛ teaspoon ground cumin
1 tablespoon lemon juice
Sprigs of fresh dill for garnish

Heat 1½ cups chicken broth and 1½ cups water to a boil in a large saucepan. Add the leeks, carrots, parsnips, celery and parsley and simmer over medium-high heat until the vegetables are very soft, about 30 to 35 minutes. Spoon the vegetables and the liquid, in two batches, into a blender jar and blend on high speed until smooth.

Pour the soup back into the same saucepan, reduce the heat to medium and add the half and half, cream, thyme, dill, salt, pepper, cayenne, cumin and lemon juice. Cook, stirring constantly, to heat and blend flavors. The soup should have the consistency of heavy cream. If the soup is too thick, use the additional chicken stock to thin.

Garnish each bowl of soup with a sprig of fresh dill and serve hot.

CREAM OF CILANTRO SOUP WITH SEAFOOD

6 servings

This simple soup explodes with flavor because of its very short cooking time. For best results, have everything ready ahead of time so the soup can be blended, heated and served as quickly as possible. The version using mussels that Robert Del Grande originally developed is equally good. The soup may also be made with chicken.

1¼ pounds bay scallops or 1½ pounds medium shrimp, peeled and deveined
1 cup vermouth
1 cup fish stock
½ cup plus 2 tablespoons chopped red onion
1 cup heavy cream
2 cloves garlic, minced
2 serrano chilies, stemmed, chopped and seeded
1 cup fresh cilantro, stemmed and rinsed
1 cup fresh parsley, stemmed
Salt
Pepper

Put the scallops or shrimp, vermouth, stock and ½ cup red onion in a large skillet over medium-high heat. Bring to a simmer, then reduce heat to low and simmer for 30 seconds. Cover and remove from heat. Let stand, covered, for 4 minutes. Remove the seafood with a slotted spoon.

Pour the liquid in a blender jar and blend on high speed. Pour back into the skillet, add the cream and heat to a simmer.

Put the garlic, chilies, cilantro, parsley and 1 cup of the liquid into a blender jar. Blend on high speed until smooth, then stir into the remaining liquid. Season to taste with salt and pepper.

Divide the seafood between 6 shallow soup plates. Ladle the hot broth over the seafood and serve immediately.

Variations
- Substitute 24 mussels, oysters or clams for the scallops or shrimp. Simmer until the shells open, then remove shellfish and proceed as in the main recipe.
- Substitute 2 cups of uncooked chicken, cut in strips, for the seafood and 1 cup chicken stock for the fish stock. Proceed as in the main recipe.

Epazote, *also called Mexican tea or wormseed, is a pungent herb with jagged leaves, native to tropical America. It is used in many Mexican dishes and is thought to take the wind out of beans.*

ROASTED PEPPER SOUP

4 servings

Soups made from roasted peppers are quite popular in the restaurants of the Southwest and chefs are fond of serving two or three soups in a bowl. This recipe may be used with red or yellow peppers. Use yellow tomatoes with yellow peppers, red with red.

2 tablespoons butter
2 tablespoons safflower oil
1 medium onion, diced
1 clove garlic, chopped
½ cup dry sherry
2 large red tomatoes, peeled and
    seeded, or 12 yellow cherry
    tomatoes, peeled and seeded
2 cups chicken stock, preferably
    homemade (page 97)
2 leaves fresh basil or ¼ teaspoon
    dried basil
1 teaspoon minced fresh thyme or ¼
    teaspoon dried thyme
4 red or yellow bell peppers, roasted,
    peeled and seeded (page 20)
2 tablespoons all-purpose flour
1 cup heavy cream
Lemon juice
Salt
White pepper

GARNISH
Basil leaves
Cilantro cream (page 112)

Heat the butter and oil in a medium saucepan over medium-high heat. Add the onion and garlic and sauté until soft and translucent, about 10 minutes. Stir in the sherry, tomatoes, chicken stock, basil and thyme and simmer, stirring occasionally, for 15 minutes.

Put half the peppers in a blender jar. Add the flour and half the onion mixture and blend on high speed until smooth. Repeat with the remaining peppers and onion.

Strain the soup through a coarse strainer into the same saucepan and place over medium-high heat. Cook, stirring occasionally, until hot and thickened, 5 to 8 minutes. Stir in the cream and season to taste with lemon juice, salt and pepper. The soup should be the consistency of chilled heavy cream; thin as necessary with chicken stock. Continue cooking until hot.

Serve the soup garnished with fresh basil or cilantro cream or prepare both a yellow and a red bell pepper soup. Use two ladles and ladle both soups at the same time into shallow serving bowls.

ROASTED RED PEPPER SOUP WITH CORN

8 servings

This soup is both colorful and flavorful and lends itself to many different garnishes. Instead of frying tortilla strips, you might want to try frying one of the chili pastas on pages 292–293.

2 tablespoons unsalted butter
1 large leek, white part only, sliced
    and rinsed
1 clove garlic, minced
5 large red bell peppers, roasted
    (page 20)
1½ tablespoons all-purpose flour
1½ tablespoons tomato paste
4 cups chicken stock, preferably
    homemade (page 97)
1 cup heavy cream
1 teaspoon salt
¼ teaspoon coarsely ground black
    pepper
2 cups corn kernels
1 tablespoon minced fresh cilantro
3 corn tortillas, cut in thin strips and
    fried crisp, for garnish (page 45).

Heat the butter in a small skillet over medium heat. Add the leeks and garlic and sauté until soft, 3 to 4 minutes. Add the peppers, tomato paste and 1 cup chicken stock and simmer for 5 minutes.

Pour the mixture into a blender jar, add flour and blend on high speed until smooth. Strain and press firmly to extract all the liquid.

Pour the pepper liquid into a medium saucepan over medium heat. Add the remaining chicken stock, cream, salt and pepper. Stir constantly until thick and smooth. Add the corn kernels and cilantro and continue to cook until the corn is tender.

Ladle the soup into bowls and garnish with tortilla strips.

TORTILLA SOUP

10 servings

This is one version of a favorite soup that originated in Mexico. It has been served in some of the most elegant restaurants in the Southwest. The rich roasted tomato and chili broth is the perfect foil for tender bits of chicken, crisp tortillas and creamy avocados.

1 large yellow or white onion, quartered
8 whole tomatoes
4 tablespoons safflower oil
1 corn tortilla, chopped
4 cloves garlic, minced
1 ancho chili, stemmed, seeded, toasted and chopped fine (page 22)
1 bay leaf
½ sprig dried *epazote* (optional)
2 teaspoons ground cumin
1 quart chicken stock, preferably homemade (page 97)
1 quart beef stock, preferably homemade (page 98)
1 can (8 ounces) tomato sauce
Salt
Cayenne pepper or coarsely ground black pepper
8 sprigs fresh cilantro for garnish

———

2 cooked chicken breasts, cut in small pieces
4 ounces Cheddar or Monterey Jack cheese, shredded
1 medium ripe avocado, peeled, pitted and cubed
2 cups fried corn tortilla strips (page 45)

Preheat an outdoor grill. Rub the onions and tomatoes with 2 tablespoons of the oil and grill on all sides until well charred, about 15 to 20 minutes. Or preheat the broiler and place onions and tomatoes on a cookie sheet and set it 4 to 6 inches from the broiling element. Broil until charred on all sides. (Leave the oven door slightly ajar.) Put the tomatoes and onions in a blender jar or food processor fitted with the metal blade and blend on high speed until smooth. Set aside.

Heat the remaining oil in a large soup pot. Add the tortilla, garlic and ancho chili and sauté for 3 to 4 minutes. Add the bay leaf, *epazote* if using, cumin, chicken and beef stock and heat to a boil. Stir in the blended tomato mixture and tomato sauce and simmer over medium heat for about 30 minutes. Add salt and cayenne or black pepper to taste, then strain through a coarse strainer. This may be done ahead and the soup reheated when ready to serve.

Warm the cooked chicken if necessary and put it in a serving bowl. Put the cheese, avocado and crisp tortillas in separate bowls. Heat the broth to a boil and ladle into large, shallow soup dishes. Garnish each one with a cilantro sprig. Invite your guests to continue garnishing the soup as they will.

SOUTHWEST VEGETABLE SOUP

10 servings

The secret to good soup is a rich homemade stock. Here you should use a stock made from game birds, smoked birds or chicken or a simple poultry stock. Canned stock makes an attractive soup presentation but the flavor inevitably falls short. Besides the vegetables listed below, you can use almost any vegetable, cut in fine dice or short julienne strips, and black beans, garbanzos or fava beans, cooked until tender but still whole. Add strips of smoked or roasted duck, poultry or game birds if you want a more substantial soup.

3 quarts clarified homemade stock
  (page 98)
2 serrano chilies, stemmed and halved
  (optional)
1 cup diced carrot, blanched
1 cup diced jícama or turnip,
  blanched
1 cup diced red, green or yellow bell
  pepper
½ cup seeded and diced zucchini,
  blanched
½ cup seeded and diced yellow
  squash, blanched
½ cup fresh green peas, blanched
2 tablespoons minced fresh cilantro
  or parsley
8 thin slices of lime, seeds removed
10 flour tortillas, thinly sliced and
  fried crisp, or 5 cups jalapeño
  pasta, fried crisp (page 45)

Put the stock in a large stockpot, add the chilies for a subtle spicy flavor, and heat to a boil.

Preheat the oven to 200° F. Put the soup bowls in the oven and warm for about 8 to 10 minutes.

Toss the vegetables together and just prior to serving, divide between the bowls. Remove the chilies from the boiling stock, then ladle the stock over the vegetables. Stir in a little minced cilantro and garnish each serving with a thin lime slice. Serve with crisp fried tortilla strips or pasta on the side.

WINTER SQUASH BISQUE WITH WILD RICE

6 servings

Instead of baking the squash, you may smoke or grill it whole for a smoky flavor. Garnish the soup with chopped pecans or pistachio nuts, or minced fresh basil or a tomato relish. Wild rice gives the soup a special touch.

4 acorn or butternut squash, halved and seeded
1 tablespoon butter
1 yellow bell pepper, stemmed, seeded and quartered, or 1 green bell pepper, stemmed, seeded and quartered
1 medium onion, quartered
1 clove garlic, cut in half
1 tablespoon vegetable oil
2 cans (14½ ounces) chicken broth
1 teaspoon minced fresh thyme or ¼ teaspoon dried
1 teaspoon minced fresh basil or 1 teaspoon dried
½ cup light cream or half and half
Lemon juice to taste
Salt
White pepper

WILD RICE
1 tablespoon butter
1 tablespoon minced onion
1 tablespoon minced fresh parsley
½ cup chopped toasted pistachio nuts or pecans (page 50)
1 cup cooked wild rice
6 sundried tomatoes, diced (optional)
Salt
Pepper

Preheat the oven to 350° F. Put the squash on a cookie sheet. Place a dab of butter in each piece. Rub the peppers, onion and garlic with oil and put them on the cookie sheet with the squash. Cover with foil and bake until the squash are tender, about 35 minutes. Cool, then scoop the pulp from the squash and put it in a blender jar. Add 1 cup water and blend on high speed until smooth. Pour into a medium saucepan.

Put the peppers, onion and garlic in the same blender jar. Add about ½ cup of the chicken broth and blend until smooth. Stir the pepper mixture, remaining chicken broth, thyme and basil into the saucepan and heat to a boil, stirring constantly. Reduce the heat to low and whisk in the cream. Cook over low heat for 10 minutes. Season to taste with lemon juice, salt and pepper. The finished soup should be the consistency of heavy cream. Thin if necessary with chicken broth.

To make the wild rice garnish, heat the butter in a medium skillet over medium heat. Add the onion and sauté until translucent. Stir in the parsley, pistachio nuts or pecans, wild rice and sundried tomatoes if using. Season to taste with salt and pepper.

To serve, ladle the soup into soup bowls and place a spoonful of wild rice in the center.

STEPHAN'S SOUTHWEST CREAMS

½ cup each cream

Stephan Pyles uses these colorful creams to swirl an attractive garnish on cream soups or black bean soups or a combination of two soups. You can use the same technique to create a flavorful garnish from almost any herb or chili.

CILANTRO CREAM
6 spinach leaves, stemmed
1 cup cilantro leaves
4 to 5 tablespoons crème fraîche (see recipe below)
Salt
Pepper

ANCHO CHILI CREAM
1 small ancho chili, stemmed, seeded and toasted (page 22)
6 tablespoons crème fraîche
Salt
Pepper

For the cilantro cream, bring 2 cups of water to a boil. Add the spinach leaves and cook 1 minute. Drain and rinse with cold water. Press spinach firmly through a strainer to remove all moisture. Put the spinach and the cilantro leaves in a blender jar. Add 2 to 3 tablespoons crème fraîche and blend until smooth. Strain the mixture into a small bowl and stir in the remaining crème fraîche to make a thick cream. Season to taste with salt and pepper. Put the cream in a clean squirt bottle and use to decorate soups.

For the ancho chili cream, bring 1½ cups of water to a boil. Pour over the chili and let soak until softened, about 10 to 15 minutes. Cut the chili in 4 pieces and place in a blender jar. Add 2 to 3 tablespoons crème fraîche and blend on high speed until smooth. Strain into a small bowl and stir in the remaining crème fraîche to make a thick cream. Season to taste with salt and pepper. Put the cream in a clean squirt bottle and use to decorate soups.

CRÈME FRAÎCHE

1 cup sour cream
1 cup heavy cream
2 tablespoons buttermilk

Stir the sour cream, heavy cream and buttermilk together in a small bowl and let stand at room temperature for 1½ hours. Refrigerate for up to 2 weeks.

BLACK BEAN SOUP WITH CILANTRO-POBLANO CREAM

10 servings

Black bean soup is a hearty meal in itself as well as a great dish around which to plan a Southwestern brunch or informal supper. In the fall, I like to serve a warm quail salad (page 141) along with the black bean soup. I garnish the soup with the cilantro-poblano cream, a ribbon of yellow bell pepper sauce and a finely diced red bell pepper. To minimize the preparation time, I make the vegetable broth while the beans are soaking.

BEANS
1 pound black beans, rinsed
3 pieces bacon, chopped

BROTH
3 medium yellow onions, peeled and chopped
3 cloves garlic, chopped
4 carrots, cut in 1-inch pieces
4 celery stalks, including leaves, cut in 1-inch pieces
1 green bell pepper, stemmed, seeded and coarsely chopped
3 fresh Anaheim chilies, roasted and peeled (page 20), or 1 can (4 ounces) diced green chilies
1 pound ham hocks or 1 ham bone
3 cups beef stock, preferably homemade (page 98)
½ cup sherry
¼ cup coarsely chopped cilantro leaves
Salt
Coarsely ground black pepper

CILANTRO-POBLANO CREAM
1 poblano chili, roasted and peeled (page 20), or 1 canned mild green chili, drained
1 cup sour cream
¼ cup heavy cream
Several sprigs fresh cilantro
Salt

Combine 7 cups of water, beans, and bacon in a large saucepan and bring to a boil. Boil for 2 minutes, remove from heat and cover. Let the beans stand undisturbed while you prepare the broth.

Place the onion, garlic, carrots, celery, bell pepper, chilies and ham hocks with the beef broth and 3 cups of water in a large stockpot or Dutch oven. Bring to a boil, then reduce the heat and simmer, uncovered, for 1½ hours. Strain the broth through a coarse strainer. Save the broth and the ham but discard the vegetables. Remove the ham from the bone and chop coarsely. Set aside.

Drain the beans and place them with the ham bones and broth in a large pot and heat to a boil over medium-high heat. Reduce the heat and simmer, partially covered, until the beans are tender, about 1½ hours.

Put some of the beans, including the liquid, in a blender or food processor fitted with metal blade. Process to puree, then pour into a bowl. Repeat until all are done. Put the soup back in the stockpot. Stir in the sherry and cilantro.

Heat the soup to a simmer over medium heat. Cook 15 to 20 minutes to combine all the flavors. Season to taste with salt and pepper. If the soup is too thick, thin it with beef stock or water.

For the cilantro-poblano cream, put the chilies in a blender or food processor fitted with the metal blade. Add the sour cream, cream and cilantro and blend smooth. Add salt to taste and let stand about 20 minutes before using. Swirl several spoonfuls on top of each serving.

DEAN'S PEPPER CHEESE AND BLACK BEAN SOUP

8 servings

Dean Fearing's combination of these two soups literally bursts with flavor. You can garnish the soup with a red bell pepper cream, thin fried corn tortilla strips, a colorful combination of diced bell peppers or if you want a hearty soup, sautéed sausages. The black bean soup takes quite a while to prepare; you may want to wait until you have some leftover black beans, which can be transformed into a soup in no time.

2 tablespoons vegetable oil
1 medium onion, minced
1 leek, white part only, minced
1 celery stalk, diced
2 cloves garlic, minced
2 jalapeño peppers, stemmed, seeded
   and minced
7 tablespoons all-purpose flour
¾ cup beer
½ cup white wine
3½ cups chicken stock, preferably
   homemade (page 97)
4 cups grated Monterey Jack cheese
White pepper

———

½ recipe black bean soup (page 113)

Heat the oil in a large saucepan over medium-high heat. Add the onion, leek, celery, garlic and peppers and sauté for 5 minutes. Stir in the flour, and then add the beer and wine. Stir constantly and heat to a boil. Add chicken stock and boil for 5 minutes. Reduce the heat and add the cheese, stirring constantly, until melted.

Put half the soup in a blender jar and blend on high speed until smooth. Remove and repeat with the rest of the soup. Season with pepper to taste. The soup should be moderately thick. If it is too thick, add more chicken stock; if too thin, add more grated cheese.

Just before serving, reheat both soups in separate saucepans over medium heat to warm. Both soups should be the same consistency. Use two ladles at the same time to ladle the soups into soup bowls. Garnish according to personal preference.

BLACK BEAN CHILI WITH RELISHES

10 servings

Black beans, cooked in a well seasoned broth and then served with relishes, shredded cheese or spicy sausages, make a delicious meal. Serve with cornsticks (page 311) or blue-cornmeal muffins (page 312).

1 pound black beans, rinsed
3 to 4 tablespoons vegetable oil
1 pound ham hocks or ham bone or
   10 to 12 ounces Canadian bacon,
   cut in 2-ounce pieces
1 large red onion, diced
1 tablespoon ground cumin
1 tablespoon leaf oregano
2 ancho chili pods, stemmed, seeded,
   toasted and chopped (page 22)
4 cloves garlic, minced
1 large carrot, finely diced
1 jalapeño chili, finely chopped
1 teaspoon crushed black
   peppercorns
8 to 9 cups chicken stock, preferably
   homemade (page 97)
1 can (14½ ounces) Italian-style
   tomatoes, chopped
¼ cup chopped fresh cilantro
Salt

Soak the beans in 6 to 8 cups water overnight. Strain and discard the water.

Heat the oil in a large stockpot over medium-high heat. Add the ham hocks or ham bone or Canadian bacon, the onion, cumin and oregano and sauté until the meat is lightly browned, about 5 minutes. Add the chili pods, garlic, carrot, jalapeño chili, peppercorns, soaked and drained beans and chicken broth. Heat to a boil, then simmer over medium heat, covered, until the beans are tender crisp, about 45 minutes. Uncover, add the tomatoes and continue to simmer until the beans are tender, 15 to 25 minutes.

Remove the ham hocks, ham bone or Canadian bacon. When the bones are cool, chop the meat and add it to the beans. Stir in the cilantro and season to taste with salt. Serve hot.

Garnishes
Serve the chili with one or more of the following:
- Three-tomato salsa (page 228)
- Tomato and green chili relish (page 227)
- Avocado relish (page 229)
- Shredded white Cheddar or Monterey Jack cheese
- Well seasoned pork sausages or wild game sausages (page 91).

GREEN CHILI SOUP

6 servings

Crème fraîche gives this soup its light and smooth texture. It may be served hot or cold. Be sure to try the chilled avocado variation at the end of the recipe. The color is bright and the flavor intriguing.

2 cups chicken stock or canned
  chicken broth
2 leeks, white part only
4 Anaheim chilies, roasted and peeled
  (page 20), or 1 can (3½ ounces)
  mild green chilies, rinsed
1 clove garlic, peeled
6 tomatillos, cored and quartered, or
  2 small green tomatoes, cored and
  quartered
1¾ cups crème fraîche, preferably
  homemade (page 112)
Salt
Pepper
2 corn tortillas, sliced in thin strips
  and fried crisp for garnish
  (page 45)

Put the chicken broth and leeks in a 2-quart saucepan over medium-high heat. Bring to a boil and allow to boil for 10 minutes. Strain.

Stem and seed the chilies and put them in a blender. Add the garlic, tomatillos, 1 cup chicken broth, crème fraîche and blend on high speed until pureed. Pour the blended soup into the remaining chicken broth and season to taste with salt and pepper.

Heat over medium-high heat to serve hot. The soup may also be served cold. To do so, chill for at least 4 hours. Taste and adjust seasoning. Serve garnished with thin strips of fried tortillas.

Variation
- Blend a ripe avocado with the chilies, tomatillos and crème fraîche. You will need to increase the amount of chicken broth. Chill well.

GREEN CHILI GUMBO

12 servings

Green chilies replace the traditional okra in this hearty gumbo. Make it in advance to give the flavors plenty of time to meld.

1½ tablespoons oil
1 pound link smoked sausage, skinned, sliced and cut in strips (¼ × 2 inches)
2 whole chicken breasts, boned, skinned and cut in bite-size pieces
¼ cup all-purpose flour
¼ cup plus 2 tablespoons butter
10 cups chicken stock, preferably homemade (page 97)
1½ cups minced onion
1 chayote squash, peeled and diced (optional)
1½ cups minced celery
½ cup minced green bell pepper
2 cloves garlic, minced
2 serrano chilies, stemmed, seeded and diced
1 tablespoon minced fresh thyme
2 bay leaves
1 can (14½ ounces) Italian-style tomatoes
1½ cups diced green chilies or 4 poblano chilies, roasted, peeled and diced (page 20)
Cayenne pepper

———

Rice for serving
Minced fresh cilantro for garnish

Heat the oil in a large skillet over medium-high heat. Add the sausage and chicken and sauté until the chicken is tender, about 3 minutes. Remove the chicken and sausage and set aside. Add the flour and ¼ cup butter to the skillet. Stir over medium heat, scraping up the browned bits in the skillet, to make a nutty brown roux. Stir in a little of the chicken stock if necessary. Set aside.

In a large saucepan, heat the remaining butter. Add the onion, chayote, celery, bell pepper, garlic and serrano chilies and cook until the onion is translucent. Add thyme, bay leaves, tomatoes, green chilies and chicken stock. Stir in the roux, and cook over medium heat, for about 15 minutes, stirring constantly for the first 5 minutes. Add the reserved chicken and sausage and remove from heat. Let stand for 1 hour or refrigerate for up to 2 days to let the flavors blend. Remove the bay leaves and reheat the gumbo before serving.

Serve the gumbo in warm bowls with a mound of rice in the center. Garnish with minced fresh cilantro.

SALADS AND SALAD DRESSINGS

Mixed Green Salad with Vinaigrette
Spring Vegetable Salad with Fresh Herb Dressing
Watercress Salad with Cheese, Grapes and Toasted Walnuts
Watercress Salad with Beets, Oranges and Herb Yogurt Dressing
Double Endive and Radicchio Salad with Blue Cheese Dressing
Spinach Salad with Pine Nuts and Warm Goat Cheese
Warm Spinach Salad with Endive and Grapes
Jícama Salad
Black-Eyed Pea Salad
Creamy Cole Slaw
Sweet and Spicy Cole Slaw
Chicken and Chili Salad
Fried Chicken Salad
Smoked Chicken Salad with Southwest Vegetables
Chicken and Wild Rice Salad with Mint and Pecans
Warm Grilled Chicken Salad
Warm Chicken Salad with Jícama and Apples
Warm Turkey Salad
Chutney-Turkey Salad in Radicchio or Endive Leaves
Duck Salad with Grapes
Warm Quail Salad
Beef Barbecue Salad with Hearts of Palm
Ceviche Pasta Salad
Seafood Pasta Salad with Basil Pesto Dressing
Warm Seafood Salad with Tangerine Vinaigrette
Zucchini and Basil Salad with Pecan Vinaigrette
Zucchini Salad
Slang Jang
Apple Pecan Salad
Southwest Fruit Salad

Dressings

Basil-Walnut Vinaigrette
Herb Vinaigrette
Roast Bell Pepper Vinaigrette
Toasted Nut Vinaigrette
Poblano Chili Dressing
Buttermilk Ranch Dressing
Poppy Seed Dressing
Pomegranate Vinegar

Salads have come a long way from the before-the-meal iceberg and, occasionally, romaine or Bibb lettuce, tomato and cucumber combination dressed with Thousand Island or Italian dressing. Actually, a salad does not have to contain any lettuce at all: it can be a colorful medley of vegetables in a light herb vinaigrette; warm tender quail on a crunchy bed of jícama and grapes, garnished with pecans; or freshly poached seafood on a cushion of greens with sliced mango and avocado. It might be oysters, lightly battered and fried, or small pieces of crisp chicken tossed into some colorful greens with a warm dressing. Or it could be a salad sampler containing several relishes or compotes served with thick, crusty croutons; or a pasta salad with several complementary relishes.

Salads in this book are no longer confined to one course. Sometimes they star as a small meal or main course; sometimes they appear as a first course, sometimes after the entree. Colorful combinations of greens with bright strips of fresh vegetables or fruit provide an edible background for grilled foods or, tossed with oil and vinegar, an edible garnish.

Feel free to mix and match these salads using different dressings or different combinations as you wish. For example, the duck salad on page 140 can be made without the cabbage, then served in endive leaves and garnished with fresh mango. Fruit combinations can be served with wedges of cheese. Crisp-fried pasta, corn or flour tortillas, toasted cornbread or croutons baked with an herb pesto complement tossed greens nicely too.

MIXED GREEN SALAD WITH VINAIGRETTE

8 servings

Almost any lettuce combination that gives a nice flavor, texture, and color contrast can be used with this basic, very flavorful dressing. I consider the greens a beginning and add whatever is in season or suits my mood of the moment. It might be a sprinkling of champagne grapes, toasted nuts or some tiny tomatoes. The salad may be garnished with a wedge of cheese or goat cheese baked in cornbread (page 273).

VINAIGRETTE

1 clove garlic, minced, or 1 shallot, minced
3 to 4 tablespoons balsamic or sherry vinegar
1 tablespoon fresh lemon juice
1 teaspoon salt or to taste
¼ teaspoon white pepper
1 to 2 teaspoons whole grain or Dijon mustard
3 tablespoons virgin olive oil
½ cup safflower oil

GREENS

1 small head red-tip leaf lettuce
1 head radicchio (optional)
1 head Bibb lettuce, leaves rinsed and separated
1 bunch watercress or ¼ pound mâche, rinsed and stemmed
12 to 14 leaves young, fresh spinach or sorrel leaves (optional)

Add plump ripe berries to salads of fresh lettuce (even a simple lettuce and tomato salad) to add color and flavor. Blackberries, blueberries and raspberries are best because of their tartness.

Heat the garlic or shallot with vinegar in a small skillet to a boil. Remove and transfer to a blender jar. Add the lemon juice, salt, pepper, mustard and oils and blend on high speed until smooth. Taste and adjust, adding salt or lemon juice to personal preference. (Dressings should always taste stronger before they are used as the taste will soften on the greens.) Refrigerate if not using immediately.

Tear the lettuce leaves into smaller pieces. Leave small leaves whole. Wash and dry the greens, then toss them together in a bowl, cover and refrigerate until crisp.

Just before serving, heat the vinaigrette to room temperature if necessary. Toss with the greens, using just enough to coat leaves.

SPRING VEGETABLE SALAD WITH FRESH HERB DRESSING

6 servings

This colorful spring salad of crisp vegetables and peppers is dressed with a light herb vinaigrette. It is as refreshing as it is beautiful. There is no substitute for the sweet, crisp taste of jícama, though a combination of turnip and apple strips might do. The salad could be turned into a light meal or entree salad by adding cooked chicken, duck or smoked turkey.

2 medium carrots
¼ pound tiny green beans, ends snipped
½ cup fresh cooked peas, or ½ cup frozen peas, thawed
4 ounces jícama, peeled
1 red bell pepper, stemmed and seeded
1 yellow bell pepper, stemmed and seeded (optional)
1 medium chayote squash, seeded, and peeled

HERB DRESSING
½ cup safflower oil
¼ cup white wine vinegar
¼ cup lemon juice
3 sprigs fresh cilantro or fresh mint, finely chopped, or ½ teaspoon dried cilantro or mint
8 sprigs fresh parsley, finely chopped
2 basil leaves, finely chopped, or ½ teaspoon dried basil
½ teaspoon dry mustard
½ teaspoon salt
⅛ teaspoon white pepper

GREENS
1 head Bibb lettuce, separated and rinsed
1 bunch watercress or 2 cups field lettuce, such as oak leaf or mâche, stemmed and rinsed

2 to 3 tablespoons toasted pine nuts (page 50)

Heat about 1 quart water in a 2-quart saucepan to a boil. Add the carrots and boil to blanch for 5 minutes. Remove with tongs and add the green beans and peas to blanch for 1 minute. Rinse all the vegetables with cold water.

Cut the carrot, jícama, red and yellow bell peppers and chayote squash in matchstick strips, ⅛ × 2½ inches. Put all the vegetables in a mixing bowl.

Whisk the oil, vinegar, lemon juice, herbs, mustard and seasonings in a small bowl until well blended.

Toss the greens in a medium bowl with enough dressing to coat each leaf lightly. Divide among 6 salad plates. Pour the remaining dressing over the vegetables and toss to coat. Mound the vegetables over the greens and scatter the pine nuts on top.

Bell peppers are naturally suited to the foods of the West and Southwest because they are compatible with so many of the other ingredients. Their vivid hues fit in a colorful cuisine. Purple bell peppers, green and purple when used raw in salads, turn all green when cooked.

WATERCRESS SALAD WITH CHEESE, GRAPES AND TOASTED WALNUTS

8 servings

The combination of a mild cheese with crunchy grapes, crisp watercress and buttery walnuts makes a light salad perfect to begin a meal. Almost any variety of grapes may be used, or a combination. Chill the cheese before grating, for more attractive shreds. If your guests are fond of moderately mild chilies, substitute the poblano chili dressing (page 152) for an exciting combination of flavor and texture.

2 bunches watercress, rinsed
  and stemmed
3 ounces Monterey Jack cheese,
  grated (about ¾ cup)
1½ cups seedless grapes, green or
  red, halved, or whole champagne
  grapes
1 tablespoon butter
¾ cup toasted walnut halves
  (page 50)
Salt

DRESSING
1 small garlic clove, minced
½ cup seedless grapes
⅓ cup white wine
1 teaspoon dry mustard
¼ teaspoon white pepper
¼ cup walnut oil
½ cup safflower oil

Combine the watercress, cheese and grapes in a large bowl.

Heat the butter in a small skillet over medium heat. Add the walnuts and sauté about 2 minutes. Place on paper towels and sprinkle lightly with salt.

For the dressing, put the garlic, grapes, and white wine in a blender and blend on high speed to puree. Add the dry mustard, pepper, walnut oil and safflower oil. Blend until smooth.

When ready to serve the salad, stir the dressing briefly and pour over the watercress, cheese and grapes. Toss to coat. Divide among 6 serving plates and garnish with walnuts.

WATERCRESS SALAD WITH BEETS, ORANGES AND HERB YOGURT DRESSING

6 servings

The fresh herbs, sharp feta cheese, sweet beets and tart oranges join forces in a light, refreshing salad. If you can obtain yellow beets, use a combination of red and yellow beets.

2 bunches watercress, rinsed and stemmed
½ cup small purple or green basil leaves (optional)
1 unwaxed cucumber, unpeeled
6 small cooked beets, quartered
1 tablespoon butter
½ cup toasted walnut halves (page 50)
Salt
1 head Bibb lettuce, rinsed
6 ounces feta cheese, drained and crumbled
1 orange, peeled and separated into segments

ORANGE-HERB DRESSING
Juice of 1 orange
1 clove garlic
¼ cup loosely packed fresh cilantro leaves
¼ cup loosely packed fresh mint leaves
2 to 3 teaspoons honey mustard
1 cup yogurt or 1 cup sour cream plus 1 tablespoon vinegar
1 teaspoon salt
¼ teaspoon white pepper

Combine the watercress and basil leaves in a large mixing bowl. Run the tines of a fork lengthwise along the skin of the cucumber. Cut in half lengthwise and slice thin. Add the cucumber and beets to the watercress and toss to combine.

Heat the butter in a small skillet. Add the nuts and sauté until golden, 1 to 2 minutes. Sprinkle lightly with salt and set aside on paper towels to drain.

Line 6 salad plates with Bibb lettuce leaves. Arrange the greens and vegetables in the center. Sprinkle the cheese and walnuts on top. Put several orange sections on the side of each plate.

For the dressing, put the orange juice, garlic, cilantro, mint, mustard, yogurt, salt and pepper in a blender jar and blend on high speed until smooth. Drizzle the dressing over the salad.

DOUBLE ENDIVE AND RADICCHIO SALAD
WITH BLUE CHEESE DRESSING

6 servings

This combination of colorful greens can really stand up to the creamy blue cheese dressing. You might add some toasted walnuts or pistachio nuts and serve it with cornbread baked in a pie pan and cut into wedges.

1 Belgian endive, leaves rinsed and
    separated
1 head curly endive, rinsed and torn in
    small pieces
1 head radicchio, leaves rinsed
1 cup buttermilk ranch dressing
    (page 152)
4 ounces blue cheese
1 cup toasted walnut halves or
    pistachio nuts, optional (see note)

———

Cornbread (pages 310–311)

Toss the Belgian endive and curly endive together in a mixing bowl; tear large radicchio leaves in half and mix with the endive. Leave small radicchio leaves whole and set aside.

Place several smaller radicchio leaves on each of 6 chilled salad plates. Toss the salad with just enough dressing to coat lightly. Divide among the salad plates. Crumble the cheese directly on the salad. Place a dollop of the remaining dressing on each plate. Garnish the greens with the nuts, if using, and serve with cornbread wedges.

NOTE: If using the nuts, sauté them in 1 tablespoon hot butter for 1 to 1½ minutes, then drain on paper towels and season lightly with salt.

Variations
- Crumble the cheese and mix it into the remaining dressing.
- Crumble some crisp bacon and sprinkle it over the greens.

SPINACH SALAD WITH PINE NUTS
AND WARM GOAT CHEESE

6 servings

This is a simple salad combining buttery pine nuts, roasted peppers and sweet onions with a mild, creamy cheese and a flavorful vinaigrette. It is just as good prepared with red onions, walnuts and pieces of feta cheese.

10 ounces fresh spinach, stemmed
   and rinsed
½ large sweet or red onion, peeled
   and sliced
3 red bell peppers, roasted, peeled
   and cut in strips (page 20)
⅓ cup toasted pine nuts (page 50)

————

4 tablespoons toasted pine nuts, finely
   chopped (page 50)
1 tablespoon fresh minced basil
6 disks mild goat cheese, about 1½
   ounces each
¼ cup virgin olive oil

VINAIGRETTE
1 clove garlic, minced
1 tablespoon whole-grain mustard
2 tablespoons red wine or sherry
   vinegar
2 tablespoons lemon juice
⅔ cup safflower oil
Salt
Pepper

Dry the spinach leaves and put them in a large bowl. Add the onion, peppers and whole pine nuts and toss to mix.

Preheat the oven to 350° F. Combine the minced pine nuts and basil. Brush each round of cheese with olive oil, then roll in the nut crumbs to coat all sides. Put the cheese rounds on a cookie sheet and bake until softened but not melted, about 2 to 3 minutes.

Whisk together the garlic, mustard, vinegar, lemon juice and safflower oil. Season to taste with salt and pepper. Toss with the spinach, using just enough dressing to coat the leaves. Place a round of cheese in the center of each salad.

WARM SPINACH SALAD WITH ENDIVE AND GRAPES

8 servings

All the ingredients for this salad may be prepared in advance and then tossed with a heated dressing at the last minute. Serve it with poultry, duck, game birds or baked ham.

1 pound fresh spinach, rinsed
1 Belgian endive, rinsed
1½ cups seedless red grapes, halved
1 tablespoon butter
¾ cup toasted pecan halves
    (page 50)

DRESSING
2 shallots, minced
1 tablespoon cider vinegar
¼ cup balsamic vinegar
½ cup plus 2 tablespoons safflower
    oil
Salt
Pepper
2 tablespoons cracklings (page 47) or
    crisp bacon, diced (optional)

Remove the tough stems from the spinach and cut the leaves into strips about ¼ to ½ inch wide. Core the endive and cut it lengthwise into strips about ¼ inch wide. Squeeze the juice from 12 of the grape halves into a saucepan and set aside. Heat the butter in a medium skillet over medium heat. Add the pecans and sauté 1 to 2 minutes. Remove to paper towels to drain and sprinkle with salt.

Toss the pecans, spinach, endive and grapes in a large, shallow dish and refrigerate, covered, until ready to add the dressing.

To make the dressing, heat shallots, grape juice and vinegars in a saucepan to a boil for 1 minute. Whisk in the oil and keep on medium heat, about 1 minute, just long enough to warm. Season to taste with salt and pepper.

Toss the greens with the warm dressing and cracklings or bacon if using. Serve immediately.

JÍCAMA SALAD

3 cups

A refreshing, crisp relish salad, this may be paired with another relish to accompany grilled fish or chicken or spicy enchiladas or soft tacos.

2 cups jícama, peeled and coarsely
    shredded or in julienne strips
¼ red bell pepper, cut in julienne
    strips
¼ yellow bell pepper, cut in julienne
    strips
¼ cup blanched julienne strips of
    nopales cactus pads (page 32)
    (optional)
Juice from 1 lime, about 2
    tablespoons
1 tablespoon finely minced fresh
    parsley
Salt
Pepper

Put the jícama in a medium bowl. Add the peppers and nopales, if using, and toss. Season with lime juice, parsley and salt and pepper to taste. Refrigerate until ready to serve or up to 12 hours.

BLACK-EYED PEA SALAD

6 to 8 servings

For people in the South, eating black-eyed peas is a tradition, particularly on New Year's Day. This salad may be served hot or cold, on its own or with almost any meat or poultry. Freshly baked cornsticks or muffins would add a traditional note. The peas can be prepared in advance, but the salad is best if combined just prior to serving. The peas may be cooked in ham stock (page 100), which makes for an exceptional flavor.

1 recipe black-eyed peas (page 272)
1½ tablespoons vegetable oil

————

1 rib celery, cut in ¼-inch dice
4 artichoke hearts, cut in ¼-inch dice
½ red bell pepper, cut in ¼-inch dice
   (about ⅓ cup)

DRESSING
1 to 2 tablespoons jalapeño jelly or 2
   tablespoons currant jelly
3 tablespoons sherry vinegar
1 shallot, minced
⅔ cup safflower oil
1 teaspoon dry mustard
1 tablespoon minced fresh parsley
½ teaspoon salt

————

Fresh artichoke leaves
Minced fresh parsley

Prepare the black-eyed peas. To finish the salad, cut the reserved smoked ham or sausage from cooking the peas into ¼-inch dice. Heat the oil in a small skillet and quickly sauté over medium-high heat until crisp.

Combine the peas, sautéed meat, celery, artichoke hearts and bell pepper. Prepare the dressing by heating the jelly, sherry vinegar, and shallot in a small saucepan over medium heat until the jelly melts. Remove from the heat and whisk in the oil, mustard, parsley and salt until well blended.

Arrange the artichoke leaves on 6 serving plates. Mound the salad in the center of each plate and sprinkle with minced parsley.

NOTE. Two cups of canned or frozen black-eyed peas may be substituted for fresh-cooked peas.

Variation
- The salad may also be served at room temperature or chilled; the preparation is the same. If serving it chilled, stir 2 tablespoons rice wine vinegar into the dressing.

CREAMY COLE SLAW

10 servings

An old-fashioned cooked cream dressing is combined with mayonnaise for a traditional cole slaw. You could also use the cream dressing for a salad of shredded carrots, raisins and pineapple. Or omit the garlic and use it for fruit salad.

1 head cabbage, quartered and cored
1 sweet white onion, halved, cored
    and thinly sliced

OLD-FASHIONED CREAM DRESSING
3 eggs, beaten
3 tablespoons sugar
1 tablespoon honey
1 tablespoon cornstarch
2 teaspoons dry mustard
2 cloves garlic, minced
1 cup heavy cream
⅓ cup vinegar
2 tablespoons butter, at room
    temperature
1 teaspoon celery seed
Pinch cayenne pepper
1 teaspoon salt
Lemon juice to taste
¼ teaspoon white pepper

––––––––

2 carrots, peeled and shredded
1 green, red or yellow bell pepper, cut
    in very fine strips (optional)
1 unpeeled Granny Smith or Red
    Delicious apple, cut in very fine
    strips (optional)
⅔ cup mayonnaise, preferably
    homemade (page 257)
Coarsely ground black pepper to
    taste

Slice the cabbage very thin and put it in a large bowl of ice water to cover. Add the onion, toss to mix and let onion and cabbage soak for at least 2 or up to 4 hours. Drain and dry thoroughly.

Put the eggs, sugar, honey, cornstarch and dry mustard in a medium saucepan and beat until smooth. Whisk in the garlic and cream over medium heat. Add the vinegar and stir constantly until the mixture begins to thicken. Lower the heat and continue to cook until thickened and smooth. Whisk in the butter, celery seed, cayenne pepper and salt. Season to taste with a squeeze of lemon and white pepper. Strain and cool. Set aside ⅔ cup for the salad and refrigerate the rest for another time.

Put the drained cabbage and onions, shredded carrots and pepper and apple if using in a large bowl and toss to mix. Combine the mayonnaise with ⅔ cup cream dressing in a small bowl and stir to mix well. Pour over the vegetables and toss to mix. Mix several times at 10-minute intervals, then season to taste with black pepper. Refrigerate until ready to serve.

Red cabbage is interchangeable with green in most recipes. Combining different varieties and colors adds interest to both raw and cooked foods. Blanching cabbage softens the taste and the odor when it is sautéed. Stir-fry red cabbage with other cabbages, Brussels sprouts and other vegetables or fruits, apples for example.

SWEET AND SPICY COLE SLAW

10 servings

This salad is a perfect example of how sweet, hot and sour flavors interact to create an extraordinary cabbage salad.

1 head cabbage, quartered and cored
2 small hot red peppers, crushed
3 tablespoons vegetable oil
⅓ cup sugar
1 large onion, quartered, cored and
    sliced thin
¼ cup rice wine vinegar
1 red bell pepper, cut in julienne
    strips
1 cucumber, peeled, halved, seeded
    and sliced
Salt
White pepper

Chinese cabbage, a catch-all term that includes celery cabbage and Napa cabbage, has an elongated, crinkly leaf with a wide, pearly white stalk. Both varieties have a mellower flavor than other cabbages, with a faint peppery undertone. The texture is light and crisp. The curly-leaved Savoy cabbage is more tender and mild in flavor.

Slice the cabbage thin and put it in a large bowl. Be sure all the shreds are dry.

Put the peppers and oil in a small saucepan over medium heat. Heat for 3 minutes, without smoking. Discard the peppers and pour the warm oil over the cabbage. Toss to coat all the cabbage.

Using the same saucepan, bring the sugar, ¼ cup water and onion slices to a boil over medium-high heat. Remove from heat, cool and then add to the cabbage. Add the vinegar, bell pepper and cucumber and toss to mix well. Season to taste with salt and pepper. Refrigerate for at least 3 hours or overnight. Toss before serving.

CHICKEN AND CHILI SALAD

6 servings

This Southwest chicken salad is quite mild when made with Anaheim chilies; use poblano chilies if you prefer a hotter taste. Serve the salad with corn muffins (pages 310–311) or grilled *quesadillas* (page 72).

4 whole chicken breasts, skinned, boned and cooked
1 large yellow onion, peeled, sliced and blanched
5 mild green chilies (Anaheim or poblano), roasted, peeled and thinly sliced (page 20)

DRESSING
1 tablespoon lime juice
1 tablespoon white wine vinegar
2 teaspoons dry mustard
1 to 1½ teaspoons salt
¼ teaspoon white pepper
Pinch cayenne pepper
½ cup mayonnaise, preferably homemade (page 257)
3½ ounces softened cream cheese
3 to 4 tablespoons milk or cream

GARNISH
Seasonal greens or watercress, washed and dried
1 papaya, seeded, peeled and diced, or ½ honeydew, cantaloupe or Cranshaw melon, peeled and sliced

Cut the chicken into bite-size pieces and put them in a mixing bowl. Add the onion, jícama and green chilies and toss to mix.

Place all the dressing ingredients in a blender or food processor. Blend on high speed. Pour half the dressing over the chicken. Cover and refrigerate until ready to assemble the salad.

Arrange greens on each of 6 plates, then divide the chicken among them. Drizzle with reserved dressing and garnish with slices of papaya or melon.

To serve a melon filled with salad, remove a slice from the bottom of each half so it will stand firm on the plate. Ripe melons, seeded and cut in chunks, can be frozen; then they are ready to make into ice with a blender or food processor.

FRIED CHICKEN SALAD

6 servings

You can make this salad with either homemade or storebought fried chicken. The combination of juicy, moist chicken, little pieces of crisp skin, toasted almonds and the fresh, crunchy jícama is delightful.

6 fried chicken breasts, boned, skin reserved
4 ounces jícama, peeled and cut in short julienne strips, or 1 can (8 ounces) whole water chestnuts, drained and cut in julienne strips
½ head iceberg lettuce, thinly sliced
4 cups curly endive, thinly sliced
1 cup sliced toasted almonds (page 50)
½ cup sliced scallions, white part and some of the green

DRESSING
1 clove garlic, finely minced
2 teaspoons whole-grain mustard
2 tablespoons soy sauce
2 tablespoons rice wine vinegar
2 to 4 tablespoons safflower oil
¼ cup chicken broth (page 97)
Salt
Pinch of cayenne pepper

———

Apple or pear slices for garnish

Cut the chicken breasts into short julienne strips. Take about half the skin and cut it into small dice. Preheat the oven to 350° F. and bake the skin 15 minutes to melt away some of the fat and crisp the skin. Drain on paper towels.

Combine the chicken, jícama or water chestnuts, lettuce and endive, almonds and scallions in a salad bowl. In a small bowl, whisk together the first 4 dressing ingredients. Add as much oil as desired. Thin with chicken broth. Season to taste with salt and cayenne pepper. Toss the salad with crisped skin pieces and dressing. Serve with fresh slices of apple or pear.

Variation
- Substitute chicken breast cutlets for fried chicken breasts. Slice the chicken thin, dust with salt and pepper and a scant amount of flour. Sauté quickly in hot oil. Add some thinly sliced fried corn tortillas or chow mein noodles in place of the crisp skin.

SMOKED CHICKEN SALAD WITH SOUTHWEST VEGETABLES

6 servings

This crisp, colorful salad will be a favorite among your friends and one they'll remember. It is stunning on the table and exciting to the taste. In the Southwest many chefs have their special versions of this salad. Create your own by adding other vegetables or fresh greens or by substituting pheasant or different game meats for the smoked chicken.

4 corn tortillas, cut in ¹⁄₁₆-inch strips, or ¼ pound jalapeño pasta (page 293) or ancho pasta (page 292)
3 cups peanut oil

VEGETABLES
1 yellow bell pepper, cut in matchstick strips
1 green bell pepper, cut in matchstick strips
1 chayote squash, peeled, seeded and cut in matchstick strips
2 carrots, peeled, blanched and cut in matchstick strips
4 ounces jícama, cut in matchstick strips
6 ounces tiny green beans, trimmed, or ¾ cup fresh peas
¹⁄₃ cup toasted pine nuts (page 50)

DRESSING
1 teaspoon salt
4 sprigs fresh summer savory, leaves removed and minced, or ¼ teaspoon dried savory
4 sprigs fresh tarragon, leaves removed and minced, or ¼ teaspoon dried tarragon
3 sprigs cilantro or basil, leaves removed and minced
1 teaspoon dry mustard
¼ teaspoon white pepper
¹⁄₃ cup white wine vinegar
²⁄₃ cup safflower oil

About 1 pound smoked chicken, cut in matchstick strips
Assorted tender lettuces such as mâche, oak leaf or Bibb to line the plate
Pine nuts for garnish

Allow the tortillas to stand, uncovered, at room temperature to dry out for at least 30 minutes. Heat oil to 350° F. Deep-fry tortillas or pasta in batches until crisp; drain on paper towels.

Toss the matchstick vegetables, green beans and pine nuts in a large bowl. Cover and refrigerate until ready to assemble the salad.

Whisk the salt, herbs, mustard, pepper, vinegar and oil in a small bowl until well mixed. Use half the dressing to coat the vegetables. Toss the chicken separately in just enough dressing to moisten. Toss the lettuce separately with just enough dressing to moisten.

Line each plate with lettuce and arrange the fried tortilla strips or pasta at random on it. Top with chicken and vegetables. Garnish with pine nuts.

Variation
- Black beans cooked in a spicy ham stock until tender but still whole add a colorful touch. Toss them with the vegetables.
- If you have some homemade game stock on hand, whisk about ¼ cup of it into the dressing; it gives a rich flavor to all the ingredients.

CHICKEN AND WILD RICE SALAD WITH MINT AND PECANS

8 servings

Fresh mint adds a subtle, refreshing flavor to wild and brown rice. I like to use grilled poultry in this salad; you may prefer poached or roasted chicken.

1 tablespoon butter
1 cup toasted pecans (page 50)

———

1 tablespoon vegetable oil
2 shallots, minced
1 cup wild rice, washed
½ cup long-grain brown rice
½ teaspoon salt
¼ teaspoon black pepper
1 cup chicken stock
2 whole cooked chicken breasts,
    preferably grilled
1 small Red Delicious apple
1 small Golden Delicious apple
Juice from 1 lemon
1 bunch scallions, white part only,
    sliced
3 tablespoons chopped fresh mint
1 tablespoon chopped fresh parsley

DRESSING
1 garlic clove, minced
4 tablespoons balsamic vinegar
2 tablespoons apple juice
4 tablespoons chicken stock
½ cup vegetable oil
Juice from ½ lemon
½ teaspoon dry mustard
1 teaspoon salt

Heat the butter to a sizzle in a small saucepan over medium heat. Add the pecans and sauté 1 minute. Place on paper towels to cool, then chop coarsely and set aside.

Heat the vegetable oil in the same saucepan over medium heat. Add the shallots, wild and brown rice and cook, stirring constantly, for about 2 minutes. Add the salt, pepper, chicken stock and 2 cups of water. Heat to a simmer and cook, covered, until the liquid is absorbed, 40 to 45 minutes. Cool.

Remove the skin from the chicken and then bone it and cut the meat into small pieces. Core and dice the apples and squeeze lemon juice over them; turn to coat. Mix the chicken, apples and scallions with the rice in a large bowl. Stir in the mint, parsley and pecans.

Heat the garlic, vinegar, apple juice and chicken stock to a boil in a small skillet. Place in a small bowl and whisk in the vegetable oil, lemon juice, mustard and salt. Add to the salad, then refrigerate at least 1 hour before serving.

Variation
- Substitute cooked duck, grilled, smoked or roasted, for the chicken and grapes for the apples.

Mint comes in many varieties: apple, orange, pineapple and spearmint, among others. Use mint in fresh chutney or relishes, steep it in tea, hot chocolate or milk for custards and custard sauces or combine it with cilantro or basil. Freshly minced mint adds a fresh taste to dishes seasoned with cumin or curry and to wild rice. It goes well with smoked meat salads and soups and stews that contain red chili pods.

WARM GRILLED CHICKEN SALAD

4 servings

The moist, tender grilled chicken and the roasted peppers are complemented by the sherry vinaigrette and toasted pine nuts. Cooking the pine nuts in a small amount of vinaigrette is one of those details that can make all the difference.

DRESSING
½ cup safflower oil
¼ cup walnut or additional safflower oil
¼ cup sherry vinegar
1 clove garlic, minced
1 teaspoon dry mustard
¾ teaspoon salt
¼ teaspoon freshly ground white pepper

———

2 red bell peppers, roasted, peeled and seeded
2 green bell peppers or mild green chilies, roasted, peeled and seeded
2 yellow bell peppers, roasted, peeled and seeded (optional)
2 heads Bibb lettuce, rinsed and dried
1 head red leaf lettuce, rinsed and dried
2 chicken breasts, split and boned, skin intact
Salt
Pepper
4 disks goat cheese baked in cornbread (page 273)

Prepare a hot fire on a gas, charcoal or indoor grill.

For the dressing, mix the oil, vinegar, garlic, mustard, salt, and pepper until emulsified. Cut the peppers and chilies into strips about ½ × 1½ inches. Reserve the juices from the peppers and add them to the dressing. Warm half the dressing in a small clean skillet over low heat. Add the pepper strips and heat through. Remove from the heat and let the peppers marinate in the dressing.

Divide the small leaves of the lettuce among 4 serving plates. Refrigerate the lettuce while you prepare the chicken.

Sprinkle the chicken lightly with salt and pepper. Gently pound to an even thickness. Place the chicken on the grill rack and grill 3 minutes on each side. Place on a cutting board and remove the skin. Cut the chicken into ½ × 1½-inch strips.

Preheat the oven to 350° F. to warm the goat cheese. Remove the peppers from the dressing. Warm the remaining dressing and toss with the lettuce, using just enough to coat the leaves.

Mound the chicken on the lettuce on each plate and drizzle a few tablespoons of dressing over the chicken. Arrange the pepper strips vertically around the chicken.

Warm the goat cheese for 2 to 3 minutes. Place one at the side of each plate and serve immediately.

NOTE. Directions for roasting peppers can be found on page 20.

WARM CHICKEN SALAD WITH JÍCAMA AND APPLES

6 servings

Fresh ginger adds a special burst of flavor to this salad. The crisp freshness of apple and jícama provides an interesting contrast to the Oriental flavor of the dressing.

1 tablespoon butter
1 cup walnut halves, toasted and
    skinned (page 50)
Salt

DRESSING
⅞ cup safflower oil
⅓ cup vinegar
1 tablespoon lemon juice
1½ teaspoons minced fresh ginger
1½ teaspoons dry mustard
1 teaspoon salt
¼ teaspoon white pepper

———

2 whole chicken breasts, boned,
    skinned and cut in strips
Salt
Pepper
1 to 1½ tablespoons vegetable oil
⅓ cup bottled Hoisin sauce
1 Granny Smith apple, cored, and cut
    in matchstick strips
1 Red Delicious apple, cored and cut
    in matchstick strips
2 ounces jícama, peeled and cut in
    matchstick strips
⅓ cup golden seedless raisins
2 heads Bibb lettuce, washed and
    separated
2 tablespoons chives for garnish

———

Ginger is best when fresh. Pieces should be large with smooth, almost shiny skin. Ginger is compatible with small, dried red chilies or cayenne pepper, fresh cilantro and citrus. Steep ginger in iced tea or candy it in a sugar syrup with citrus.

Heat the butter in a large skillet over medium heat. Add the walnuts and sauté 2 minutes. Drain on paper towels and sprinkle lightly with salt. Set aside.

Put the oil, vinegar, lemon juice, ginger, mustard, salt and pepper in a blender and blend on high speed to mix. Divide the dressing in half.

Sprinkle the chicken strips with salt and pepper. Heat the oil in a large skillet over medium heat. Add the chicken and sauté for 1½ minutes. Remove from heat. Mix half the dressing with the Hoisin sauce and pour over the chicken. Toss to coat all the pieces.

Put the apples, jícama, and raisins and remaining dressing in a small bowl and toss to coat. Arrange around the edge of each plate. Place the lettuce leaves in the center and mound the warm chicken on top. Garnish with chives and walnuts.

Variations
- To prepare this salad with leftover chicken or turkey, cut the meat into strips and drizzle with chicken stock. Wrap tightly in foil and heat in a 400° F. oven for 10 minutes.
- To prepare a cold salad with leftover chicken or turkey, marinate strips of meat in the dressing for 1 hour before assembling the salad.

WARM TURKEY SALAD

8 servings

This salad may be made with any cooked poultry, not just turkey. It is a fine way to turn leftovers into a light meal.

2 small heads Boston lettuce, rinsed and leaves separated

1 head radicchio lettuce, rinsed and leaves separated, or 1 cup thinly sliced red cabbage

1 head romaine lettuce, rinsed and cut in 1-inch strips, or 6 cups young spinach leaves, rinsed

½ pound thick-sliced pepper bacon or ½ pound thick-sliced smoked bacon or pancetta

1 cup toasted pecan or walnut halves (page 50)

1 pound fresh mushrooms cut in half (see note)

2½ cups cooked turkey meat, cut in julienne strips

⅓ cup balsamic vinegar

Salt

Several turns of freshly ground pepper

12 thin slices of sweet onion for garnish

You can make your own Southern-style pepper bacon. Grind black peppercorns or a combination of black, red and green peppercorns over one pound of bacon at room temperature. Cover with wax paper and rap with a meat pounder, then turn and repeat on the other side. Wrap in wax paper and place on a plate. Weigh down with another plate and refrigerate for at least 5 hours before using.

Tear large Boston and radicchio leaves in half; leave small leaves whole. Toss with romaine or spinach in a large bowl.

Slice the bacon into strips about ½ inch wide. Cook over medium heat in a large skillet until browned and crisp, about 8 to 10 minutes. Remove and drain on paper towels. Add the pecans to the skillet and sauté over medium heat 1 to 2 minutes, then remove and drain on paper towels. Add the mushrooms and cook over low heat until soft, 5 to 8 minutes. Add the turkey and bacon and heat to warm, stirring often. Add the vinegar and stir to incorporate. Season to taste with salt and pepper. Cool about 1 minute, then add to the greens and toss to mix well.

Arrange salad on dinner plates and sprinkle with toasted pecans or walnuts. Garnish with onion rings.

NOTE.   If possible, use a combination of wild and cultivated mushrooms for richer flavor.

Variation
- You may also prepare this salad with chicken, duck, quail or pheasant. Bone and cut the meat into julienne strips. Sauté until tender in a separate skillet using clarified butter. Deglaze with balsamic vinegar and water, and season to taste with salt and pepper. Arrange meat on top of the greens and garnish with nuts.

CHUTNEY-TURKEY SALAD IN RADICCHIO OR ENDIVE LEAVES

6 to 8 servings

No one will guess what the ingredients of this salad are but they may say it is the best turkey salad they have ever had. Serve it in radicchio leaves as an entree or in endive leaves for an appetizer.

4 cups turkey meat, white or dark, cut in small strips
1½ cups finely diced jícama
1½ cups sliced seedless grapes, red or green
¾ cup toasted pine nuts, walnuts or pecans, chopped (page 50)
1 cup mayonnaise, preferably homemade (page 257)
¼ cup mango chutney
3 tablespoons chopped fresh mint
Salt
Pepper
½ cup crisply cooked bacon, diced, or ½ cup duck cracklings (page 47)
Radicchio or Belgian endive leaves for serving

Put the turkey, jícama, grapes and nuts in a large bowl. Stir mayonnaise and chutney together in a small bowl. Add the mint, then add to the turkey and mix well. Season to taste with salt and pepper.

Just prior to serving the salad, stir in the crisp bacon or cracklings. Mound the salad in radicchio leaves or spoon it into endive leaves.

NOTE. Appetizers may be assembled 12 hours in advance and refrigerated. In that case, sprinkle with bacon or cracklings just before serving.

DUCK SALAD WITH GRAPES

6 servings

Duck is particularly good with cabbage and grapes in a salad. Serve it with homemade biscuits or muffins. To save time, you could buy a roasted duck from a Chinese restaurant. Then, of course, you lose out on the duck fat for sautéing.

1 head Napa cabbage or red cabbage, rinsed
3 tablespoons sugar
1 teaspoon salt
2 cups diced jícama
2 cups halved seedless red grapes

DRESSING
1 tablespoon olive oil
1 shallot, minced
3 tablespoons balsamic vinegar or sherry vinegar
1 teaspoon dry mustard
1 teaspoon salt
¼ teaspoon white pepper
½ cup safflower oil
1 egg

———

3 cups cooked duck cut in julienne strips
¼ cup toasted pine nuts (page 50)
⅓ cup duck cracklings (page 47) or crisp bacon
1 tablespoon minced fresh parsley
Salt

Cabbage can be sautéed in butter and seasoned with maple syrup, fruits, walnuts and onions to serve with wild game or duck. Cabbage keeps in the refrigerator 1 to 2 weeks, unwashed, first wrapped in paper towels, then in sealed plastic bags. Once it is washed and cut, cabbage wilts and turns brown, often bitter.

Core and slice the cabbage ½ inch thick to make strips. Put the strips in a colander.

Heat 1 quart water, sugar and salt to a boil. Pour it over the cabbage to blanch and sweeten. Shake the colander to remove all the water, then place cabbage strips in a large mixing bowl. Add the jícama and grapes and toss to combine.

Heat the olive oil in a small skillet over medium heat. Add the shallot and sauté until soft, about 1 minute. Add the vinegar and cook about 30 seconds, then pour the mixture into a blender jar. Add the mustard, salt and pepper and blend on high speed, adding the oil and egg through the top. Pour half the dressing over the duck and mix the other half with the cabbage and grapes. Cover and refrigerate both for at least 1 hour or up to 12 hours.

When ready to assemble the salad, combine the duck and cabbage, using all the dressing. Mix in the pine nuts, cracklings and parsley. Season to taste with salt. Divide the salad among 6 salad plates and serve it with homemade biscuits or muffins.

WARM QUAIL SALAD

4 servings

The quail may be grilled until almost done, then warmed in a skillet or oven instead of sautéed. This salad can also be made with breast of pheasant or duck.

4 quail
Salt
Pepper
2 tablespoons safflower oil
1 tablespoon unsalted butter
8 clumps mâche lettuce, rinsed, or 1 bunch watercress, rinsed and stemmed
1 head red-tip leaf lettuce, rinsed and leaves separated, or 2 bunches oak leaf lettuce, rinsed and separated
2 heads Bibb lettuce, rinsed and leaves separated
3 ounces jícama, peeled and cut in short julienne strips
1 cup seedless red grapes, halved
1½ tablespoons butter
24 toasted pecan halves (page 50)

DRESSING
1 shallot, minced
¼ cup white wine
2 tablespoons balsamic vinegar
2 teaspoons whole-grain Dijon mustard
½ teaspoon salt
¼ teaspoon white pepper
2 teaspoons lemon juice
½ cup safflower oil

———

¾ cup chicken stock, preferably homemade (page 97)
2 tablespoons balsamic vinegar

Cut each quail in half at the breast bone, then trim away the wing tips and separate the legs from the body. Bone the breast and reserve all bones and trimmings. Sprinkle the breast and leg with salt and pepper. Heat oil and butter in a medium skillet over medium-high heat. Add the quail breast, legs and trimmings and sauté until browned, about 1½ minutes per side. Remove the breasts and legs and seal in foil. Set the skillet and contents off the heat to finish later. Preheat the oven to 400° F.

Cut the large lettuce leaves in half; leave small ones whole. Put them in a large bowl, add the jícama and grapes and toss to mix. Cover and refrigerate until ready to assemble the salad.

Heat butter in a small skillet. Add the pecans and sauté for about 1½ minutes. Drain on paper towels.

Put the quail in the oven to reheat for 8 to 10 minutes. Bring the shallot, wine and balsamic vinegar to a boil. Strain into a small bowl and discard the shallot. Whisk in the mustard, salt, white pepper, lemon juice and safflower oil. Set aside.

Put the skillet back on medium-high heat. Add the chicken stock and balsamic vinegar and heat to a boil. Boil for 8 minutes, then strain into a bowl and discard all the trimmings. Whisk in half the reserved dressing and set aside.

Pour just enough of the remaining dressing over the greens to coat; mix well. Put the greens on four large dinner plates. Slice 2 quail breasts and place them in the center of the greens. Put two legs on the side of each plate. Warm the remaining dressing and drizzle over the salad. Garnish with pecans.

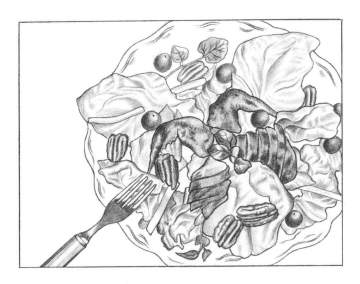

BEEF BARBECUE SALAD WITH HEARTS OF PALM

6 servings

The charcoal flavor of the meat and the hint of barbecue flavor in the dressing make a tasty beef salad that keeps both the cook and the kitchen cool. You can serve the meat 10 to 15 minutes after taking it from the grill or at room temperature or chilled. Serve the salad with French bread, biscuits or herb rolls (page 304).

DRESSING
1 serrano chili, stemmed, seeded and chopped
1 clove garlic
1 egg
3 tablespoons tarragon vinegar
1 tablespoon coarse or whole-grain mustard
1 teaspoon Worcestershire sauce
1½ tablespoons barbecue sauce
¾ cup safflower oil
Salt

————

1 can (14 ounces) hearts of palm
14 fresh mushrooms, sliced
1 red bell pepper, cut in julienne strips, or 4 sundried tomatoes, drained and cut in thin strips
1 tablespoon minced fresh parsley
2 tablespoons chopped fresh chives
2 bunches watercress, rinsed and stemmed
3 cups sunflower greens or green sprouts (not alfalfa sprouts)
1 tablespoon safflower oil
1 tablespoon red wine vinegar

————

2 pounds boneless sirloin steak, 1 inch thick, grilled (page 196)
Salt

Put the serrano chili, garlic, egg, vinegar, mustard and Worcestershire sauce in a blender jar. Blend on high speed, adding the barbecue sauce and oil through the top. Season to taste with salt.

Slice the hearts of palm and put them, the mushrooms, pepper, parsley and chives in a bowl. Add about ⅔ of the dressing and mix well.

Toss the watercress and sunflower greens together in another bowl. Drizzle with oil and vinegar and toss to coat the greens.

Trim the fat from the steak and cut into thin slices about 3 inches long. Arrange slices on 6 large plates. Mound the mushroom mixture on a third of the plate, the greens on another. Drizzle remaining dressing over the beef.

CEVICHE PASTA SALAD

8 servings

This colorful mélange of seafood, salmon and peppers may also be served without pasta. In a ceviche, the fish cooks enzymatically in lime juice.

½ pound fresh salmon, boned
½ pound firm-flesh fish (whitefish, seabass or orange roughy), boned
1 pound medium to large sea scallops, rinsed
1½ cups lime juice
2 serrano chilies, stemmed and seeded
Salt
Pepper

———

1 pound angel's hair pasta (cappellini) or thin spaghetti, cooked al dente
1 yellow bell pepper, cut in ⅛-inch strips
1 green bell pepper, cut in ⅛-inch strips
1 red bell pepper, cut in ⅛-inch strips
1 bunch watercress, rinsed and stemmed
⅓ cup vegetable oil
1 teaspoon Dijon mustard
2 tablespoons rice wine vinegar
Salt
Pepper

GARNISH
Lime wedges
Freshly cracked black pepper

Cut the fish into bite-size pieces and slice the scallops. Put all the fish in a shallow glass or porcelain dish. Add the lime juice and chilies. Toss to coat all the fish and marinate, stirring 4 or 5 times, for at least 4 hours or up to 8 hours. No more than 1 hour before serving, drain all but several tablespoons lime juice from the fish. Season the fish to taste with salt and pepper.

Transfer the cooked, drained pasta to a large bowl. Add all the peppers, the watercress and drained seafood. Whisk the oil, mustard and vinegar together in a small bowl and pour it over the pasta and seafood. Toss gently to combine. Season to taste with salt and pepper. Serve with lime wedges and freshly cracked black pepper.

NOTE. So much seafood is frozen but sold as fresh that I feel it is safer to blanch it for ceviche, unless I am sure about it. To do so, place the fish and scallops in a large sauté pan and cover with water. Tie 1 tablespoon *each* peppercorns and mustard seeds in a spice bag or piece of cheesecloth and add to the pan, along with a sliced lemon and broken bay leaf. Bring to the boil and remove immediately from the heat. Let stand, uncovered, for 5 minutes, then drain and cool. Proceed with the recipe.

SEAFOOD PASTA SALAD WITH BASIL PESTO DRESSING

12 servings

The pesto really makes the seafood and pasta come alive. Use any shape pasta, depending on the kind of look you want.

1 pound pasta, preferably fresh
1 tablespoon safflower oil

DRESSING
½ cup basil pesto (page 25)
¼ cup vinegar
1 teaspoon dry mustard
⅔ cup safflower oil
1 teaspoon salt
¼ teaspoon white pepper
1 large egg

———————

1½ cups white wine
2 tablespoons butter
2 shallots, sliced
¾ pound medium shrimp, shelled and deveined
1½ cups lobster meat, cut up
¾ pound bay scallops, rinsed
2 Roma or plum tomatoes, seeded and cut in strips
1 cup sliced young spinach or sorrel leaves (optional)

Roma or plum tomatoes usually have better flavor, texture and taste than the average supermarket tomato; use them when homegrown tomatoes are not available. Quartered but left intact at the core, they make a colorful plate garnish.

Cook the pasta in lightly salted boiling water until al dente or tender to the bite. Drain and put in a mixing bowl. Toss with oil so the pasta does not stick together. This may be done 3 to 4 hours in advance.

Put the pesto in a small bowl and whisk in the vinegar, mustard, oil, salt, pepper and egg until emulsified.

Heat 2 cups water, the wine, butter and shallots to a boil in a large saucepan. Add the shrimp, lobster and scallops and turn immediately to cover both sides with the liquid. Remove from the heat, cover and let stand for 10 to 12 minutes. Drain.

Add the seafood and the dressing to the pasta and toss to combine. Gently mix in the tomatoes and spinach if using. Chill one hour before serving.

WARM SEAFOOD SALAD WITH TANGERINE VINAIGRETTE

8 servings

Tangerine juice gives succulent shrimp and scallops an indescribable tang that is echoed by the mango garnish. Dressing the seafood with butter sauce instead of vinaigrette dressing, as in the variation at the end of the recipe, makes the salad even richer.

1 bunch watercress, rinsed and
    stemmed
1 Belgian endive, rinsed and cut in
    julienne strips
4 cups red-tip leaf lettuce, rinsed

DRESSING
2 tablespoons white wine vinegar
1 tablespoon lemon juice
½ cup safflower oil

———————

1½ pounds medium shrimp, peeled
    and deveined
1 pound sea scallops, rinsed
½ cup tangerine juice
½ cup vermouth
1 garlic clove, minced
1 shallot, minced
1½ tablespoons whole-grain mustard
1 tablespoon minced orange zest
1 tablespoon minced fresh parsley
Salt
Pepper

GARNISH
2 mangos, peeled and sliced
1 avocado, pitted, peeled and sliced

Put the watercress and endive in a large bowl. Tear the lettuce into small pieces. Toss. Cover and refrigerate to crisp.

Put the vinegar, lemon juice and oil in a small bowl and whisk to combine. Divide into 2 equal portions and set aside.

Put the shrimp and scallops in a large skillet. Add ½ cup water, tangerine juice, vermouth, garlic and shallot and heat to a boil. Turn the shellfish to coat, then cover tightly and immediately remove from the heat. Let stand for 12 minutes.

Uncover the shellfish and remove with a slotted spoon. Wrap tightly in aluminum foil to keep warm. Strain the liquid. Heat ¾ cup to a boil and reduce to about 3 tablespoons. Whisk in the mustard, orange zest and parsley and cool 5 minutes. Transfer to a blender jar and add half the vinaigrette dressing. Blend on high speed until smooth. Season to taste with salt and pepper. Combine with seafood in a large bowl and toss to coat. Adjust salt and pepper to taste.

To assemble, toss the greens with the remaining vinaigrette dressing. Sprinkle lightly with salt and pepper, then arrange the greens on a large platter. Spoon the shellfish and sauce in the center and drizzle any remaining sauce over the top. Garnish with slices of mango and avocado.

Variations
- Cook the seafood as directed; drain and wrap in foil. Boil liquid to reduce to 3 tablespoons. Reduce the heat to low and whisk in 6 tablespoons unsalted butter, about 2 tablespoons at a time. Strain, then season to taste with salt and pepper. Stir in the orange zest, mustard and parsley. Add the seafood and toss to coat with sauce. Prepare half the amount of dressing and toss to coat the greens. Assemble and garnish the salad as directed.
- If tangerine juice is not available, use orange juice.

ZUCCHINI AND BASIL SALAD WITH PECAN VINAIGRETTE

8 servings

This salad is an excellent accompaniment to grilled fish or chicken. You can use feta cheese instead of goat cheese if desired.

4 small zucchini, thinly sliced
Salt
4 cups romaine lettuce, ribs removed, rinsed and sliced wide
About 15 leaves fresh basil, cut in thin strips
1 red bell pepper, cut in short julienne strips
½ cup chopped toasted pecans (page 50)
1 tablespoon butter
Toasted-nut vinaigrette, made with pecans (page 151)
Pepper
12 ounces fresh mild goat cheese, molded in 8 disks and warmed, or 8 ounces feta cheese (see note)

Put the zucchini in a colander and sprinkle with salt. Toss to lightly coat all the slices. Let stand for 30 minutes, then rinse under cool water. Blot dry. Place in a large bowl with romaine lettuce, basil and red pepper. Toss to mix.

Put the pecans and butter in a small skillet over medium-high heat. Sauté for about 1 minute, then remove and drain pecans on paper towels.

When ready to serve, toss the salad with enough vinaigrette to coat lightly, then add pecans and season to taste with salt and pepper. Divide the salad among 8 plates with a disk of warmed goat cheese in the center of each.

NOTE.   Do not warm feta cheese. Drain it, then crumble it over the salad.

ZUCCHINI SALAD

4 servings

This is an easy little salad that is just perfect with grilled stuffed chilies and other dishes from the grill.

1 medium zucchini, cut in julienne strips
Salt
1 head romaine lettuce, small inner leaves only, rinsed
2 large tomatoes, seeded and cut in strips
¼ cup toasted pine nuts (page 50)
¼ cup safflower oil
2 tablespoons mild vinegar
Pepper
Lemon juice to taste

Sprinkle the zucchini with salt and let stand for 30 minutes. Drain and press to extract the juices. Blot dry. Put the zucchini in a mixing bowl. Remove the ribs from the lettuce and slice thin. Add to the zucchini along with the tomato strips and pine nuts. Toss to combine.

Whisk the oil and vinegar together in a small bowl. Drizzle over the salad to moisten, then season to taste with salt, pepper and lemon juice. Cover and refrigerate for up to 30 minutes.

SLANG JANG

6 servings

Slang jang is one of those home-style regional dishes that you never find in a restaurant but that everyone makes at home. It is a relish-type salad made up of strips of tomatoes, peppers and onions. If different colored tomatoes and peppers are available, you can make a really beautiful one by using a combination of green and red and yellow tomatoes and an assortment of peppers. In the Southwest, slang jang usually acompanies hamburgers, steaks or grilled meats; it is also great on its own. Several serving suggestions are given at the end of the recipe.

6 to 8 tablespoons safflower oil
1 small yellow onion, halved, cored
    and cut in strips
1 green or yellow bell pepper, cored
    and cut in strips
3 tablespoons red wine or balsamic
    vinegar
1 tablespoon rice wine vinegar
20 Roma tomatoes or 8 large vine-
    ripened tomatoes, seeded, cored
    and cut lengthwise in julienne
    strips
1 to 2 tablespoons fresh basil leaves
    cut in thin strips
Salt
Coarsely ground black pepper
1 cup julienne strips hearts of palm
    (optional)

Heat 3 tablespoons oil in a large skillet. Add the onion and pepper and cook about 30 seconds. Add the vinegar and remove from heat. Put the onion, pepper and tomatoes in a bowl and add the remaining oil. Season to taste with basil, salt and pepper. Stir in hearts of palm if using and then marinate the salad, refrigerated, for at least 2 hours or overnight.

Serving Suggestions
When ready to serve the salad, assemble in one of the following ways:
- Add 6 ounces mozzarella or feta cheese and serve as a salad.
- Drain juices and serve as a condiment with buttered and toasted French bread croutons.
- Add the drained juices to the pan drippings of sautéed steaks or hamburgers along with a little beef stock and minced hot chilies and reduce. Strain and whisk in a little butter. Serve the salad with the meat.
- Serve undrained in bowls with hot crusty French bread.

There are many varieties of basil, the most popular being Italian basil, with large, smooth, dark green leaves. Opal basil is purple with slightly fringed leaves and a spicier taste. Lemon basil has a clean, lemon-mint flavor and delightful aroma. Use small leaves whole in salads or to steep in wine for a mulled-wine flavor.

APPLE PECAN SALAD

6 servings

Jícama has a crisp, apple-like flavor and chayote one reminiscent of fresh cucumber. Combined with pecans, apple and melon, they make a light salad that is perfect for warm summer evenings.

1 tablespoon butter
⅔ cup toasted pecans (page 50)
Salt

DRESSING
½ cup safflower oil
2 tablespoons lemon juice
2 tablespoons white wine vinegar
1 teaspoon dry mustard
1 teaspoon salt
¼ teaspoon white pepper
2 sprigs fresh mint, leaves finely
    chopped

———

½ cup cantaloupe melon, cut in ¼-
    inch dice
1 chayote, peeled, seeded and cut in
    matchstick strips
1 large Red Delicious apple, unpeeled,
    cut in matchstick strips
4 ounces jícama, peeled and cut in
    matchstick strips

Apples came to America with the early settlers and have been a part of meals from Colonial days to our time because they keep so well. They are widely grown in America and the tree is surrounded by many myths and legends. There are countless varieties, though many are no longer grown commercially and supermarkets carry only a few.

Heat the butter in a medium skillet over medium heat. Add the pecans and sauté about 1 minute. Sprinkle lightly with salt and place on paper towels. When cool, cut in quarters.

Put the oil, lemon juice, vinegar, mustard, salt, pepper and mint in a blender jar and blend on high speed until well mixed.

Combine the cantaloupe, chayote, apple, jícama and pecans in a large bowl. Pour the dressing on top, and mix gently. Serve immediately.

SOUTHWEST FRUIT SALAD

6 servings

The honey-orange dressing is a good match for almost any fruit salad. Suggested combinations follow the recipe.

DRESSING
1 orange
2 tablespoons orange juice
1 shallot, minced
½ cup safflower oil
3 tablespoons white wine vinegar
1½ to 2 tablespoons honey
½ teaspoon dry mustard
½ teaspoon salt
¼ teaspoon white pepper
1 teaspoon mustard seeds

———

2 ripe papaya, each cut into 9 slices
3 pink grapefruit, peeled and sectioned
18 large strawberries
6 fresh mint sprigs for garnish

———

Figs are available in two varieties, Calimyrna (yellow-green) and Mission (purple-black), from summer through late fall. They are delicious in a sauce for duck or poultry, in a fruit compote or chutney with wild birds, or with fresh raspberries and cream. Figs must be refrigerated when ripe and used within a few days.

Cut the peel and pith from the orange and then cut the orange sections from the membranes. Place the orange sections, juice and shallot in a blender or food processor fitted with the metal blade. Add the rest of the dressing ingredients and process until very smooth. If you prefer, strain to remove the mustard seeds.

Use enough dressing to coat each of 6 salad plates and reserve the rest. Fan 3 slices of papaya on each plate and place the grapefruit sections between the papaya slices. Halve or quarter strawberries and arrange them at the tops of the fans. Drizzle lightly with dressing. Garnish each salad with a fresh mint sprig.

Variations
Use the following combinations of fruits according to what is in season:
- Honeydew, cantaloupe or Cranshaw melon, fresh figs and blueberries
- Mango, avocado and raspberries
- Papaya, honeydew melon and blueberries, blackberries or raspberries

BASIL-WALNUT VINAIGRETTE

1 cup

This dressing is particularly good on salads that include tomatoes, bacon, mushrooms, mangos or toasted walnuts. Use it also with sliced ripe tomatoes and fresh mozzarella cheese. Make the dressing just before using as fresh basil discolors rapidly.

3 tablespoons white wine vinegar
1 tablespoon lemon juice
1 clove garlic, minced
8 fresh basil leaves
1 teaspoon dry mustard
¾ teaspoon salt
¼ teaspoon white pepper
½ cup safflower oil
3 tablespoons walnut oil

Put the vinegar, lemon juice, garlic, basil, mustard, salt and pepper in a blender jar. Blend on high speed, while adding the oil through the top. Use immediately or refrigerate. Bring back to room temperature and mix before using.

HERB VINAIGRETTE

1 cup

Mint, basil and cilantro give this vinaigrette a fresh, crisp taste that is delicious on fruits and marinated vegetables as well as seasonal greens garnished with grapes or toasted nuts.

4 tablespoons white or red wine
  vinegar
1 shallot, minced
5 fresh basil leaves
⅛ cup cilantro leaves
⅛ cup mint leaves
1 teaspoon dry mustard
¾ teaspoon salt
¼ teaspoon white pepper
⅔ cup safflower oil
1 to 2 teaspoons lemon juice

Put the vinegar, shallot, basil, cilantro, mint, mustard, salt, pepper and oil in a blender jar and blend on high speed to combine. Season to taste with lemon juice. Use immediately or refrigerate in a screwtop jar. Bring to room temperature and shake before using.

ROAST BELL PEPPER VINAIGRETTE

1 cup

Yellow and red bell peppers make an excellent vinaigrette sauce for cold meats, poultry, seafood and vegetable or seafood pâtés and terrines. It is also good drizzled on chilled julienned vegetables in a salad. Use chilled peppers for better color.

2 red bell peppers, roasted, peeled and chilled (page 20)
1 clove garlic
1 tablespoon lemon juice
3 tablespoons white wine vinegar
¾ teaspoon salt
1 teaspoon dry mustard
¼ teaspoon white pepper
1 large egg
1 sprig Mexican mint marigold (optional) or 1 sprig tarragon (optional)
½ cup safflower oil

Cut the peppers into several pieces and put them in a blender jar. Add the garlic, lemon juice, vinegar, salt, mustard, pepper, and egg. Add the leaves of the herb if using. Blend 1 to 1½ minutes or until pureed, then add the oil and blend again. Strain. Use immediately or refrigerate.

NOTE.   Bell peppers vary in flesh thickness. If the dressing seems too thick, thin with chicken broth or water.

TOASTED NUT VINAIGRETTE

2½ cups

Toasted nuts add great flavor to a simple vinaigrette, especially one that is served warm over seasonal greens garnished with fresh berries and more toasted nuts. Almost any kind of nut can be used; walnuts, hazelnuts, pecans, almonds and pine nuts are best. Use the sauce on salads, with grilled fish or chilled blanched vegetables.

NUT ESSENCE
¼ cup vinegar
¼ cup white wine
1 shallot, minced
1 cup chicken stock
½ cup chopped toasted and peeled nuts (page 50)
1 teaspoon lemon juice

VINAIGRETTE
1 teaspoon dry mustard
¼ cup vinegar
Salt
¼ teaspoon white pepper
⅔ cup safflower oil
1 tablespoon finely chopped toasted nuts (page 50)

Heat the vinegar, wine, shallot and chicken stock in a saucepan to a boil. Add the nuts and simmer over medium heat for 5 to 8 minutes. Remove from heat and let cool. Add lemon juice and refrigerate for 3 hours or overnight. Strain the mixture in a small bowl. Press to extract all the liquids.

Whisk the dry mustard, vinegar, ½ teaspoon salt, pepper, and oil into the strained nut essence. Taste and add salt if needed. Add the chopped nuts when dressing the salad or garnishing the fish.

POBLANO CHILI DRESSING

¾ cup

The poblano chili has a mild, subtle hotness that perks up a simple vinaigrette dressing. Use this on your favorite greens, on cold rice or pasta salad or over avocados and tropical fruits like mango and papaya.

1 tablespoon virgin olive oil
1 shallot, minced
1 poblano chili, roasted, peeled and
    cut in ⅛-inch dice (page 20)
½ cup safflower oil
¼ cup rice wine vinegar
2 teaspoons minced fresh cilantro
½ teaspoon dry mustard
½ teaspoon sugar
1 teaspoon salt

Heat the olive oil in a medium skillet over medium heat. Add the shallot and sauté for 1 minute. Stir in the diced poblano chili and immediately remove from the heat. Transfer to a small bowl and whisk in the safflower oil, vinegar, cilantro, mustard, sugar and salt. Use immediately.

BUTTERMILK RANCH DRESSING

3 cups

Ranch dressing and iceberg lettuce are as much a part of the Southwest as barbecue and have been around a long, long time. This is a mild dressing that gets its refreshing taste from buttermilk. It goes quite well with some of the spicy foods and sauces that often come before or after a salad. Use it on salads, cole slaw (to be served with barbecued meats) or as a dipping sauce for grilled chicken wings (page 59).

1 tablespoon safflower oil
½ white onion, minced
3 cloves garlic, minced
½ teaspoon dried thyme
¼ teaspoon celery salt
1 teaspoon cornstarch
½ cup heavy cream
1⅔ cups buttermilk
⅔ cup mayonnaise, preferably
    homemade (page 257)
Salt
White pepper
Minced fresh parsley

Heat the oil in a small saucepan over medium-high heat. Add the onion and garlic and sauté until golden brown, about 8 to 10 minutes. Stir in the thyme and celery salt and lower the heat to medium-low. Stir the cornstarch into the cream, then whisk into the onion and spice mixture and stir constantly to make a paste. Remove from heat and whisk in the buttermilk. Cool, then strain and press to extract all the juices. Whisk in the mayonnaise and season to taste with salt, pepper and minced parsley.

Variation
- You can make this with a crème fraîche base, omitting the heavy cream and the cornstarch, which is needed to keep the buttermilk dressing from becoming too watery. Crème fraîche makes a much richer dressing. Prepare 1½ cups crème fraîche (page 112); add 1½ cups buttermilk to it. Stir in the garlic and onion mixture, let stand for 1 hour, then strain and add the mayonnaise, salt, pepper and parsley.

POPPY SEED DRESSING

3½ cups

This sweet-sour dressing is used throughout the South and Southwest on fruit salads.

1½ cups minced onion
1 cup sugar
1 tablespoon dry mustard or
    1½ tablespoons grainy mustard
2 teaspoons salt
⅔ cup pomegranate or raspberry
    vinegar
2 cups safflower oil
3 tablespoons poppy seeds

Heat the onion, sugar, mustard, salt and vinegar in a medium saucepan to a boil. Boil until the sugar is dissolved, then let stand to cool completely. Strain and put the mixture in a blender jar. Add the oil and blend until smooth. Stir in poppy seeds. Store refrigerated for several weeks.

Variation

- Add 2 jalapeño or 3 serrano chilies to the onion and sugar mixture. Do not seed them, simply stem and halve them, then strain and discard as directed.

POMEGRANATE VINEGAR

4 quarts

Pomegranates make a delicious fruit-flavored vinegar. It has all the flavor of raspberry vinegar and may be substituted in any recipe.

1 gallon apple cider vinegar
8 pomegranates, washed and
    quartered
¼ cup sugar

Heat the vinegar to a boil in a large saucepan and boil 5 minutes. Stir in pomegranates and sugar, then remove from heat and cool. Leave the vinegar covered with a cheesecloth overnight.

Strain the vinegar through a fine sieve or cheesecloth before transferring to clean bottles.

Variation

- Use 4 cups cranberries or the pulp and juice from 6 prickly pears in place of pomegranates.

ENTREES

Panfried Pepper Steaks
Sizzling Beef Fajitas
Roast Tenderloin in Mustard Sauce
Loin of Venison with Blackberry and Port Wine Sauce
Texas Brisket
Chile Con Carne
Robert's Game Ragout
Roast Leg of Lamb
Roast Pork with Tangerine Sauce
Honey-Baked Ham
Veal in Lime and Serrano Chili Butter Sauce
Veal Cutlets
Fried Chicken
Chicken with Pomegranates
Chicken in Pecan Butter Sauce
Roast Chicken Breasts with Spice-Nut Gratin
Chicken Fajitas
Stephan's Wild Turkey with Blue Cornmeal–Bourbon Stuffing
Braised Turkey Breast
Turkey with Pasta, Tomatoes and Walnut Cream Sauce
Smoked Birds with Fettuccine and Pistachio Nuts
Mushroom Pasta with Chicken and Toasted Walnuts
Walnut-Baked Salmon Trout
Salmon with Herb Sauce
Apple-Mint Poached Salmon
Halibut with Saffron Sauce and Tomato Salsa
Halibut in Nut Gratin
Sautéed Trout with Walnuts and Pancetta
Panfried Catfish
Shellfish with Peppers
Seafood Chili
Seafood Risotto with Peppers and Chilies

PANFRIED PEPPER STEAKS

4 servings

Fresh green chilies and green peppercorns make a slightly spicy sauce for panfried steaks that is sure to please. The flavor is quite different from that of peppercorns alone. You can always tone it down by reducing or omitting the chilies if you like, but I urge you to try the recipe full strength first.

4 strip steaks, ¾ to 1 inch thick
Salt
2 teaspoons green peppercorns,
    crushed
1 tablespoon minced fresh parsley
2 tablespoons vegetable oil
3 tablespoons butter
1 large shallot, minced
3 serrano chilies, stemmed, seeded
    and finely minced
½ cup dry white wine
¼ cup beef stock, preferably
    homemade (page 98)
2 teaspoons whole-grain mustard
Salt
Pepper
Three tomato salsa (page 228) or
    pico de gallo (page 159)
Watercress for garnish

For a delicious accompaniment, shred potatoes into very fine strips, dust lightly with flour and cayenne pepper and deep-fry.

Trim the excess fat from the steaks and sprinkle with salt, crushed peppercorns and parsley. Heat the oil and 1 tablespoon butter in a large skillet over medium-high heat. Add the steaks and cook to brown on both sides, about 4 minutes per side. Remove the steaks to a warm platter.

Put the shallot and chilies in the skillet and deglaze with the wine and beef broth. Simmer about 2 to 3 minutes, then whisk in the mustard and cook until the sauce thickens, about 3 to 4 minutes. Whisk in the remaining butter and season to taste with salt and pepper. Drain the relish and stir the juices and several spoonfuls of the relish into the sauce.

Arrange fresh relish around the edges of each plate, then put a steak in the center. Garnish with watercress. Spoon some sauce over each steak and put the rest in a sauceboat.

SIZZLING BEEF FAJITAS

8 servings

Sizzling *fajitas* have swept the country like mesquite wildfire and now many cuts of meat, fish and poultry are called *fajitas*. The term actually refers to a cut of beef, the skirt steak, which is the diaphragm of the animal. Tenderloin or a half-inch-thick piece of top sirloin can be substituted for skirt steak, but not flank steak, which is too tough. These are *fajitas* with all the trimmings but you can adapt it as you wish: it's really the sizzling platter that makes the dish. Use individual steak platters or an iron skillet or flat griddle with a handle. Be sure to put a thick hot pad down on your table first.

2 to 3 pounds skirt steak, or top sirloin steak, ½ inch thick

MARINADE
4 garlic cloves, minced
1 tablespoon lime juice
⅓ cup Worcestershire sauce or ⅓ cup soy sauce
4 serrano chilies, stemmed and minced
¼ cup apple cider vinegar
1 can (14 ounces) beef broth

GUACAMOLE
2 moderately ripe avocados, peeled and pitted
1 clove garlic, minced
2 tablespoons minced white onion
1 green chili, roasted, peeled and minced (page 20)
Lemon juice
Salt
Pepper

At least 3 hours before grilling the meat, trim to remove all fat and gristle. For skirt steak, use a flat meat pounder to tenderize; this is not necessary with sirloin. Put the meat in a shallow glass dish or plastic bag. Combine the marinade ingredients and pour over the meat. Marinate for about 3 hours.

To make the guacamole, put the avocados, garlic, onion and green chili in a mixing bowl. Combine with a fork until well mixed but not necessarily free of lumps. Season to taste with lemon juice, salt and pepper. Cover and set aside.

For the *pico de gallo,* combine the onion, tomatoes, chilies and vinegar in a bowl. Add cilantro and stir to mix well. Season to taste with salt.

About 45 minutes before serving, clean the grill surface and rub it with an oil-dampened cloth. Preheat the grill for about 30 minutes. Remove the meat from the marinade and put ½ cup marinade, including most of the garlic, in a bowl. Stir in ½ cup oil and cilantro. Sprinkle the meat with salt and pepper and place it on the grill. Baste with the marinade, then turn and grill on the opposite side, basting again. Grill until medium rare, about 5 to 6 minutes in all. Remove, cover with foil and keep warm.

Heat the remaining 2 tablespoons oil in a cast-iron skillet over medium-high heat. Add the onions and cook until browned but

PICO DE GALLO

½ sweet onion (Vidalia, Maui or
    Texas sweet), finely chopped
2 tomatoes, cut in ¼-inch dice
3 serrano chilies or 2 jalapeño chilies,
    stemmed, seeded and minced
1 tablespoon rice wine vinegar
1 tablespoon minced fresh cilantro
Salt

———————

½ cup plus 2 tablespoons safflower
    oil
4 tablespoons minced fresh cilantro
Salt
Pepper
2 large yellow or white onions, thinly
    sliced
2 bell peppers, thinly sliced
4 limes, cut in half
Flour tortillas (page 300) or 8
    warmed pita breads, cut in half
1 cup sour cream

still crisp. Remove and add bell peppers. Sauté about 2 minutes and add to onions. Remove the skillet from the heat.

Preheat the oven to 450° F. Wrap the tortillas or pita breads in foil and heat until warm, 8 to 10 minutes.

Cut the beef across the grain into strips about ¼ inch thick. Reserve all the juices. Put the skillet back on high heat long enough to get hot, then add the meat. It will sizzle. Turn immediately, then put the onions and peppers on top. Pour about 2 tablespoons of the marinade plus reserved juices on top to create a sizzle. Carry the skillet immediately to the table. Squeeze lime juice on top. Advise guests to make a sandwich using tortillas or pita breads to enclose meat strips, peppers, onions, *pico de gallo,* guacamole and sour cream.

NOTE.   For an even more dramatic sizzle, you can drizzle 2 to 4 tablespoons hot melted butter or butter and marinade combined over the *fajitas.* For extra sizzle that lasts longer, drizzle the meat and onions with 2 tablespoons oil instead of the marinade.

ROAST TENDERLOIN IN MUSTARD SAUCE

8 servings

The interesting variety of mustards available today makes it possible to create a flavorful mustard sauce that is anything but "ho-hum." A whole roasted or grilled tenderloin is always a favorite for entertaining, and the mustard sauce is a winner.

1 whole beef tenderloin (about 6 pounds), untrimmed

MUSTARD SAUCE
1 tablespoon vegetable oil
1 shallot, minced
½ carrot, sliced
1 can (14 ounces) beef broth
½ cup white wine
Several sprigs fresh parsley
1½ cups cream
1 tablespoon whole-grain mustard
1 tablespoon tarragon or wine mustard
1 tablespoon Dijon mustard
2 teaspoons minced fresh parsley
Salt
Pepper
Vegetable oil
Coarsely ground pepper
Coarse salt

———

½ cup white wine
Watercress or parsley sprigs for garnish

———

Garlic and its less pungent cousin, shallots, add flavor to relishes and sauces. They may also be roasted or grilled to serve as an accompaniment to grilled or roasted foods.

Trim the tenderloin, reserving the fat and marbled meat trimmings. (See note at end of recipe.)

Heat the oil in a medium saucepan over medium heat. Add the shallot and cook briefly. Add the carrot, beef broth, ½ cup water, wine and sprigs of parsley and simmer over medium heat until reduced to ½ to ¾ cup, 20 to 25 minutes. Strain and pour back into the saucepan. Stir in the cream and mustards and heat to a boil. Add the minced parsley and season to taste with salt and pepper. Remove from heat.

Preheat the oven to 500° F. Tuck the thinner end of the tenderloin under the roast. Rub the meat with vegetable oil, and pepper. Place it in a lightly oiled roasting pan, uncovered, and put in the center of the oven for 5 minutes. Reduce the heat to 375° F. and roast for 30 to 45 minutes or until a meat thermometer registers 130° F. for rare, 135° F. for medium. Sprinkle lightly with coarse salt and transfer to a heated platter. Cover to keep warm.

Skim all the fat from the roasting pan and place it over medium-high heat. Add wine and ½ cup water to deglaze the pan, stirring to incorporate all the pan drippings. Boil for 5 minutes. Strain. Put the mustard sauce over medium heat to reheat. Add the strained pan drippings and stir until hot.

To serve, slice the roast and place 2 or 3 slices at least 1 inch from the edge of each plate. Spoon the sauce on top and let it spill towards the edge of the plate. Mound vegetables or potatoes on the rest of the plate and garnish with fresh watercress or parsley.

NOTE.   If you are roasting the tenderloin, wrap the trimmings and freeze. Use them for stock another time. If you are grilling the meat, brown the trimmings in oil with the shallot for the sauce.

LOIN OF VENISON WITH BLACKBERRY
AND PORT WINE SAUCE

6 servings

Blackberry and port wine sauce is ideal for venison and it is very good with beef tenderloin as well. Serve the meat with vegetables and parsleyed potatoes.

3 cups unsweetened blackberries,
    fresh or frozen and thawed
2 shallots, peeled and sliced
2 cups port wine
1 loin of venison or beef tenderloin
    (about 3 to 4 pounds), trimmed
Oil
Salt
Pepper
Minced garlic
1½ cups beef stock, preferably
    homemade (page 98)
3 tablespoons unsalted butter
Blackberries for garnish

All berries intensify in flavor when seasoned lightly with chilies. Let one or two chilies steep in a sugar syrup for making ices, strain and discard before making ice, or add small amounts of finely seeded, diced chilies to berry chutneys, relishes, vinaigrettes or meat juices, particularly from game or game birds.

Set aside ½ cup blackberries for garnish. Put the remaining blackberries, shallots and wine in a saucepan and bring to a boil. Boil, uncovered, until the liquid is reduced to ¼ to ½ cup. Set aside.

Preheat the oven to 500° F. Rub the meat with oil, salt, pepper, and garlic. Lightly oil a roasting pan, put in the roast and place it in the center of the oven. Roast 5 minutes and reduce the heat to 375° F. Roast 6 to 8 minutes per pound until a meat thermometer registers 130° F. for rare, 135° F. for medium, about 25 minutes. Transfer the meat to a serving platter while finishing the sauce.

Place the roasting pan over high heat and add the beef stock. Stir to deglaze the pan and incorporate all browned bits from the pan. Whisk in the blackberry sauce and heat to a boil. Reduce heat and simmer for 2 to 3 minutes. Strain the sauce into a small skillet. Whisk in butter over medium-low heat. Season to taste with salt and pepper.

Slice the roast thin. Spoon some of the sauce onto half of each plate. Place 4 to 5 slices on each plate, stopping the sauce from covering the entire plate. Garnish with the remaining blackberries. Serve vegetables and parsleyed potatoes on the other half of the plate.

TEXAS BRISKET

8 to 10 servings

There are few things more economical—and appreciated—for casual entertaining than a barbecued brisket. The beauty part is that you can do so much ahead and leave the brisket to cook by itself. All you need to go with it is hot-water cornbread (page 310), fresh from the oven, and creamy cole slaw (page 130).

1 whole brisket (5 to 6 pounds), untrimmed

MARINADE
1 cup Worcestershire sauce
1 cup red wine
1 can (14 ounces) beef broth
¼ cup liquid smoke (only if searing indoors)
Juice from 2 limes
¼ cup chopped parsley
6 green onions, white and green part, chopped
4 tablespoons brown sugar
1 tablespoon salt
1 tablespoon coarsely ground black pepper
4 cloves garlic, chopped
2 serrano chilies, stemmed and halved
¼ cup bottled barbecue sauce or triple-pepper relish (page 240) (optional)

———

Oil for searing
2 tablespoons barbecue sauce (pages 264–265)
2 tablespoons butter, at room temperature
Salt
Pepper
Tender greens or watercress and red-tip leaf lettuce for garnish

Texans and many Southerners have always made their hash from brisket or beef roast rather than corned beef. Mix the meat with potatoes, red, green or yellow bell peppers, onions and a dash of cayenne pepper. Cook it in hot butter and oil for a crisp crust.

At least 30 hours ahead of time, put the brisket, fat side up, in a large pan at least 2 inches deep or a heavy-duty plastic bag. Combine the marinade ingredients and pour over the brisket. Cover or seal tightly and marinate for 30 to 36 hours.

Preheat an outdoor grill. Remove the brisket from the marinade and rub with oil. Sear on a grill by placing fat side down for about 6 to 8 minutes, then turning and searing the opposite side for 6 to 8 minutes. You may also sear the meat in a large skillet or roasting pan over medium-high heat.

Preheat the oven to 200° F. Lay out several overlapping sheets of heavy-duty aluminum foil large enough to enclose the brisket completely. Pour about ½ cup of the marinade over the meat, then wrap securely in foil. Refrigerate the remaining marinade for another use (within 1 week). Put the brisket in a roasting pan and place in the center of the oven. Roast, undisturbed, for 8 hours.

After 8 hours, remove the brisket and let stand for 10 minutes. Pour off and reserve all the juices. You can either stir them into a prepared barbecue sauce and cook to incorporate over medium heat for 10 to 12 minutes or put all the juices and ½ cup of the reserved marinade in a saucepan to make a sauce. In that case, boil the juices for 12 to 15 minutes to reduce and thicken. Whisk in barbecue sauce and soft butter. Season to taste with salt and pepper.

Slice the brisket across the grain. Use a large plate and garnish it with a combination of tender greens or watercress and red-tip leaf lettuce. Place overlapping slices of brisket on the plate and then drizzle with sauce.

CHILE CON CARNE

12 servings

This chili recipe calls for beef and pork but you may use any combination of venison, antelope, beef or pork. Since game tends to be quite lean, you will need to add more pork to compensate. Chili recipes are as personal as the cook, each one usually claiming his or hers to be *the* authentic chili. Use this recipe as a guide to develop your own.

5 ancho chili pods, stemmed, seeded and toasted (page 22)
2 to 3 tablespoons safflower oil
2 pounds beef chuck, trimmed and cut in small cubes or coarsely ground
2 pounds pork shoulder, trimmed and cut in small cubes or coarsely ground
4 cloves garlic, minced
1 large yellow or white onion, diced
1 can (14 ounces) beef broth or 2 cups homemade beef stock (page 98)
1 can (12 ounces) beer
2 tablespoons apple cider vinegar
1 bay leaf
1 tablespoon minced fresh oregano or 1 teaspoon dried leaf oregano
1 or 2 serrano or jalapeño chilies, stemmed and minced
Salt
1 teaspoon ground cumin
1 large ripe tomato, peeled, seeded and chopped, or 1 cup canned tomatoes, chopped, including juice

---

4 to 5 cups cooked pinto or kidney beans
2 cups grated Cheddar or Monterey Jack cheese or 12 ounces mild goat cheese, crumbled
2 cups chopped sweet onion

The Chili Queens gathered with their charcoal braziers in the Military Plaza in San Antonio to peddle their chile con carne. This original chili was made with braised meat, cooked in a brick-red chili sauce made from ancho chili pods.

Bring about 1 quart water to a boil. Add the toasted chili pods, cover and remove from heat. Let stand until the skins loosen from the pods, about 1 hour. Remove as much peel as possible and discard it.

Heat oil in a large stockpot. Add the meat, garlic and onion in several batches; cook on all sides to brown. Add 2 cups water, beef broth, beer, vinegar and bay leaf and heat to a simmer. Stir in the oregano, serrano or jalapeño chilies, ancho chilies and salt to taste. Simmer over medium heat, uncovered, stirring occasionally, until the sauce has thickened, about 1 hour. Add the cumin and tomatoes and continue to simmer until there is a moderately thick broth, but still plenty of liquid. Taste and adjust salt, pepper and other seasonings to personal taste.

Place beans, cheese and onions in separate bowls to accompany the chili. Fill chili bowls about half full to allow for the garnishes. Serve with chilled beer and cornbread (page 311).

ROBERT'S GAME RAGOUT

4 servings

Robert Del Grande from Cafe Annie in Houston uses a combination of venison, duck and squab for his ragout. It is very good served atop blue- or yellow-corn tamales (pages 287–289) or one of the flavored pastas (pages 292–293). Toss the flavored pasta with goat cheese sauce (page 262) instead of cream sauce for a more exotic taste.

2 tablespoons duck fat or unsalted butter
1 large shallot, minced
8 tart berries (cranberries, raspberries or currants)
1½ pounds mixed game (choose from duck, squab, pheasant, venison) or ½ pound each chuck roast, duck breast and dark turkey meat, cut in very small pieces (see note)
1½ cups red wine
2 cups homemade stock, either game or beef or a combination of beef and veal (page 98)
2 tablespoons fresh minced thyme or 1 teaspoon dried thyme
½ cup tawny port wine
Salt
Coarsely ground black pepper

CREAM SAUCE
1 cup heavy cream
1 teaspoon minced garlic
¼ cup grated Parmesan cheese

———

Salt
½ pound fettuccine or thin spaghetti, preferably fresh
4 fresh thyme sprigs for garnish

Early Texas settlers lived on buffalo, deer, fish, fowl, wild grapevines, herbs, grasses and various native plants. The first planting of grapevines in Texas can be traced to the El Paso Valley in 1662.

Melt the butter or duck fat in a deep saucepan or large sauté pan over medium-high heat. Add the shallots and berries and sauté several minutes. Add the meat and sauté until browned on all sides, 5 to 8 minutes. Deglaze with the red wine and heat to a boil. Boil until about half of the wine has evaporated. Add the stock, thyme and port wine and cook, uncovered, until the meat is tender and the juices have thickened, about 35 to 40 minutes. Season to taste with salt and pepper. Reduce the heat to low and keep warm.

Put the cream and garlic in a medium saucepan and heat to a boil. Add the Parmesan cheese and cook, stirring constantly, until the sauce thickens, about 5 minutes.

Bring 2 to 3 quarts lightly salted water to a boil. Add the pasta and cook over medium-high heat until tender to the bite, about 1½ to 2 minutes for fresh pasta, 5 to 6 minutes for dried pasta. Drain, then stir into the cream sauce.

Arrange the pasta on 4 large plates, leaving a round space in the center of each. Spoon the ragout in the center and garnish each serving with a fresh sprig of thyme.

NOTE. Use less tender cuts of meat for a ragout: the long cooking time makes them tender, particularly if the ragout is made a day ahead and reheated.

ROAST LEG OF LAMB

8 to 10 servings

Cooking a roast for family or friends fills your kitchen with the delicious aroma of meat and herbs. I like to start the meat in a very hot oven, then reduce the heat to cook it at a lower temperature: it makes for a tender, juicy roast. I also like to make a sauce from the pan juices. Minted-pear-and-papaya chutney (page 242) is excellent with roast leg of lamb. Traditional vegetables, such as peas and carrots seasoned with fresh mint, and grilled eggplant (page 273) also go well with lamb.

1 leg of lamb (6 pounds), bone in
2 to 3 tablespoons vegetable oil
2 cloves garlic, cut in 4 slivers each
3 to 4 sprigs fresh rosemary, crushed,
   or ½ teaspoon dried rosemary
Salt
Coarsely ground black pepper

ORANGE-POMEGRANATE SAUCE
3 large oranges, juiced (1 to 1½ cups)
⅓ cup pomegranate vinegar
   (page 153), see note
1 cup port wine
¾ cup beef stock, preferably
   homemade (page 98)
12 fresh mint sprigs
½ tablespoon cornstarch
2 tablespoons unsalted butter
2 tablespoons minced fresh mint
Salt
Freshly ground black pepper

———

Sprigs of mint or rosemary or mixed
   greens for garnish

Preheat the oven to 450° F. Rub the lamb with oil, then make 8 slivers in the fat with a sharp knife. Insert garlic and rub the lamb with rosemary, salt, and pepper. Put the roast in a roasting pan and place on the center rack of the oven. Reduce the heat to 350° F. and roast until a meat thermometer registers about 140° to 145° F. for medium to medium-rare, 160° to 165° F. for well done, about 1½ hours. Transfer the lamb to a serving platter and cover it with foil to keep warm.

Skim the excess fat from the pan juices. Place the roasting pan on medium-high heat and add the orange juice, vinegar, port wine and beef broth to deglaze. Stir to loosen and incorporate all the caramelized bits from the pan. Add mint sprigs and boil over high heat until liquid thickens, about 10 to 12 minutes. Strain the reduced sauce into a smaller saucepan. Taste and add water if the sauce tastes too strong. If quite thin, dissolve ½ tablespoon cornstarch in 2 tablespoons water and stir into the sauce over medium heat, until thickened. Whisk in the butter and minced mint, and season to taste with salt and pepper.

To serve, slice the roast and arrange slices on each plate with vegetables. Garnish with fresh mint or rosemary or mixed greens.

NOTE.   If you do not have pomegranate vinegar, substitute raspberry vinegar or red wine vinegar mixed with 2 tablespoons currant jelly.

ROAST PORK WITH TANGERINE SAUCE

10 servings

I am especially fond of tangerine-flavored sauce with a pork roast; it also works well with oranges. Try blood oranges, too, when they are in season. Serve the pork with stir-fried spinach and apple-potato relish (page 231) or red-onion chutney (page 241).

3 cloves garlic, minced
2 teaspoons minced fresh sage or ½ teaspoon dried sage
2 teaspoons minced fresh rosemary or ½ teaspoon dried rosemary
2 teaspoons minced fresh tarragon or ½ teaspoon dried tarragon
2 tablespoons flour
1 teaspoon salt
½ teaspoon pepper
1 rolled boned pork loin (about 5 pounds), at room temperature
2 tablespoons butter
½ cup chicken stock, preferably homemade (page 97)
2 to 3 tablespoons unsalted butter, at room temperature

TANGERINE SAUCE
4 fresh tangerines or 4 oranges
2 cups dry white wine
2 shallots, chopped
¼ cup golden raisins
2 tablespoons butter
Salt
Pepper

STIR-FRIED SPINACH
1 pound fresh spinach
2 tablespoons safflower oil
1 tablespoon unsalted butter
Salt
Pepper

Preheat the oven to 475° F. Combine the garlic, minced sage, rosemary, tarragon, flour, salt and pepper. Rub the roast with butter, and then roll in herb mixture. Place fat side up in a large roasting pan. Pour the chicken stock in the roasting pan. Place in the center of the oven and reduce the heat to 300° F. Roast, basting several times, until a meat thermometer registers an internal temperature of 165° F., 2½ to 3 hours.

While the meat is roasting, squeeze the tangerines, reserving 4 strips of peel (½″ × 1½″). Place juice and peel in a skillet with wine, shallots, and raisins. Bring to a boil and boil for 10 minutes, then cool and strain. Set aside.

Place the cooked roast on a serving platter and cover with foil to keep warm. Skim the excess fat from the pan juices, and place the roasting pan over medium-high heat. Add the tangerine-wine mixture to deglaze the roasting pan, stirring to loosen all browned bits. Remove from heat and strain the sauce into a small saucepan. Place over medium heat and whisk in the unsalted butter. Season to taste with salt and pepper. Keep the sauce warm over medium-low heat.

Stem and rinse the spinach. Dry thoroughly. Heat the safflower oil and butter in a large skillet over medium heat. Add the spinach and stir-fry until just wilted, about 1½ to 2 minutes. Season to taste with salt and pepper. Mound the spinach loosely in the center of each plate. Slice the roast and lay overlapping slices on the spinach. Serve with the relish of your choice.

Variation
• Substitute Swiss chard for the spinach.

HONEY-BAKED HAM

10 to 12 servings

Honey-glazed hams are very popular in the Southwest. Adding maple syrup and spicy mustard to the honey makes a flavorful crusty glaze as well as a delicious sauce. Serve the ham with sweet-potato and jícama pancakes (page 277) or grits cakes (page 313) and cranberry-apricot relish (page 234) or fresh-berry chutney (page 245).

1 ready-to-eat (13 to 15 pounds)
   smoked ham
3 cups white wine

GLAZE
5 tablespoons whole-grain Dijon
   mustard or Creole-style mustard
⅓ cup honey
⅓ cup maple syrup

SAUCE
1¼ cups chicken stock
3 tablespoons maple syrup
2 tablespoons mustard
2 teaspoons cornstarch

Preheat the oven to 400° F. With a sharp knife, remove the rind from the ham, then score with diagonal cross-cuts. Put the ham in a roasting pan and pour the wine over the top. Cover with foil. Reduce the heat to 350° F. and bake the ham 1¼ hours.

Combine the mustard with honey and maple syrup. After 1¼ hours remove the foil and brush the ham with the glaze, using all of the mixture. Return the ham to the oven and continue baking for an additional 1½ hours, or until the internal temperature reaches 140° F. Baste occasionally after the glaze is set, about 45 minutes. If the glaze becomes too dark before the meat thermometer registers 140° F., cover the ham again with foil. When the ham is done, transfer it to a serving platter and cover it with foil to keep warm.

Skim the fat from the pan juices and reserve all meat juices or caramelized bits from the glaze that have accumulated. Heat to a boil. Add 1 cup chicken stock, maple syrup and mustard. Dissolve the cornstarch in the remaining chicken stock and whisk it into the glaze to thicken it if necessary. The sauce will have a rich, dark color. Strain before serving.

Serve ham slices with the sauce and suggested accompaniments.

VEAL IN LIME AND SERRANO CHILI BUTTER SAUCE

4 to 5 servings

A simple butter sauce made with chilies, mango and lime is a nice complement to veal. The serrano chili adds a subtle hint of spice and keeps the mango from making the sauce too sweet. Use more serrano chilies for a spicier sauce. Serve with an assortment of vegetables, such as cauliflower, green beans and wedges of red bell pepper, and a few mango slices.

1½ pounds veal sirloin, ½ inch thick

LIME-CHILI SAUCE
Juice of 2 limes (5 to 6 tablespoons)
4 to 6 serrano chilies, stemmed, halved and seeded
¼ cup white wine vinegar
3 shallots, chopped
¾ cup (1½ sticks) unsalted butter, at room temperature
1 fresh mango, pureed (about ½ cup)
Salt
White pepper

———

2 tablespoons minced fresh parsley
2 tablespoons flour
1 teaspoon salt
1 teaspoon pepper
½ cup fine dry breadcrumbs
2 tablespoons sesame seeds (optional)
2 tablespoons oil
2 tablespoons butter
Watercress, mâche or fresh parsley for garnish

Use a meat pounder and pound the veal about ¼ inch thick. Trim away fat and membrane and cut into medium-size medallions. Allow 3 to 4 medallions per person.

Heat the lime juice, chilies, vinegar and shallots in a medium saucepan to a boil and boil until reduced to ¼ cup liquid, 3 to 4 minutes. Lower the heat and lift the pan from the burner to cool. Whisk in the butter, 2 tablespoons at a time, over low heat, to make a smooth, creamy sauce. Strain, then return the saucepan to low heat and whisk in the mango puree. Season to taste with salt and pepper. Place the sauce over hot water on low heat to keep warm. If it becomes too thick upon standing, thin with a few drops of hot water.

Combine the parsley with flour, salt, pepper, breadcrumbs and sesame seeds if using. Spread out on a shallow plate. Heat 1 tablespoon oil and 1 tablespoon butter in a large sauté pan until sizzling. Dip each medallion in the flour mixture to coat lightly. Shake off the excess, then add to the skillet and sauté, turning once, until browned, about 2 minutes. Remove to a warm platter. Repeat with remaining oil, butter, and medallions.

Spoon some of the sauce on serving plates, then arrange medallions overlapping each other. Garnish with fresh greens.

VEAL CUTLETS

6 servings

The bland nature of veal makes it a perfect foil for spicy chilies. These cutlets take just minutes to prepare and are excellent with a plate of colorful grilled bell peppers.

3 cloves garlic, minced
3 serrano chilies, minced
2 tablespoons minced fresh parsley
2 cups breadcrumbs or 1 cup each breadcrumbs and cornbread crumbs
⅔ cup all-purpose flour
Salt
White pepper
2 eggs, beaten
4 tablespoons vegetable oil
12 veal cutlets, pounded to even thickness, just under ¼ inch
1 cup clarified butter (page 49)

Place the garlic, chilies, parsley, breadcrumbs, flour, 2 teaspoons salt and 1 teaspoon pepper in a blender or food processor and blend or process until finely minced. Spread out in a shallow plate. Combine the egg and oil in another shallow plate. Sprinkle each cutlet lightly with salt and pepper, then brush with the egg and oil mixture. Place in the crumbs and coat both sides.

Heat about half the clarified butter in a large skillet over medium-high heat. Add half the cutlets and sauté quickly until browned and crisp on both sides, about 1 to 1½ minutes per side. Repeat with the rest of the cutlets. Serve immediately.

Variation
- Use chicken breast cutlets or medallions from the loin of rabbit instead of veal cutlets. Soak the chicken or rabbit in buttermilk first to make the meat more tender.

FRIED CHICKEN

6 to 8 servings

Soaking the chicken in buttermilk both tenderizes it and helps give it a crispy coating. When chicken is fried at a high enough temperature, it is not greasy.

1 quart buttermilk
16 pieces chicken including breasts
and thighs, bone in (see note)

SEASONED FLOUR
1½ cups all-purpose flour
1½ tablespoons salt
1 tablespoon coarsely ground black
pepper
2 teaspoons garlic powder
1 teaspoon chili powder
1 teaspoon paprika
1 teaspoon cayenne pepper
2 teaspoons dry mustard

Peanut oil for frying
Cream gravy, page 48 (optional)

Pour the buttermilk in a shallow pan large enough to hold all the chicken. Add the chicken, turning once to coat all the pieces. Marinate, refrigerated, for at least 2 hours or up to 6 hours. About 1 hour before serving, remove the chicken from the buttermilk, letting excess liquid drain off.

Combine the flour, salt, pepper, garlic powder, chili powder, paprika, cayenne pepper and dry mustard in a large paper bag and shake to combine. Dip each piece in the bag to coat lightly.

Heat about 1 to 1½ inches of oil over medium-high heat in a sauté pan or two pans large enough to hold all the chicken. When a bread cube dropped in the oil turns brown in 40 to 50 seconds, add the chicken, skin side down, and fry until golden, about 8 to 10 minutes. Use tongs to turn all the chicken pieces and continue to cook, bone side down, partially covered, for up to 20 to 25 minutes. Smaller pieces will take less time. Remove the chicken to drain on paper towels, pour off all but 3 tablespoons of the fat in one of the pans and prepare the cream gravy if using. Serve the chicken on a large platter garnished with fresh watercress and tomato wedges.

NOTE.   Remove the skin and surface fat if you like, to reduce calories.

CHICKEN WITH POMEGRANATES

6 servings

Pomegranate sauce turns chicken into an elegant dish. The same sauce may be used for game birds, Cornish hens or turkey. When pomegranates are out of season (most of the year), substitute unsweetened cranberries, currants or raspberries. Serve the chicken with creamy scalloped potatoes (page 278) and spinach flan (page 294).

6 whole chicken breasts, split, boned
   and skinned
Vegetable oil
Salt
Pepper

POMEGRANATE-PECAN SAUCE
3 fresh pomegranates (see note)
2 cups white or rosé wine
1 large shallot, peeled and chopped
Natural juices from the chicken
1½ cups chicken stock, preferably
   homemade (page 97)
2 teaspoons cornstarch
3 tablespoons unsalted butter
Salt
Pepper
12 pecan halves, coarsely chopped
Roasted pecans (page 50) for garnish

Preheat the oven to 425° F. Rub the chicken lightly with oil, then season with salt and pepper. Put the chicken in an oiled roasting pan in the center of the oven. After 5 minutes, reduce the heat to 325° F. and roast for 30 to 35 minutes.

To prepare the sauce, cut the pomegranates in quarters and set ½ cup seeds aside for garnish. Separate and discard the peel and membrane and put the remaining seeds in a medium saucepan over medium-high heat. Add the wine and shallot and heat to a boil until the liquid is reduced to about ¾ cup, 20 to 25 minutes. Strain and press to extract all flavor from the seeds. This concentrated essence will flavor the sauce.

Remove the chicken and transfer it to a warm platter. Cover with foil to keep warm while finishing the sauce.

Skim the fat from the pan drippings, then heat to a boil. Deglaze the pan with the pomegranate essence and chicken stock. Stir to scrape all the browned bits from the pan and boil several minutes. Strain and pour the strained liquid into a smaller saucepan. If the sauce is too thin to coat the spoon, dissolve cornstarch in ¼ cup water, whisk it into the sauce and cook over medium-low heat until thickened in a shiny glaze that coats the spoon. Whisk in the butter and season to taste with salt and pepper. Stir in the pecans, and keep the sauce warm over low heat.

To serve, place 2 chicken cutlets on each plate. Spoon the sauce over the chicken and garnish the plate with the reserved pomegranate seeds and roasted pecans.

NOTE.   Fresh pomegranates or berries are always best for a sauce reduction, but when they are not available or you are in a hurry, you may substitute 2 tablespoons currant jelly, cooking it with the cup of wine and the shallot long enough to melt the jelly.

CHICKEN IN PECAN BUTTER SAUCE

6 servings

This is an impressive yet easy dish for entertaining. The technique for cooking the chicken gives a perfectly moist result and the pecan butter sauce is a lovely accompaniment. Both the sauce and the rice may be made in advance and reheated.

Nutty brown and wild rice (page 283)
Pecan butter sauce (page 259)

————

6 large chicken breasts, split
Salt
Pepper
2 tablespoons minced fresh parsley
2 tablespoons vegetable oil
2 tablespoons butter
2 tablespoons chopped chives for garnish

Prepare both the rice and the pecan butter sauce and set aside.

Turn on the broiler. Bone the chicken breasts, reserving the skin and bones. Put the skin and bones on a large cookie sheet and place 4 to 6 inches under the broiling element. Broil, leaving the door ajar, until lightly browned, 6 to 8 minutes.

Set the oven temperature at 275° F. Sprinkle the chicken cutlets lightly with salt, pepper and 1 tablespoon parsley. Heat the oil and butter in a large sauté pan over medium-high heat. Add the chicken and sauté to brown on both sides for a total of 1½ to 2 minutes. Put the chicken cutlets on top of the browned bones on the cookie sheet. This helps keep the chicken moist. Bake for 15 minutes or up to 20 minutes. Discard the bones and skin or reserve to make chicken stock.

Arrange 2 pieces of chicken on each plate, leaving a 1½-inch space at the plate edge. Spoon the sauce over the chicken and allow it to spill onto the outer edge of the plate. Add a large spoonful of rice. Sprinkle the chicken with parsley or chives for garnish.

ROAST CHICKEN BREASTS WITH SPICE-NUT GRATIN

4 servings

Pecans and cornbread crumbs pep up simple baked chicken. This is an easy dish to do ahead for fall entertaining. The spicing is very subtle. Serve the chicken with cranberry-apricot relish (page 234) and a tossed green salad.

¾ cup finely chopped toasted pecans, about 20 pecan halves (page 50)

1½ cups coarse cornbread crumbs (about 4 muffins)

½ cup grated Parmesan cheese

1 tablespoon minced fresh parsley or cilantro

1 garlic clove, minced

2 jalapeño chilies, stemmed, seeded and diced

Salt

Coarsely ground black pepper

4 chicken breasts, split, boned and skinned

1 egg, beaten

6 to 7 tablespoons melted butter

Preheat the oven to 375° F. Combine the pecans, cornbread crumbs, cheese, parsley or cilantro, garlic and chilies in a mixing bowl to make a coarse crumb mixture. Transfer to a shallow plate. Lightly salt and pepper the chicken breasts. Dip each chicken breast first in the egg, then in the crumbs. Do not mold crumbs together—maintain a coarse, loose coating.

Arrange chicken in a buttered baking dish large enough to hold all 8 pieces in a single layer. Sprinkle remaining crumbs over the top, then drizzle evenly with melted butter. Replace crumbs that fall off but do not press them into the chicken. (The chicken may be prepared 3 to 4 hours ahead of time and refrigerated until ready to bake.) Bake the chicken for 35 to 40 minutes, basting several times.

CHICKEN FAJITAS

8 servings

The popularity of beef *fajitas* has encouraged many variations, including chicken. This spectacular chicken dish may be served as an appetizer course for an elegant dinner party or as an entree for casual entertaining.

**Three tomato salsa (page 228) or
tomato and green chili relish (page
227)**
**Guacamole (page 158) or avocado
relish (page 229)**

MARINADE
1 cup safflower oil
2 tablespoons soy sauce
⅓ cup lime juice
Freshly cracked black pepper
3 serrano chilies, halved
2 cloves garlic, minced

———

**4 chicken breasts, boned and split,
with skin**
2 tablespoons butter
2 tablespoons oil
**24 flour tortillas, preferably
homemade (page 300) or 8 pita
breads, quartered**
1 head Bibb lettuce, rinsed and dried
**8 sprigs fresh cilantro, with long
stems, for garnish**
1 lime, cut in half

*Slice moderately firm avocados for salads,
relishes or garnish; use firmer ones on pizzas,
which will be briefly cooked. Puree soft
avocados for guacamole, soups or sauces.*

Prepare relish accompaniments and guacamole and refrigerate for up to 2 hours. Combine the marinade ingredients in a shallow glass dish. Place the chicken breasts in the marinade, turn over, and let marinate for 30 minutes to 1 hour, no longer.

Remove chicken breasts from the marinade; reserve the marinade. Heat the butter and oil in a large sauté pan or skillet. Add the chicken breasts and sauté 3 minutes per side, until medium rare. The center portion should be slightly pink. Remove the chicken from the pan and cut away the skin. Cut chicken into strips approximately ½ inch wide.

Preheat the oven to 400° F. Warm the tortillas or pita breads in the oven.

Put two small lettuce leaves on the edge of each plate. Fill each with a spoonful of salsa or guacamole. Remove tortillas or pita from oven and divide among the plates. Garnish each plate with a long-stemmed sprig of cilantro.

Heat a lightly oiled griddle on the stove over high heat. Combine melted butter with 2 tablespoons of the marinade. Place the chicken strips on the hot griddle, turn once, then pour the butter marinade over them. Bring the griddle sizzling to the table and squeeze the lime juice over the chicken. Advise your guests to use the tortillas or pita bread to enclose the chicken and some salsa or guacamole.

Variation
- The chicken breasts may be grilled instead of sautéed if more convenient. For more flavor, brush them with chili-cilantro basting pesto (page 204) while grilling. Cook 3 minutes on each side.

STEPHAN'S WILD TURKEY WITH BLUE CORNMEAL–BOURBON STUFFING

6 to 8 servings

Blue corn muffins or cornbread make a delicious stuffing for game. This one was developed by Stephan Pyles of Dallas's Routh Street Cafe. You may substitute a roasting chicken for the turkey or bake the stuffing in individual timbale molds.

1 wild turkey (8 to 10 pounds)
Salt
Freshly ground black pepper

STUFFING
½ cup plus 2 tablespoons butter
1 pound bulk chorizo or spicy pork
   sausage
1 cup chopped onions
¼ cup diced celery
¼ cup diced carrots
4 serrano chilies, stemmed, seeded
   and minced
6 cloves garlic, minced
¼ cup diced chayote (optional)
¼ cup Bourbon whisky
8 cups coarsely crumbled cornbread,
   preferably made from blue
   cornmeal (page 311)
1 teaspoon fresh thyme leaves
1 teaspoon minced fresh sage
2 teaspoons chopped fresh cilantro
½ cup chicken or turkey stock,
   preferably homemade (page 97)
Salt
White pepper

———

¼ cup softened butter for coating
   turkey

Wash turkey well and season cavity with salt and freshly ground pepper.

Heat 1 tablespoon butter in a large skillet over medium heat. Add the sausage and sauté, breaking up with a fork, until browned, about 5 minutes. Drain and set aside. Heat the remaining butter in the same skillet over medium-high heat. Add the onions, celery, carrots, chilies, garlic and chayote if using and sauté for 2 to 3 minutes. Deglaze with Bourbon and cook 5 minutes to reduce liquid. Remove from heat and put in a large bowl. Add sausage, cornbread, thyme, sage and cilantro. Moisten with stock and season to taste with salt and papper. Toss to mix well.

Preheat oven to 350° F. Stuff the turkey and truss it. Rub with generous amount of softened butter, then season outside with more salt and freshly ground pepper. Place turkey on rack in baking pan and roast until done, allowing about 20 minutes per pound to reach an internal temperature of 170° F. Baste every 15 minutes during baking. When done, transfer to platter and allow to rest 10 to 15 minutes.

Prepare a gravy with the pan juices (see page 47). Slice the turkey and serve with stuffing and gravy.

BRAISED TURKEY BREAST

8 to 10 servings

Now that turkey parts are being marketed virtually everywhere, you do not have to buy a whole bird just to have the white meat. The technique in this recipe gives you a very moist turkey breast without frequent basting. What is more, the cooking time can be easily adjusted to meet the schedule of family or guests. You could serve the turkey with pomegranate-pecan sauce (page 171) instead of the simple berry sauce in the recipe.

3 tablespoons vegetable oil
1 turkey breast (4 to 6½ pounds),
    bone in
Salt
Freshly cracked pepper

BERRY SAUCE
1 cup white wine or 1 cup water plus 2
    tablespoons vinegar
½ cup fresh berries (raspberries or
    cranberries) or pomegranate seeds
1 shallot, minced
1 cup chicken stock, preferably
    homemade (page 97)
1 teaspoon cornstarch
2 tablespoons unsalted butter
Salt
Pepper

GARNISH
Cornbread-pecan stuffing (page 285)
Cranberry sauce or cranberry-apricot
    relish (page 234)

Preheat oven to 450° F. Heat the oil in a large ovenproof sauté pan or small roasting pan. Sprinkle the turkey breast with salt and pepper, then brown in the hot oil, turning to brown all sides, about 8 to 10 minutes. Add more oil if necessary to prevent the skin from sticking.

Remove turkey, place a rack in the pan and set the turkey, skin side down, on the rack. Pour ½ cup water in pan. When the steam subsides, put the pan in the oven. Roast at 450° F. for 20 minutes, then reduce the heat to 275° F. and continue to cook for 30 to 45 minutes, depending on size, until internal temperature reaches 160° to 165° F. Remove the turkey and place it on a platter. Cover with foil and let stand for 15 minutes before carving. This resting time is important as the juices baste the turkey internally as it continues to cook.

For the sauce, skim the fat from the roasting pan. Heat the natural juices to a boil over medium-high heat. Deglaze the pan with wine or water and vinegar. Add the berries and cook until thick and syrupy, about 5 to 8 minutes. Add the shallot and chicken stock and heat to a boil for 5 minutes. Strain into a smaller saucepan. If the juices are quite thin, remove ½ cup and dissolve the cornstarch in it. Stir the mixture into the sauce and cook an additional 3 to 4 minutes. Whisk in the butter and season to taste with salt and pepper.

To serve, slice the turkey and arrange several slices on each plate. Drizzle with sauce. Put a spoonful of cornbread-pecan stuffing on each plate. Serve with cranberry sauce or cranberry-apricot relish.

NOTE. It is also possible to roast the turkey breast at 275° F. for 1½ to 2 hours, as long as you baste it every 15 minutes. In that case, omit the initial 20 minutes of roasting at 450° F. Preheat oven to 450° F. and turn it down to 275° F. when you put the turkey in.

TURKEY WITH PASTA, TOMATOES AND WALNUT CREAM SAUCE

6 servings

This is one of my favorite ways to serve leftover turkey. The sauce is rich, but the fresh tomatoes give it a light taste.

1 recipe walnut cream sauce (page 263)

1 tablespoon minced fresh basil

1½ pounds fettuccine or spaghetti, preferably fresh

1 tablespoon vegetable oil

1½ pounds thin strips of cooked turkey, white meat only

¼ cup white wine

¼ cup turkey or chicken stock, preferably homemade (page 97)

Salt

Pepper

½ pound fresh young spinach leaves, rinsed well and dried thoroughly

½ cup toasted walnuts (page 50)

3 tablespoons walnut or vegetable oil

2 tablespoons clarified butter (page 49)

4 tomatoes, seeded and cut in strips

6 single basil leaves or toasted walnut halves for garnish

To peel, seed and juice fresh tomatoes, plunge them first into boiling water for 20 to 30 seconds, long enough for the skin to loosen. Quickly transfer tomatoes to a small bowl of ice-cold water and peel. Cut the tomatoes in half crosswise and squeeze to extract juice and seeds. Strain if desired. Or hold a single tomato with a long-handled fork and char the skin with a cook's blowtorch. Rinse under cold water to remove the skin.

Heat the walnut sauce in a medium saucepan over medium heat. Whisk in the basil. Keep the sauce warm over low heat.

Preheat the oven to 400° F. Heat lightly salted water to a boil in a large saucepan. Add the pasta and cook until tender to the bite, 2 to 3 minutes. Drain and toss with oil to prevent it from sticking together.

Put the turkey in aluminum foil. Sprinkle with wine, broth, salt and pepper. Seal and place in the oven to warm for 10 minutes.

Put the spinach and walnuts in a large bowl. Add the oil and clarified butter and toss to coat all the leaves. Heat a large non-stick skillet over medium-high heat. Add the spinach mixture and sauté, tossing constantly, until heated but not limp, about 2 to 3 minutes. Arrange around the edge of each plate.

Use the same skillet on medium-high heat. Add the pasta and walnut cream sauce. Stir constantly until all the pasta is coated and hot. Add the tomatoes and toss to combine.

To serve, overlap slices of turkey on top of the spinach, leaving a border of spinach showing. Mound the pasta in the center. Garnish with a single basil leaf.

SMOKED BIRDS WITH FETTUCCINE
AND PISTACHIO NUTS

6 servings

This is a very simple recipe for fall or winter when smoked birds are likely to be available at specialty stores, even the supermarket. You might want to smoke the birds yourself, following the directions on page 192.

2½ cups heavy cream

1¼ cups chicken stock, preferably homemade (page 97)

3 large leeks, white part only, rinsed and sliced

Salt

White pepper

2 tablespoons unsalted butter

1 cup toasted pistachio nuts, shelled and coarsely chopped

1½ cups sliced button mushrooms or 18 small pleurotte or chanterelle mushrooms, rinsed and dried thoroughly

1½ pounds smoked birds, such as quail and pheasant, or a combination of turkey and quail or pheasant, meat only, cut in slivers

¼ cup dry white wine

1½ pounds fettuccine, preferably fresh

2 ounces pâté de foie gras

2 teaspoons minced fresh thyme or ¼ teaspoon dried thyme leaves

2 tomatoes, diced, for garnish (optional)

Heat the cream, 1 cup chicken stock and leeks to a boil in a 3-quart saucepan. Stir in ½ teaspoon salt and ¼ teaspoon pepper, reduce heat and simmer until reduced to about 2½ to 3 cups, about 20 to 25 minutes.

Heat 1 tablespoon butter in a small skillet. Add the pistachios and sauté for several minutes. Remove to paper towels. Heat the remaining butter in the skillet. Add mushrooms and sauté until softened, 1 to 2 minutes.

Preheat oven to 425° F. Drizzle the meats with remaining chicken stock and wine; wrap in foil. Place in the oven to warm for 10 minutes.

Meanwhile, cook the fettuccine in lightly salted boiling water until tender to the bite, 2 to 2½ minutes for fresh or 4 to 4½ minutes for dried pasta. Place fettuccine in a colander to drain, then return to the same pan. Add half the cream mixture, toss to coat all the pasta and cook over medium heat 1 to 2 minutes. Season to taste with salt and pepper. Divide among 6 dinner plates.

Whisk the pâté and thyme into the remaining cream over medium heat. Add warmed meats, including juices, and mushrooms; heat for several minutes. Pour the sauce with the meat and mushrooms over the pasta and sprinkle with pistachios. Spoon the diced tomatoes in a ring around the plate as a garnish.

MUSHROOM PASTA WITH CHICKEN AND TOASTED WALNUTS

6 servings

Pasta dishes are very easy to prepare for company, as both the pasta and the sauce may be made ahead and reheated. I myself am very fond of the combination of mushrooms and sundried tomatoes; if you cannot get sundried tomatoes, you can substitute red bell peppers, either fresh or canned. Wild mushrooms such as chanterelles, morels or cèpes will give the dish a very intense flavor.

1 tablespoon cornstarch

2 cups heavy cream

1½ pounds fresh mushroom pasta (page 293) or 1 pound dried fettuccine, preferably spinach

2 tablespoons vegetable oil

2 tablespoons butter

3 chicken breasts, skinned, boned, split and cut in thin strips

1 pound cultivated or wild mushrooms, sliced

3 tablespoons minced fresh parsley or 1½ tablespoons minced fresh summer savory

8 sundried tomatoes, drained and diced, or 4 tablespoons red bell pepper, diced

Salt

White pepper

Minced fresh parsley or summer savory for garnish

½ cup toasted walnuts (page 50), chopped

Stir the cornstarch in the cream to dissolve and set aside.

Heat 3 quarts water to a boil in a large saucepan. Add the pasta and cook over high heat until tender to the bite, about 4 minutes for fresh or 8 to 10 minutes for dried. Drain and transfer to a bowl. Toss the pasta with 1 tablespoon oil to prevent it from sticking together.

Heat the remaining vegetable oil and the butter in a large skillet over medium heat. Add the chicken and mushrooms and sauté for 2 to 3 minutes. Add 1 cup of the cream mixture. Cook over medium heat until thickened, about 5 minutes. Stir in parsley or summer savory and tomatoes or bell pepper.

Rinse the oil from the pasta.

Heat the remaining cream to a boil, stirring constantly. Reduce the heat to medium and add the pasta. Toss to coat evenly with the cream and cook long enough to heat and thicken the cream, about 3 minutes. Season to taste with salt and pepper. Divide the pasta among 6 serving plates. Spoon the warm chicken mixture on top and sprinkle with minced fresh parsley or summer savory and toasted walnuts.

WALNUT-BAKED SALMON TROUT

4 servings

Baby salmon trout is a delicate fish with a distinctive flavor. Baking it this way keeps the fish moist under an attractive coating. Serve it with corn sauce (page 254), roast-bell-pepper sauce (page 253) or sliced vine-ripened tomatoes.

1 cup dry white wine
2 tablespoons white wine vinegar
3 sprigs fresh parsley
2 slices leek or onion, about ¼ inch
   thick
Butter for the broiler rack
4 whole baby salmon trout, filleted
1 tablespoon lemon juice

WALNUT-BASIL BREADING
1 cup coarse soft breadcrumbs
6 fresh basil leaves, minced
3 tablespoons finely chopped
   toasted walnuts (page 50)
¼ teaspoon salt
⅛ teaspoon white pepper
2 to 3 tablespoons butter, melted

Fresh basil leaves for garnish

The French called basil the herb of kings, but the Greeks and Romans thought it symbolized hate and misfortune and that it could cause madness. Basil is more easily grown than stored. Cut as close to time of use as possible since the leaves wilt easily. Shred or mince with scissors.

Preheat the oven to 375° F. Put the wine, vinegar, parsley and leek in a broiler pan large enough to accommodate all the fish. Butter the rack and put on top. Arrange trout on the rack and add water so fish is partially submerged. Squeeze lemon juice over the fish. Cover loosely with foil and place in the oven; bake 6 minutes. Meanwhile, combine the crumbs, basil, nuts, salt and pepper. Remove foil, then peel the skin from the fish and sprinkle seasoned crumbs on top. Drizzle with melted butter.

Turn the broiler on. Broil 1½ to 2 minutes, leaving the door ajar, until the crumbs are lightly browned.

Carefully transfer the fish to individual serving plates. Garnish with basil. Accompany with a fresh seasonal vegetable.

SALMON WITH HERB SAUCE

6 servings

Fresh poached salmon, chilled and marinated for several hours and then served with a fresh tomato relish, makes a cool, refreshing summer meal. Serve it with your favorite cornbread or a basket of different kinds of muffins. The salmon is also nice as an appetizer or fish course; in that case, reduce the portion size to 3 to 4 ounces.

6 salmon fillets (6 ounces), ¾ to 1 inch thick (do not use steaks)

MARINADE
1 tablespoon olive oil
2 cloves garlic, minced
1 shallot, minced
⅓ cup white wine vinegar
½ teaspoon salt
¼ teaspoon white pepper
1 to 2 tablespoons minced fresh basil or tarragon or Mexican mint marigold

———

White wine
Water
3 tablespoons lemon juice
⅔ cup safflower oil
2 egg yolks
Salt
Pepper
Watercress or fresh basil for garnish
Three tomato salsa (page 228)

About 4 hours before serving time, remove salmon from refrigerator and pat dry.

Heat oil in a small skillet. Add the garlic and shallot and cook to sweat, about 1 minute. Put in a small bowl and whisk in the vinegar, salt, pepper and fresh herbs. Brush the salmon with the marinade, then wrap in plastic wrap and refrigerate until ready to cook, no more than 3 hours. Reserve marinade.

When ready to cook the fish, heat equal amounts of wine and water to a boil in 2 large skillets. Remove the skillets from the heat and put the fillets in, skin side down. Cover immediately and let stand for 10 minutes.

Remove fillets from the skillets, place on a platter and squeeze lemon juice on top. Pour the rest of marinade over the fish and let stand at room temperature to cool. Cover and refrigerate for no more than 1½ hours.

Drain all the marinade from the salmon and put it in a blender jar. Add the oil and egg yolks and blend on high speed to combine. Season to taste with salt and pepper.

To serve, place 1 salmon fillet on each plate with a generous clump of watercress or basil. Put the salsa on the side. Ladle some sauce over the fish and serve the rest in a sauceboat.

Variation
• The salmon may also be grilled. Clean the grill surface and rub with an oil-dampened cloth. Preheat the grill. Brush the salmon with the marinade again. Grill skin side up for about 3 minutes, then turn, brush with marinade and grill about 3 minutes on the opposite side. Be careful not to char the fish. See page 205 for more information about grilling salmon.

APPLE-MINT POACHED SALMON

4 servings

Apple and mint lighten a butter sauce and cut the richness of salmon. The technique here is foolproof, even for an inexperienced cook, and ensures moist fish with a marvelous flavor. It may be served with fresh peas or asparagus. If you choose to double the recipe, use two skillets.

1 cup apple juice
16 fresh mint sprigs, including stems (see note)
¾ cup white wine
¼ cup white vinegar
2 large shallots, chopped
4 portions (8 ounces) salmon, 1 inch thick, filleted and skinned
Salt
Pepper
3 tablespoons heavy cream
¾ cup (1½ sticks) unsalted butter, at room temperature
Sprigs of mint for garnish

Preheat the oven to 200° F. Bring the apple juice, mint, wine, vinegar and shallots to a boil in a skillet large enough to hold all the fillets. Sprinkle the salmon with salt and pepper. Place the salmon fillets in the boiling liquid. Immediately turn the fillets over with a spatula and cover them with a tight-fitting lid. Remove the skillet from the heat and let the salmon poach, covered and undisturbed, for 12 minutes. Remove the fillets and wrap in foil. Place them in the oven to keep warm for up to 20 minutes.

Strain the liquids, then heat them to a boil in the same skillet until reduced to about ⅓ cup, about 10 minutes. Add the cream and boil 2 minutes. Strain again and place in a small saucepan over low heat. Whisk in the butter, 2 tablespoons at a time, to make a smooth, creamy sauce. Season to taste with salt and pepper.

To serve, spoon the sauce onto 4 warm dinner plates. Place the salmon on the sauce, and garnish with a sprig of mint.

NOTE. Mint varies considerably in intensity of flavor, particularly at the end of the season. You may need to use as much as double the amount indicated to obtain enough flavor. Do not substitute dried mint, though; use another fresh herb such as basil or tarragon instead.

HALIBUT WITH SAFFRON SAUCE AND TOMATO SALSA

6 servings

The colors and flavors in this dish make it spectacular. The butter sauce, lightly seasoned with saffron, is easily made from the poaching liquid; it complements any tomato-based salsa, spicy or mild. Serve with a green vegetable in season to complete the spectrum.

1 cup white wine
¼ cup white vinegar
2 shallots, sliced
About ½ teaspoon saffron threads
Salt
Pepper
6 halibut fillets (8 ounces), 1 inch thick
1 lobster tail, shelled and cut up (optional)
1½ cups heavy cream
½ cup (1 stick) unsalted butter, at room temperature
Grilled tomato relish (page 227) or pico de gallo (page 159)

Heat 1½ cups water, the wine, vinegar, shallots and saffron threads to a boil in a skillet large enough to hold all the fillets, or use two skillets. Lightly salt and pepper the fillets, and lobster, if using, and place them in the boiling liquid. Immediately turn the fillets with a spatula and remove the pan from the heat. Cover with a tight-fitting lid and let stand undisturbed for 12 minutes. Remove the fish to a warm platter and cover with foil. Place the platter in a warm (200° F.) oven to keep warm for up to 15 minutes.

To finish the sauce, heat 1 cup of the poaching liquid to a boil and reduce to about ⅓ cup, 8 to 10 minutes. Add the cream and continue boiling until the cream is thickened, about 10 minutes. Strain through a fine sieve and put sauce back in the same skillet over medium-low heat. Whisk in the butter, 2 tablespoons at a time, until the sauce is smooth and creamy. Season to taste with salt and pepper.

To serve, spoon some sauce on each plate. Arrange the fish on the sauce, then mound relish over a portion of the fish. If using lobster, spoon the lobster on top of the halibut, and serve the relish on the side.

Variation
- Whitefish or seabass may be substituted for halibut. Monkfish may be substituted for lobster.

HALIBUT IN NUT GRATIN

6 servings

Ground pine nuts give this light coating a toasted, buttery flavor. The fish does not actually need a sauce; if you prefer to serve one, either the roast-bell-pepper sauce (page 253) or the lime-chili sauce with mangos (page 168) is a good match.

½ cup finely ground toasted pine nuts (page 50) or other nuts, such as pistachios or pecans
1½ cups fine dry breadcrumbs
6 halibut fillets (5 to 6 ounces), ¾ inch thick
Salt
Black pepper
2 tablespoons butter
2 tablespoons oil

Combine the nuts and breadcrumbs and place on a large shallow plate or cookie sheet. Sprinkle the fillets with salt and pepper, then place in the crumbs and turn to coat both sides lightly. This may be done 3 to 4 hours ahead. Refrigerate the fish, covered, until ready to cook.

Preheat the oven to 400° F. Heat the butter and oil in a large ovenproof skillet or griddle that will hold all the fish without crowding or use 2 skillets. Add the fillets and sauté over medium-high heat for 20 to 30 seconds, then carefully turn over. Place the skillet in the oven and bake for 6 minutes. Serve the fish immediately or cover with foil and keep warm for up to 10 minutes in a warm (200° F.) oven.

To serve, cover each plate with sauce, if using, and place the fish in the center.

NOTE.   Be sure to toast and cool the nuts before attempting to grind them.

SAUTÉED TROUT WITH WALNUTS AND PANCETTA

6 servings

Pancetta is a lightly spiced Italian bacon that is cured rather than smoked. If you cannot get it (it is hard to find), substitute regular bacon. A simple tomato relish like the one on page 226 goes very well with trout prepared this way.

¼ **pound pancetta or bacon, diced**
2 **limes**
6 **trout fillets (6 ounces), about**
   ½ inch thick
Salt
Pepper
3 **tablespoons unsalted butter**
2 **tablespoons vegetable oil**
2 **cloves garlic, finely minced**
2 **tablespoons minced fresh parsley**
1 **cup walnuts, toasted and skinned**
   (page 50)
6 **sprigs fresh parsley for garnish**
Lime wedges for garnish

Put a medium skillet on medium-high heat. Add the pancetta and cook until crisp, about 5 minutes. Drain on paper towels.

Squeeze limes over both sides of the fillets. Sprinkle with salt and pepper. Heat 2 tablespoons butter and the oil over medium-high heat in 1 or 2 skillets large enough to hold all the fish. Add the fillets and sauté for 1½ to 2 minutes on each side. Put the fillets on a heated platter to keep warm.

Heat the remaining butter in a medium skillet over medium heat. Add the garlic, parsley, walnuts and bacon. Sauté just long enough to warm, about 1½ minutes.

Serve 1 fillet per person. Spinkle the walnut-bacon mixture on top and garnish with fresh parsley and lime wedges.

PANFRIED CATFISH

6 servings

Most catfish today is farm-raised and it is easy to buy filleted fish. For the breading, you can use blue cornmeal in place of the usual yellow or white cornmeal for a change of pace: the texture is slightly more grainy. Fried catfish is very good with roast-bell-pepper sauce (page 253) and ricotta-ranch compote (page 255).

3 **tablespoons safflower oil**
2 **beaten eggs**
⅔ **cup yellow, white or blue cornmeal**
1 **cup fine breadcrumbs**
½ **cup all-purpose flour**
¼ **teaspoon cayenne pepper**
6 **catfish fillets (6 ounces)**
Salt
Pepper
⅓ **cup clarified butter (page 49)**

Combine the oil and eggs in a medium bowl and set aside. Mix together the cornmeal, breadcrumbs, flour and cayenne pepper on a shallow plate. Sprinkle the catfish with salt and pepper, dip in the egg mixture, then coat both sides with crumbs.

Heat half the clarified butter in a large skillet over medium-high heat. Add three fillets and sauté until golden brown, then turn and cook on the opposite side, about 2½ to 3 minutes per side. Remove and cover with foil to keep warm while sautéeing the remaining fillets. Serve plain or with sauce or compote.

SHELLFISH WITH PEPPERS

6 servings

This is a colorful stir-fry of peppers, corn and shellfish with a hint of smoky pepper flavor from the ancho chili. You may serve it over rice or pasta or with crusty French bread or homemade tortillas.

1½ pounds raw lobster meat or peeled and deveined shrimp
2 tablespoons butter
2 tablespoons safflower oil
1 yellow or white onion, cut in half and thinly sliced
1 red bell pepper, thinly sliced, or 1 red bell pepper, roasted, peeled and thinly sliced
1 green bell pepper, thinly sliced, or 2 poblano chilies, roasted, peeled and thinly sliced
2 cups fresh corn niblets, cut from the cob, about 3 ears
1 ancho chili, toasted, stemmed, seeded and minced (page 22)
¼ cup heavy cream
Salt
Pepper
1 tablespoon minced fresh cilantro for garnish

Store bell peppers unwrapped, away from all moisture, for up to 1 week (only 2 to 3 days for riper peppers, especially red peppers). Never store in plastic bags.

Pat the shellfish dry with paper towels. Heat the butter and oil in a large skillet or sauté pan over medium-high heat. Add the onion and sauté for several minutes, then add the peppers, corn, shellfish and ancho chili and stir-fry until the shellfish is tender, about 6 to 8 minutes, allowing more time if using shrimp. Add the cream and toss to coat all the ingredients. Season to taste with salt and pepper. Spoon the mixture onto large plates or wide shallow bowls. Garnish with minced fresh cilantro.

NOTE. Methods of roasting fresh peppers and chilies are described on page 20.

SEAFOOD CHILI

6 servings

The rich, full flavor of poblano chilies and the piquancy of cayenne pepper blend with cool tomatillos to make a delicious base for fresh shellfish. Choose fish that is fresh and in season.

1 tablespoon virgin olive oil
1 tablespoon vegetable oil
2 shallots, minced
2 cloves garlic, minced
2 poblano chilies, roasted, peeled and diced (page 20)
1 red bell pepper, diced
1 yellow bell pepper, diced
2 cans (14½ ounces) Italian-style tomatoes, chopped
4 fresh tomatillos, husks removed and diced, or 2 green tomatoes, peeled and diced
1½ cups white wine
1 tablespoon minced fresh basil or 1 teaspoon dried basil
1 tablespoon minced fresh oregano or 1 teaspoon dried oregano
1 tablespoon minced fresh cilantro or 1 teaspoon dried cilantro
2 tablespoons tomato paste
1½ teaspoons salt
½ teaspoon pepper
Pinch cayenne pepper
2 teaspoons chili powder
½ pound scallops
18 large shrimp, peeled and deveined
½ pound firm-flesh fillets such as redfish (channel bass), orange roughy or halibut
12 mussels, scrubbed and debearded, or clams, scrubbed
Sprigs of basil, oregano or cilantro for garnish
Ancho-chili mayonnaise, page 257 (optional)

Heat the oils in a large skillet over medium heat. Add the shallots and garlic and sauté until softened, about 2 minutes. Stir in the poblano chilies and the red and yellow bell peppers and sauté for 3 minutes. Add the tomatoes, tomatillos, wine, basil, oregano, cilantro, tomato paste, salt, pepper, cayenne pepper and chili powder. Simmer over medium heat until the vegetables are softened, about 5 minutes. This step may be done ahead and the sauce refrigerated for up to 2 days.

When ready to finish the chili, bring the liquid to a full boil in a large sauté pan or Dutch oven. Pat the scallops, shrimp and fish dry and add, gently turning them. Place the mussels or clams on top and cover with a tight-fitting lid. Remove from the heat and let stand, undisturbed, for 20 minutes. Remove the cover and heat back to a simmer over high heat. As soon as the liquid begins to simmer, remove the scallops, shrimp and fish and spoon into warm serving bowls. When the broth boils, spoon it over the fish, add the mussels or clams and then garnish each bowl with a fresh herb sprig. Serve with bread or rolls and ancho-chili mayonnaise if desired.

Oregano has a sharp, somewhat bitter flavor that goes well with catsup-based barbecue sauces and sauces made with dried or fresh red chilies. The American Indians used oregano as a medicinal tea and to flavor meats. Soaked sprigs add flavor to a charcoal fire.

SEAFOOD RISOTTO WITH PEPPERS AND CHILIES

8 servings

Despite the fact that there are a lot of ingredients in this recipe, it is very easy to make and guaranteed to please your guests.

4½ cups chicken stock, preferably
    homemade (page 97)
½ cup (1 stick) unsalted butter
1 tablespoon olive oil
2 shallots, minced
2 cloves garlic, minced
2 cups Italian Arborio rice
1½ cups white wine
½ cup toasted pine nuts (page 50)
½ cup cilantro leaves, finely minced
1 teaspoon minced fresh rosemary or
    3 tablespoons minced fresh basil
2 tablespoons minced fresh parsley
2 red bell peppers, sliced in ⅛-inch
    strips
2 yellow bell peppers, sliced in
    ⅛-inch strips
2 serrano chilies, stemmed and finely
    minced (seeds optional)
2 poblano chilies, roasted (page 20),
    peeled and diced
1½ pounds medium shrimp, peeled
    and deveined
2 cups lobster meat or swordfish, cut
    in chunks
8 to 10 basil or rosemary sprigs for
    garnish

Heat the chicken stock and 2 cups water to a boil. Melt 2 tablespoons butter and the oil in a large saucepan or Dutch oven over medium heat. Add the shallots, garlic, and rice and cook, stirring constantly, until the rice is opaque, 5 to 6 minutes. Add the wine and simmer until most of the liquid is absorbed. Add 1 cup diluted stock and simmer until most of the liquid is absorbed, about 6 minutes. Continue to add liquid in 1 cup amounts, simmering each time until most of the liquid is absorbed. Do not allow all the liquid to be absorbed.

With the last addition of stock, add the pine nuts, cilantro, rosemary or basil, parsley, red and yellow peppers, chilies, shrimp and lobster. Stir to mix in. Cook until the rice is tender, about 6 to 8 minutes.

To serve, spoon the risotto onto 8 dinner plates, covering the entire plate. Place a single sprig of basil or rosemary in the center for garnish.

Variation
- Instead of cooking the seafood with the rice, grill it and combine them on the plate. To grill the seafood, clean and preheat the grill. About 10 minutes before the risotto will be done, combine ¼ cup clarified butter (page 49), 2 tablespoons lime juice, 1 teaspoon *each* minced fresh basil and cilantro, 1 minced serrano chili and 1 minced clove of garlic. Brush the seafood with this mixture, skewer the pieces and grill, brushing again with the sauce, for 2 to 2½ minutes per side. To serve, remove from skewers and arrange on top of the risotto.

GRILLING AND BARBECUE

Grilled Sirloin Steak
Grilled Tenderloin
BBQ Short Ribs
Grilled Lamb Chops
Grilled Pork Tenderloin
Grilled Veal Chops with Lemon Basil Vinaigrette
Rosemary-Smoked Chicken
Grilled Cornish Game Hens
Grilled Salmon
Grilled Swordfish

Marinades

Dry Rub
Achiote Paste
Barbecue Rub
Barbecue Mop
High-Acid Marinade
Oriental High-Acid Marinade
Low-Acid Fruit Marinade
Vinaigrette
Herb Mayonnaise
Smoky Chili Pesto
Herb Pesto

People who live in warmer climates or who have grown up in the Southwest take cooking outdoors for granted. Local smokehouses and barbecue places are important cultural landmarks in many communities and both the ribs and colorful atmosphere are tough to reproduce at home. Traditional barbecue is slowly cooked over indirect, wood-burning fires and drenched in spicy sauces that have long simmered with smoky meat drippings. In other parts of the country, barbecue has become a catch-all term that can mean a place, a technique or a piece of equipment. But to barbecue fanatics, there is a clear distinction between barbecue and grilling.

Barbecue

In the traditional sense, barbecue is closer to smoking than to grilling and was reserved for tougher cuts of meat or those that required slow cooking. Authentic barbecue in the Southwest uses slow, indirect heat in a covered grill, with smoke supplied by aromatic woods. The temperature can be medium to low. For the home cook the closest approximation is obtained with a long, drum-type grill, a covered charcoal grill with a damper or adjustable rack or a charcoal-water smoker where the heat is maintained at about 180° to 220° F. Charcoal-water smokers cook with steam; no basting is required. Food stays moist but does not get a crusty exterior. You can simulate barbecue with smaller game birds, fish or small pieces of poultry by using a covered grill: add soaked chips for smoke and partially close the damper to reduce the temperature. Small birds or poultry can be put on the grill when the fire has cooled to about 230° F. and left there with the dampers partly or completely closed and the grill covered until the fire burns away. If they are not fully cooked by then, finish them in the oven. This way you get smoky flavor with very little bother.

Spit Roasting

This is another type of barbecuing and an excellent way to cook roasts, birds, poultry, or anything more than 2½ to 3 inches thick. It uses indirect heat, at a temperature between 250° and 350° F. The meat bastes itself as it rotates, keeping the flesh moist. Since it is a slow method, it is particularly useful for less tender roasts like pork loin or sirloin tip and for birds, poultry, duck and brochettes. The food is cooked evenly, with marvelous flavor.

Grilling

Strictly speaking, grilling is fast cooking over a hot-to-medium direct fire. It is suited to tender cuts of meat, poultry pieces, shellfish and fish. Generally, beef is grilled over a hotter fire than fish, chicken or vegetables. Meat and poultry will be crisp on the outside and juicy within.

Foil Grilling

Delicate or fragile items can be cooked on a medium-hot grill in sealed aluminum foil packages. The result is like steaming or poaching, with all the natural flavors captured by the foil. Little, if any, smoky flavor will penetrate the foil. Packages must be turned frequently to cook evenly. This is an excellent method for flaky fish, shellfish, boned poultry, vegetables or a combination of fish or poultry and vegetables. Aromatic herbs, citrus, wine or herb butters can be added for extra flavor.

Cold Smoking

Professional cold smoking is done at a very low heat for days or weeks and calls for a brine. For home cooks, the grill must be covered and the temperature kept below 140° F.; home cold smoking does not preserve the meat. It is, however, an excellent way to retain all the moisture in roasts, large turkeys or game and game birds that have little moisture or are quite lean. It requires some attention as you need to add live coals to keep the temperature constant as well as soaked chips to keep the smoke going.

Hot Smoking or Grill Smoking

This is a compromise between barbecue and grilling. Soaked wood chips or chunks are added to a gas or charcoal fire to add flavor and moisture to the dry heat. The dampers are usually partly closed to reduce the heat to about 200° to 250° F. and retain smoke; this makes for a slightly longer cooking time. Results are close to barbecue though less controlled. If the grill does not have a cover, you can tent the foods with foil to trap the smoke and retain more moisture during longer cooking times. This is best for small game birds and poultry pieces.

Hearth Cooking

The overwhelming popularity of grilling and barbecue may stimulate a revival of hearth cooking or grilling over the coals in a fireplace. This is not a suitable way to cook beef or lamb, mainly because of the lower heat and the inevitable mess from the fat, but fish or vegetables are fun to grill. If you have a glass screen, you can slow-smoke small birds or poultry overnight.

Types of Grills

Grills come in all different sizes and shapes, require different kinds of fuel and have different features —and carry different price tags. Whether you are getting your first grill or a replacement or a supplementary one, you can now pick one that suits your budget, your lifestyle and your culinary ambitions.

Open barbecues.   The hibachi is probably the least costly of all types and can be used both indoors in your fireplace, with the flue open, or outdoors on a boat, campsite or patio. Since it has a small cooking surface, it is best suited to appetizers for small groups of people or dinners for two. The heat is hard to regulate but you will obtain charcoal flavor and the fun of easy grilling. The brazier or adjustable grill comes in both table-top and free-standing models. Usually the grill surface can be moved up and down so you can sear the food over hot coals, then raise the grill surface, thereby lowering the temperature. These are designed for charcoal briquettes; some less expensive models may not be able to withstand the intense heat of mesquite wood or mesquite charcoal. It can take from 20 to 60 minutes for the fire to be ready.

Covered grills.   These are probably the most popular and are generally available in two types, kettle grills and rotisseries. Both have a cover and vents to help control the heat. The kettle type usually does not have an adjustable rack. That is not necessarily a disadvantage. The rotisserie type can be used for both spit-roasting and grilling. You can also simulate a traditional barbecue in these covered grills by building a fire on the sides with a drip pan in the center. They are not so effective as the oil-drum type of grill that is often found in the Southwest. In those long grills you can build a good fire at either end for what is sometimes referred to as hot smoking, only you use charcoal instead of the traditional wood.

Gas grills have become very popular because they are so convenient. Many are portable and come in different sizes, some with small propane tanks. The small ones are handy for apartment dwellers despite the lack of true charcoal flavor. You can add wood chips or chunks for smoke, and herb branches for flavor and since they have covers, you can enjoy the benefits of grill-smoking. Large gas grills have adjustable heat controls and can be used much like an oven.

Electric indoor grills never reach the heat level of an outdoor grill so you do not have the possibility of searing. You do get the ambience and health advantages of grilling, though. Times may be slower for beef, but fish takes about the same time as on a charcoal or gas grill.

Charcoal-water smokers.   Smokers are designed for controlled temperature smoking but they do not preserve the foods. This type can double as a kettle grill with a small grill surface. The water is placed in a pan between the food and the heat; both coals and soaked wood chips or chunks are easily added. There are also electric smokers with temperature controls that relieve the cook of the task of replenishing coals; the flavor, however, does not compare.

Wood-burning grills.   These are not available for home or backyard use unless you have a brick one built for the express purpose. Wood cooking is superior to charcoal for several reasons: Wood coals have a natural draft that gives more efficient heat that is less likely to be too hot or drying to the food. Wood fires have an advantage of a fine aroma, an essential ingredient in barbecue and smoking. When Texans talk about mesquite grilling they mean mesquite wood, not mesquite wood charcoal. The only wood-burning grill most of us have is the fireplace—not to be ignored for the aficionado of grilling and smoking. After the fire has burned to glowing coals, you can grill fish, vegetables or poultry with little effort or excess equipment. If you have a closed screen, you can do some home smoking overnight as well.

Instructions in this section are for grilling in general rather than for a specific type of grill. To adapt these general cooking techniques and recommendations to your own grill, consult the instruction booklet that came with it.

Tools

Useful tools for cooking on the grill include:

- Long restaurant-style turner
- Long-handled tongs
- Wooden or bamboo and stainless skewers
- Long-handled basting brush
- Hinged grill for vegetables and flaky fish
- Heavy-duty foil for foil-grilling fish and vegetables
- Instant-read meat thermometer
- Wire brush and soft brush for cleaning the grill
- Electric starter
- Heavy mitts or gloves
- Drip pan

Fuel

Other than gas and electricity, there are two kinds of fuel for the grill: wood and charcoal. There are several kinds of charcoal and charcoal briquettes. Those made with petroleum distillates are undesirable. Some are labeled wood charcoal; it is less dense with more natural draft, which creates a hotter fire. Mesquite charcoal burns at about 900° F., regular charcoal at about 600° to 700° F. There is however quite a bit of sparking with mesquite charcoal and the sources are varied enough to make it inconsistent.

A wood fire is the best for all-purpose grilling and barbecue, but backyard grills are not made for wood fires. The benefits include significant flavor from the wood, added moisture and a natural draft that makes the fire efficient. The initial heat is very intense, but after the fire burns down, the coals are less hot. That is why wood cooking is excellent for barbecue where longer cooking times are desired. That is also why mesquite wood is so popular in the Southwest. It burns hotter and gives better results for the direct heat method, grilling. If you are lucky enough to have a grill that will burn wood, try some chunks of aromatic wood or combine them with charcoal. Wood chips create a little smoke but will not impart a significant amount of flavor to the foods. Soak them in water for 15 minutes before adding them to charcoal or gas fires.

Wood chunks burn slower and will add some flavor. Soak these for about 1 hour and add sparingly to avoid lowering the heat of the fire too much.

Preparing the Grill and Building a Fire

It is essential to begin cooking on a clean grill surface. Old or neglected grills end up with clogged air vents and charcoal-crusted grids. Both can ruin the taste of the food and efficiency of the grill. I find it easier to clean the grill after cooking so it is ready for the next time. My method is to use a wire brush to remove charred bits, then clean with a softer brush and water, giving attention to both sides of the surface. Then I rub the surface with an oil-dampened cloth to season it and prevent foods from sticking. Before cooking I either rub the grill again with an oil-dampened cloth, or spray with a nonstick vegetable spray.

Whether the fire is direct or indirect, it is best not to use charcoal starter: it can adversely affect the taste of the food. Instead, soak wads of paper in oil and put them among the briquettes or use an electric starter. Start a direct fire by mounding the coals in the center. Once they are hot, spread them out to make an even fire. Start an indirect fire by arranging the coals on one side with a drip pan on the other or on both sides with a drip pan in the center. In charcoal-water smokers, the fire is at the bottom with water between the fire and the food.

Always allow ample time for building a fire; with charcoal it can take from 25 to 60 minutes to get a grey-white hot ash on the coals. If you need to replenish the coals for extended cooking or smoking (over 1 hour), start new coals at the edge of existing ones just before you begin to cook or start them in another barbecue and transfer them with tongs. Gas grills need 15 to 20 minutes to reach a maximum heat. Close the grill to preheat. If you plan to use wood chips or chunks, allow 20 minutes for soaking the chips, about 45 minutes to 1 hour for chunks.

To determine when the fire is ready, hold your hand about 4 inches from the grill surface; if you can tolerate 2 seconds, it is hot enough to sear beef; 3 seconds, ready to grill most foods (medium to high); 4 seconds, medium; 5 seconds, low heat.

Cooking Time

It is hard to be exact about cooking time because there are so many variables: the wind, the type of grill, the rack height, the amount of water-soaked wood added and whether the grill is covered and for how long. In the table that begins on page 212, general recommendations are given as a guide for each category of meat and poultry. If you enjoy grilling, jot down the time and temperature each time you prepare something; that way you will have your own guide for future reference.

Testing has confirmed that the old rules for internal temperature are too high. Food will continue to cook for 10 to 15 minutes after being taken off the heat. Remove the food at 10° F. below the desired temperature. Rather than piercing the meat to see how the juices run, which causes some to be lost, use the touch test. Meat, fish and boneless pieces of poultry feel soft and limp when rare, springy or more elastic when medium and firm when well done. When fully cooked, fish and poultry should feel not quite firm. The inside should be moist, not flaky or dry.

Some other points to remember:

- All meat needs a resting period before slicing. This is especially true for bone-in pieces.
- Fish begins to exude natural juices when fully cooked. Time fish by the rule of 8 to 10 minutes per 1 inch of thickness. You can remove fish from the heat at the minimum time, cover it tightly with foil, leaving no air space, and keep it warm in a 200° F. oven for 12 minutes without its drying out.
- Tougher cuts of meat or game need low temperatures (no more than 212° F.) and additional moisture to ensure tenderness. More tender cuts of game, such as a venison loin, are best seared and grilled at high temperatures. The most common problem with all grilled foods is too hot a fire. Brisket, for example, can be cooked for up to 24 hours on low heat.

Tips about Grilling

Here are a few tips gleaned from my experience that may be helpful to you when you are cooking on the grill. The recipes that follow are sort of master recipes for different kinds of meat, poultry and fish; more details can be found in the table that begins on page 212. Directions for grilling and foil-grilling vegetables are on pages 51–52.

- Always clean the grill before using.
- Spray turning tools with a corn-oil cooking spray, especially when turning fish.
- Handle items with tongs: forks pierce the flesh and cause a loss of juices.
- Skewer small items and keep size uniform.
- Always use fresh fish, meat, poultry or birds. Frozen foods lose moisture more quickly.
- Leave items out at room temperature 30 minutes before grilling. When marinating fish in the refrigerator, wrap in plastic and place on ice.
- Start grilling with foods that take longer, then add the remaining items. Prepare all sauces, relishes, and condiments first.
- Flatten boneless cutlets or whole birds and some roasts to cook evenly. Bone-in items always retain more moisture.
- When cooking large pieces of poultry bone-in, begin flesh side to the grill, then turn. This reduces heat loss and makes the juices run towards the flesh.
- When preparing boneless chicken breasts, reserve the skin. After searing the flesh side, turn and cover with skin to keep the meat from drying while grilling the other side. Poultry skin may also be used this way for boneless wild duck breasts, which have very little fat, rabbit pieces or small game birds like dove or quail.
- When entertaining large groups, where you need to prepare a lot of meat (too much for an average-size grill), choose thick filet steaks 1½ to 2 inches thick or bone-in chicken breasts. Sear them on both sides over a hot fire, brush with a seasoned pesto and refrigerate to finish later in the oven.
- Most items do best with hot heat at first, then a more moderate temperature for the remainder of the cooking time.
- Baste sparingly with high-oil-content marinades to prevent the fire from flaring up.

GRILLED SIRLOIN STEAK

6 servings

A thick top sirloin steak is ideal for grilling. Serve the tender, flavorful slices of meat with ranch-style tomato sauce (page 252) or roasted peppers (page 276), fresh corn and homemade biscuits for a meal your friends will remember as one of the best they have ever had.

**1 top sirloin steak, 1 inch thick, about
  2 to 2½ pounds
1 tablespoon vegetable oil
Coarsely ground black pepper
Coarse salt
About ½ cup Dijon mustard**

Baby onions, red or white, make an attractive accompaniment to grilled or roasted meats, in chutneys or relishes.

Prepare a hot fire in a gas or charcoal grill. Be sure the grill rack is clean. Let the steak come to room temperature. Rub both sides with oil, pepper, salt and Dijon mustard. When the fire is ready, place the steak over the hottest portion of the grill surface. Grill 5 to 6 minutes on each side, allowing less time for rare, more for medium rare. Transfer the steak to a carving board and let it stand 5 minutes before carving. Slice the steak rather thin and serve with roasted peppers and fresh corn.

NOTE. This cut of meat may also be grilled indoors on an electric grill. Allow 8 to 10 minutes per side for rare, 12 to 15 minutes for medium rare.

GRILLED TENDERLOIN

8 servings

A whole tenderloin, cooked on the grill, is always perfect for entertaining. This method of grilling produces a flavorful, moist tenderloin with a peppery crust. Serve it with grilled scallions (page 280), roasted peppers (page 276) and a tomato and chili relish (page 227) for a Southwestern meal. You can use the same seasoning and barbecue mop and roast the tenderloin indoors.

1 whole beef tenderloin, trimmed (about 4 pounds)
Barbecue rub (page 208)
Barbecue mop (page 209)
1 to 2 tablespoons vegetable oil

Take the meat out of the refrigerator and let it come to room temperature. Clean the grill surface and then rub it with an oil-dampened cloth. Prepare a hot fire, allowing 20 to 25 minutes for charcoal to burn down and create a white ash on the coals. Prepare the barbecue rub in one bowl, the barbecue mop (doubling the recipe) in another. Oil your hands and rub the dry seasonings into the tenderloin, coating it well. Tuck the long end of the filet under and tie with string. Let stand 20 minutes.

Put the tenderloin on the grill and cook 5 to 6 minutes or until marked. Use a brush to moisten the roast wth the barbecue mop. Turn the roast ¼ turn to make criss-cross marks and grill another 5 minutes. Continue to moisten with the mop every 4 to 5 minutes. Turn the roast over and grill 5 minutes, then turn 2 more times to sear all sides, cooking a total of 25 to 30 minutes (or 8 minutes per pound for a rare roast). The internal temperature should be 120° F. Transfer the roast to a preheated 275° F. oven and let it rest for 15 minutes or at 250° F. for about 25 to 30 minutes. Or move to a cooler portion of the grill until the internal temperature reaches 125° to 130° F. Let meat stand 5 to 8 minutes before slicing. (If you prefer a medium-rare roast, take it off the grill when the internal temperature is 135° F. Remember that the roast will continue to cook when removed from the grill: the internal temperature will rise 10° F.)

You may also grill the tenderloin for about 30 minutes and finish it in a 425° F. oven. This method may be helpful in pulling the dinner together if you are eating indoors.

To serve, slice the tenderloin and serve with grilled scallions and red peppers and a tomato and chili relish. Stir meat juices into the relish.

BBQ SHORT RIBS

4 to 6 servings

The preliminary cooking indoors shortens the grilling time without robbing too much moisture from the meat. Use the same technique for baby back ribs.

2 pounds short ribs, trimmed
½ red onion, sliced
1 bay leaf
2 cloves garlic, minced
1 cup red wine
¼ cup Worcestershire sauce
2 serrano chilies, stemmed and
    chopped
1 lemon or lime, quartered
2 teaspoons liquid smoke (optional)
1 teaspoon salt

BARBECUE SAUCE
2 tablespoons vegetable oil
½ red onion, chopped
1 clove garlic, minced
Juice and peel of 1 lemon
1 tablespoon brown sugar
¼ cup red wine
¼ cup Worcestershire sauce
1 tablespoon whole-grain mustard
1½ cups bottled catsup
4 tablespoons butter
½ teaspoon chili powder
½ teaspoon dried oregano
¼ teaspoon cayenne pepper
Salt
Coarsely ground black pepper

———

Oil

Put the short ribs, onion, bay leaf, garlic, red wine, Worcestershire sauce, chilies, lemon, liquid smoke, if using, and salt in a large saucepan. Add enough water to cover ribs; heat to a boil. Skim the foam that rises to the top, then reduce the heat and cook, covered, over low heat until ribs are tender, about 1 to 1½ hours. Remove ribs from cooking liquid and cover. Bring cooking liquid to a boil and boil for 15 to 20 minutes. Strain and set aside about ¾ cup for the sauce.

Heat the oil in a medium saucepan over medium heat. Sauté onion and garlic for 8 to 10 minutes. Add the lemon juice and several strips of peel, brown sugar, wine, Worcestershire sauce, mustard and reserved cooking liquid and cook about 10 minutes. Stir in the catsup, butter, chili powder, oregano and cayenne pepper and cook, stirring often, until thickened, about 10 to 15 minutes. Season to taste with salt and pepper.

When ready to finish the ribs, prepare an outdoor grill. Put wood chips or chunks in water to soak. When the fire is medium-hot, rub the meat with oil and then sear for 5 to 6 minutes on both sides. Spoon barbecue sauce over the top and cool the fire by adding wood chips or chunks that have been soaked in water. Cook, covered, until the meat is heated through, about 15 to 30 minutes. (Time varies according to whether the ribs have been refrigerated.)

Variation
- To finish the ribs indoors, preheat the oven to 400° F. Place the ribs on a baking pan and spread with sauce. Cook, covered, for 20 minutes, then reduce the heat to 300° F. and cook, uncovered, until heated through, about 10 to 15 minutes.

GRILLED LAMB CHOPS

4 to 5 servings

Lamb chops may be expensive but they are so good when grilled over charcoal, it is worth the expense. The fat content is high enough to keep the meat tender and moist. Serve the lamb with wild rice with pears and pistachio nuts (page 284). The minted-pear-and-papaya chutney (page 242), eggplant-and-black-bean relish (page 237) and tomato-mint chutney (page 243) are all good relish accompaniments.

2 racks of lamb, cut into single chops
   ¾ inch thick or double chops 1½
   inches thick

MARINADE
1 tablespoon freshly cracked black
   pepper
Several sprigs fresh rosemary
Several sprigs fresh thyme
6 mint leaves
1 bay leaf, crushed
2 cloves garlic, crushed
¾ cup vegetable oil
¼ cup sherry vinegar
1 tablespoon Worcestershire sauce
½ cup beef stock

———

1 clove garlic, minced
1 tablespoon minced fresh rosemary
1 tablespoon minced fresh thyme
1 tablespoon minced fresh parsley
1 teaspoon coarse salt
Sprigs of mint or rosemary for
   garnish

Remove the lamb chops from the refrigerator to let them come to room temperature. Combine the pepper, rosemary, thyme, mint, bay leaf, garlic, oil, vinegar, Worcestershire sauce and beef stock in a shallow pan. Add the lamb chops and marinate at least 45 minutes or up to 2 hours, turning once.

Mince together the garlic, rosemary, thyme, parsley and salt to make a paste.

Prepare a hot fire on a gas, charcoal or indoor grill. If using charcoal, let the fire burn until a white ash forms over the coals. Remove the lamb chops from the marinade. Strain the marinade and stir ½ cup into the minced herbs. Brush one side of the chops with the herb mixture. Grill, 3 to 4 minutes for single chops, 5 to 6 minutes for double chops. Brush the chops again with marinade. Turn and grill for same amount of time on second side. If you prefer lamb medium or well done, grill 1 to 2 minutes longer on each side.

To serve, put the relish or accompaniment in the center of the plate. Arrange the chops so the bones face upward and towards the center of the plate. Use fresh mint or rosemary sprigs for garnish.

NOTE.   Use the same marinade and basting sauce for sautéing the chops or broiling them indoors.

GRILLED PORK TENDERLOIN

8 servings

Pork tenderloins are much more tender than pork chops when grilled. The basting marinade leaves a lovely, shiny glaze on the tenderloin and makes a delicious, light sauce. Serve with hot-water cornbread (page 310).

3 whole pork tenderloins

MARINADE
2 garlic cloves, minced
**1 ancho chili, toasted, soaked and
  mashed (page 22)**
3 tablespoons minced onion
⅓ cup Worcestershire sauce
½ cup apple cider
¼ cup red wine vinegar
1 cup beef stock
3 sprigs fresh thyme

———

Vegetable oil
Barbecue rub, page 208 (optional)
Salt
Pepper
1 shallot, minced
½ cup chopped apple
1 tablespoon bottled barbecue sauce
**2 tablespoons unsalted butter, at
  room temperature**
**Fresh watercress or mixed lettuce for
  garnish**

Thyme is a savory companion for honey and apples in a sauce for game or pork. Use lemon thyme for a lighter, faint citrus flavor.

Trim each tenderloin to remove all gristle and connective tissue. Turn the thinner end under and tie with string.

Combine the garlic, ancho chili, onion, Worcestershire sauce, cider, vinegar, beef stock and thyme in a shallow dish. Put the tenderloins in the marinade, turn and marinate for 12 to 18 hours.

At least 30 minutes in advance, clean the grill surface and rub with an oil-dampened cloth. Preheat the grill. Remove the pork from the marinade and reserve the marinade. Rub tenderloins with oil, then coat with barbecue rub, if using, or sprinkle with salt and pepper. Grill to sear, turning on all sides and basting with the marinade each time. Grill about 30 minutes or until the internal temperature registers 165° F. Continue to baste occasionally. Put the tenderloins on a heated platter and cover with foil while preparing the sauce.

Put about half the reserved marinade in a medium saucepan over medium-high heat. Add the shallot, apple and barbecue sauce and heat to a boil. Boil until reduced by about half. Strain and whisk in the butter, then season to taste with salt and pepper.

To serve, slice the meat and arrange slices on a platter. Garnish the platter with generous clusters of watercress or a combination of several lettuces. Pour the juices from the meat into the sauce. Drizzle some of the sauce over the meat slices and serve the remainder with the roast. Accompany with cornbread.

NOTE. You may use the same marinade and sauce for pork roast, with or without the barbecue rub.

GRILLED VEAL CHOPS WITH LEMON BASIL VINAIGRETTE

6 servings

The flavors of mango or papaya, veal and basil complement and enhance each other. Crisp lettuce and jícama are a refreshing contrast to the flavor of mesquite- or hickory-grilled veal.

6 veal rib chops, bones trimmed

VINAIGRETTE
¾ cup safflower oil
1 clove garlic, minced
2 shallots, minced
1 serrano chili, stemmed, seeded and minced
⅓ cup rice wine vinegar
½ teaspoon salt
¼ teaspoon white pepper
1 tablespoon lemon zest
1 tablespoon minced fresh lemon basil

GARNISH
2 heads young Bibb lettuce, rinsed and leaves separated, chilled
1 bunch watercress, rinsed and stemmed, chilled
⅓ cup small opal basil leaves or 1 small head radicchio lettuce, rinsed, leaves separated and cut in half (optional)
2 mangos or papayas, peeled and cut in cubes
1 cup short julienne strips of jícama
6 sprigs of basil for garnish

When preparing veal or lamb chops for a large crowd, sear the chops first on the grill or in a hot skillet. Refrigerate, covered, until later in the day, then finish in a hot oven.

Clean the grill surface and rub with an oil-dampened cloth. At least 30 minutes in advance, preheat the grill. Heat 3 tablespoons of the oil in a small skillet over medium-high heat. Add the garlic and shallots and cook about 30 seconds. Do not brown. Put the garlic and shallots in a small bowl and whisk in the serrano chili, vinegar, salt, pepper and remaining oil. Divide the vinaigrette and set aside ⅓ of it to dress the greens. Stir the lemon zest and basil into the greater amount of vinaigrette. Brush it on the veal on both sides. Let stand for 10 minutes.

Grill the veal on both sides, basting with the vinaigrette several times, for about 5 to 6 minutes per side or until the internal temperature is 130° F. Remove and cover to keep warm while preparing the garnish.

Put the lettuce, watercress, basil or radicchio if using, mango or papaya and jícama in a large bowl. Add the reserved vinaigrette and toss to coat everything. Arrange on large plates, leaving a place in the center for the veal chop. Warm the rest of the vinaigrette used for basting in a small skillet over medium heat. Brush on top of the veal chop. Garnish each plate with a sprig of fresh basil.

NOTE.   If lemon basil is not available, substitute plain basil, summer savory, cilantro or tarragon.

Variation
•   Substitute salmon or tuna or pheasant for the veal. The vinaigrette will keep the tuna moist.

ROSEMARY-SMOKED CHICKEN

12 servings

Boneless whole chickens are available in some parts of the country; they are wonderful for grilling and easy to serve. If you cannot find them already boned, you might persuade the butcher to bone them for you, leaving the skin and fat intact. Use an aromatic wood or wood chips if you do not have rosemary on hand, soaking them in the same way. I like to serve the chicken pieces on a platter together with a colorful assortment of grilled bell peppers, tossed with balsamic vinegar and fresh rosemary.

3 boneless chickens, skin intact
3 tablespoons virgin olive oil

SEASONING SALT
1½ tablespoons salt
½ teaspoon black pepper
1 teaspoon chili powder
2 teaspoons dry mustard
1 teaspoon garlic powder

———

2 tablespoons chopped fresh rosemary
12 to 14 woody sprigs fresh rosemary or 1 quart wood chips

———

Grilled bell peppers (page 20)
3 tablespoons balsamic vinegar
1 tablespoon minced fresh rosemary

Rosemary is considered the symbol of friendship, loyalty and remembrance. It is very good with chicken and lamb. Whole branches are wonderful in a barbecue. Rosemary and mint in a butter or vinaigrette go well with tuna or salmon.

Rub the chickens with olive oil. Combine the seasoning salt ingredients in a small bowl or shaker and sprinkle the chicken with seasoning salt and rosemary on both sides. Let stand for 1 hour.

Clean the grill surface and rub it with an oil-dampened cloth. Preheat the grill at least 20 to 30 minutes in advance. Soak the rosemary sprigs or wood chips in water for at least 30 minutes. When the fire is ready, place the chickens "frog-style" on the grill and sear for 5 minutes, then turn and sear on the other side. Place the rosemary branches around the chickens. If using wood chips, place them directly on the coals, under the rack. Before the smoke subsides, cover the grill and cook about 20 minutes, turning at least once. After 20 minutes, turn the chicken again. Turn gas grills off and leave covered and undisturbed for 25 minutes. For charcoal grills, douse a little water on the coals to cool, then close the grill and open the vents. Leave undisturbed for 25 minutes.

To serve, cut each chicken into 4 serving pieces. Toss the grilled peppers with balsamic vinegar and minced rosemary and arrange with chicken on a large platter.

NOTE. You may want to grill the peppers in advance and reheat them, covered with foil, in a preheated 400° F. oven for 5 minutes.

GRILLED CORNISH GAME HENS

8 servings

This makes a delicious and colorful mixed grill. The grill-oven technique makes it possible for everything to be ready at the same time.

4 Cornish game hens, cut in half
8 cloves garlic, minced
¼ cup virgin olive oil
¾ cup safflower oil
1 fresh pineapple, cored and peeled
¼ cup lemon juice
4 sage leaves

GRILLED VEGETABLES
3 green bell peppers, cut in 4 or 5
** wedges**
2 red bell peppers, cut in 4 or 5
** wedges**
¼ cup safflower oil
2 unpeeled yellow zucchini or
** crookneck squash**

———————

Salt
Pepper
2 tablespoons minced fresh sage
¼ cup balsamic vinegar (optional)
1 tablespoon safflower oil (optional)
Fresh sage leaves for garnish

Put the hens in a large shallow baking dish.

Combine the garlic, olive oil and safflower oil in a bowl.

Cut half the pineapple into 8 long strips about 1 inch by 5 inches long. Set aside.

Cut the remaining pineapple, including the core, into small chunks and put them in a blender jar. Add the lemon juice and sage leaves and blend on high speed until smooth. Add the oil and garlic and then pour the marinade over the game hens and marinate for 30 minutes or up to 1½ hours.

Put the pepper wedges in another shallow pan. Brush on both sides with safflower oil. Cut ends diagonally from squash, slice on the bias ½ inch thick and cut into strips 3 inches long. Pour enough water to cover squash in a large skillet. Heat to a boil, add squash and cook until water returns to a boil. Drain and rinse with cold water. Put the squash in the pan with the peppers and brush with safflower oil.

Clean the grill surface and rub with an oil-dampened cloth. Preheat the grill and allow the coals to burn to a white ash, about 20 minutes. Preheat the oven to 375° F. Remove the game hens from the marinade and sprinkle with salt, pepper and minced sage. Grill flesh side down for 15 minutes. Baste with the marinade several times. Turn and grill on the other side 15 minutes, continuing to baste. Remove game hens after a total of 30 minutes and wrap each piece individually in foil. Reduce the oven temperature to 300° F. and continue to bake for 10 minutes.

Before grilling the peppers, brush any residue from the grill. Sprinkle the peppers and squash lightly with salt and pepper and place on the grill, peppers skin side down. Grill on both sides until lightly charred or browned, and just tender when pierced with a fork. This takes from 5 to 15 minutes, depending on the type of grill and whether it is covered or open.

If you want to finish the game hens on the grill, continue cooking until the internal temperature is 150° F, then remove, cover and keep warm in a 250° F. oven while cooking the vegetables. If you wish, toss the peppers gently in vinegar and oil.

To serve, put half a game hen on each plate with some grilled red and green peppers and squash and one of the reserved pineapple strips. Garnish with fresh sage leaves.

GRILLED SWORDFISH

6 servings

The chili and cilantro basting marinade used on the swordfish is quite versatile: it is just as good with grilled chicken, chicken *fajitas* and almost any meat, fish or poultry. I prefer grilled fish served with a simple salsa, but if you like both a sauce and relish, lime butter sauce (page 259) is delicious with this.

Three-tomato salsa (page 228)

CHILI-CILANTRO BASTING PESTO
1 garlic clove, minced
2 shallots, minced
3 serrano chilies, stemmed, seeded and diced
½ teaspoon coarse salt
½ cup cilantro sprigs, minced
¼ teaspoon white pepper
¼ cup (½ stick) butter, melted
¼ cup lime juice

———

6 swordfish steaks (6 to 8 ounces), 1 inch thick
Corn-oil cooking spray

At least six hours in advance prepare the three-tomato salsa and refrigerate.

Prepare a grill with a hot fire, allowing 25 to 30 minutes for a charcoal fire to burn to a white ash. Gas or indoor grills should be turned to the highest setting. Put the garlic, shallots, chilies, salt and cilantro on a cutting board and use a sharp knife to mince them into a paste. Put this paste or pesto in a small bowl and stir in the pepper and melted butter. Add the lime juice just prior to use as it will discolor the cilantro.

Trim the swordfish and remove the dark sections. Brush both sides with the basting pesto. Grill about 4 minutes on one side, until the edges turn opaque. Spray a spatula with corn-oil cooking spray and turn the fish. Brush again with the pesto and grill until the natural juices begin to exude, about 4 minutes. Drain the accumulated juices from the salsa and pour them over the steaks before you remove them from the grill. Put the steaks on a warm platter and serve immediately.

GRILLED SALMON

6 servings

Fresh salmon that has been grilled to perfection does not really need a sauce since the natural juices make it moist and succulent. I prefer a relish such as grilled-corn-and-pepper relish (page 238) or melon relish (page 232) with fresh tomatoes or seasonal vegetables. If you prefer a sauce, tomatillo butter sauce (page 260) complements the fish and adds a Southwestern twist.

1 salmon (5 to 7 pounds), filleted and cut in 1-inch-thick portions
Salt and pepper
4 tablespoons (½ stick) butter, melted
2 tablespoons fresh lemon juice
Corn-oil cooking spray

To make zucchini fans, parboil zucchini, then slice to within 1 inch of the stem, leaving stem intact. Spread out to make a fan, then brush with oil, salt and pepper and place on the grill just long enough to warm. Sprinkle with freshly grated Parmesan cheese and serve with a red roasted pepper catsup (page 241).

Set a gas grill on the highest setting. If using charcoal, start the coals at least 25 minutes before you plan to cook. If you are grilling on an indoor grill, preheat the grill at the highest setting. (Indoor grills do not get as hot and the fish may take a little longer to cook.) Remove the grill rack and clean it with a wire brush. Dampen a cloth with oil and wipe the grill surface. When the coals form a white ash, spread them out to make an even fire. Place the grill rack about 5 to 6 inches from the coals.

Sprinkle the fillets lightly with salt and pepper. Mix the butter and lemon juice and brush the salmon on both sides. Place fillets on the grill skin side up and cook until the edges become opaque, about 4 minutes. Brush a spatula with corn-oil cooking spray before using it to turn the fillets. Grill until the natural juices begin to exude, about 4 minutes. Stay with the fish to be sure it does not overcook: it will continue to cook after it is removed from the grill. It is better to undercook it slightly than to overcook it.

Serve the fish immediately or keep it warm up to 10 minutes on a heatproof platter covered with foil in a 200° F. oven.

Marinades

There are as many marinades and barbecue sauces as there are backyard chefs and the problem of which to use for what can be confusing to even an experienced cook. Marinades, no matter what the regional differences, are used for three reasons: to add flavor; to tenderize tough cuts of meat; and to maintain moisture during grilling. The marinating process is much quicker at room temperature than under refrigeration. Despite popular opinion, food cannot be marinated indefinitely; some food cannot withstand even several hours of marination. Check individual recipes and the instruction guide carefully so you do not find that your chicken has turned to mush or your beef paled to light gray in a high-acid marinade. Marinades fall into several categories.

Dry Seasoning Rubs

These are either made from dried seasonings and spices or a combination of fresh minced herbs and dried seasonings. Then during grilling, the meat or poultry is kept moist with a flavorful barbecue mop. If these rubs have salt, they act like a brine. The salt enables the seasonings to penetrate the meat. When using a seasoning rub, first rub the food with oil and liberally coat with the seasonings. Do not leave the rub on too long: lean, low-moisture meats risk losing moisture and turning dry when grilled.

Barbecue Mops

Mops are often high in acids but are used for basting to insure moisture. They may have a flavorful stock as a base with acids that complement the food to be grilled. Small amounts of barbecue sauce or a spicy condiment can be added without the possibility of scorching that is associated with basting with pure barbecue sauce. These mops can be combined with additional stock or broth and then strained and reduced to make a sauce. The acids or strong ingredients necessary to make them flavorful can be softened by finishing the sauce with a little unsalted butter. Mops may also contain small amounts of sugar or maple syrup, molasses or honey, which when combined with a little oil add a sheen during grilling.

Acid Marinades

Acid marinades serve to tenderize meat; they are especially good for game. They should contain some oil if used for chicken or fish to prevent it from breaking down. Acids that are used include vinegar, soy sauce, Worcestershire sauce, wine, citrus juices, yogurt or buttermilk; they are infused with herbs and spices. High-acid citrus marinades can be used on firm-fleshed or oily fish both to tenderize and to add moisture; they should not be used as a marinade for fish for more than 15 minutes or it will cook enzymatically before you have a chance to grill it.

Poultry can also benefit from high-acid marinades but should not be left too long in the marinade. That is why it is best to add a little oil if you intend to marinate for any length of time. Do not use salt when marinating meat, chicken or fish if you plan to leave it more than 30 minutes; the salt will draw precious moisture out. Use salt sparingly and season with pepper just prior to grilling.

Game and some game birds can be lean and tough, particularly those felled by the weekend hunter. High-acid marinades made with berries or wine both reduce the gamey flavor and tenderize the meat. After marination, the meat or birds should be rubbed with oil, salt and pepper; they should be basted often during grilling. Acid marinades for dark meat should not contain fresh lime if marinated for more than 15 to 30 minutes; it will discolor the meat. Use red-wine or berry-infused vinegar instead. Lime may be added to the basting medium if desired during cooking.

Vinaigrettes

A vinaigrette sauce is a low-acid marinade that can double as a basting medium. These sauces supply moisture and acid to tenderize meat and add flavor; they are excellent for firm-fleshed or oily fish.

There is enough oil or butter in them to compensate for lean cuts. Enriched by some reduced stock, vinaigrettes work as a sauce for warm salads. Use them also to baste vegetables during grilling.

Sweet-and-Sour Marinades

Such marinades are made with a base of fruit such as plum puree or orange marmalade and are usually used on pork, ribs or duck. Orange marmalade is usually combined with grainy mustard and vinegar; plums with chili paste (page 23), oil and vinegar.

Seasoned Ground Fat

A mixture of ground pork fat, beef fat, salt pork or bacon with fresh or dried herbs, garlic, peppers or chilies and spices can be used to preserve moisture in small birds, poultry or game that require more than 8 to 10 minutes cooking time. The seasoned fat is either stuffed under the loosened skin of poultry or used to coat a roast that is to be grilled or barbecued. Such mixtures add excellent flavor while maintaining moisture.

Aromatic Oils

Flavored oils can be used to keep low-fat foods (fish, game, poultry, boneless and skinless chicken breasts or lean roasts) from drying out. These are oil in which fresh herbs, garlic or shallots, onions, citrus zest or chilies, either dried or fresh, have been left to steep. They are not so much marinades as basting mediums, brushed on 10 to 15 minutes before grilling and then later used for basting. Virgin olive oil is preferred for flavor and its natural resistance to high temperatures. You can use clarified butter or butter if you prefer the flavor but their heat tolerance is not as great. The danger with an oil basting marinade is that drips of oil cause the fire to flare up, and if delicate food such as fish is grilled on a high heat, the result may be a burned-oil taste. Some chefs in the Southwest use an herb mayonnaise or a garlicky chili aioli to baste with. If this approach appeals to you, use the white barbecue sauce on page 264 or an herb mayonnaise (page 210) when oil-based marinades are recommended.

Pestos

These pastes are dense concoctions of herbs, garlic or shallots, onions and seasonings like ginger or other spices combined with just enough oil to bind them so they will adhere to the meat. They may also be used as stuffing: make an incision in the meat and spread with a small layer of pesto to season and moisten the meat. If more moisture is needed, add additional oil or a combination of oil and citrus and use for basting during grilling. See Texas tapas (page 63) and *fajitas* (page 158 and page 174) for other examples of how pestos can be used.

Herb Butters

Compound-butters or pestos made with additional melted butter, oil and chicken broth are suitable for basting vegetables during grilling. They slow the evaporation of natural juices and prevent the food from sticking to the grill.

Barbecue Sauces

Such sauces should be used only during the final 10 to 12 minutes of cooking time since they often contain catsup or sugar and may burn during grilling.

Recipes for different kinds of marinades follow. Consider them a guide and feel free to make substitutions and create new ones on your own. There really is no right or wrong way: it is a matter of personal taste. This is a time when cooking can be fun!

Dry Rub

½ cup

10 bay leaves, coarsely ground
1 tablespoon black pepper
1 tablespoon dried basil
1 tablespoon garlic powder
1 tablespoon dried thyme
1 tablespoon dried leaf oregano
2 teaspoons ground cloves
2 teaspoons ground nutmeg
1 teaspoon ground mace
½ teaspoon ground cinnamon
½ teaspoon ground cumin

Combine all the ingredients and use as a dry rub for pork or game.

Achiote Paste

1¼ cups

⅓ cup ground annatto seeds
½ teaspoon cayenne pepper
3 cloves garlic, minced
2 tablespoons minced fresh cilantro
4 tablespoons safflower oil or clarified butter
4 tablespoons fresh lemon or orange juice
1 teaspoon coarsely ground salt

Make a paste of all the ingredients and use on fish, lamb, chicken or game.

Variation
- Add ¼ cup beef or lamb broth, preferably homemade (page 98) and use as a mop for beef or lamb when using indirect heat.

Barbecue Rub

½ cup

3 tablespoons salt
3 tablespoons black pepper or coarsely ground pepper
1 tablespoon garlic powder or 2 tablespoons finely minced fresh garlic
1 tablespoon Hungarian paprika
2 teaspoons minced dried bay leaf
1½ teaspoons cayenne pepper
1½ teaspoons dry mustard

Mix all the ingredients together and use as a dry rub in conjunction with a barbecue mop.

NOTE. You may use prepared Cajun spices in place of this combination for a spicy rub.

Barbecue Mop

2½ cups

1 cup stock (beef, veal, chicken or
    smoked game), pages 97–98
¼ cup wine or citrus, apple or
    pineapple juice
¼ cup Worcestershire sauce or
    teriyaki, soy or tamari
⅛ cup vinegar
⅓ cup oil (optional)
2 green chilies or dried red chilies,
    crushed (optional)
2 crushed garlic cloves or 2
    tablespoons minced onions
2 to 3 tablespoons bottled barbecue
    sauce or prepared condiment, such
    as Tabasco or Pickapeppa Sauce
Salt
Pepper (optional)

Mix together all the ingredients to use as a marinade. You may want to increase or decrease the acid ingredients depending on the meat.

High-Acid Marinade

1¼ cups

½ cup vinegar or red or white wine
⅓ cup lemon juice
1 white or yellow onion, minced
¼ cup Worcestershire sauce
Black pepper
Salt
3 tablespoons oil or clarified butter
½ cup stock or wine

Combine the first 7 ingredients and use as a marinade. Add stock or wine and use to baste during grilling.

Oriental High-Acid Marinade

1¼ cups

½ cup soy sauce
½ cup sake or ½ cup wine and 1
    tablespoon molasses
2 tablespoons chopped fresh ginger
¼ teaspoon cayenne pepper
1 tablespoon sesame oil

Whisk all the ingredients together and use as a spicy marinade. Use also to baste during grilling.

NOTE.   For a similar marinade, see fire shrimp (page 76).

Low-Acid Fruit Marinade

1¼ cups

½ cup fruit vinegar (page 153) or
  wine
1 cup fresh crushed berries
3 shallots, minced
1 clove garlic, minced
2 or 3 crushed peppercorns
Salt
3 to 4 fresh herb sprigs
⅓ cup oil
1 tablespoon honey (optional)

Combine the first 8 ingredients. Add honey if desired when basting.

NOTE.   Serve with a compound-butter using the same herb or herbs and 2 to 3 tablespoons of the fresh pureed berries. Sweeten with honey or maple syrup.

Suggested Combinations
- Blackberries, raspberries or cranberries with thyme
- Mango puree thinned with vinegar and basil
- Blackberries with sage
- Cranberries or raspberries with mint
- Port wine or reduced white wine with berries

Vinaigrette

1 cup

1½ cloves garlic, minced
1 shallot, minced
2 teaspoons grainy mustard (optional)
¼ cup vinegar (balsamic or sherry
  vinegar, herb- or fruit-flavored
  vinegar)
½ cup virgin olive oil or safflower oil
½ teaspoon salt
¼ teaspoon white pepper
Fresh herbs (optional)
Finely diced fruits or roasted peppers

Mix together the first 7 ingredients. Add minced fresh herbs to taste. Enhance with fruits or peppers and serve warm with grilled fish or poultry.

Herb Mayonnaise

¾ cup

1 egg yolk
1 teaspoon vinegar
1 teaspoon lemon juice
¼ teaspoon salt
Pinch of pepper
¾ cup oil
1 cup fresh herbs, finely minced

Blend the egg yolk, vinegar, lemon juice, salt and pepper in a blender jar until light and thick. With the motor running, add the oil in a slow, steady stream. Blend until thick. Stir in the minced herbs.

Smoky Chili Pesto

¾ cup

2 cloves garlic, minced
½ cup minced onion
3 ancho chilies, toasted, soaked and
    pureed (page 22)
1 tablespoon minced fresh cilantro
1 teaspoon minced fresh mint
3 tablespoons safflower oil
4 tablespoons vinegar or lime juice
Salt
Pepper
Beef, chicken or veal stock (pages
    97–98) to moisten

Mix together garlic, onion, chilies, cilantro, mint and oil. Add vinegar to use as a marinade for tough meats. Or brush on tender cuts, chicken or fish after seasoning with salt and pepper. Add stock to remaining herb mixture and use for basting.

Herb Pesto

¾ cup

2 cloves garlic, minced
1 cup minced fresh herbs (basil,
    tarragon, mint, rosemary)
2 tablespoons finely minced pine nuts
    or almonds
4 tablespoons virgin olive oil
Ground fresh or dried chilies
    (optional)
⅓ cup vinegar or lemon or lime juice
Salt
Pepper
Stock (pages 97–98) to moisten

Mix garlic, herbs, nuts, oil and chilies, if using. Add vinegar if using pesto as a marinade for tough meats. For tender cuts of meat or for chicken or fish, season with salt and pepper and brush with herb mixture. Squeeze lemon or lime juice directly on meat to avoid discoloring. Add stock to remaining herb pesto to use for basting.

NOTE. Add 2 tablespoons grated Parmesan cheese to the pesto to garnish grilled meals.

POULTRY

1. Poultry is the most versatile of meats, as it may be grilled, smoked or barbecued with a wide variety of seasonings or marinades, with equal success.

2. All poultry benefits from a rest, either after the initial cooking over high heat and before being moved to a lower heat to finish cooking or at least 10 minutes and up to 30 minutes (for a large turkey) after cooking.

3. Poultry grilled or cooked bone-in will have better flavor and be more moist. Boneless breasts are, however, convenient for large crowds and cook quickly. Boned whole chickens cook evenly over direct heat and are easy to serve.

4. Standard internal temperatures for all poultry are usually 175° F. or 185° F., which if adhered to would risk resulting in a dry, overcooked chicken. Remove when temperature is at 160° F. to 170° F. The temperature will rise 10 degrees as the meat continues to cook by retained heat. Chicken should be pink when slashed upon removal. White pieces cook faster than dark.

5. All poultry can be cooked initially on the grill for flavor, then finished in the oven or kept warm in a 200° F. oven until ready to serve. Baste often.

6. Stuff whole birds with herb sprigs, onions or garlic cloves, or a combination of apples, squash and onions.

7. Any marinade can be used on poultry. Suggested herbs and seasonings include: basil, tarragon, Mexican mint marigold, savory or chilies, dried or fresh. Leaner poultry or boneless breasts require a higher fat marinade or basting mop.

8. When spit-roasting, add 5 or 6 briquets to the fire to maintain temperature.

ITEM OR CATEGORY	METHOD	SPECIAL PREPARATION	MARINADE	TIPS	TIME	INTERNAL TEMPERATURE
Whole chicken	Indirect, spit or smoke		Any type, marinate for 2 hours or less with high-acid marinade; up to 12 hours for oil-based marinade or pesto.	1. Cook breast side down for first 45 minutes so juices run into breast. 2. Start on hotter part of grill then move to cooler part. 3. Baste often for moisture.	Indirect 15–20 minutes/pound (1½–2 hours) Spit 20 minutes/pound (1½–2 hours) Smoke 30–45 minutes/pound (3–5 hours)	Remove at: 160° F.–165° F.
Whole chicken, cut in half or in pieces	Direct, covered	Remove wings.	See general information for poultry (Number 7).	Begin meat side down and finish bone side down. Baste often.	Halves 15–20 minutes each side Small pieces 8–12 minutes total Large pieces 15–20 minutes total	Not applicable Not applicable
Boneless chicken breasts	Direct or foil-grill	Pound to flatten to an even thickness, if de-	Oil-based herb pesto or vinaigrette	For foil-grilling, boneless pieces can be cut up or	Direct 4–5 minutes total	Not applicable

Type	Method	Preparation	Seasoning / Marinade	Notes	Time	Temperature
(continued from previous page)				for 30 to 40 minutes and cooked with tomatoes, onions, mushrooms, herbs or a relish and a small amount of butter. Cook quickly, then let rest: chicken will continue to steam inside packet once taken off grill.	8–9 minutes (if flattened)	
Whole chicken, boneless	Direct, indirect	None	Season with salt and pepper or rub with olive oil and herbs.	Turn several times. Leave skin on.	Direct 20–45 minutes; Indirect 20 minutes	160° F.–165° F.
Whole turkey or breast halves, bone in	Indirect, spit or smoke	Flatten boned breasts, if desired.	Same as whole chicken	Same as whole chicken	Indirect 15–20 minutes/pound; Spit 8–10 minutes/pound (over hot coals); Smoke 30–45 minutes/pound	160° F.–165° F.
Whole domestic duck or goose	Indirect, spit or smoke	Score skin for self-basting.	Use high acid for flavor.	Watch for flare-ups. Tie legs together; twist wings under back.	Indirect: Duck 15–20 minutes/pound (1½–2 hours), Goose 25 minutes/pound (2½ hours); Spit: Duck 30 minutes/pound, Goose 18–25 minutes/pound; Smoke: Duck 35–45 minutes/pound, Goose 30–45 minutes/pound	145° F.–160° F. (medium rare)
Wild duck or goose	Indirect or smoke	Usually smaller and leaner than domestic birds with a stronger taste: if very lean, loosen skin and stuff herbs and ground fat under skin.	Use an acidic marinade, berries and wine or citrus.	Baste often.	Indirect 30–40 minutes for a 1½-pound bird; Smoke 1–1½ hours (hot smoke), depending on size of bird	Not applicable

ITEM OR CATEGORY	METHOD	SPECIAL PREPARATION	MARINADE	TIPS	TIME	INTERNAL TEMPERATURE
Domestic duck pieces, bone in	Direct	Remove wing.	Marinate for tenderness with a medium-acid marinade for 6 to 10 hours.	Start on hot part of grill and finish over lower heat. Leave skin on or use seasoned ground fat.	Direct 30–40 minutes	145° F–160° F.
Boneless duck breast	Direct	None	Same as duck pieces	Serve with berry and herb compound-butter	Direct 5–6 minutes (on very hot grill)	
Cornish game hens or poussins, whole or halves	Direct, indirect or smoke	Flatten frog style (see squab), if desired.	Stuff seasoned fat under loosened skin.	When using direct heat, grill skin side down first, finish with bones to grill.	Direct 20–30 minutes Indirect 40–60 minutes Smoke 45 minutes to 1½ hours (depending on temperature)	Not applicable

GAME BIRDS

1. Domestic or pen-raised game birds are more tender and less gamy and usually have more moisture than wild birds. Sometimes a stronger game flavor is desired and can be introduced with wine and berry marinades.
2. Small game birds can be grill-smoked briefly for flavor and then finished in the oven.
3. Always allow 10 to 15 minutes resting time to be sure birds are done. This can be done in a 200° F. oven to keep warm.

ITEM OR CATEGORY	METHOD	SPECIAL PREPARATION	MARINADE	TIPS	TIME	INTERNAL TEMPERATURE
Squab	Direct, indirect or split	Flatten frog style. Turn breast side up and break breast bone to flatten. Make a slit in the skin between the base of the breast and the thigh to tuck leg in. Tuck wing tips in or remove.	For flavor, use wine and berries or a sweet-and-sour marinade.	Serve with compound-butter of herbs and berries. See general information for game birds (Number 3).	Direct 8–10 minutes/side (16–20 minutes total) Indirect or spit 45–60 minutes	Remove at: 135° F.–155° F. (Squab should be served medium rare for best color and flavor.)

ITEM OR CATEGORY	METHOD	SPECIAL PREPARATION	MARINADE	TIPS	TIME	INTERNAL TEMPERATURE
Small game birds (dove and quail)	Direct or smoke	Flatten frog style.	Aromatic oil, salt and pepper	See general information for game birds (Number 3).	Direct 8–10 minutes / Smoke 35–40 minutes (hot smoke)	150° F. / 160° F.
Pheasant, capon and guinea hens	Direct, indirect, spit or smoke	Flattened, whole or halves	Aromatic oil, pesto or berry marinade	Cover with bacon or loosen skin and stuff with herbed fat; baste often.	Direct 15–20 minutes/pound 30–45 minutes / Indirect 20 minutes/pound / Spit 1½ hours / Smoke 30–45 minutes/pound	160° F. / Not applicable / Not applicable / Not applicable

RABBIT

ITEM OR CATEGORY	METHOD	SPECIAL PREPARATION	MARINADE	TIPS	TIME	INTERNAL TEMPERATURE
Rabbit: whole, pieces, boned loin, or boned leg meat	Direct, spit or smoke	None	Wine marinade for flavor or oil-based marinade	Baste often. Treat rabbit pieces like chicken pieces. Mustard sauces blend well.	Direct Small pieces: 12–15 minutes total Loin: 5–6 minutes on hot fire / Spit Whole: 1–1½ hours / Smoke Whole: 30–35 minutes/pound (medium heat)	Remove at: 160° F.–165° F.

VEAL

ITEM OR CATEGORY	METHOD	SPECIAL PREPARATION	MARINADE	TIPS	TIME	INTERNAL TEMPERATURE
Veal Chop	Direct	None	Marinate to season	Use thick 1-inch chops	Direct Rare: 8–10 minutes/inch Medium: 11-12 minutes/inch	Remove at: 125°F.

BEEF

1. The most tender cuts are steak, tenderloin and rib roast, boned or bone in. Cuts of uniform thickness (1 to 3 inches) are best for grilling over direct heat.
2. Always bring meat to room temperature before cooking.
3. Rub all cuts first with oil, then sear over direct high heat.
4. Turn frequently as this aids in continuous basting.
5. Suggested herbs and seasonings: all peppers and chilies, dried or fresh, garlic, onions, shallots, bay leaf, rosemary, tarragon, oregano and marjoram or a combination of oregano or marjoram with savory and thyme.
6. Dry seasoning rubs are excellent with roasts.
7. Let rest 10 to 20 minutes before carving and serving. This may be done in a 200° F. oven.

ITEM OR CATEGORY	METHOD	SPECIAL PREPARATION	MARINADE	TIPS	TIME	INTERNAL TEMPERATURE
Large roasts, irregular shapes	Spit roast	None	Marinate less tender cuts with a medium-acid marinade.	Sear first.	Boneless Rare: 12 minutes/pound Medium: 14 minutes/pound Well done: 15 minutes/pound Bone in Rare: 7–10 minutes/pound Medium: 13–15 minutes/pound	Remove at: Rare: 125° F.–135° F. Medium: 155° F.–160° F. Well done: 160°F.–165° F.
Chuck roast	Direct or indirect	Choose 1½–2½ inches thick.	Marinate with a high-acid marinade for 24 hours and baste with mop.		Direct 10–12 minutes/inch thickness Indirect 1–2½ hours total	
Brisket	Indirect or smoke	None	Marinate with high-acid marinade for 48 hours and baste often with mop.	Can start on grill and finish in 250° F. oven or sear first then wrap in foil to finish on indirect heat, covered.	Indirect 4 hours with grill covered TK 6–8 hours, carefully monitoring grill temperature at 180° F.–200° F. Smoke 4–5 hours	

Cut	Heat	Preparation	Marinade / Seasoning	Notes	Timing
Beef ribs	Direct (low heat), indirect or smoked	Simmer in broth for 10 to 15 minutes, then finish on grill	Use a high-acid marinade, 12 to 24 hours; baste with a barbecue mop during the last 10 minutes or with a sweet-and-sour sauce.	Sear first and finish in oven as an alternative. Baste often.	Direct 30–40 minutes / Indirect 3–4 hours over low heat
Steaks, tender cuts	Direct	Trim excess fat; slash fat to prevent curling.	Marinate for flavor, use dry seasoning rub for spice just prior to grilling.	Sear first on all sides.	Rare: 8–10 minutes/inch thickness / Medium: 10–12 minutes/inch thickness
Hamburgers	Direct		Use aromatic oil or dry seasoning rub just before grilling.	Avoid high-fat hamburger meat: burgers will fall apart. Or use barbecue plate to avoid fat fire.	Direct / Rare: 7–8 minutes total / Medium: 10 minutes total / Well done: 15 minutes total
Skirt steaks	Direct (high heat)	Pound lightly to even thickness.	Use high-acid marinade for 15 minutes and baste with thinned herb pesto.	None	Direct 2 minutes per side
Flank steak	Direct (high heat)	Pound to tenderize.	High acid for at least 15 minutes or up to 48 hours	None	Direct 8–10 minutes total
Tenderloin: roast or 2-inch thick steaks	Direct	None	Aromatic oil or dry seasoning rub and mop for flavor only	Sear first and/or sear first and finish in oven.	Direct / Rare: 9–10 minutes/inch thickness / Medium: 11–12 minutes/inch thickness / See general guide above
Brochettes	Direct		None	Use tender cuts only, ¾ inch thick.	Direct / Rare: 8–10 minutes/inch thickness (6–8 minutes total) / Medium: 10–12 minutes/inch thickness (8–9 minutes total)

LAMB

1. Lamb is wonderfully suited for grilling and barbecue and has enough fat to keep it moist and tender. The best cuts for grilling are the loin chops, tenderloin and leg, boned and butterflied. Chops should be at least 1½ to 2 inches thick.
2. Sear all cuts on all sides, including fat portions, first.
3. Herbs and seasonings for lamb: dried chilies (ground or combined with achiote paste), rosemary, cumin, mint, coriander and basil.
4. Make lamb *fajitas* using butterflied leg of lamb in place of the traditional beef skirt steak.

ITEM OR CATEGORY	METHOD	SPECIAL PREPARATION	MARINADE	TIPS	TIME	INTERNAL TEMPERATURE
Whole leg, bone in	Indirect in covered grill or spit roast	None	Rub with oil and seasonings and baste with herb pesto mop.	Sear first. Replenish coals every 45 minutes.	Indirect Rare: 16–18 minutes/pound Medium: 18–24 minutes/pound Well done: 24–28 minutes/pound Spit 1½–2 hours, depending on size	Remove at: Rare: 130° F. Medium: 150° F. Well done: 160° F.
Boneless leg	Indirect in covered grill or spit	None	Same as whole leg, bone in	Sear first.	Indirect 6–10 minutes/pound Spit 1–1½ hours, according to size	
Butterflied leg, boned and trimmed (4–4½ pounds), 2 to 3 inches thick	Direct or indirect on covered grill		Acid marinade, then seasoned rub or chili paste	Sear first and baste often for moisture.	Direct Rare: 11 minutes/inch thickness Well done: 14–15 minutes/inch thickness Indirect 16 minutes/pound	See general guide above
Loin or rib chops	Direct	None	Marinate for flavor.	None	Direct Rare: 10 minutes/inch thickness Medium: 12 minutes/inch thickness	See general guide above
Lamb shanks	Direct	Simmer first for 30 minutes, then reduce cooking time 10–15 minutes.	Marinate for four hours.	None	Direct 30–40 minutes	See general guide above

| Lamb kabobs | Direct | Place cubes on skewers, alternating with vegetables. | None | None | Direct For ¾- to 1-inch cubes: 12–15 minutes |

PORK

1. Pork and barbecue sauces or chili-based sauces and marinades are well matched. The best cut for quick grilling is the tenderloin. Pork is lean and does best with low heat and extended cooking time. Roasts and chops need a 10-minute rest before slicing to relax the proteins.
2. Grilled roast pork and thick pork chops are both excellent thinly sliced and served in barbecue sauce or barbecue sauce thinned with veal stock or natural pan juices.
3. Be careful not to overcook pork. Remove it before the desired internal temperature is reached. It will continue to cook by retained heat. Test again after 10 minutes.
4. Herbs and seasonings: ginger, sage, garlic, dried chilies, achiote, rosemary, anise, cumin, nutmeg, and thyme. Use marinades or basting mops with apple, citrus juices, tropical fruits or combinations of soy, orange and ginger.
5. Marinades: use high-acid for less tender cuts (shoulder, chops, loin roasts). Use a ground-fat and herb mixture during grilling. Sear meat first, then rub with oil and barbecue seasoning or salt and pepper.

ITEM OR CATEGORY	METHOD	SPECIAL PREPARATION	MARINADE	TIPS	TIME	INTERNAL TEMPERATURE
Boneless roast	Direct, indirect, spit roast or smoke	None	Marinate to tenderize and season.	Sear first. Baste frequently. Check roast at 150° F., close the dampers to kill the fire, then leave roast on the grill (covered) for 15 minutes or up to 1 hour.	Direct 25–30 minutes/pound; Indirect 2½–3 hours; Smoke 45–60 minutes/pound	Remove at: 155° F.–160° F.; 155° F.–160° F.; 155° F.–165° F.
Bone-in roast (butt, shoulder)	Direct, indirect	None	Marinate to tenderize and season.	Baste frequently.	Direct 1½–2 hours; Indirect 15–18 minutes/pound	Same as for boneless roast; Same as for boneless roast
Boneless tenderloin	Direct, indirect	None	To season	None	Direct 10–15 minutes/inch thickness; Indirect 18–25 minutes/inch thickness	155° F.–165° F.; 155° F.–165° F.

ITEM OR CATEGORY	METHOD	SPECIAL PREPARATION	MARINADE	TIPS	TIME	INTERNAL TEMPERATURE
Shoulder chops	Direct heat (low)	Slash fat, sear on all sides first.	Optional, to tenderize and season.	Baste frequently.	35 minutes/inch thickness	
Loin chops	Direct heat (low)	Slash fat, sear on all sides first.		Baste frequently with herb pesto.	35 minutes/inch thickness	
Baby back ribs	Direct, smoke (hot)	Parboil 15 minutes to reduce grilling time by 20 to 30 minutes.		Baste often for moisture, using barbecue sauce last 10 minutes.	Direct 35–50 minutes at 6 inches above coals Smoke (hot) 1–1½ hours Smoke (cold) 6–7 hours	
Sausages (uncooked)	Direct heat	None	None	May use barbecue plate to avoid fat fires.	15 minutes/inch	
Small suckling pig	Spit roast	None	None	Suitable for a large barbecue only	10 minutes/pound	

LARGE GAME

ITEM OR CATEGORY	METHOD	SPECIAL PREPARATION	MARINADE	TIPS	TIME	INTERNAL TEMPERATURE
Venison: steaks (1½ to 2 inches) or ground for hamburger	Direct, indirect or smoke	None	Use high-acid marinade for tenderness and flavor; season with chilies, garlic, berries and wine or port; baste with spicy barbecue sauces or sweet-and-sour sauces.	Rub with oil and sear first. The loin is best for grilling. Treat venison like an eye of round (a less tender cut of beef). Venison is very low in fat and moisture; compensate with lots of basting. Do not overcook as meat will get tough.	See guidelines for beef.	See general guide for beef.
Antelope	Direct	Grill loin; use other portions to grind for hamburger. Is generally less dry than venison.	Marinate for flavor with chili pesto.	Sear on all sides first. Treat like a small beef tenderloin.	Rare: 9–10 minutes/inch thickness Medium: 11–12 minutes/inch thickness	See general guide for beef. See general guide for beef.

Wild boar	Direct, indirect and smoke	Treat like pork loin.	High acid for tenderness and flavor or seasoned rub	Loin is best cut. Sear on all sides first. Baste often.	See guidelines for pork	See temperatures for pork.

FISH

1. Fish, like poultry, is moister if grilled whole, with the bone in; however many people prefer boneless fillets for convenience.
2. Firm-fleshed fillets are best for grilling. Thicker fillets (¾ to 1 inch) dry out less.
3. Fish that is going to be grilled must be fresh, not frozen, and as fresh as possible. Grilling intensifies all flavors.
4. Fish needs moisture and enough fat to compensate for its leanness during grilling, but it usually should not be marinated in oil for more than 30 minutes; it can become oil soaked, which spoils the flavor of grilled fish. Melted butter, clarified butter and olive oil are best, though light oils (safflower oils) are fine when used with spices and seasonings.
5. Suggested herbs and seasonings: basil, chilies (fresh or dried), cilantro, rosemary (alone or combined with mint), savory, tarragon and Mexican mint marigold.

ITEM OR CATEGORY	METHOD	SPECIAL PREPARATION	MARINADE	TIPS	TIME	INTERNAL TEMPERATURE
Whole lobster	Direct, indirect (with covered grill)	Crack large claws; remove sac in head. Slit lengthwise to flatten tail.	Baste with aromatic oil or clarified butter.	If grilling over direct heat, parboil first by immersing in boiling water and removing when water returns to a boil.	Direct 5–6 minutes, shell side down (after parboiling); 1–2 minutes, meat side down. Indirect 20–25 minutes	
Mussels, oysters, and clams in shell	Direct	Clean, scrub well.	None	None	Until shells open, 8–10 minutes	
Shrimp (shelled and deveined), scallops, oysters (shucked)	Direct, smoke, or foil-grill	Skewer smaller pieces.	Herb pestos, aromatic oils, or vinaigrettes	For foil-grilling, add roasted or smoked tomatoes or relishes or compound butters.	Direct 5–10 minutes. Smoke 30–45 minutes (hot smoke). Foil: 10 minutes	
Whole soft-shell crabs	Direct in foil tent	None	Seasoning salt or salt and pepper	None	45 minutes	

ITEM OR CATEGORY	METHOD	SPECIAL PREPARATION	MARINADE	TIPS	TIME	INTERNAL TEMPERATURE
Lobster tails	Direct	Crack shell; do not parboil.	Aromatic oil, vinaigrette or pesto	Accompany with relish.	5 minutes shell side down, 4–5 minutes more, basting often	
Firm-fleshed fish: shark, monkfish, halibut, sea-bass, orange roughy, mahi mahi	Direct	Trim away any black portions (cut away membrane on monkfish).	Vinaigrette, herb pesto, herbed mayonnaise, or aromatic oil for flavor	Accompany with relish.	9–10 minutes/inch thickness, (slightly longer for monkfish)	
Oilier firm-fleshed fish: salmon, bluefish, tuna, trout, catfish, whitefish, swordfish	Direct or smoke	Same as firm-flesh fish	Low acid to balance fat (just before grilling), vinaigrettes or herb pestos	Baste tuna and swordfish often for moisture.	9–10 minutes/inch thickness	
Whole fish	Direct, indirect or smoke	None	None	Baste often for moisture and flavor.	Direct 9–10 minutes/inch thickness Indirect 30 minutes Smoke 30–45 minutes (hot smoke)	
Flaky, delicate fish	Direct (in foil packets)	Season and wrap in foil.	Add herb butter, pesto, citrus, relish or julienne vegetables (carrots, jicama, celery, zucchini) to packs or stuff fish with vegetables or crabmeat.	Be careful not to cook too long; the fish continues to steam inside the pack after it is taken off the grill.	7–8 minutes	
Brochettes of firm-fleshed fish	Direct	Cut fish at least ¾ inch thick.	Aromatic oils for flavor and moisture	Baste often.	9–10 minutes/inch thickness	

RELISHES, CHUTNEYS AND SAUCES

Relishes and Chutneys

Tomato Relish *(Pico de Gallo)*
Grilled Tomato Relish
Tomato and Green Chili Relish
Three Tomato Salsa
Avocado Relish
Tomatillo Relish
Tomatillo and Pepper Relish
Apple-Potato Relish
Melon Relish
Papaya-Melon Relish
Papaya and Red Pepper Relish
Cranberry-Apricot Relish
Pomegranate-Pecan Relish
Cucumber-Onion Relish
Black Bean Relish with Jícama and Mango
Black Bean and Pepper Relish
Eggplant and Black Bean Relish
Grilled Corn and Pepper Relish
Green Chili and Corn Relish
Roasted Pepper and Chili Relish
Triple Pepper Catsup
Roasted Pepper Catsup
Red Onion Chutney
Minted Pear and Papaya Chutney
Papaya and Ancho Chutney
Tomato-Mint Chutney
Tomatillo-Mango Chutney
Berry Chutney
Pepper-Spiced Pears
Maple-Spiced Peaches
Mango-Orange Marmalade
Red Pepper and Orange Jelly
Hot Pepper Jelly
Ancho Pepper Jam

Sauces

Stephan's Smoked Tomato Salsa
Ranch-Style Tomato Sauce
Serrano Chili and Cilantro Sauce
Roast Bell Pepper Sauce
Corn Sauce with Chilies, Peppers and Mango
Ancho Chili Sauce
Ricotta Ranch Compote
Dean's Pecan and Virginia Ham Compote
Triple Mustard Sauce
Mayonnaise
Ancho Chili Mayonnaise
Chardonnay Mayonnaise
Hollandaise Sauce
Cilantro Hollandaise
Lime Butter Sauce
Pecan Butter Sauce
Tequila-Orange Butter Sauce
Tomatillo Butter Sauce
Veracruz Butter Sauce
Maple-Pecan Butter
Amy's Mexican Mint Marigold Pesto
Goat Cheese Sauce
Cheese and Pepper Sauce
Walnut Cream Sauce
White Barbecue Sauce
Jim's Barbecue Sauce
Hill Country Barbecue Sauce

Relishes and chutneys are part of our American culinary heritage. In the Southwest, tomato- or chili-based relishes called *salsas* are either the combination of diced fresh tomatoes, small hot chilies, onions and herbs (usually cilantro) called *pico de gallo* or a blended combination of fresh tomatoes and chilies. Many of the relishes in this book are based on the *pico de gallo* principle, but they are made from a variety of fruits, vegetables and seasonings besides tomatoes.

Inspired cooks and chefs have focused much of their creative energy on relishes. In contemporary Southwest regional cooking, these are often more like a little salad of crisp diced vegetables or a medley of tomatoes, chilies, onions and herbs or a colorful concoction of fruits and vegetables. Relish ingredients can be finely diced or coarsely diced or cut in julienne strips.

Relish may be used as an accompaniment for meat or poultry or eggs or added to a vinaigrette for basting grilled fish or poultry (page 210). Relishes often garnish pasta dishes, rice or risotto, beans and soup. They can also be drained and whisked into a butter sauce (pages 259–261).

Relish sometimes replaces a sauce; sometimes it is served alongside a light butter sauce or vinaigrette. If the relish has a tomato base and exudes juices, these are often added to the sauce or vinaigrette to pull the dish together.

Chutneys are cooked relishes. Mine are often cooked for less time than traditional chutneys, which are stewed for hours. Fruits such as mangos, papayas, pears and peaches are paired with fresh and dried chilies to create wonderful chutneys to serve with hot or cold meats.

Small fresh chilies are used in Southwest cooking the same way as black pepper or hot-pepper sauce is used in other regions, to give a peppery twist. But beware: fresh green chilies are notorious for their unpredictability. One serrano may be very hot and the next one, identical in shape and size, not so hot at all. Tomatoes and tomatillos, which are often used in relishes, are equally unpredictable. Some are sweet, some acid, some salt.

Once a relish is put together, therefore, it is necessary to balance the flavors to taste. If the tomatoes are not sweet enough, a little maple syrup or orange juice or a touch of sugar syrup may be needed. Chilies that are too harsh can be tempered with a little salt, oil, lime juice or vinegar. Chilies, which are low in acid, are often paired with onions or tomatoes. Sometimes a touch of oil is needed to soften strong flavors.

Relishes change in intensity of flavor as they age, particularly those that include beans, jícama or fruit. All relishes need to be tasted just before serving and adjusted to taste for spice and balance.

Relishes and Chutneys

TOMATO RELISH *(PICO DE GALLO)*

2 cups

This simple, uncooked relish is best when tomatoes are at their peak. If available, Roma tomatoes are good because of their thick flesh and rich flavor. Use it to accompany almost any grilled or roasted poultry, fish or beef.

1 tablespoon vegetable or olive oil
1 clove garlic, minced
1 shallot, minced (optional)
1 cup diced onion
1½ tablespoons minced fresh cilantro
6 firm, ripe tomatoes, peeled, seeded and cut in ¼-inch dice
Salt
White pepper

Heat the oil in a small skillet over medium heat. Add the garlic, shallot, if using, and onion and toss. Stir in the cilantro and remove from heat. Let cool.

Put the tomatoes in a mixing bowl. Add the onion mixture and toss gently to mix. Season to taste with salt and pepper. Serve warm or at room temperature.

Variation
- Add 2 avocados, diced, to the tomato-onion-cilantro mixture.

Yellow tomatoes may be small and pear-shaped or round like cherry tomatoes or standard size. They are slightly less acid than red tomatoes. They make colorful tomato relishes and salads when combined with red tomatoes. Use a fresh basil vinaigrette on a yellow and red tomato salad.

GRILLED TOMATO RELISH

2½ cups

Grilling the tomatoes gives this relish a subtle outdoor flavor that is excellent with grilled meats. You could also serve the relish with egg dishes or fish or poultry or use it to garnish soups.

4 large ripe tomatoes, left intact
½ cup unsalted tomato juice
¼ cup diced green bell pepper
½ cup diced seeded cucumber
1 serrano chili, seeded and finely minced
½ cup cilantro leaves, chopped
2 leaves fresh basil, chopped
Salt
Pepper

You can make a pureed sauce from any leftover relish that contains chilies, tomatoes, onions, tomatillos or bell peppers. Puree the sauce in a blender, then cook it briefly. If you want more tomato flavor or more herbs, add some tomato sauce and fresh minced herbs. Cool and refrigerate the sauce for up to 1 week.

Heat a grill to medium-hot and place the tomatoes on it for 6 minutes, turning once. Cool, then peel, quarter and remove the seeds. Chop the pulp and put it in a glass bowl. Stir in the tomato juice, pepper, cucumber, serrano chili, cilantro and basil. Season to taste with salt and pepper. Refrigerate at least two hours before serving. Stir once or twice before serving.

TOMATO AND GREEN CHILI RELISH

2 cups

This is my favorite fresh tomato and chili relish. I prefer to use poblano chilies but if they are not available, canned or fresh Anaheims are an acceptable substitute.

2 tablespoons safflower oil
½ small red onion, diced
3 poblano or Anaheim chilies, roasted, peeled, seeded and cut in ¼-inch dice (page 20), or 1 can (4 ounces) diced green chilies
6 ripe tomatoes, seeded and cut in ¼-inch dice
1 tablespoon red wine vinegar
Salt
White pepper
1 to 2 tablespoons minced fresh basil or cilantro

Heat the oil in a skillet over medium heat. Add the onion and sauté just until softened, 1 to 2 minutes. Stir in the chilies and remove from the heat. Stir in the tomatoes and vinegar. Season to taste with salt and pepper. Refrigerate at least 1 hour but no longer than 3 hours. Just before serving, stir in basil or cilantro to taste.

NOTE. If ripe tomatoes are not available, use whatever is available fresh and add 2 sundried tomatoes, diced. Taste the relish before seasoning as sundried tomatoes are salty. You may peel the tomatoes if you wish but it is not necessary for this relish.

THREE TOMATO SALSA

About 3 cups

Yellow cherry tomatoes make for a colorful, appealing salsa and the sweetness of red onion balances out the acidity of the tomatillos. This is a salsa that can be served with grilled meats or poultry or fish: drain the juices from the relish and use them to baste during grilling. It can also be used in a ceviche: drain the lime marinade and toss the fish with salsa.

2 tablespoons extra virgin olive oil
½ small red onion, peeled and diced
2 tablespoons white wine
8 tomatillos, husked, cored and cut in
    ¼-inch dice, or 3 firm, unripe
    green tomatoes, seeded and cut in
    ¼-inch dice
4 tomatoes, seeded and cut in ¼-inch
    dice
1 pint yellow cherry tomatoes, seeded
    and cut in ¼-inch dice
Salt
Coarsely ground white pepper
6 sprigs fresh basil, minced

Heat the oil in a medium skillet over medium-high heat. Add the onion and cook 1 to 2 minutes. Add the wine and tomatillos; stir to combine. Remove from heat. Add the red and yellow tomatoes to the skillet while the mixture is still warm but do not heat or cook. Season to taste with salt and pepper and stir in the basil.

Let the relish stand 15 to 20 minutes so the flavors will meld or refrigerate for up to 2 hours before using. If you refrigerate the salsa, use it within 6 hours. It will still taste good the next day but it will have lost its fresh, crisp characteristics.

NOTE. If yellow cherry tomatoes are not available, substitute yellow bell peppers, roasted and peeled (page 20), or mild green chilies.

AVOCADO RELISH

2 cups

This relish tastes and looks best if the avocados are cut just before serving. The onion mixture may be prepared in advance and kept at room temperature until you are ready to combine the relish. The slight touch of honey takes some of the sharpness from the poblano chilies. If the chilies are mild, as they sometimes are depending on where they are grown, replace the honey with a pinch of sugar. I like to use this relish with chicken or beef *fajitas*. It is also good on hamburgers or with grilled fish or shrimp.

1 tablespoon vegetable or light olive oil
1 medium red onion, chopped
6 tablespoons rice wine vinegar
1 teaspoon honey
2 poblano chilies, roasted, peeled and cut in ¼-inch dice (page 20)
2 medium-ripe avocados
Salt
Pepper

Heat the oil in a small skillet over medium heat. Add the onion and sauté until softened, about 2 minutes. Stir in the vinegar, honey and poblano chilies and remove from heat. Cool.

Just before serving the relish, peel the avocados and cut them into small pieces. Do not use any overripe parts. Place the avocado in one layer in a shallow dish and pour the onion mixture on top. Stir gently to combine, taking care not to mash the avocados. Season to taste with salt and pepper.

Variation
• Add 1 papaya, peeled, seeded and diced.

Haas avocados have bumpy skin that blackens as it ripens, with flavor superior to the Fuerte, which has a thin, green skin. It is always safer to buy avocados when firm, even rock hard, and let them ripen at room temperature in a dark place or in a paper bag. Do not refrigerate: use at peak of ripeness.

TOMATILLO RELISH

1½ cups

Tomatillos are generally used unripe, which is when they have their best green color and tart flavor. They make a lively relish that is good with fish, poultry or cheese. Adding mango gives the relish an unusual twist. You may want to add a pinch of sugar or a teaspoon of maple syrup if the tomatillos are very tart. Some people add 2 to 3 tablespoons of white wine when they serve this relish with a dish accompanied with wine.

1 tablespoon vegetable or virgin olive oil
1 shallot, minced, or ⅓ cup minced red onion
1 pound fresh tomatillos, husks removed, cored and quartered
3 pieces (½ inch) mango (optional)
2 teaspoons to 1 tablespoon fresh cilantro, minced
Salt
White pepper
2 serrano chilies, stemmed and finely minced (optional)

Use unripe tomatoes as a substitute for tomatillos in relish and chutney. Add lime juice to achieve the acidity characteristic of tomatillos.

Heat the oil in a small skillet over medium heat. Add the shallot or onion and cook until softened, about 1 to 2 minutes. Put the tomatillos and mango, if using, in a blender or food processor fitted with the metal blade. Process until pureed. Add the softened shallot and cilantro; stir to mix. Season to taste with salt and pepper. For a spicier relish, stir in the serrano chilies. Refrigerate the relish for up to 24 hours.

TOMATILLO AND PEPPER RELISH

1½ cups

Fresh tomatillos with a bit of shallot and cilantro make a crisp refreshing relish. Bell peppers add color and a nice blend of flavors.

1 tablespoon vegetable oil
1 shallot, minced
½ pound fresh tomatillos, husks removed, cut in ¼-inch dice
2 serrano chilies, stemmed, seeded and finely minced
½ red bell pepper, cut in ¼-inch dice
½ yellow bell pepper, cut in ¼-inch dice
1 teaspoon rice wine vinegar
Salt
Pepper
Fresh herbs such as basil or cilantro (optional)

Heat the oil in a small skillet over medium heat. Add the shallot and sauté until softened, about 2 minutes. Remove from heat and immediately stir in the tomatillos, chilies, and bell pepper. Stir in vinegar, then season to taste with salt and pepper. Add herbs to taste.

APPLE-POTATO RELISH

3 cups

A warm, cinnamon-flavored relish that takes just a short time to cook, this pairs beautifully with pork, game birds or Cornish hens. It is also good with homemade sausages.

4 small red potatoes (about 1 pound), peeled and cut in ¼-inch dice
3 tablespoons butter
1 tablespoon vegetable oil
1 small red onion, chopped
3 Granny Smith apples, peeled and cut in ¼-inch dice
½ teaspoon salt
¼ teaspoon white pepper
⅛ teaspoon cinnamon
Freshly grated nutmeg

Heat the potatoes with enough water to cover to a boil; boil until tender but still quite firm, about 8 minutes. Drain. Heat the butter and oil in a large skillet over medium heat. Add the onion and sauté until translucent, 2 to 3 minutes. Stir in the apples, potatoes, salt, pepper, cinnamon and nutmeg to taste and cook over medium heat until tender. Serve warm.

Small Pippin (Yellow Newton) apples have a wine-like flavor and make an attractive garnish for wild-bird or meat platters. They may also be baked and served with caramel sauce and toasted pecans.

MELON RELISH

5½ cups

This relish is particularly good with grilled fish, chicken or duck; it is a colorful, refreshing addition to a summer barbecue. The sweetness of the melon tends to dilute the hotness of the chilies; you may want to add another minced jalapeño chili if you prefer a hotter flavor. Begin 6 to 8 hours ahead of time to allow the flavors to blend.

½ medium cantaloupe, cut in ¼-inch dice (about 2½ cups)
½ medium honeydew, cut in ¼-inch dice (about 1¼ cups)
1 large cucumber, peeled, seeded and cut in ¼-inch dice
1 red bell pepper, cut in ¼-inch dice
2 green jalapeño chilies, seeded and cut in ¼-inch dice
Salt
White pepper

Combine the melons, cucumber, red pepper and jalapeño chilies in a 2-quart mixing bowl. Season to taste with salt and pepper. Refrigerate, covered, for several hours or overnight. Taste before serving, adding salt or pepper if needed.

NOTE.   If red jalapeño chilies are available, use ½ small red bell pepper for color and one red and one green jalapeño chili.

Southwest markets are usually filled with many different shapes and varieties of melons. Their cool, sweet taste goes well with the assertive flavors of regional foods and they pair well with grilled dishes, other fruits, tomatoes and tomatillos. Melons are best vine ripened. Choose firm, sweet-smelling melons.

PAPAYA-MELON RELISH

2½ to 3 cups

1 papaya, ripe and firm, cut in ¼-inch
    dice
½ honeydew melon, cut in ¼-inch
    dice
½ cantaloupe or Cranshaw melon,
    cut in ¼-inch dice
1 cucumber, peeled, seeded and cut in
    ¼-inch dice
½ red bell pepper, stemmed, seeded
    and cut in ¼-inch dice
Piece of gingerroot (1½ inches long),
    peeled and minced
1 to 2 tablespoons rice wine vinegar
Salt
White pepper
Sugar

Combine the papaya, honeydew, cantaloupe, cucumber, red bell pepper and ginger in a medium bowl. Add vinegar, salt, pepper and sugar to taste. Refrigerate for at least 8 hours before serving.

PAPAYA AND RED PEPPER RELISH

4 cups

Red peppers and papaya make a refreshing relish that has many uses. It goes well with grilled veal and poultry, as well as spicy sausages. It is a colorful appetizer when served with toasted French bread.

3 cups cider vinegar
1 cup sugar
2 yellow onions, peeled and thinly
    sliced
1½ teaspoons salt
6 red bell peppers, roasted, peeled
    and sliced (page 20)
2 jalapeño chilies, stemmed, seeded
    and cut in ⅛-inch dice
2 fresh papayas or mangos, peeled,
    seeded and cut in strips
Freshly ground black pepper

Heat the vinegar and sugar to a boil in a 2-quart saucepan. Add the onions and salt. Immediately remove from the heat and let stand for 15 minutes. Add the peppers and chilies and mix well. Transfer to a mixing bowl and refrigerate.

Just prior to serving, drain and gently mix in the papaya or mango strips. Season with black pepper to taste.

NOTE. For a different appearance, all the ingredients may be diced in ¼-inch pieces. I prefer using strips when the relish will accompany meats and dice when it will be served otherwise.

CRANBERRY-APRICOT RELISH

3½ cups

Dried fruits such as apricots are used in many Southwestern dishes. They combine quite well with cranberries, for example, and they help absorb some of the juices. Chopped pecans or diced cooked chestnuts may be added for even more substance. Diced small chilies may also be added for a hint of spice; they seem to intensify the berry flavor. Serve this relish with holiday ham or turkey or with game, such as venison, antelope or duck.

4 ounces dried apricots or sundried pears
3 seedless oranges
1 cup sugar
1 package (12 ounces) fresh cranberries, rinsed
1 Red Delicious apple, cored but not peeled, diced

Cut the apricots into small pieces and put them in a large bowl. Cut the peel and white pith from the oranges. With a small sharp knife cut the segments from the membrane and place in a small bowl.

Squeeze the juice from the membrane into a saucepan and heat to a boil. Add sugar, cranberries and ½ cup water. Reduce the heat to medium-low and cook just until berries begin to pop, about 5 minutes. Remove from the heat and let cool 5 minutes. Pour the cranberry mixture over the apricots and let stand 10 minutes. Stir in the oranges and apple. Refrigerate at least 2 hours. The relish will thicken as it cools.

POMEGRANATE-PECAN RELISH

2½ cups

Since pomegranates unfortunately are not available all year round, you may have to substitute fresh raspberries or cherries. When they are in season, on the other hand, you could add diced cooked chestnuts to the relish. Whichever way you make it, the relish goes well with ham, turkey or game.

1 tablespoon unsalted butter
1 cup toasted pecans (page 50)
1 tablespoon vegetable oil
1 small red onion, chopped
2 tablespoons red wine vinegar
3 pomegranates or 1½ pints fresh raspberries
1½ tablespoons chopped fresh basil or mint
Salt

Heat the butter in a small skillet over medium heat. Add the pecans and sauté until golden, about 1 minute. Cool and chop coarsely.

Using the same skillet, heat the oil over medium heat. Add the onion and cook until softened, about 1½ minutes. Add the vinegar and remove from heat.

Cut the pomegranates in quarters. Scoop out the seeds and put in a mixing bowl. Add the pecans, onion and fresh basil; mix well. Season to taste with salt.

CUCUMBER-ONION RELISH

4 cups

This crisp relish provides a nice contrast to grilled fish (particularly salmon) or poultry or cold sliced chicken or pork. When using to accompany spicy foods, drain and stir in a cup of sour cream.

2 tablespoons rice wine vinegar
4 tablespoons white wine vinegar
1 tablespoon minced gingerroot
1 tablespoon sugar
1 teaspoon celery seed
1 teaspoon mustard seed
1 medium onion, cut in ¼-inch dice
1 large cucumber, peeled, seeded and
   cut in ¼-inch dice (about 2½
   cups)
1 Red Delicious apple, cut in ¼-inch
   dice (about ½ cup)
Salt
White pepper

Heat the vinegars in a small skillet over medium heat. Add the gingerroot and sugar and simmer for 3 to 4 minutes. Stir in the celery seed, mustard seed and onion and toss to mix well. Remove from heat. Combine the cucumber and apple in a mixing bowl. Stir in the ginger-onion mixture and toss to mix. Season to taste with salt and pepper. Refrigerate for at least 1 hour or up to 24 hours.

BLACK BEAN RELISH WITH JÍCAMA AND MANGO

2 cups

If you cook the beans in a spicy ham stock (page 100), this relish is spectacular. The rich beans, hot chilies, and crisp jícama make an exciting combination. Serve with game or pork.

4 ounces jícama, peeled and cut in
   ¼-inch dice
2 fresh red or green jalapeño chilies,
   stemmed, seeded and cut in ¹⁄₁₆-
   inch dice
1 cup cooked black beans (page 271)
1 to 2 tablespoons champagne vinegar
2 to 3 tablespoons chopped fresh
   cilantro
Salt
White pepper
2 ripe, medium-firm mangos or
   papayas, cut in ¼-inch dice (see
   note)

Combine the jícama, jalapeño chilies, beans, 1 tablespoon vinegar, and 2 tablespoons cilantro in a glass bowl. Toss to combine and season to taste with salt and pepper. Refrigerate for at least 1 hour or up to 24 hours.

Cut the fruit no more than 1 hour before you plan to serve the relish. Gently mix into the relish. Taste again and correct seasoning, adding more vinegar, cilantro, salt or pepper as needed.

NOTE.   If the mangos or papayas are less than ripe or lack full fruit flavor, add 1 to 2 tablespoons fresh orange juice.

BLACK BEAN AND PEPPER RELISH

2 cups

The variety of colors and textures in this relish looks appetizing and is interesting with beef, game or grilled fish. I particularly like the subtle flavor of maple syrup with black beans and ham.

½ **yellow bell pepper, cut in ¼-inch dice**
½ **green bell pepper, cut in ¼-inch dice**
½ **red bell pepper, cut in ¼-inch dice**
1 **cup cooked black beans (page 271)**
2 **tablespoons olive oil**
1 **clove garlic, minced**
2 **shallots, minced**
⅓ **cup rice wine vinegar**
1 **tablespoon maple syrup**
1½ **tablespoons minced fresh cilantro**
Salt
Pepper

———

1 **teaspoon olive oil (optional)**
3 **tablespoons ham, cut in ⅛-inch pieces (optional)**

Put peppers and black beans in a shallow dish. Heat the olive oil in a small skillet over medium heat. Add the garlic and shallots and cook until soft, about 2 minutes. Add vinegar and maple syrup and remove from heat. Pour the mixture over the peppers, add cilantro and mix gently to combine. Season to taste with salt and pepper. Refrigerate the relish at least 2 hours. Stir several times to coat the ingredients with dressing.

If you are using the ham, heat the olive oil and sauté ham over medium-high heat until browned, about 2 minutes. Stir into the relish.

EGGPLANT AND BLACK BEAN RELISH

3 cups

Eggplant and black bean relish with chilies and peppers makes a savory accompaniment to lamb or beef.

1 large or 2 small eggplants (about 1 pound), peeled
Salt
1 tablespoon virgin olive oil
2 tablespoons vegetable oil
2 cloves garlic, minced
1 medium onion, cut in ¼-inch dice
2 Anaheim or poblano chilies, roasted, peeled and cut in ¼-inch dice (page 20)
2 red bell peppers, cut in ¼-inch dice
1 yellow bell pepper, cut in ¼-inch dice (optional)
1½ cups cooked black beans (page 271)
2 red tomatoes, peeled, seeded and cut in ¼-inch dice
1 tablespoon minced fresh basil
Salt
Pepper

Eggplant is delicious with spicy chilies. Grill eggplant and serve it with a bell-pepper catsup (page 240) and grilled squash.

Cut the eggplant in ¼-inch dice. Do not use heavily seeded portions. Put the eggplant in a colander and sprinkle lightly with salt. Fill a small mixing bowl with water and place on top of the eggplant to weigh down. Let stand 30 minutes, then rinse and blot dry.

Heat the oils in a large skillet over medium-high heat. Add the eggplant, garlic and onion and sauté until softened, about 3 minutes. Add the chilies, red and yellow peppers and sauté another 1 to 2 minutes. Reduce the heat to low and stir in the black beans, tomatoes and basil. Cook a few minutes to blend the flavors. Season to taste with salt and pepper. Serve warm or at room temperature.

GRILLED CORN AND PEPPER RELISH

3 cups

This relish will take on a light smoky flavor if the corn is grilled outdoors. If it is not practical or possible to do so, brown the corn under the broiling element of the stove. The relish is excellent with many kinds of poultry, fish or barbecued meat and is as good cold as it is warm or at room temperature.

5 ears fresh corn, shucked with silks removed
3 tablespoons safflower oil
2 tablespoons minced onion
3 poblano chilies, roasted, peeled and cut in ¼-inch dice (page 20), or 1 can (4 ounces) diced green chilies
1 red bell pepper, stemmed, seeded, and cut in ¼-inch dice
6 fresh tomatillos, husked, rinsed and cut in ¼-inch dice
2 teaspoons cider vinegar
½ teaspoon salt
⅛ teaspoon white pepper

Rub the corn lightly with oil. Heat a charcoal grill to medium hot. Put the cobs on a clean rack and grill, turning to brown lightly on all sides, for a total of 5 minutes. (If using the stove, preheat the broiling element; place the corn 4 to 6 inches from the element and brown on all sides until tender-crisp, about 4 minutes.) Cool the corn, then cut the kernels from the cobs.

Heat the remaining oil in a small skillet over medium heat. Add the onion and sauté about 2 minutes. Add the corn, chilies, pepper, tomatillos and vinegar and cook 3 minutes. Season to taste with salt and pepper. Serve warm or at room temperature.

NOTE. Substitute 1 medium green tomato for the tomatillo or omit altogether if neither is available.

GREEN CHILI AND CORN RELISH

6½ cups

Corn and green chilies pair up to make a simple little relish that could almost be a salad. This is the kind of relish you might use as a condiment with an entree salad, one of the warm salads or on a casual buffet table with various dishes to choose from.

2 tablespoons corn oil
16 green onions, sliced, white and green portions separated
5 cups corn niblets
3 Anaheim chilies, roasted, peeled, seeded and cut in ¼-inch dice, or ¾ cup diced canned green chilies, drained
½ cup mayonnaise, preferably homemade (page 257)
2 tablespoons sour cream
⅛ teaspoon cayenne pepper
Salt

Heat the corn oil in a medium saucepan over medium heat. Add the white portion of the green onion and sauté until barely softened, about 1 minute. Add the corn niblets and enough water to prevent sticking and cook until the corn is tender-crisp, about 4 to 5 minutes. Stir in the chilies, then remove from heat and cool. Drain off any excess liquid and put in a bowl. Stir in the mayonnaise, sour cream and sliced green onion tops. Season to taste with cayenne pepper and salt.

ROASTED PEPPER AND CHILI RELISH

1 cup

Here is an inviting relish that may be used with pâtés, sausages or grilled fish, with roasted meats or poultry. Vary the herbal seasoning according to what you are serving the relish with: rosemary, for example, would be a good choice with lamb sausages or chops. The relish is also good on a hamburger or with melted cheese in a *quesadilla*.

1 red bell pepper, roasted, peeled and
    cut in ¼-inch dice
1 green bell pepper, roasted, peeled
    and cut in ¼-inch dice
1 poblano chili, roasted, peeled and
    cut in ¼-inch dice
2 serrano chilies, stemmed, seeded
    and minced
2 tablespoons vegetable or virgin
    olive oil
½ medium yellow onion, diced
2 tablespoons balsamic or sherry
    vinegar
2 tablespoons rice wine vinegar
Salt
Pepper
2 teaspoons minced fresh basil or
    cilantro or 1 teaspoon fresh
    rosemary

Toss the peppers and chilies together in a mixing bowl. Heat the oil in a large skillet over medium heat. Add the onion and sauté just until softened, about 2 minutes. Add the balsamic and rice wine vinegars and heat to a boil. Pour over the peppers and mix well. Season to taste with salt and pepper. Stir in one of the herbs.

NOTE. Instructions for roasting peppers and chilies can be found on page 20.

TRIPLE PEPPER CATSUP

4 cups

This is a fiery hot condiment to use on all types of meat or with cream cheese on crackers. You will find many uses for it. You can, for example, stir ¼ to ½ cup into a marinade or add 2 to 3 tablespoons to a sauce for meat, game or poultry. Freeze in one-cup containers or process in sterilized jars for shelf storage.

3 tablespoons unsalted butter
4 serrano chilies, stemmed, seeded and chopped
2 garlic cloves, minced
1 white onion, peeled and chopped
2 poblano chilies, roasted, peeled and chopped (page 20)
8 red bell peppers, roasted, peeled and chopped (page 20)
1 can (14½ ounces) Italian-style tomatoes, chopped
6 tablespoons brown sugar
¼ cup lemon or orange juice
⅔ cup vinegar
1 tablespoon minced fresh basil
2 teaspoons dry mustard
¼ teaspoon ground allspice
¼ teaspoon ground cloves
¼ teaspoon ground coriander
½ teaspoon dried thyme
1 bay leaf
¼ cup warm virgin olive oil
Salt
Pepper

Heat the butter in a large saucepan or Dutch oven over medium heat. Add the serrano chilies, garlic and onion and sauté until onion is soft, about 5 minutes. Stir in the poblano chilies, red bell peppers, tomatoes, brown sugar, lemon or orange juice, vinegar, basil, mustard, allspice, cloves, coriander, thyme and bay leaf. Cook partially covered to prevent spattering, stirring several times, for about 15 minutes. Reduce the heat to medium-low and continue cooking until thick and chunky and most of the liquid has evaporated, about ½ hour. Put in a blender jar, add the oil and blend on high speed until smooth. Season to taste with salt and pepper.

Bay leaves have long been regarded as a symbol of wisdom and the wearer believed to be protected from accident or misfortune. California leaves are stronger and oilier than the European variety. The Mexican bay leaf is the mildest.

ROASTED PEPPER CATSUP

2 cups

This is a quicker, milder version of triple-pepper catsup that may be made with red or yellow peppers and used with French fries, grilled scallions (page 280) or other grilled vegetables such as eggplant and zucchini. It is important to roast and peel the peppers according to the directions on page 20 in order to capture all the natural juices. They are essential to a flavorful catsup.

4 red or yellow bell peppers, roasted, peeled and chilled (page 20)
1 tablespoon minced shallot or 1 tablespoon minced garlic
2 tablespoons virgin olive oil
3 tablespoons safflower oil
2 tablespoons lemon juice
1 tablespoon minced fresh cilantro or 1 tablespoon minced fresh Mexican mint marigold
Salt
Pepper

Pour all the juices from the peppers into a blender jar. Stem and remove the seeds from the peppers without rinsing them in water, then add the peppers to the blender jar along with the shallot or garlic, olive oil, safflower oil and 1 tablespoon lemon juice. Blend on high speed until smooth, about 2 minutes. Add the cilantro or marigold and then season to taste with salt and pepper. Add more lemon juice if desired. Serve warm or at room temperature.

RED ONION CHUTNEY

3½ to 4 cups

This is a versatile chutney that is very easy to make, even though the cooking time is long. Just remember to stir it several times as it cooks. Serve it warm or cold and dress it up with herbs, purple basil when available or green basil or mint. Rosemary, always good with onions, is another possibility.

2 to 3 tablespoons vegetable oil
1 large yellow or Maui onion, roughly chopped
4 large red onions, roughly chopped
2 large lemons, juice and peel
⅔ cup cranberry or pomegranate vinegar (page 153) or rice wine vinegar
½ cup light brown sugar
½ teaspoon ground cumin
Coarsely ground black pepper
Salt
Hot-pepper sauce
Minced fresh basil or mint or rosemary (optional)

Heat the oil in a large skillet or sauté pan over medium-high heat. Add the onions and sauté, stirring constantly, until golden brown, 10 to 15 minutes. Add lemon juice and peel. Stir in the vinegar, brown sugar and cumin. Cover and simmer over medium heat, stirring occasionally, for 45 minutes. Uncover and season to taste with pepper, salt and hot-pepper sauce. Cook uncovered, stirring occasionally, until all the liquid has evaporated and the onions begin to take on a glazed, caramelized look. Add fresh herbs if using. Cool and store refrigerated for up to 2 weeks.

Sweet onions are more perishable than other varieties and are best stored individually wrapped in foil. Those famed for sweetness are the Maui (available in winter only), Vidalia, Walla Walla and Texas onions. Use them raw or cooked.

MINTED PEAR AND PAPAYA CHUTNEY

1½ to 2 cups

I particularly like this chutney with roast or grilled lamb. It is also excellent with duck, pork and spicy sausages, smoked or fresh, especially those made with game. If you are using an underripe papaya that is quite firm, cook it along with the pears.

1 ancho chili pod, stemmed and seeded
1 tablespoon maple syrup
1 tablespoon butter
4 large firm pears, cored, peeled and cut in ¼-inch dice
2 shallots, minced
¼ cup fresh orange juice
¼ cup white wine
1 medium-ripe papaya, peeled, seeded and cut in ¼-inch dice
⅓ cup slivered toasted almonds (page 50)
20 leaves fresh mint, chopped
Salt
Pepper

Cover the chili pod with boiling water in a small bowl and let stand until the skin loosens from the pulp, about 30 minutes to 1 hour. Peel and place pulp and maple syrup in a blender and blend on high speed to puree.

Heat the butter in a medium skillet over medium-high heat to a sizzle. Add the pears and shallots and sauté 1 minute. Add orange juice, wine, and ancho chili pulp and continue cooking until the pears are tender-crisp. Remove the chutney from the heat and cool 5 minutes. Gently stir in papaya, almonds and mint. Refrigerate for 30 minutes to 1 hour. Season to taste with salt and pepper.

NOTE. Substitute 3 tablespoons ancho pepper jelly (page 250) for the ancho chili pod and maple syrup, if you have some on hand.

PAPAYA AND ANCHO CHUTNEY

2½ cups

Ancho chilies give a smoky flavor to this distinctive chutney. The cooking time is short, leaving the fruits intact. This is superb with roast lamb, poultry, game or pork or on a turkey sandwich.

3 ancho chilies, seeded and stemmed
½ cup packed brown sugar
1 tablespoon lime juice
1 tablespoon clarified butter
1 clove garlic, minced
1 small onion, chopped
2 Granny Smith apples, peeled and cut in ¼-inch dice
¼ cup seedless golden raisins
½ cup dry white wine
2 papayas, peeled and cut in ¼-inch dice

Heat the chilies and 2 cups water to a boil in a small saucepan. Remove from the heat and let stand, covered, until the skin begins to separate from the pulp, 20 to 30 minutes. Drain the chilies and remove as much of the skin as you can.

Place the chilies, sugar and lime juice in a blender or food processor and process until pureed.

Heat the butter in a large skillet over medium heat. Add the garlic, onion and apples and sauté 3 to 4 minutes. Stir in the raisins, chili puree and white wine and simmer for 5 minutes. Add the papaya and simmer, stirring occasionally, until chutney thickens but the fruit remains firm, 15 to 25 minutes. Cool and refrigerate until ready to serve. The relish may be served cold or at room temperature.

TOMATO-MINT CHUTNEY

1 cup

This chutney is cooked rather briefly compared to traditional ones that are sometimes stewed for an hour or more. The flavors remain fresh and bright and the relish colorful. It goes well with lamb, pork and duck.

½ cup seedless golden raisins, minced
½ cup white wine
1 mint sprig
2 tablespoons olive oil
1 small red onion, chopped
1 teaspoon brown sugar
¼ cup balsamic vinegar
1 large green tomato, seeded and diced, or 4 tomatillos, husked and diced
2 red tomatoes, peeled, seeded and diced
Salt
Pepper
Pinch cayenne pepper
6 sprigs fresh mint, chopped

Combine the raisins, white wine, ½ cup water and whole mint sprig in a small bowl and let stand for at least 1 hour. Strain and discard the liquid and mint sprig.

Heat the oil in a medium skillet over medium heat. Add the onion and sauté until translucent, about 3 minutes. Add brown sugar, vinegar and green tomato. Cook over medium heat until most of the liquids have been absorbed, about 2 minutes. Stir in the red tomatoes and cook an additional 2 minutes. Season to taste with salt, pepper and cayenne. Stir in raisins and chopped mint. Refrigerate for up to 12 hours.

Before serving, drain the juices from the chutney. Place them in a small skillet over medium heat and heat to a boil. Boil to thicken, about 2 minutes. Stir the thickened juices back into the chutney. Taste and adjust seasonings.

TOMATILLO-MANGO CHUTNEY

1½ quarts

This chutney derives a mild spiciness from the serrano chilies. It is delicious with cold meats, sausages, grilled poultry or game.

4 ripe tomatoes, peeled, seeded and chopped

20 tomatillos, husked and chopped fine

2 green or red bell peppers, chopped fine

1 large or 2 medium yellow onions, coarsely chopped

3 mangos, pitted, peeled and coarsely chopped

1 Granny Smith apple, peeled, cored and chopped

2 cups brown sugar

½ pint apple cider vinegar

2 teaspoons salt

2 whole cloves

2 teaspoons whole mustard seed

2 tablespoons tamarind paste (page 35) or 1 tablespoon crystallized ginger

5 serrano or jalapeño chilies, stemmed but not seeded, ground

3 cups fresh corn kernels, cut from the cob (optional)

Combine all ingredients except the corn in a large saucepan. Heat to a boil, then reduce the heat and simmer, stirring occasionally, for 2 hours. If using corn, stir the kernels into the chutney after 1¾ hours. Pack into sterilized jars and seal or refrigerate for up to 2 weeks.

BERRY CHUTNEY

3 cups

This chutney is barely cooked, so the berries stay plump and juicy. Ripe mango is added when the chutney is served, giving it a very fresh taste and appearance. It is wonderful with grilled Cornish hens, chicken, duck or any game birds. When grilling or roasting the poultry or birds, puree about ½ cup of the chutney in a blender, then use it either to make a butter for basting or for melting over the hot cooked birds or to whisk into the basting marinade.

1 shallot, minced
2 tablespoons unsalted butter
5 plums, peeled, pitted and diced
5 tablespoons brown sugar
¼ cup port wine
2 teaspoons balsamic or rice wine
vinegar
⅓ cup seedless raisins
2 cups blueberries, rinsed and
stemmed
⅓ cup raspberries or halved
strawberries
Salt
Pepper
1 ripe mango, peeled, pitted and diced

Tiny red or white onions and small champagne grapes are attractive and taste good in fresh chutney.

Heat the shallot and butter in a large skillet over medium-high heat. Cook until softened, then add the plums, brown sugar, port wine, vinegar and raisins. Simmer over medium heat for 10 minutes, until the sauce thickens. Stir in the blueberries and cook an additional 5 to 6 minutes, then remove from the heat and stir in the raspberries or strawberries. Cool to lukewarm. Season to taste with salt and pepper. Stir in the mango when ready to serve.

PEPPER-SPICED PEARS

2 to 2½ cups

Spiced fruits are a good accompaniment for grilled sausages or smoked meats. They have character enough to stand up to meat or to balance sausage.

1 cup white wine
1 orange, juice and peel
1¼ cups cranberry vinegar (page 153) or apple cider vinegar
¾ to 1 cup sugar
1 teaspoon minced gingerroot
3 serrano chilies, stemmed, seeded and cut in julienne strips
2 sticks cinnamon
4 unblemished pears, peeled, cored and sliced

Pears are wonderful in homemade chutneys, preserves or relishes. Poached, they are good with a caramel sauce and fresh raspberries. A pear ice can be spiced with hot chilies as pears go well with both fresh and dried peppers.

Heat the white wine and orange juice in a large skillet to a boil. Boil until reduced by half, 10 to 15 minutes. Cut the orange peel into julienne strips. Add the orange peel, vinegar, ¾ cup sugar, ginger, chilies and cinnamon to the skillet and heat to a simmer. Remove from heat and cool 2 minutes. Add the pears and spoon the liquid over them so all are well basted. Let stand to marinate, basting several times, for 45 minutes. Taste and add more sugar if needed. Refrigerate for up to 24 hours. Strain before serving.

NOTE. The strained liquid from the pears may be used in place of vinegar in salad dressings to be used on seasonal greens, warm or cold meat or poultry salads or fruit salads.

MAPLE-SPICED PEACHES

3 cups

These are delicious with sausages or meats as well as with waffles, pancakes, quiches and other brunch dishes.

1 piece gingerroot (about 2 inches), cut in julienne strips
1½ cups gewürztraminer or other white wine
1 cup pomegranate vinegar (page 153)
½ cup pure maple syrup
¼ cup diced red onion
5 whole cloves
2 cinnamon sticks
½ teaspoon ground allspice
8 large peaches or nectarines (about 4 pounds)
Sugar

Add julienne strips of gingerroot to fresh steamed vegetables or chop and use in marinades and vinaigrettes.

Heat the ginger and wine in a large skillet to a boil. Boil until reduced by half, 10 to 15 minutes. Add the vinegar, maple syrup, onion, cloves, cinnamon and allspice. Bring back to a boil, then remove from heat. Cool 2 minutes.

Peel and cut peaches or nectarines into ½-inch dice. Add to the syrup and spoon the liquid over them so all are coated. Marinate for 30 minutes, basting several times. Taste and add sugar, a tablespoon at a time, if need be. Refrigerate for up to 24 hours. Drain before serving.

MANGO-ORANGE MARMALADE

2 quarts

Oranges and mangos combine to make marmalade with a Southwestern touch. Grapefruit and tequila are another felicitous combination.

3 large navel oranges, cut in half and seeded
2 lemons, halved and seeded
4 cups sugar
1 large mango, peeled, pitted and diced

Use a food processor, meat grinder or food mill to grind the oranges and lemons. Put them in a large stainless steel saucepan or kettle and stir in sugar and 2 cups water. Let stand overnight or up to 24 hours at room temperature. Stir in the mango.

Put the saucepan over medium-high heat and heat to a boil, stirring constantly. Reduce the heat to low and cook, stirring occasionally to prevent scorching, for 45 to 60 minutes or until the marmalade begins to jell on the sides of the pan (200° F. to 220° F. on a candy thermometer). Spoon into sterilized jars and refrigerate for up to 1 month.

GRAPEFRUIT-TEQUILA MARMALADE

2 quarts

2 thin-skinned grapefruit, preferably pink
1 pomegranate, juiced
4 cups sugar
3 ounces tequila

Grind the grapefruit, using a food processor, meat grinder or food mill. Put the pulp in a large stainless steel saucepan and stir in pomegranate juice, sugar, tequila and 2 cups water. Let stand overnight or up to 24 hours, at room temperature.

Put the saucepan on medium-high heat and bring to a boil, stirring constantly. Reduce the heat to low and cook, stirring occasionally to prevent scorching, for 45 to 60 minutes or until the marmalade begins to jell on the sides of the pan (200° F. to 220° F. on a candy thermometer). Spoon into sterilized jars and refrigerate for up to 1 month.

RED PEPPER AND ORANGE JELLY

About 1 quart

A mildly spiced jelly that is flecked with orange peel and red pepper, this is good with cornbread, cold pork and pâtés or on top of cream cheese as an appetizer.

2 seedless oranges
2 large red bell peppers, seeded and stemmed
8 or 9 dried red chilies (arbol or japone chilies), stemmed and halved
5 cups granulated sugar
1¼ cups cider vinegar
3 ounces liquid pectin

Peel the oranges, including the white pith. With a sharp knife, cut away all the pith from several strips of orange peel. Cut into ¹⁄₁₆-inch dice. (You should have about 2 tablespoons.) Discard the rest. Trim away the fleshy portion from several strips of red bell pepper. Cut enough pepper to make 2 tablespoons of ¹⁄₁₆-inch dice. Set aside both diced orange and pepper to finish the jelly.

Cut the peeled oranges and remaining red pepper in 4 pieces. Use a food processor fitted with the metal blade to chop very fine. Transfer to a large saucepan.

Add the dried chilies, sugar and vinegar. Bring to a boil over high heat and boil for 10 minutes, stirring occasionally. Do not allow the jelly to stop boiling. Remove from heat and skim the foam. Strain, pressing hard to extract all the liquid.

Pour back into the saucepan and bring to a boil that cannot be stirred down. Add the pectin and boil, stirring constantly, for exactly 1 minute. Stir in the diced orange peel and red pepper.

Spoon the jelly into sterilized jars and seal. Invert for at least 45 minutes, until the jelly begins to set. Turn right side up and allow to cool. This will distribute the flecks of orange peel and red pepper evenly.

NOTE.   If the jelly does not jell, pour it back in the saucepan, bring it back to a boil and boil for 2 minutes. Stir in 1 ounce more of pectin and boil for exactly 1 minute. Pour back into jars, reseal and invert.

HOT PEPPER JELLY

About 1 quart

Really good pepper jellies are hard to find even in many specialty shops. Bits of finely diced green, red and yellow pepper seem to float in this pale green jelly. It would make a perfect gift.

Several strips green bell pepper
Several strips red bell pepper
Several strips yellow bell pepper or
**   small hot yellow pepper**
1 green bell pepper, stemmed, seeded
**   and coarsely chopped**
1 Granny Smith apple, peeled, seeded
**   and coarsely chopped**
8 jalapeño chilies, preferably fresh,
**   stemmed and halved**
1½ cups cider vinegar
5 cups granulated sugar
3 ounces liquid pectin

Trim away most of the fleshy part from the bell pepper strips, and cut skin in ⅛- to 1⁄16-inch dice. Set aside to add to the finished jelly.

Place the remaining pepper and the apple in a food processor fitted with the metal blade and process with 5 to 6 pulses to chop very fine. Transfer to a 5-quart saucepan. Add the jalapeño chilies, ¼ cup water, vinegar and sugar and heat to a boil over high heat. Stir occasionally and boil for 10 minutes. Do not allow the jelly to stop boiling. After 10 minutes, remove the pan from heat and skim the foam from the top. Strain, pressing firmly to extract all liquid from the peppers. Pour back into the same saucepan and bring to a boil that cannot be stirred down. Add the pectin and boil, stirring constantly, for exactly 1 minute. Stir in the diced pepper.

Pour the jelly into sterilized jars and seal. Invert for at least 45 minutes, until the jelly begins to set. Turn right side up and allow to cool. This will distribute the pepper flecks throughout the jelly.

ANCHO PEPPER JAM

1 pint

This pepper jam is used in much the same way as Hoisin or plum sauce is used in Chinese cooking. It adds a smoky, slightly sweet flavor to game ragouts, barbecue sauces, hearty bean soups, mayonnaise and chutneys.

12 to 14 ancho chilies
3 tablespoons fresh orange juice
3 tablespoons currant jelly
1 tablespoon cider vinegar
2 to 3 tablespoons maple syrup
Salt

Place the chilies in a large saucepan, add water to cover and heat to a boil. Remove from the heat and let stand covered for about 1 hour. Grasp the base of each chili and pull the stem to remove it and most of the seeds. Rinse to remove the remaining seeds and peel off as much of the skin as possible. Discard any liquid.

Place the orange juice, jelly, and vinegar in a small saucepan. Cook over low heat, stirring constantly, until jelly melts. Remove from the heat and pour in blender. Add the chili pulp and 2 tablespoons maple syrup and blend on high speed to combine. Season to taste with salt and add more maple syrup if needed. Pour into sterilized jars. Store for up to 1 week, refrigerated, or in the freezer for up to 3 months.

Sauces

STEPHAN'S SMOKED TOMATO SALSA

1½ cups

Stephan Pyles of the Routh Street Cafe in Dallas often smokes tomatoes and bell peppers for a relish or salsa. They have a slightly smoky flavor that goes well with both grilled meats and bell-pepper ice (page 324).

1½ pounds very ripe tomatoes
2 tablespoons virgin olive oil
1 small red bell pepper, diced
1 small green bell pepper, diced
1 small yellow bell pepper, diced (optional)
3 tablespoons diced onion
3 serrano chilies, stemmed, seeded and diced
1 teaspoon tomato paste (optional)
2 tablespoons minced cilantro or basil
Salt
Freshly ground black pepper

Allow unripe tomatoes to ripen on a sunny windowsill, then keep at room temperature. Meatier tomatoes are better for sauces and relishes, juicier ones better for salads.

Prepare a smoker with soaked chunks of aromatic woods such as mesquite, hickory, cherry or apple (page 192). Rub the tomatoes with oil and place on top of the grill surface. Cover the grill and smoke for 10 minutes. Peel the tomatoes, then cut in half and squeeze to remove the seeds. Dice the tomato pulp and set aside.

Heat the remaining oil in a large skillet over medium heat. Add the peppers, onion and serrano chilies. Cook for 3 minutes, then add tomatoes. If the tomatoes lack good red color, stir in tomato paste. Add cilantro or basil and season to taste with salt and pepper.

NOTE. If it is inconvenient to smoke the tomatoes, roast them and roast the peppers as well (page 20).

RANCH-STYLE TOMATO SAUCE

3 cups

The rich taste of the poblano chilies makes this an exceptionally flavorful tomato sauce to use with grilled meat, omelets or fish.

2 tablespoons safflower oil
1 red onion, chopped
2 cloves garlic, peeled
2 large poblano chilies, roasted, peeled and diced (page 20)
5 red tomatoes, peeled and diced, or 1 can (14½ ounces) Italian-style tomatoes
1 teaspoon fresh oregano or ½ teaspoon dried oregano
1 teaspoon minced fresh basil or ½ teaspoon dried basil
1 cup tomato sauce
1 tablespoon red wine vinegar
Salt
Pepper

Heat the oil in a medium saucepan over medium-high heat. Add the onion and garlic and sauté until translucent, about 5 minutes. Add the chilies, tomatoes, oregano, basil, tomato sauce and vinegar and cook over medium-low heat until the sauce thickens and the flavors blend, about 10 minutes. Season to taste with salt and pepper.

NOTE. The sauce keeps well under refrigeration for about 1 week. If it thickens, thin it with about ½ cup tomato juice when reheating. Taste and adjust seasoning.

SERRANO CHILI AND CILANTRO SAUCE

5 cups

This is a rich, creamy, and subtly spiced sauce that is good with shellfish, grilled fish or poultry.

2 shallots, quartered
3 garlic cloves, cut in half
6 serrano chilies, stemmed and seeded
2 cups heavy cream
3 tablespoons all-purpose flour
2 small bunches fresh cilantro leaves, rinsed
5 spinach leaves, rinsed
3 cups chicken stock, preferably homemade (page 97)
Lime juice
Salt
Pepper

Put the shallots, garlic, chilies, cream, flour, cilantro and spinach in a blender jar. Blend on high speed until very smooth. Stir the cream mixture into the chicken stock. Cook over medium heat, stirring constantly, until the sauce is smooth and coats a spoon, about 3 to 4 minutes. Season to taste with fresh lime juice, salt and pepper.

NOTE. If using a canned chicken broth, bring two 14½-ounce cans of broth with 2 tablespoons chopped celery, 2 tablespoons chopped carrot, ¼ onion, sliced, and 2 parsley stems to a boil in a medium saucepan. Boil for 5 minutes, then strain and return to the same saucepan.

ROAST BELL PEPPER SAUCE

3 cups

Sauces made from bell peppers are colorful, light and full flavored. You can use either red, yellow or green bell peppers. When peppers are plentiful, use two sauces, each a different color, at the same time. They are particularly good with seafood and chicken or a special dish like the Santa Fe tortillas with Gulf crabmeat (page 71).

4 large red, yellow or green bell peppers, roasted, peeled and chilled (page 20)
1 clove garlic, chopped
1½ cups chicken broth, preferably homemade (page 97)
2 tablespoons all-purpose flour
1 tablespoon cornstarch
2 serrano chilies, stemmed and seeded (optional)
2 tablespoons tomato paste (see note)
¼ to ½ cup heavy cream
Salt
Pepper

All bell-pepper sauces and those made with bell peppers and chilies are naturally very low in calories. For a bell-pepper sauce lower in calories, omit the cream and blend with lemon juice and reduced chicken stock, using 1 to 2 teaspoons of cornstarch to thicken as necessary.

Cut the peppers in several pieces and place them in a blender jar. Be sure to add any juices that may have accumulated after roasting the peppers. Add the garlic, chicken broth, flour, cornstarch, serrano chilies and tomato paste, if using, and blend on high speed until very smooth.

Put the pureed peppers in a medium saucepan over medium-high heat. Stir in ¼ cup cream and cook, stirring constantly, until thickened, about 5 minutes. Add additional cream if necessary to make a sauce the consistency of heavy cream. Season to taste with salt and pepper. Strain the sauce through a fine strainer and then put it back in the same saucepan over low heat to keep warm until ready to use.

NOTE.   Use tomato paste only with red peppers.

CORN SAUCE WITH CHILIES, PEPPERS AND MANGO

About 2 cups

This is a light, creamy sauce with the rich taste of corn. The mango offsets that richness, yet blends in with the pepper and chilies. Serve it together with tomatillo relish (page 230) with grilled or poached fish.

4 ears white or yellow corn
2 tablespoons butter
1 shallot, minced
2 serrano chilies, stemmed, seeded and minced
¼ cup chopped onion
1½ cups heavy cream
2 teaspoons cornstarch
1 tablespoon diced roasted and peeled green chilies (Anaheim or poblano), page 20
1 tablespoon diced roasted and peeled red bell pepper (page 20)
2 tablespoons diced mango or papaya
1 tablespoon minced fresh herb, such as cilantro, basil or tarragon
Salt
Pepper

Cut the corn from the cob and set aside 1 cup to finish the sauce. Heat the butter in a large skillet over medium heat. Add the shallot, serrano chilies, onion and corn and sauté until the onion is translucent. Stir in ⅔ cup water and ½ cup cream. Cook for 8 minutes. Cool, then pour into a blender jar and blend on high speed about 1 minute. Strain and press to extract all the juices.

Pour the liquid into a saucepan. Whisk the cornstarch into the remaining cream, then stir it into the strained sauce. Cook over medium heat, stirring constantly, until thickened. Stir in the green chili, red bell pepper, mango, reserved corn and herb of choice. Season to taste with salt and pepper and remove from the heat.

To serve, pour some sauce on each dinner plate, enough to cover the bottom. Center the fish on top.

Variation

- To transform the sauce into a seafood bisque, omit the cornstarch and stir poached seafood (lobster or chunks of crab) into the finished sauce. Heat to warm.

ANCHO CHILI SAUCE

2 cups

The ancho chili gives the sauce a rich, smoky flavor that is well suited to game, beef, steaks, game birds or veal. You might also stuff corn crêpes with goat cheese and spoon the sauce on top.

2 tablespoons bacon fat or pork or duck fat
1 shallot, minced
1 clove garlic, minced
1 ancho chili, toasted and soaked (page 22)
3 tomatillos, quartered
3 cups beef or veal stock, preferably homemade (page 98)
3 tablespoons unsalted butter
Salt
Black pepper
Pinch cayenne pepper
¼ cup fresh corn kernels
2 tablespoons diced roasted and peeled red bell pepper (page 20)

Heat the fat in a medium saucepan over medium-high heat. Add the shallot and garlic and sauté until softened, about 1 to 2 minutes.

Put the ancho chili and tomatillos in a blender jar and blend on high speed until smooth. Add some of the stock if necessary to facilitate blending. Stir the blended mixture into the shallot and garlic, then add the rest of the stock and heat to a boil. Boil until reduced by about a third and thickened, 12 to 15 minutes. Strain, then return to the same saucepan over medium-low heat and whisk in the butter. Season to taste with salt, black pepper and cayenne pepper. Stir in the corn and bell pepper.

Variation
- For a creamier sauce, use ½ cup cream in place of the butter. Add it with the stock.

RICOTTA RANCH COMPOTE

3 cups

This refreshing combination of ricotta cheese and homemade crème fraîche seasoned with roasted peppers, jícama and cucumber is a perfect accompaniment to spicy fish or chicken.

½ cup ricotta cheese
1½ cups crème fraîche (page 112)
Salt
Pepper
1 tablespoon safflower oil
1 clove garlic, minced
½ cup peeled, seeded and diced cucumber
¼ cup diced jícama
¼ cup diced roasted red bell pepper (page 20)
¼ cup diced roasted yellow or green bell pepper (page 20)
½ cup diced papaya or mango
2 teaspoons minced fresh basil
1 teaspoon minced fresh mint

Stir the ricotta cheese into the crème fraîche and season to taste with salt and pepper. Heat the oil and garlic in a small skillet over medium-high heat until softened, about 1½ minutes. Stir the garlic, cucumber, jícama, roasted peppers, papaya or mango, basil and mint into the ricotta mixture. Serve immediately or refrigerate for up to 8 hours.

NOTE. Ripe cantaloupe melon may be substituted for papaya or mango.

DEAN'S PECAN AND VIRGINIA HAM COMPOTE

1½ to 2 cups

Dean Fearing has come up with a versatile and delicious compote that will turn a simple chicken breast into an elegant dish. It goes with everything from game birds to breakfast pancakes. Add wild mushrooms or roasted chestnuts for a compote that is sensational with turkey.

1 tablespoon vegetable oil
1 shallot, minced
½ cup Virginia or smoked ham, cut in
   ⅛-inch dice
1 cup toasted pecan halves
½ cup chopped fresh chanterelle or
   cèpe mushrooms or ½ cup
   chopped roasted and peeled
   chestnuts (optional)
2 to 5 tablespoons heavy cream
1½ to 2½ tablespoons maple syrup

Heat the oil in a medium skillet over medium heat. Add the shallot and ham and sauté 1 minute. Add pecan halves, mushrooms or chestnuts, if using, cream and maple syrup. (Use the greater amount of both cream and syrup if adding mushrooms or chestnuts.) Simmer over medium-low heat until almost all the liquid is gone, about 2 minutes. The pecans should be glazed but not caramelized.

NOTE. If fresh mushrooms are not available, substitute 1 tablespoon dried mushrooms. Cover them with boiling water and let soak for 30 minutes. Drain and chop.

TRIPLE MUSTARD SAUCE

1 cup

A versatile sauce that may be served warm or cold, and may be varied with different fresh herbs, this goes well with cold meats, poultry or seafood or on a mixed appetizer plate of smoked or grilled sausages, chilled seafood and crabcakes (page 80).

1½ cups heavy cream
2 tablespoons whole-grain mustard
1 tablespoon Dijon mustard, coarse-
   or fine-grain
1 tablespoon peppercorn mustard,
   Creole mustard or wine mustard
3 tablespoons unsalted butter, at
   room temperature
Salt
Pepper
2 teaspoons minced fresh herbs, such
   as dill, tarragon, basil, cilantro,
   garlic chives or chives

Heat the cream to a boil in a medium saucepan and boil over medium heat until thickened and reduced by half, about 8 minutes. Whisk in the mustards and cook over low heat for several minutes, then whisk in the butter. Season to taste with salt and pepper and add the fresh herb of choice. Serve the sauce warm or cold.

Garlic chives, also called Chinese chives or Oriental garlic, have full garlic flavors, with edible, slightly hot flowers. Leaves are broader, longer and flatter than common onion chives.

MAYONNAISE

2 cups

2 egg yolks
1 whole egg
1 tablespoon vinegar
2 tablespoons lemon juice
½ teaspoon salt
1 teaspoon dry mustard
¼ teaspoon white pepper
1¾ cups safflower oil

In a blender jar, blend the egg yolks, whole egg, vinegar, lemon juice, salt, mustard, and pepper until light and thick. With the blender running, remove the cover and very slowly add the oil in a slow, steady stream. Blend until thick.

ANCHO CHILI MAYONNAISE

1½ cups

I particularly like this on hamburgers but it is also good with chicken salad and seafood.

1 ancho chili, stemmed and seeded
1 serrano chili or 1 jalapeño chili,
    stemmed and seeded
1½ teaspoons dry mustard
1 clove garlic, minced
1 tablespoon lemon juice
1 tablespoon vinegar
½ teaspoon salt
2 whole eggs
¾ cup safflower oil
Leaves from 5 sprigs cilantro
    (optional)

Heat 1½ cups water in a small saucepan to a boil. Add the ancho chili and let it soak until you can peel off the skin, 20 to 25 minutes. Discard the skin and put the ancho chili pulp in a blender jar. Add the serrano chili, dry mustard, garlic, lemon juice, vinegar, salt and eggs. Turn the blender on and add the oil through the top. Add cilantro, if using, and blend until thick and smooth. Season to taste with more salt. Store in the refrigerator for up to 10 days.

Variation
- For jalapeño mayonnaise, omit the ancho chili and use 3 jalapeño or serrano chilies.

CHARDONNAY MAYONNAISE

About 1½ cups

You can vary the light wine flavor by using different wines. For a sweeter flavor, use Riesling or a Moselle wine.

⅔ cup chardonnay wine
1 shallot, minced
2 egg yolks
1 whole egg
2 tablespoons lemon juice
1 teaspoon dry mustard
½ teaspoon salt
¼ teaspoon white pepper
1 to 1½ cups safflower oil

Heat the wine and shallot in a saucepan over medium-high heat to a boil. Boil until reduced to about ¼ cup. Cool 5 minutes. Strain and pour the reduced wine, egg yolks, egg, lemon juice, mustard, salt and pepper in a mixing bowl. Slowly add the oil, whisking constantly and vigorously, until the mayonnaise is thick and emulsified. You would also have excellent results using a blender or food processor. Refrigerate the mayonnaise until ready to use. It keeps for about 2 weeks.

HOLLANDAISE SAUCE

¾ cup

2 egg yolks
2 tablespoons lemon juice
½ cup (1 stick) unsalted butter, melted (keep hot)
Salt
Pinch of cayenne pepper

In a blender jar, blend the egg yolks and lemon juice until thick and light. With the blender running, slowly add the hot melted butter. Continue to blend until thick. Season to taste with salt and cayenne pepper.

CILANTRO HOLLANDAISE

1¼ cups

This is very easy to make: it may be blended a day ahead and heated just prior to serving.

¾ cup (1½ sticks) unsalted butter
4 tablespoons lemon juice
1 teaspoon vinegar
2 egg yolks
1 small shallot, minced
Salt
1½ tablespoons diced roasted and peeled red bell pepper (page 20)
1½ tablespoons diced roasted and peeled poblano chili (page 20)
1 tablespoon minced fresh cilantro

Heat the butter in a small skillet over medium heat to melt. Put the lemon juice, vinegar, egg yolks, shallot and ¼ teaspoon salt in a blender. Blend on high speed, adding the melted butter through the top, until smooth and emulsified, about 15 seconds. Stir in the pepper, chili and cilantro. Season to taste with more salt if needed.

When ready to heat the sauce, put it in a medium saucepan over medium-low heat. Cook, stirring constantly, until the sauce melts and then thickens, about 5 minutes. Use immediately.

LIME BUTTER SAUCE

¾ cup

An intense, lime-flavored butter sauce, this goes well with grilled swordfish, tuna, grouper or orange roughy or with poultry. If you choose to serve a relish or relish accompaniment as well, the spicy melon relish (page 232) or avocado relish (page 229) would be a good choice. Prepare the sauce as close to serving time as possible.

1 shallot, minced
¼ cup lime juice
2 tablespoons white tarragon vinegar
2 tablespoons dry white wine
¾ cup (1½ sticks) unsalted butter, at room temperature
Salt

Heat the shallot, lime juice, vinegar and wine to a boil in a small saucepan for 3 to 4 minutes until reduced by half. Reduce the heat to low and let the skillet cool. Whisk in the butter, 3 tablespoons at a time. Do not let the sauce boil or it will separate. If it does start to break, add ½ to 1 tablespoon ice-cold butter or crushed ice to bring it back to a creamy consistency. Strain the sauce to remove the shallot. Season to taste with salt and serve immediately or keep the sauce warm over hot water, off the heat, or in a thermos for up to 1 hour.

PECAN BUTTER SAUCE

About 1 cup

This is a rich, nutty sauce that is as good with chicken as it is with fish. Add the natural juices from the chicken or fish to enhance the sauce.

1½ cups pecans, toasted and chopped (page 50)
1 cup heavy cream
¼ cup white wine
1 cup chicken or veal stock, preferably homemade (pages 97–98)
1 cup beef stock, preferably homemade (page 98)
1 mushroom, chopped
1 small piece carrot
1 large shallot, chopped
1 teaspoon tomato paste
1 sprig plus 1 tablespoon chopped fresh tarragon (see note)
3 tablespoons unsalted butter
Salt
White pepper

At least 1½ hours in advance, heat 1 cup pecans, cream and ½ cup water in a small saucepan to a boil. Boil for 5 minutes, then remove from the heat and let stand for 1½ hours or up to 2 hours. Strain and press all the liquid from the pecans; discard them.

Heat the wine, chicken and beef stock, mushroom, carrot, shallot, tomato paste and tarragon sprig to a boil. Boil until reduced to about ½ to ¾ cup, 8 to 10 minutes. Stir in the strained cream mixture, then whisk in the butter, 1 tablespoon at a time, over medium-low heat. When all the butter has been added, stir in the remaining pecans and chopped tarragon. Season to taste with salt and pepper. Keep the sauce warm in the top of a double boiler until ready to use.

NOTE.   If Mexican mint marigold is available, substitute it for the tarragon. Use slightly more mint marigold than tarragon.

TEQUILA-ORANGE BUTTER SAUCE

1 cup

Here tequila keeps the orange juice from tasting too sweet and the serrano chilies add just a hint of spice. The sauce is good on scallops, fresh grilled tuna, swordfish or shrimp. One of my favorite little meals is servings of four grilled shrimp with two miniature cornbread muffins, each on a plate filmed with this sauce and garnished with fresh corn.

1 shallot, minced
2 serrano chilies, stemmed, cut in half
   and seeded (veins intact)
⅔ cup fresh orange juice
¼ cup white wine vinegar
2 tablespoons tequila
¼ cup heavy cream
¾ cup (1½ sticks) unsalted butter, at
   room temperature
Salt
White pepper

Heat the shallot, serrano chilies, orange juice, vinegar and tequila to a boil in a medium skillet. Boil until reduced to ¼ cup, about 2 minutes. Strain and discard the peppers. (For a hotter sauce, let the peppers steep in the liquid for 10 minutes.) Return the strained sauce to the same skillet. Add the cream and boil until thickened, about 3 to 4 minutes. Reduce the heat to low and let the pan cool. Whisk in the butter, 2 tablespoons at a time, to make a smooth and creamy sauce. Season to taste with salt and pepper. Keep the sauce warm in a double boiler over hot water or in a thermos bottle until ready to use.

TOMATILLO BUTTER SAUCE

2½ cups

Tomatillos have a tartness that counterbalances the cream and butter, but they are not always consistent in flavor. You may need to adjust the amount of butter, salt and cilantro to maintain an intense tomatillo flavor. The sauce holds better than most butter sauces but is best used within several hours. Serve it with chicken or fish.

1 pound tomatillos, washed with
   husks removed, quartered
2 tablespoons minced fresh cilantro
2 serrano chilies or 1 jalapeño chili,
   stemmed, cut in half and seeded, or
   2 poblano chilies, roasted, peeled
   and seeded (page 20)
5 tablespoons heavy cream
1 large shallot, minced
2 tablespoons white vinegar
¼ cup white wine
¾ cup (1½ sticks) unsalted butter, at
   room temperature
Salt
Pepper

Place tomatillos, cilantro and chilies in a blender and blend on high speed until liquefied. Heat the cream, shallot, vinegar and wine in a medium saucepan to a boil. Add the tomatillos and boil until the cream is thickened, 3 to 4 minutes. Reduce the heat to low and cool the pan several minutes. Whisk in the butter, 2 tablespoons at a time, stirring constantly to make a smooth, creamy sauce. Season to taste with salt and pepper. Serve immediately or warm in a double boiler or reheat over low heat; the sauce does not break easily.

VERACRUZ BUTTER SAUCE

1½ cups

This delicious and unusual butter sauce uses some of the ingredients of a tomato-based Veracruz sauce; the richness of the butter tames the chilies. It is a good sauce to serve with poached or grilled fish or shellfish, poached oysters, catfish mousse (page 83) or crabcakes (page 80).

1 cup (2 sticks) unsalted butter, at room temperature
4 scallions, white part only, thinly sliced
1 shallot, minced
¼ cup dry white wine
3 tablespoons white vinegar
2 poblano chilies, roasted, peeled, seeded and cut in ¼-inch dice (page 20) or ¼ cup diced canned green chilies
4 stuffed green olives, chopped
½ cup peeled, seeded and diced tomatoes
1 tablespoon capers

Heat ½ tablespoon of the butter in a small skillet over medium heat. Add the scallions and sauté about 30 seconds. Set aside. Heat the shallot, wine and vinegar to a boil in a small saucepan. Boil until the liquid is reduced to about ¼ cup, 3 to 4 minutes. Turn the heat to low and let the skillet cool. Whisk in the butter, 2 to 3 tablespoons at a time. If the sauce starts to break, add a bit of crushed ice or ½ to 1 tablespoon ice-cold butter to bring it back to a smooth, creamy consistency. Strain the sauce and return it to the saucepan. Stir in the scallions, chilies and olives; drain the tomatoes and slice them in. Stir in the capers. Cook over low heat just long enough to warm all the ingredients. To keep the sauce warm, place it in the top of a double boiler over hot water on very low heat for up to 30 minutes, stirring occasionally.

MAPLE-PECAN BUTTER

1½ cups

Use this on muffins, pancakes or waffles. It is also surprisingly good on hot-water cornbread (page 310) or grits cakes (page 313).

¾ cup (1½ sticks) unsalted butter, at room temperature
¼ cup pure maple syrup
½ cup finely chopped toasted pecans (page 50)
½ teaspoon vanilla

Put the butter and maple syrup in a mixing bowl and beat with an electric beater until thoroughly creamed. Stir in the pecans and vanilla. Refrigerate until ready to use or up to 1½ weeks.

AMY'S MEXICAN MINT MARIGOLD PESTO

¾ cup

Amy Ferguson, chef at Baby Routh's in Dallas, likes to whisk this pesto into a butter sauce (pages 259–261) and serve it with grilled redfish. It may also be used to stuff a split chicken breast or season risotto or rice that is going to accompany poultry or game.

1 cup Mexican mint marigold leaves
½ cup toasted pecans (page 50)
2 tablespoons grated Parmesan cheese
¼ cup virgin olive oil
Pinch of salt

Put the mint marigold, pecans, cheese, olive oil and salt in a food processor fitted with the metal blade. Process until finely chopped. Keeps about 4 days, refrigerated.

NOTE.   If Mexican mint marigold is not available, substitute a combination of ⅔ cup tarragon leaves, ⅓ cup parsley leaves and ⅓ cup chervil leaves.

GOAT CHEESE SAUCE

2 cups

This is delicious over a smoky ancho-chili pasta (page 292) and julienne strips of smoked chicken or rabbit. It is also good with mushroom pasta and strips of ham.

1 clove garlic, minced
¼ cup white wine
¼ cup chicken stock, preferably homemade (page 97)
2 cups heavy cream
8 to 10 ounces goat cheese, preferably mild
Salt
White pepper
2 tablespoons grated Parmesan cheese (optional)

Heat the garlic, wine and stock in a medium saucepan to a boil. Boil for 3 minutes, then add the cream and heat to a simmer over medium heat. Whisk in the goat cheese, about 2 ounces at a time, stirring constantly. Season to taste with salt and pepper and add more goat cheese if desired. Stir in the Parmesan cheese if using.

NOTE.   Gorgonzola cheese may be substituted for the mild goat cheese. In that case, do not add Parmesan cheese.

CHEESE AND PEPPER SAUCE

4 cups

Here you may cut the peppers and onions in strips instead of dicing them, depending on the look you want the finished sauce to have. It is excellent over enchiladas filled with seafood, or with wild-rice crêpes (page 64) filled with seafood. You may also use it to dress vegetables such as cauliflower or broccoli.

1 cup white wine
1 cup heavy cream or half and half
1 cup milk
3 tablespoons all-purpose flour
3 tablespoons melted butter
4 ounces soft white cheese, such as Havarti or Monterey Jack, cut in cubes
4 ounces sharp Cheddar, grated
¼ cup minced onion
1 cup diced red, green or yellow bell pepper or a mixture
2 green chilies (poblano or Anaheim), roasted, peeled and diced (page 20)
¼ teaspoon cayenne pepper
1 tablespoon minced fresh parsley

Put the wine, cream or half and half, and milk in a 1½-quart saucepan and stir to mix. Heat to a boil. Pour 2 cups of the hot liquid into a blender jar; add the flour and melted butter. Blend smooth on high speed, then pour the blended mixture back into the saucepan over medium heat. Add both cheeses and stir constantly until they melt and the sauce is smooth. Stir in the onion, bell pepper, chilies and ⅛ teaspoon cayenne pepper and cook, stirring constantly, for about 1 minute. Stir in the parsley. Taste and add more cayenne pepper if desired. Use immediately or cool and refrigerate for up to 3 days.

WALNUT CREAM SAUCE

2½ cups

The crisp, clean flavor of chayote (or cucumber) lightens this nutty cream sauce. Use it on pasta, or with chilies stuffed with meat (pages 66–68).

1 medium chayote, peeled and chopped, or 1 medium cucumber, peeled, seeded and chopped
1 leek, white part only, sliced
1 shallot, minced
1 cup chicken or turkey broth, preferably homemade (page 97)
3 cups heavy cream
4 tablespoons finely chopped toasted walnuts (page 50)
Salt
Pepper

Put the chayote or cucumber, leek, shallot and broth in a medium saucepan and heat to a boil. Boil for 5 minutes, then add the cream and walnuts. Continue to boil, stirring occasionally, until reduced and thickened, about 15 minutes. Use a fine sieve to strain the sauce. Season to taste with salt and pepper. Keep the sauce warm over low heat or refrigerate it. It keeps well refrigerated for 2 days. It will thicken then but it thins somewhat when reheated.

Variation
- If using on pasta, add about 1 tablespoon minced fresh basil when reheating the sauce.

WHITE BARBECUE SAUCE

1 cup

Barbecue sauce with a mayonnaise base is one of those unusual concoctions found in isolated areas of the South. It is served with warm or cold barbecued meats, on hamburgers or grilled meats or as a dipping sauce for fried onion rings or fried vegetables.

1 garlic clove, finely minced, or ¼
    teaspoon garlic powder
1½ tablespoons balsamic or red wine
    vinegar
1 teaspoon minced fresh thyme or ¼
    teaspoon dried thyme leaves,
    crushed
¼ teaspoon cayenne pepper
2 tablespoons bottled smoky
    barbecue sauce
1 teaspoon grainy mustard
Several drops Worcestershire sauce
1 cup mayonnaise, preferably
    homemade (page 257)
Coarsely ground black pepper

Stir all the ingredients into the mayonnaise, then add black pepper to taste. Refrigerate until ready to use.

JIM'S BARBECUE SAUCE

7 cups

Jim Nassikas of Stanford Court in California and Deer Valley Resort in Park City, Utah, uses this semi-sweet, spicy barbecue sauce to brush on meats or poultry during the final minutes of cooking. It can also be served as a condiment. It will char if you use it when grilling, because of the sugar and tomato catsup. I use Jim's sauce on brisket and hamburgers and to finish ribs.

¼ cup vegetable oil
1½ tablespoons finely minced garlic
1½ cups chopped onion
½ cup minced gingerroot
2 tablespoons prepared horseradish
2 tablespoons leaf oregano
1 teaspoon salt
2 tablespoons dry mustard
¾ cup red wine vinegar
3 cups tomato catsup
1 cup honey
½ cup dark brown sugar
¼ cup Worcestershire sauce
2½ tablespoons chili paste (page 23)

Heat the oil in a 2-quart saucepan over medium-high heat. Add the garlic and onion and sauté until soft, 4 to 5 minutes. Add the gingerroot, horseradish, oregano, salt and mustard and stir to combine. Deglaze the pan with vinegar and cook until thickened, 5 minutes. Add the catsup, honey, sugar, Worcestershire sauce and chili paste. Simmer over medium-low heat, stirring occasionally, for 1 hour.

HILL COUNTRY BARBECUE SAUCE

4 cups

This is a typical Texas barbecue sauce, which always incorporates good amounts of smoke-flavored drippings collected while brisket or ribs cook slowly. Liquid smoke is optional but it does add a bit of that smoky flavor that is pretty hard to come by without an elaborate set-up. Use this zesty sauce on anything from brisket to duck.

2 tablespoons vegetable oil
3 cloves garlic, minced
1½ cups chopped onion
2 serrano chilies, stemmed and
  chopped, or 1 jalapeño chili,
  stemmed and chopped
3 fresh tomatoes, peeled and seeded,
  or 1 can (14½ ounces) Italian-style
  tomatoes
Juice and 4 strips of peel from 1
  lemon
3 tablespoons brown sugar or maple
  syrup
¼ cup balsamic or red wine vinegar
½ cup Worcestershire sauce
3 cups beef stock, preferably
  homemade, from grilled or smoked
  meats (page 98)
1 bay leaf
1½ cups tomato catsup
2 teaspoons liquid smoke (optional)
2 tablespoons fresh oregano or ½
  teaspoon dried leaf oregano
Drippings from barbecued or grilled
  meats
1 teaspoon salt
1 teaspoon coarsely ground black
  pepper
Pinch of cayenne pepper

Heat the oil in a large saucepan over medium-high heat. Add the garlic, onions and chilies and sauté until softened, about 5 minutes. Stir in the tomatoes, lemon juice and peel, brown sugar or maple syrup and cook another 5 minutes. Add the vinegar, Worcestershire sauce, stock and bay leaf and heat to a boil. Cook the sauce, uncovered, over medium heat until it has reduced and thickened, about 35 to 40 minutes. Stir in the catsup, liquid smoke if using, oregano, drippings, salt and pepper. Cook about 10 minutes, or until the ingredients are well blended. Add cayenne pepper to taste, then cool the sauce for 10 minutes. Pour half the sauce into a blender jar and blend on high speed until smooth. Repeat with remaining sauce. Refrigerate for 2 to 3 weeks.

Variation

- For a sweeter sauce, add ¼ cup fresh orange juice, 3 additional tablespoons brown sugar and 2 whole cloves. Discard the cloves before blending.

ACCOMPANIMENTS

Vegetable Medley
Vegetable Sauté
Black Beans
Black-Eyed Peas
Fresh Corncakes
Goat Cheese Baked in Cornbread
Grilled Eggplant
Herbed Eggplant Ratatouille
Panfried Eggplant with Basil Salsa
Dean's Tobacco Onions
Roasted Peppers
Sweet-Potato and Jícama Pancakes
Fire Fries
Herb-Roasted Potatoes
Creamy Scalloped Potatoes
Grill-Roasted Potatoes and Onions
New Potatoes with Peppers and Brie
Grilled Scallions
Glazed Acorn Squash
Acorn Squash Stuffed with Wild Rice and Pecans
Zucchini-Walnut Gratin
Zucchini Fans
Panfried Summer Squash
Nutty Brown and Wild Rice
Wild Rice with Pears and Pistachio Nuts
Cornbread-Pecan Stuffing

Tamales

Vegetable Tamales
Blue-Corn Tamales
Shrimp Tamales with Corn Sauce
Sweet-Potato and Corn Tamales

Pasta

Ancho Chili Pasta
Jalapeño Pasta
Mushroom Pasta

Flans

Spinach Flan
Corn and Pepper Flan
Sweet-Potato Flan
Onion and Chili Flan

The traditional American meal used to be meat, a vegetable, potato and maybe bread but now there is growing emphasis on eating for enjoyment or entertainment rather than merely for sustenance. When peas or asparagus are at their peak nowadays, they might star as a first course rather than take a back seat. Juicy grilled chicken might follow, accompanied by several colorful relishes. Plump tamales might serve as an accompaniment or as an entree, with a relish or a thick, chunky vegetable sauce or both. An assortment of seasonal vegetables and black-eyed peas or a combination of beans served with fresh cornbread might make up a meal (a revival of the old-fashioned vegetable plate).

Certainly the increased availability of vegetables and the emphasis on whole grains and simple foods have created a new place for vegetables and a renewed appreciation for freshness. There is nothing more visually appealing than a plate of tiny, tender carrots and fresh garden peas or broccoli seasoned with slivers of fresh ginger or herbs. Thick slices of grilled or sautéed eggplant served with a bright, red pepper catsup or a tomato and green chili relish or black beans simmered in a savory broth are attractive and satisfying.

An accompaniment can be as simple as fresh goat cheese, baked in herbs and cornbread crumbs, on a bed of sautéed greens or as unusual as blue cornmeal pancakes chock-full of fresh corn and roasted peppers or as easy as a ragout of wild mushrooms simmered in shallots, basil and cream. There are 36 recipes for accompaniments in this chapter and other suggestions appear throughout the book. The possibilities are endless.

VEGETABLE MEDLEY

6 servings

A colorful assortment of fresh vegetables, both hot and cold, is the perfect accompaniment to any meat, poultry or fish. Pick vegetables that are at their peak of freshness, with an eye to color, texture and shape.

3 carrots, thinly sliced
1½ cups cauliflower florets
1 turnip or 1 rutabaga, cut in ½-inch dice
1 cup Sugar Snap peas or 1 cup asparagus tips or 1 cup broccoli florets
2 tablespoons butter
Salt
Pepper
6 red cherry tomatoes, quartered, for garnish

Heat enough water to cover all the vegetables and bring to a boil in a medium saucepan. Add the carrots and cauliflower and boil 1 minute. Add the turnip or rutabaga and cook another 1½ minutes. Add the peas or asparagus tips or broccoli last, cooking just until vegetables are tender-crisp but still have their bright color, about 1 minute. Rinse immediately under cold water and set aside until ready to serve.

Heat the butter and 2 tablespoons water in a large skillet to a boil. Add the vegetables and cook to warm, stirring frequently, about 2 minutes. Season to taste with salt and pepper. Arrange the vegetables on each plate and garnish with cherry tomatoes.

VEGETABLE SAUTÉ

6 servings

Vegetables sautéed quickly in butter keep their vivid color and their crunch. They may be cut in advance and kept refrigerated in sealed plastic bags for 4 to 5 hours before cooking.

2 large carrots, peeled, or 12 baby carrots, peeled
2 chayote, peeled
2 small or 1 large zucchini, unpeeled
1 red bell pepper, stemmed and seeded
1 cup broccoli florets
1 tablespoon unsalted butter
¼ teaspoon salt
Pinch cayenne pepper
1 tablespoon minced fresh dill or basil

Heat 4 cups water to a boil over high heat. Add the carrots and cook to blanch for 2 minutes. Cut carrots, chayote, zucchini and pepper into matchstick strips about 1/16 inch × 2½ to 3 inches.

Heat the butter in a medium skillet to a sizzle. Add all the vegetables and sauté until tender-crisp, about 2 to 3 minutes. Season with salt, cayenne pepper and fresh dill or basil. Serve immediately.

BLACK BEANS

6 to 8 servings

Black beans have a rich, earthy flavor and they may be used in many ways: in soups, bean salads, relishes and bean cakes. The beans need to be simmered in a flavorful broth. Try the spicy ham stock on page 100 or add bones from smoked meats or birds to the broth. If the beans are to be used for a relish, cook them just to the point of being tender. For accompaniments, cook them longer; for bean cakes, longer still.

1 pound (2 cups) dried black beans, well rinsed
2 tablespoons vegetable oil
1 pound ham hocks or ham bone or 4 to 5 ounces Canadian bacon
1 red onion, diced
2 cloves garlic, minced
½ large carrot, diced
2 bay leaves
1 tablespoon ground cumin
1½ teaspoons crushed peppercorns
2 serrano or jalapeño chilies, stemmed and cut in half (optional)
4¼ cups chicken broth (page 97) or spicy ham stock (page 100)
Salt

Soak the beans in water to cover overnight. Drain, discarding the water.

Heat the oil in a large stockpot over medium-high heat. Add the ham hocks, ham bone or Canadian bacon, onion and garlic and cook about 5 minutes. Add the beans, carrot, bay leaves, cumin, peppercorns, chilies if using, and broth. Simmer over medium heat, covered, for 45 minutes. If beans are to be used in relish, uncover and simmer until beans are tender but the skins are intact, 5 to 8 minutes. If they are to serve as an accompaniment, uncover and simmer until very tender but still whole, 10 to 15 minutes. If they are to be used to make bean cakes, uncover and simmer until the beans are very soft and begin to fall apart, 35 to 45 minutes.

When the beans are done, remove the ham hocks, ham bone or bacon and bay leaves and season to taste with salt. Cool the beans in their broth. Beans may be served as is or accompanied with a tomato and chili relish, sour cream or minced cilantro.

BEAN CAKES

6 to 8 servings

2 cups black beans, cooked as directed above
2 tablespoons bacon fat or 2 tablespoons freshly rendered pork fat
1 tablespoon sour cream
1 tablespoon minced fresh cilantro
1 tablespoon minced fresh basil
Vegetable oil or bacon fat for frying

GARNISH
Tomato and green chili relish (page 227)
Avocado relish (page 229)
Sour cream

Pour the beans and their liquid in a mixing bowl or into a food processor fitted with the metal blade. Add the bacon or pork fat, sour cream, cilantro and basil. Mash or process until pureed enough for the beans to be formed into cakes.

Heat the oil or fat in a large skillet over medium heat. Shape the puree into cakes and sauté on both sides until warmed. Serve bean cakes with one or both of the relishes and sour cream.

BLACK-EYED PEAS

6 to 8 servings

Black-eyed peas can be served in many ways—hot, cold in a relish or warm in salad (page 129). Fresh black-eyed peas are found nowadays in more and more parts of the country; they are far superior to the dried ones.

1 pound black-eyed peas, rinsed
6 ounces salt pork or smoked sausage
   or bacon
1 jalapeño chili, stemmed and minced
3 cloves garlic, chopped
1 onion, chopped
1 carrot, cut in 4 pieces
2 bay leaves
1 stick cinnamon or 1 teaspoon
   ground cinnamon
½ teaspoon black peppercorns
1 teaspoon salt

If using dried peas, soak in cold water to cover, overnight. Drain, discarding the water. Fresh peas do not need to be soaked.

Put the salt pork or bacon or sausage in a Dutch oven over medium-high heat. Add water to cover and heat to a simmer. Simmer for 15 minutes, then add the peas, jalapeño chili, garlic, onion, carrot, bay leaves, cinnamon stick and peppercorns. Continue to simmer for 1 to 1½ hours or until the peas are tender. Stir in the salt.

Discard the carrot, bay leaf and cinnamon stick. Reserve the sausage if using. Let it cool, then dice it and combine with peas. Refrigerate the peas and sausage in about 2 cups of the cooking liquid until ready to use, up to 3 days.

FRESH CORNCAKES

16 to 18 four-inch or 22 to 24 three-inch pancakes

These pancakes seem made to go with game birds, turkey, or chicken. Try them also with poached eggs and the cilantro hollandaise sauce (page 258) or tomato and green chili relish (page 227). The vegetables in these corncakes are quite crisp; if you prefer them softer, sauté them 2 to 3 minutes before adding them to the batter.

1 cup all-purpose flour
½ cup yellow or blue cornmeal
1 tablespoon sugar
1 tablespoon baking powder
½ teaspoon salt
1 cup milk
2 eggs, separated
¼ cup (½ stick) butter, melted
1 cup corn kernels
4 scallions, white part only, thinly
   sliced
¼ cup chopped red bell pepper
¼ cup roasted, peeled and diced
   green chilies (page 20)
¼ cup diced zucchini or yellow
   squash (optional)
Vegetable oil
Butter

Preheat the oven to 200° F. Combine the flour, cornmeal, sugar, baking powder, and salt in a mixing bowl. Stir in the milk, egg yolks and melted butter until mixed but not necessarily smooth. Fold in corn, scallions, red pepper, green chilies and squash if using. Beat the egg whites in a separate bowl until stiff. Fold the batter into the whites.

Heat equal amounts of oil and butter, beginning with 1 teaspoon each, in a medium skillet over medium-high heat. Drop batter into the skillet by the spoonful and cook until bubbles appear on the surface, about 1 to 1½ minutes. Turn and cook on the remaining side until golden brown. Keep the pancakes warm in the oven while continuing to prepare the rest. Use additional oil and butter for each batch.

NOTE.   Green chilies may be fresh or canned.

GOAT CHEESE BAKED IN CORNBREAD

10 to 16 rounds

A cornbread and nut coating is a nice counterpoint to mild, creamy cheese. Cut into 1½-ounce disks, the cheese is good as an appetizer that you might serve with a tomatillo relish (page 230) or a warm ancho chili sauce with tomatillos (page 255). Smaller 1-ounce disks are good for garnishing tossed salads or for combining with smoked meats, sausages and relishes on a sampler plate.

2 cups coarse cornbread crumbs, made from cornmeal muffins or cornbread (pages 310–312)
1 teaspoon cayenne pepper
½ cup toasted pecans or walnuts, chopped (page 50)
2 tablespoons minced fresh cilantro or parsley
1 pound mild goat cheese, cut into disks
¼ cup vegetable or extra-virgin olive oil

Combine the cornbread crumbs with cayenne pepper, chopped nuts and herbs on a large cookie sheet or plate. Cut or shape the cheese into sixteen 1- or ten 1½-ounce disks, depending on use. Set aside. Dip each piece of cheese first in oil, then in crumbs, lightly coating both sides. Transfer to a baking sheet and refrigerate for up to 24 hours.

Preheat the oven to 300° F. Place the cookie sheet on the top rack of the oven and bake for 5 to 6 minutes or until cheese is soft and warm. Remove and serve immediately.

GRILLED EGGPLANT

6 servings

Grilled eggplant is particularly good and goes well with almost anything. You can spice it any way you want.

2 medium eggplant (1 pound), unpeeled, sliced ½ inch thick
2 tablespoons salt, preferably sea salt
Garlic powder
Lemon or lime juice
Teriyaki sauce
¼ cup safflower oil
¼ cup butter, melted
2 teaspoons freshly ground black pepper
1 tablespoon minced fresh thyme

Arrange the eggplant slices in a single layer on a cookie sheet. Sprinkle lightly and evenly with salt, then put another cookie sheet on top and weigh it down with a heavy bowl or several books. Let stand for at least 30 minutes, then blot dry.

Sprinkle the eggplant evenly with garlic powder, lemon or lime juice and teriyaki sauce on both sides. Combine the oil, butter, pepper and thyme in a small bowl to brush on the slices while grilling.

Clean the grill surface and rub with an oil-dampened cloth. Prepare the grill, allowing the charcoal to burn down to a white ash, about 20 minutes. Brush the eggplant with oil and butter mixture and grill on both sides until lightly browned and tender.

Variation

- For spicier eggplant slices, use barbecue rub and mopping sauce (pages 208–209) to season and moisten the eggplant. Substitute barbecue rub for the salt. Season both sides again after blotting dry.

HERBED EGGPLANT RATATOUILLE

6 servings

Cooking each vegetable separately keeps the flavors intact. The generous fresh-herb seasoning creates a lively vegetable dish that is equally good hot or cold. Balsamic vinegar, with its mild, rich taste, is quite distinctive.

1 medium eggplant (½ pound), unpeeled
Coarse salt
1 red bell pepper
1 yellow bell pepper
1 green bell pepper
1 zucchini squash, unpeeled
1 yellow crookneck squash, preferably small, unpeeled
3 tablespoons virgin olive oil
3 tablespoons vegetable oil
1 red onion, chopped
1 clove garlic, minced
1 tablespoon fresh rosemary or ½ teaspoon dried rosemary
1 tablespoon fresh thyme or ½ teaspoon dried thyme
1 tablespoon minced fresh basil or ½ teaspoon dried basil
¼ cup balsamic vinegar
¼ cup beef broth
Salt
Coarsely ground black pepper

Quarter the eggplant lengthwise into long wedges; cut each wedge into 8 to 10 pieces. Sprinkle lightly with coarse salt and put pieces on a cookie sheet. Cover with another cookie sheet. Fill a large bowl with water and put it on top of the cookie sheet to weigh down. Let stand for 30 to 45 minutes, then blot dry. Cut the peppers and squash into bite-size wedges.

Heat 2 tablespoons olive oil and 1 tablespoon vegetable oil in a large sauté pan over medium-high heat. Add the onion and garlic and sauté until softened, about 3 minutes. Add the eggplant and sauté until brown on all sides, 5 to 6 minutes. Remove the onion and eggplant to a large bowl. Stir the rosemary, thyme and basil into the pan. Deglaze the pan with half the vinegar and broth. Add to the eggplant mixture.

Heat the remaining oil in the same pan over medium-high heat. Add the peppers and sauté until softened, 3 or 4 minutes. Stir in the zucchini and yellow squash. Cook until the peppers and squash are tender but still firm, 4 to 5 minutes. Stir in the remaining vinegar and broth, then add the peppers and squash to the eggplant mixture and toss to mix. Season to taste with salt and pepper.

You may serve the ratatouille immediately or refrigerate it for up to 3 days. Serve at room temperature or preheat the oven to 375° F. and reheat for 15 to 20 minutes and serve warm.

PANFRIED EGGPLANT WITH BASIL SALSA

8 servings

Sautéed eggplant, lightly breaded with herbs and toasted nuts, is delicious with a spicy tomato and basil salsa.

2 medium eggplant or 8 Japanese
    eggplant (1 to 1½ pounds),
    unpeeled
1 to 2 tablespoons fine sea salt

SALSA
1 tablespoon butter
2 shallots, minced
2 tomatoes, seeded and diced
2 serrano chilies, stemmed, seeded
    and cut in ⅛-inch dice
2 teaspoons minced fresh basil
Salt
Pepper

———

½ cup toasted walnuts, chopped
    (page 50)
2 cups fresh breadcrumbs
2 cloves garlic, minced
2 tablespoons minced fresh basil or
    2 teaspoons dried basil
1 tablespoon minced fresh parsley
1 teaspoon freshly ground black
    pepper
¼ cup heavy cream
2 large eggs, beaten
⅓ cup vegetable oil
⅓ cup butter
8 sprigs fresh basil for garnish

Cut the eggplant into slices about ¼ inch thick. Cut on the diagonal if using small Japanese eggplant. Put the slices on a cookie sheet and sprinkle with sea salt. Cover with wax paper and place another cookie sheet on top. Fill a large saucepan with water and put it on top of the cookie sheet to weigh it down. Set aside for at least 30 minutes, then blot dry.

For the salsa, heat butter in a medium skillet over medium-high heat. Add the shallots and sauté 1 minute, then add tomatoes, chilies and basil. Toss to combine, and remove from heat. Season to taste with salt and pepper. Set aside.

Preheat the oven to 200° F. Combine the nuts, crumbs, garlic, herbs and pepper in a bowl, then spread out on a cookie sheet. Beat the cream with eggs in a small bowl. Dip each eggplant slice first in the egg mixture, then in the crumbs and coat evenly. Heat equal amounts of oil and butter, starting with 1½ tablespoons each, in a large skillet or in two skillets over medium-high heat. Add the eggplant slices and sauté 1½ to 2 minutes on each side or until golden brown. Put cooked eggplant on a cookie sheet and keep warm in the oven while continuing to sauté the rest of the slices.

Serve each person 2 to 3 eggplant slices topped with salsa. Garnish each plate with a sprig of fresh basil.

DEAN'S TOBACCO ONIONS

6 servings

Dean Fearing, who was raised in Kentucky, calls these tobacco onions because when the onions are fried, they look like loose tobacco. Try them as an alternative to French fries with steak or hamburgers.

1 cup sifted flour
1½ teaspoons salt
½ teaspoon white pepper
½ teaspoon cayenne pepper
2 yellow onions, peeled and thinly sliced
1 red onion, peeled and thinly sliced
Peanut oil for frying

Combine the flour, salt and both peppers in a large bowl. Toss the onions in the flour mixture in 4 batches. Shake off the excess and lay onions out on paper towels.

Heat enough oil for deep-frying to 375° F. in a medium skillet or deep-fat-fryer. Fry the onions in 4 batches until golden brown, about 1½ to 2 minutes for each batch. Drain on paper towels.

Vidalia or other sweet onions make a savory sauce for game or smoked poultry. Simmer the onions in a game- or smoked-bird stock with a carrot, a celery stalk and herbs until reduced and thick, then strain and finish with unsalted butter and minced fresh herbs.

ROASTED PEPPERS

6 servings

In the Southwest, roasted peppers and onions accompany everything from *fajitas* to grilled fish. I particularly like the flavor of balsamic vinegar with peppers and I always use the juices from roasted peppers in the dressing: they add important flavor.

2 tablespoons vegetable oil
½ yellow onion, roasted, peeled and cut in strips
2 tablespoons cider vinegar
¼ cup balsamic vinegar
All juices from the peppers
¼ teaspoon salt
Freshly ground black pepper
1 tablespoon fresh thyme or rosemary (optional)
2 red bell peppers, roasted, peeled and cut in ¾-inch strips
2 yellow bell peppers, roasted, peeled and cut in ¾-inch strips
2 green bell peppers, roasted, peeled and cut in ¾-inch strips

Heat the oil over medium heat in a 10-inch skillet. Cook the onion strips until they just lose their crispness, about 1 minute. Add all the vinegar and juices from the peppers, and simmer 1 minute. Add salt, pepper, herbs if using and all the peppers. Remove from the heat and put the peppers in a bowl. Let them marinate at room temperature for 15 minutes. Refrigerate until ready to use. Serve the peppers in their dressing at room temperature.

NOTE.   Directions for roasting peppers are on page 20.

Serving Suggestions
- Use as an appetizer with warmed mild goat cheese or on top of toasted French bread.
- Serve with grilled foods, steaks, or *fajitas*.
- Combine with seasonal greens in a salad.

SWEET-POTATO AND JÍCAMA PANCAKES

10 four-inch pancakes

Combine sweet potatoes, cinnamon and allspice with crisp jícama for a potato pancake that is excellent with ham or spicy sausages. If jícama is not available, substitute turnips.

4 tablespoons butter
3 tablespoons minced yellow onion
1 medium sweet potato (8 ounces), peeled and shredded
8 ounces jícama, peeled and shredded
1 large egg, beaten
6 tablespoons all-purpose flour
⅛ teaspoon cinnamon
½ teaspoon salt
¼ teaspoon allspice
¼ teaspoon cayenne pepper
2 to 3 tablespoons vegetable oil

Heat 1 tablespoon of butter in a medium skillet over medium heat. Add the onion and sauté 2 to 3 minutes. Transfer to a mixing bowl. Add the sweet potato, jícama, egg, flour and seasonings; mix well. Let the batter rest for 10 minutes. Heat 2 teaspoons butter and 2 teaspoons oil to a sizzle in a large skillet or griddle over medium heat. Pour the batter by the spoonful in the hot skillet and cook on both sides until golden brown, about 5 minutes. Add additional butter and oil to the skillet as necessary to cook the rest of the pancakes.

The nutty, almost sweet flavor of parsnips goes well with sweet potatoes, pecans or walnuts and with carrots in a cold or hot vegetable dish.

FIRE FRIES

6 servings

4 medium russet potatoes (about 2 pounds), peeled
Peanut oil for frying
1 teaspoon cayenne pepper
2 tablespoons chili powder
1 teaspoon salt

Cut the potatoes in strips, about ⅛ inch × 2½ inches. Soak in cold water for 10 minutes. Drain and pat dry.

Heat enough oil for deep-frying to 350° F. in a medium skillet or deep-fat-fryer. Fry the potatoes in 3 batches until golden brown, about 1½ minutes for each batch. Drain on paper towels.

Blend cayenne pepper, chili powder, and salt. Sprinkle liberally over hot fries. Serve immediately.

HERB-ROASTED POTATOES

4 servings

These crusty, herb-flavored potatoes are a winner with beef, lamb or game.

12 to 16 tiny new potatoes (about 2 pounds), scrubbed

¼ cup virgin olive oil

2 tablespoons coarse salt

¼ cup fresh thyme or 4 teaspoons dried thyme

2 tablespoons fresh rosemary or 2 teaspoons dried rosemary

1 tablespoon fresh basil or 1 teaspoon dried basil

2 teaspoons freshly ground white pepper

4 sprigs of fresh rosemary or thyme for garnish

Place the potatoes in a bowl and sprinkle with oil, salt, herbs and pepper. Turn several times and let marinate for at least 2 hours or overnight.

Preheat the oven to 400° F. Place the potatoes in a shallow baking dish with all the marinade. Place in oven and turn the heat down to 350° F. and roast the potatoes, turning every 10 to 15 minutes, for 45 minutes to 1 hour, or until fork tender. Serve garnished with sprigs of fresh rosemary or thyme.

Variation

- Cut a cross in the top of each potato and sprinkle with ¼ cup of finely grated Romano cheese just before serving.

CREAMY SCALLOPED POTATOES

8 servings

Thinly sliced potatoes become very light and tender when baked with cream. They are delicious as is or you may add a light cheese sauce. For a Southwest touch, try the cheese and pepper sauce (page 263) or the goat cheese sauce (page 262).

2 shallots, peeled and chopped, or 2 tablespoons minced onion

2 tablespoons all-purpose flour

4 egg yolks

2 cups milk

1½ cups heavy cream

1½ tablespoons minced fresh parsley

4 baking potatoes, peeled and thinly sliced (see note)

Salt

White pepper

2 tablespoons minced fresh parsley for garnish

Preheat the oven to 350° F. Whisk the shallots, flour, egg yolks, milk, 1 cup cream and parsley in a mixing bowl. Pour ⅓ of the mixture into an oblong 2-quart casserole dish. Make a layer of potatoes on top of the cream. Sprinkle with salt and pepper, then add the remaining egg-milk mixture and potatoes in 3 or 4 layers. Press the top layer down to be sure all the potatoes are moistened. Cover with foil.

Fill a pan larger than the casserole dish half full with warm water. Place the casserole in the larger pan and bake for one hour. Uncover and pour the remaining cream on top and continue baking until the top is lightly browned, about 30 minutes. Sprinkle with additional minced parsley.

NOTE.   If potatoes are peeled and sliced in advance, set them aside in cold water to cover.

GRILL-ROASTED POTATOES AND ONIONS

6 servings

This is a good way to cook potatoes along with steaks or anything else that takes about 15 minutes to cook. You do not get any outdoor flavor to speak of since the potatoes and onions steam in their own juices with the herbs but it is an easy way to prepare everything outdoors.

6 medium to large white potatoes, scrubbed

1 large yellow or white onion, peeled and sliced ⅛ inch thick

6 thin slices butter

Salt

Pepper

3 fresh herb sprigs, such as rosemary or thyme

Minced rosemary or thyme for garnish

Slice the potatoes about ¼ inch thick. Put them in a saucepan and cover with cold water. Heat to a rolling boil, then remove from the heat, cover and let stand for 15 minutes. Tear off 3 strips (12 inches × 16 inches) of heavy-duty aluminum foil.

Drain the potatoes and arrange potato and onion slices on the foil. Dot with thin slices of butter and sprinkle with salt and pepper. Put an herb sprig on top, then fold edges in and seal. Cook the packages on the grill for about 15 minutes. Unwrap and discard the herb sprigs. Sprinkle with minced herbs and divide among 6 plates.

NEW POTATOES WITH PEPPERS AND BRIE

6 servings

Rich, creamy Brie with spicy peppers makes a nice contrast to the potato. The dish really dresses up simple grilled meat or poultry.

8 ounces Brie cheese, skin removed

18 tiny new potatoes (2½ pounds), white or red, scrubbed with peel left intact

1 or 2 jalapeño chilies, stemmed, seeded and diced

Salt

Black pepper

Put the Brie in the freezer so it will cut more easily. Put the potatoes in a medium saucepan, then fill ¾ full with cold water. Bring to a boil and boil until the potatoes are barely tender, about 8 minutes. Drain. Preheat the oven to 350° F. Put the potatoes directly on the rack to keep warm and finish cooking for up to 12 minutes. Cut the cheese into pieces. Toss with diced chilies.

Cut a cross in the top of each potato, season with salt and pepper and place on a heatproof plate. Top with cheese and chilies. Return to the oven for about 1½ minutes, just long enough to melt the cheese.

GRILLED SCALLIONS

6 servings

This is a simple recipe and yet it is incredibly delicious. Serve as an appetizer with fresh flour tortillas or French bread or serve with grilled meats.

6 bunches scallions
3 tablespoons safflower oil
Juice from 1 lime
Coarsely ground black pepper
Coarse salt
3 limes, quartered, for garnish

Rinse the scallions and remove any brown or wilted leaves. Do not remove whiskers. Trim the green ends to make them even and place in a glass dish. Add the oil, lime juice and black pepper and toss to coat.

Prepare a hot fire. Lay the scallions on the grill and grill until charred on both sides, about 5 to 6 minutes. Close the cover of a gas grill if necessary to increase the heat. Serve the scallions with coarse salt and lime wedges.

GLAZED ACORN SQUASH

6 servings

This method of cooking acorn squash is very quick and the texture is far more pleasing than when squash has been baked for hours. You will be surprised that such a small amount of brown sugar is enough to bring out the full flavor of the squash. If you want a garnish for flavor or color, use diced bell peppers or nuts. This is also a good way to cook pumpkin.

2 medium acorn squash
1 teaspoon salt
2 tablespoons butter
1 tablespoon light brown sugar,
   loosely packed
¼ teaspoon freshly grated nutmeg or
   ground coriander
¼ teaspoon white pepper
Juice from ½ orange (about 3
   tablespoons)
2 tablespoons diced red or green bell
   pepper or 4 tablespoons coarsely
   chopped toasted pecans (optional)

Cut the squash in half and seed it, removing the stringy center portion. Cut the squash into wedge-like sections, about ½ inch thick. Peel and place in a large skillet, and cover with cold water. Add salt and bring to a boil. Boil until fork tender, about 5 minutes. Remove the skillet from the heat and drain off all but 3 tablespoons of the water, leaving just enough to coat the bottom of the skillet. Add the butter, sugar, nutmeg and pepper and return the skillet to medium heat. Simmer, lifting the pan from the heat as necessary to prevent the squash from sticking; cook 3 to 4 minutes until nearly all the liquid has boiled down to a glaze.

Arrange the squash on a warm serving platter. Deglaze the skillet with orange juice and add the peppers or pecans if using. Leave the pan on the heat just long enough for the pan drippings to blend with the orange juice, then pour over the squash.

ACORN SQUASH STUFFED WITH WILD RICE AND PECANS

6 servings

The delightful combination of wild rice, apples and pecans gives acorn squash a rich and succulent flavor. It is an especially welcome addition to a game dinner.

3 small to medium acorn squash, cut in half and seeded
Salt
Coarsely ground black pepper
5 tablespoons melted butter
¼ teaspoon cayenne pepper
1½ tablespoons minced fresh parsley
1 shallot, minced
¾ cup toasted pecans, chopped (page 50)
2¼ cups cooked wild rice (page 284)
¾ cup minced unpeeled Red Delicious apple
18 toasted pecan halves for garnish (page 50)

Preheat the oven to 375° F. Slice a thin portion from the bottom of each squash half so it will stand. Put the squash in a buttered baking pan and sprinkle with salt and pepper. Combine 3 tablespoons melted butter with cayenne pepper and 1 tablespoon parsley. Brush on each squash. Cover with foil and bake until very tender when pierced with a fork, about 35 to 45 minutes.

Meanwhile, heat the remaining butter in a medium skillet. Add the shallot and pecans and sauté until shallots are soft and translucent, about 2 to 3 minutes. Add the rice, apple and remaining parsley and heat to warm, about 3 to 4 minutes. Spoon into the squash and garnish each serving with 3 pecan halves. Squash may be covered with foil and kept in a warm (200° F.) oven for 20 to 25 minutes.

ZUCCHINI-WALNUT GRATIN

6 servings

Zucchini with walnuts, mushrooms and blue cheese—what a splendid accompaniment for meat or poultry!

5 tablespoons unsalted butter
1 cup toasted and skinned walnuts, coarsely chopped (page 50)
2 shallots, minced
3 tablespoons minced fresh parsley
6 white mushrooms, chopped
4 medium zucchini, cut in matchstick strips
½ teaspoon salt
6 tablespoons crumbled blue cheese

Heat 2 tablespoons butter in a small skillet over medium heat. Add the walnuts, shallots and parsley and sauté a few minutes. Stir in the mushrooms, toss to combine and cook 1 to 2 minutes. Heat the remaining butter in a large skillet over medium-high heat. Sprinkle the zucchini lightly with salt and add. Sauté quickly until tender-crisp, 1 to 2 minutes. Mound the zucchini on a warm flameproof serving platter and put the walnut mixture on top. Sprinkle with cheese.

Preheat the broiler to the highest setting. Place the platter 6 inches from the broiling element and broil just long enough to warm the topping, about 30 seconds.

ZUCCHINI FANS

6 servings

This is an attractive way to serve zucchini. These fans are baked but they could be grilled (page 34).

2 tablespoons soft breadcrumbs or 1 tablespoon each cornbread and white-bread crumbs

2 tablespoons grated Parmesan cheese

1 tablespoon finely chopped pecans or hazelnuts

1 stick unsalted butter, at room temperature

1 tablespoon minced fresh oregano or basil or ¼ teaspoon dried leaf oregano

2 tablespoons minced fresh chervil or ½ teaspoon dried chervil

2 tablespoons minced fresh parsley or ½ teaspoon dried parsley

1 clove garlic, minced

¼ teaspoon cayenne pepper

6 small zucchini

Salt

Pepper

2 tablespoons lemon juice

Preheat the oven to 400° F. Put the breadcrumbs, cheese and nuts in a small bowl and toss to mix. Cream the butter with oregano or basil, chervil, parsley, garlic and cayenne pepper.

Drop the zucchini in boiling water and boil over high heat for 2 minutes. Remove and cool. Cut each zucchini lengthwise up to but not through the stem into 4 slices, each about ¼ inch thick. Carefully spread each slice with herb butter. Place zucchini on a buttered pan with the slices fanned out. Sprinkle with salt and pepper. Combine lemon juice with ⅓ cup water and pour in the pan. Bake until tender, about 15 to 20 minutes.

Remove the pan from the oven and turn on the broiler. Sprinkle the breadcrumb mixture over the squash. Melt remaining herb butter and drizzle over zucchini. Broil about 4 inches from the heating element until golden brown, about 1 minute. Serve the fans garnished with sprigs of fresh herb.

Squash blossoms are wonderful sautéed (lightly coated with seasoned flour first) or stuffed and deep-fried. Soak blossoms in ice water to make them open. Stuff with soft cheeses and fry. Serve with toasted hazelnuts or pistachio nuts.

PANFRIED SUMMER SQUASH

6 servings

Fresh summer squash, panfried with onions until lightly browned, is a delicious accompaniment to almost any meat or fish. Serve it with a *pico-de-gallo* type of tomato relish (page 226).

Safflower oil for frying
½ medium yellow onion, sliced thin
3 medium zucchini, sliced ⅛ inch thick on the diagonal
3 medium yellow squash, sliced ⅛ inch thick on the diagonal
Salt
Pepper

Heat 2 tablespoons oil in a large skillet over medium-high heat. Add the onion, zucchini, and yellow squash and cook over medium heat, turning frequently, until browned and crisp on both sides. Add additional oil if necessary. Season to taste with salt and pepper, then add a few drops of water, cover, and remove from heat. Remove the cover after 4 or 5 minutes and serve with the tomato relish.

NUTTY BROWN AND WILD RICE

6 servings

Fruit, nuts and fresh herbs give the rice a light, delicious flavor that blends quite well with fish, poultry or game. Vary the nuts and herbs depending on what is available fresh.

1 tablespoon vegetable oil
1 tablespoon butter
1 cup wild rice
½ cup brown rice
½ cup minced red onion
¼ cup minced celery
1 clove garlic, minced
2 cups chicken stock, preferably homemade (page 97)
½ cup chopped peeled apple or pear
½ cup pecans, walnuts or hazelnuts, toasted and chopped (page 50)
2 tablespoons minced fresh parsley or 2 tablespoons chopped fresh mint or basil
½ teaspoon dried thyme
Salt
Pepper
2 tablespoons unsalted butter

Heat the oil and butter in a medium saucepan over medium-high heat. Add the wild and brown rice, onion, celery and garlic. Sauté until the rice is golden and the onion translucent, about 5 minutes. Add the chicken stock and 1½ cups water and simmer over medium-low heat, covered, for 35 minutes. Stir in the apple or pear and nuts, cover again and continue to simmer until the rice is tender, about 10 to 15 minutes. Add additional hot water if all the liquid evaporates and the rice is not yet tender. Stir in the herbs and season to taste with salt and pepper. Stir in the butter just before serving.

WILD RICE WITH PEARS AND PISTACHIO NUTS

6 servings

This dish could be used either as an accompaniment or as a stuffing for poultry, boned lamb or Cornish hens. Use firm, ripe pears.

WILD RICE
2 tablespoons butter
¾ cup wild rice
⅓ cup minced red onion
½ celery stalk, diced
1 cup chicken stock, preferably
   homemade (page 97)

———

1 tablespoon butter
1 large or 2 small pears, peeled and
   cut in ¼-inch dice
1 cup toasted pistachio nuts, coarsely
   chopped
1 tablespoon lemon juice
1½ tablespoons fresh thyme leaves,
   chopped, or ½ teaspoon dried
   thyme leaves
1 tablespoon chopped fresh mint
   leaves
Salt
Cracked white pepper

Heat 2 tablespoons butter in a 2-quart saucepan over medium heat. Add the rice, red onion and celery and sauté until the onion is soft, about 5 minutes. Stir in the chicken broth and 1 cup water; cover and simmer until all but about ½ cup of the liquid has been absorbed and the rice is tender, 40 to 45 minutes.

Heat 1 tablespoon butter in a small skillet over medium heat. Add the pears, nuts, lemon juice, thyme and mint. Cook until the pears are tender, about 5 minutes. Stir the pear-nut mixture into the rice and cook over low heat an additional 5 to 6 minutes to combine the flavors. Season to taste with salt and pepper.

CORNBREAD-PECAN STUFFING

2½ quarts, enough stuffing for a 14-pound turkey or 12 six-ounce servings

You may use this stuffing for almost any birds, including your Thanksgiving turkey. Or you might make individual servings to accompany grilled chicken breasts, pork or lamb chops or fish. For a spicier stuffing use 2 or 3 finely minced jalapeño or serrano chilies.

8 cups cornbread (page 311)
6 English muffins
½ cup butter
8 ribs celery, finely chopped
2 onions, finely chopped
1½ cups toasted pecans, chopped
    (page 50)
2 red bell peppers, finely chopped
2 mild green chilies, roasted, peeled
    and diced, or 2 poblano chilies,
    roasted, peeled and diced (page
    20)
1 pound bulk pork or chorizo sausage
1 tablespoon fresh oregano or ¼
    teaspoon dried oregano
6 fresh sage leaves or ½ teaspoon
    dried sage
2 tablespoons fresh basil or ½
    teaspoon dried basil
2 tablespoons parsley or 1 teaspoon
    dried parsley
½ teaspoon black pepper
¼ teaspoon cayenne pepper
Salt
½ cup turkey or chicken stock,
    preferably homemade

———

Butter for the molds
2½ cups heavy cream

Break or crumble cornbread and English muffins into coarse crumbs and place in a large bowl. Heat 4 tablespoons butter in a skillet. Add celery, onions, and pecans and sauté until translucent. Add with the red bell peppers and chilies to the bread.

Sauté the sausage in a medium skillet over medium-high heat, to brown. Add the sausage, oregano, sage, basil, parsley, pepper, cayenne pepper, salt to taste and stock to the dressing and mix well. Melt the remaining butter and stir in.

For individual servings, preheat the oven to 350° F. Butter 12 six-ounce custard cups or soufflé molds and fill with stuffing. Pour about 2 tablespoons cream in each one. Bake for 20 to 25 minutes or until tops are well browned.

If stuffing a turkey or baking in a casserole, add cream to stuffing before baking. Bake casserole for 30 to 35 minutes in preheated 350° F. oven.

Tamales

Tamales are traditionally made from freshly ground *masa harina* with a bean or meat filling. In some regions, freshly ground corn is used instead to make a so-called green corn tamale. After many years of testing, tasting and teaching, my personal preference is for a dough made by combining freshly ground corn with cornmeal; it is a sort of compromise between Southern cornbread and Italian *polenta*.

Tamales made with fresh corn may be steamed in the oven or on top of the stove. They cook faster than their traditional *masa* cousins and are more tender. They are an excellent choice for entertaining as they may be held in a warm oven (150° F.) for 30 to 45 minutes or reheated in the oven. (Wrap them first in a damp towel, then in heavy-duty foil. Preheat the oven to 400° F. and heat for 10 to 12 minutes.) They may also be reheated in the microwave oven.

Preparing tamales is a time-consuming process that involves several steps besides preparing the dough filling. They are explained in detail here and referred to in the recipes that follow.

Soaking the husks.   Dried corn husks for tamales must be separated, cleaned and soaked prior to use. There will always be some rejects and many that are not standard size. Clean husks first under running water and remove all the silks. Discard any badly damaged ones. Place the rest in a large bowl of warm water and weigh down with a smaller bowl. Soak until flexible, about 2 hours. Drain and press on towels to remove excess moisture.

Wrapping the tamales.   Tamales may be wrapped in the husks several ways. For flavor and fun, I prefer to roll them and tie the ends like an English cracker. To do this, place the dough in the center of 2 overlapping husks, leaving about 2 inches at each end and 1½ inches at the sides. Roll one edge over, then roll the other edge on top to make a round, fat cigar shape. Cut strips from imperfect soaked husks to tie the ends. Push the dough towards the center very gently, tie one end and then the other. Fringe the ends.

Tamales may also be folded in a husk with one end left open or completely encased in a husk; the envelope is then tied with a strip of husk.

Steaming the tamales.   You may use a traditional steamer, a bamboo steamer, a fish poacher, or make your own steamer from a broiler pan or large baking pan with a wire rack. The pan must be deep enough to hold at least 1½ inches of water and the rack high enough to keep the tamales out of the water. Arrange the wrapped tamales in up to 3 layers on the rack, cover with a thin kitchen towel, and then seal tightly with foil. Simmer over medium to medium-low heat or place in a preheated 450° F. oven for 25 to 30 minutes. Check the water level after 15 minutes and refill with hot water if necessary. After about 20 minutes, unwrap a tamale to test it. The filling should be puffed, moderately firm, but tender. It should not crumble, but remember that tamales do firm up upon standing. Rewrap the tamale after checking. If you plan to hold the tamales for 30 minutes or so before serving, check the water level after 20 minutes, then cover tightly and turn the oven off. Leave the tamales undisturbed until ready to serve.

Traditionally, tamales have been served with other tamales, probably because they were so much work the cook was less than enthusiastic for accompaniments. I, too, like the tamale to be the star of the meal but more from an aesthetic point of view. Plain tamales may be served with grilled fish or poultry or a game ragout (page 164). Tamales made with vegetables or seafood may be served with a simple corn sauce. Steamed lobster is especially good served that way.

VEGETABLE TAMALES

12 tamales

Vegetables steam inside the tamale, adding additional flavor and texture to a dough made from cornmeal and freshly ground corn.

½ package dry tamale husks or 30 husks

DOUGH
1½ cups fresh corn kernels
¾ cup chicken stock, preferably homemade (page 97)
1 cup white cornmeal
½ cup yellow cornmeal
½ cup unsalted butter (1 stick), at room temperature
3 tablespoons vegetable shortening
1 teaspoon sugar
½ teaspoon baking powder
½ teaspoon salt
¼ teaspoon white pepper
½ cup diced zucchini
¼ cup diced red bell pepper
¼ cup diced carrot

SAUCE
2 tablespoons butter
1 shallot, minced
1½ cups corn kernels
1½ cups heavy cream
¼ cup diced red bell pepper
¼ cup diced yellow bell pepper or ¼ cup diced yellow squash
¼ cup diced zucchini squash
2 teaspoons minced fresh cilantro
Salt
Pepper

Clean and soak the husks as explained on page 286.

Put 1 cup corn kernels in a food processor fitted with the metal blade or blender jar. Process until the kernels are finely ground. Add some of the chicken stock if using a blender to facilitate grinding. Pour into a mixing bowl. Add the cornmeal, butter, and shortening. Beat to mix well. Combine the chicken stock, sugar, baking powder, salt and pepper in a small bowl. Pour it into the cornmeal batter and stir to make a thick batter. Fold in the remaining corn, zucchini, red pepper and carrot. Let the dough rest for 20 minutes, until firm enough to hold its shape.

Use 2 corn husks for each tamale. Overlap them and spoon about ½ cup dough in the center. Roll the edges inward to make a fat cigar shape. Tie the ends with string or strips of leftover or imperfect husks. Fringe the ends.

Steam on top of the stove or in the oven for about 25 to 35 minutes. Check water after 15 minutes and add more if necessary to maintain the steam level. After about 20 minutes, remove a tamale and open to see if it is done: the filling should be firm and fall away from the wrapper. Rewrap and return to pan. When done, tamales should be removed from heat and kept covered for up to 20 minutes before serving.

For the sauce, heat the butter in a saucepan over medium-high heat. Add the shallot and corn and sauté for 1 minute. Add ½ cup water and heat to a boil. Boil 3 to 4 minutes, then add the cream and continue to boil, stirring frequently, until the sauce thickens, about 8 minutes. Stir in the peppers, zucchini and cilantro and reduce the heat to low. Cook over low heat until the vegetables are tender, about 5 minutes. Season to taste with salt and pepper.

To serve, cut each tamale down the center with a sharp knife. Pinch the ends and gently pull the opening apart to loosen the filling. Spoon the sauce over the tamales, allowing it to spill onto the entire plate.

BLUE-CORN TAMALES

12 tamales

Blue-corn tamales are wonderful with game, beef or grilled poultry. They may be served as is or with the corn sauce from the recipe for vegetable tamales.

2 tablespoons minced onion
1¾ cups white corn kernels
¾ cup chicken stock, preferably homemade (page 97)
1 cup blue cornmeal
½ cup white cornmeal
½ cup unsalted butter (1 stick), at room temperature
4 tablespoons vegetable shortening, at room temperature
1 teaspoon sugar
½ teaspoon baking powder
½ teaspoon salt
¼ teaspoon white pepper
Pinch cayenne pepper

———

½ package dry corn husks or 30 husks, cleaned and left to soak for 2 hours (page 286)

Place the onion and ¾ cup corn kernels in a food processor or blender jar and process the kernels until finely ground. Add some of the chicken stock if using a blender, to facilitate grinding. Pour the corn mixture into a mixing bowl. Add the cornmeal, butter and shortening and beat to mix. Combine the chicken stock, sugar, baking powder, salt, pepper and cayenne pepper in a small bowl. Pour it into the cornmeal batter and stir to make a thick batter. Fold in the remaining corn kernels and let the dough rest for 20 minutes until firm enough to hold its shape.

Select two husks the same size and overlap the wide ends. Spoon about ½ cup dough in the center. Roll the edges inward to make a fat cigar shape. Tie the ends with string or strips of leftover husks. Fringe the ends.

Steam on top of the stove or in the oven (preheated to 450° F.) until the tamales are puffed, moist and firm, 25 to 35 minutes. Check after about 15 minutes to be sure the water has not boiled away; add more water if needed. Keep the tamales covered for up to 20 minutes before serving.

To serve, cut the tamales down the center with a sharp knife. Pinch the ends and gently pull the opening apart to loosen the filling. Accompany with corn sauce or a tomato and chili relish.

Variation
- Substitute 1 cup yellow cornmeal for the blue.
- Place a ½-ounce stick of Monterey Jack cheese in the center of the dough of each tamale.

SHRIMP TAMALES WITH CORN SAUCE

12 tamales

Tamales are a good dish for entertaining. The dough may be made 5 or 6 hours before filling the tamales, and the tamales may be rolled and refrigerated 12 hours before steaming them. They hold quite well covered after steaming and may even be reheated in a microwave oven. This sauce also reheats quite well. Don't ever be discouraged by the length of a tamale recipe!

½ package dry tamale husks, at least 30 husks

DOUGH
1 shallot, minced
1½ cups fresh corn kernels
¾ cup chicken stock, preferably homemade (page 97)
1 cup yellow cornmeal
½ cup unsalted butter (1 stick), at room temperature
4 tablespoons, vegetable shortening, at room temperature
1 teaspoon sugar
½ teaspoon baking powder
½ teaspoon salt
¼ teaspoon white pepper
Pinch cayenne pepper
½ cup diced red bell pepper
¼ cup roasted, peeled and diced poblano chili or green bell pepper (page 20)
1 cup chopped raw shrimp (about ½ pound)

SAUCE
2 tablespoons butter
1 shallot, minced
24 medium to large shrimp (1½ pounds)
¾ cup water and white wine mixed or water only
1½ cups corn kernels
2 cups heavy cream
¼ cup roasted, peeled and diced poblano chili (page 20)
¼ cup diced red bell pepper
1 tablespoon chopped fresh cilantro
Salt
Pepper

---

12 fresh cilantro sprigs for garnish

Following the directions on page 286, clean and soak the husks.

Put the shallot and 1 cup of the corn kernels in a food processor bowl fitted with the metal blade or in a blender jar. Process until the kernels are finely ground. If you are using a blender, add some of the chicken stock as well. Pour into a mixing bowl. Add the cornmeal, butter and shortening. Beat to mix well. Combine the chicken stock, sugar, baking powder, salt and white and cayenne peppers in a small bowl. Pour into the cornmeal mixture and stir to make a dough the consistency of thick cake batter. Fold in the remaining corn, the red pepper, chili and chopped shrimp. Let the dough rest until firm enough to hold its shape, about 20 minutes.

Select two husks of approximately the same size and overlap the wide ends in the middle. Spoon about ¼ cup of the dough in the center. Roll the edges inward to make a fat cigar shape. Tie each end with a piece of string or strip of husk and fringe them.

Steam on top of the stove or in a preheated (450° F.) oven until the tamales are puffed and moist and hold their shape, about 25 to 35 minutes. Check water level after 15 minutes and add more hot water if necessary. Keep tamales covered for up to 20 minutes before serving.

To prepare the sauce, heat the butter in a large skillet over medium heat. Add the shallot and shrimp and sauté for 2 minutes. Remove shrimp. Add the water and wine and corn to the skillet and cook over high heat until half the liquid evaporates, about 5 minutes. Add the cream and chilies and continue to cook over high heat, stirring often, until the cream thickens, 5 to 8 minutes. Add the red bell pepper, shrimp and cilantro. Season to taste with salt and pepper.

To serve, cut the tamales down the center with a sharp knife. Pinch the ends and gently pull them apart to loosen the filling. Place one tamale on each plate and spoon the warm sauce on top, allowing it to spill onto the plate. Garnish each serving with a sprig of fresh cilantro and fresh tomatillo relish, if desired.

SWEET-POTATO AND CORN TAMALES

12 tamales

The combination of freshly ground corn, cornmeal, and sweet potatoes makes a colorful and intriguing accompaniment to a fall meal. Serve these with ham or roast turkey.

½ package dry tamale husks or 30
   husks

DOUGH
1½ cups diced sweet potatoes (about
   1 pound)
4 tablespoons minced onion
1½ cups fresh corn kernels
¾ cup chicken stock, preferably
   homemade (page 97)
½ cup yellow cornmeal
1 cup white cornmeal
½ cup unsalted butter (1 stick), at
   room temperature
4 tablespoons vegetable shortening, at
   room temperature
2 teaspoons sugar
½ teaspoon baking powder
½ teaspoon salt
¼ teaspoon white pepper
Pinch cayenne pepper

SAUCE
2 tablespoons butter
1 shallot, minced
½ cup diced sweet potato (1 small
   sweet potato)
½ cup white wine
½ cup corn kernels
1 cup heavy cream
½ cup diced red bell pepper or ¼
   cup diced sundried tomatoes,
   drained
Salt
Pepper

Clean and soak the husks as described on page 286.

Put the sweet potatoes in water to cover. Bring to a boil and cook 5 minutes. Drain and let cool.

Put the onion and corn kernels in a food processor bowl or blender jar. Process until the kernels are finely ground. Add some chicken stock if using a blender. Pour into a mixing bowl. Add the cornmeal, butter and shortening. Beat to mix well. Combine the chicken stock, sugar, baking powder, salt, white pepper and cayenne in a small bowl. Pour into the cornmeal mixture and stir to make a dough the consistency of thick cake batter. Fold in the sweet potatoes and let the dough rest until firm enough to handle, about 20 minutes.

Take two husks the same size and overlap the wide ends in the middle. Spoon about ½ cup dough in the center. Roll the edges inward to make a fat cigar shape. Tie the ends with string or strips of husks. Fringe the ends.

Steam on top of the stove or in a 450° F. oven until tamales are puffed, moist and firm, 25 to 35 minutes. Check water level after 15 minutes and add more hot water if necessary. Keep tamales covered for up to 20 minutes before serving.

To prepare the sauce, melt the butter in a saucepan. Add the shallot and diced sweet potato and sauté 1 minute. Add wine and simmer over medium heat until it has nearly all evaporated, 5 to 6 minutes. Add ½ cup water and corn kernels. Heat to a boil and cook until the vegetables are soft, about 5 minutes. Add the cream and red peppers or sundried tomatoes. Reduce the heat to low. Season to taste with salt and pepper. Keep warm over low heat for up to 8 minutes.

To serve, cut the tamales down the center with a sharp knife. Pinch the ends and gently pull the opening apart slightly to loosen the filling. Place on individual plates and spoon the sauce on top, allowing it to spill over.

Pasta

It is much easier now to have fresh pasta than ever before. The surge of popularity of pasta has encouraged pasta shops to open in many large cities. In some areas you can order the kind you want; you can even find pasta-makers who are willing to venture into pastas made with chilies, mushrooms or fresh herbs.

Making pasta at home is not difficult, but it does need time (unless you have an extruder). There are many kinds of machines for making pasta. Some mix and extrude the dough; others roll and cut it. Some are electric, others hand cranked.

Making pasta. Although machines vary, the techniques are similar. First you prepare the dough, either plain or flavored, and shape it into a flat oval. Let it rest, covered in plastic wrap, for 20 minutes. Lightly flour the dough and roll it into an oval that will pass through the widest opening of your pasta machine's rollers. Roll the dough, then fold it in thirds, flatten it, lightly dust with flour if it is still a bit wet, and pass through the rollers again. Repeat two more times. Then pass the dough through the rollers twice without folding. You are now ready to begin decreasing the opening of the rollers. Decrease one notch each time you pass the pasta through the rollers until you reach the desired thickness. If you are making a pasta salad, for example, you should roll the pasta thicker than you would for a hot pasta dish.

Once the desired thickness is reached, let the long strip of dough rest at room temperature for 5 minutes. Select the cutting attachment, then cut the dough into the desired shape. Sprinkle with white cornmeal to prevent sticking. The pasta may be used within a few hours or covered and refrigerated until ready to cook. It will not dry for 10 to 12 hours when stored this way. Or you may air-dry the pasta by placing it on racks and leaving it at room temperature until dry. Pasta may also be frozen in heavy-duty plastic bags, about half a pound per bag.

Cooking pasta. Fresh pasta takes much less time to cook than dried pasta and dried homemade pasta cooks much faster than commercially dried pasta. Very thin fresh pasta that is going to be cooked in a cream sauce often does not need to be parboiled at all: it will cook in the cream as it boils to reduce and thicken. Exact times are difficult to give because there are so many variables.

Use enough water so that the pasta is not crowded; bring it to a fast boil and add the pasta. Test a strand and drain the pasta as soon as it is tender to the bite (al dente). Most fresh pasta will be done in 1 or 2 minutes; very thin fettuccine can be tender in as little as 30 to 45 seconds.

If you are not using the pasta immediately, rinse it with cold water and toss with a little oil. Let stand at room temperature until you are ready to use it. To reheat pasta that was tossed in oil, place in a colander and rinse the oil off with hot water. Heat the rinsed pasta directly in the sauce or in a small amount of boiling water for about 30 seconds.

When cooking frozen pasta, shake off any excess cornmeal but do not thaw. Drop frozen pasta directly into boiling water and cook until tender to the bite.

ANCHO CHILI PASTA

1 pound

Ancho chili pasta has a rich chocolate color with a roasted, smoky flavor when it is made with fresh toasted ancho chilies rather than chili powder. The chili pods need to be crisp to grind easily. Take extra care not to burn them while toasting. The pasta is delicious with a simple cream sauce, grated cheese and pine nuts or with game and a natural meat sauce. I particularly like ancho pasta with mild goat-cheese sauce (page 262).

3 ancho chili pods, stemmed, seeded and toasted (page 22)
3 large eggs
Salt
1 teaspoon sugar
2 to 2¼ cups all-purpose unbleached flour
2 to 4 tablespoons safflower oil

Break the toasted pods in 5 pieces and put them in a food processor fitted with a metal blade. Process until finely ground, scraping the sides of the bowl as necessary. Add the eggs, 1 teaspoon salt, sugar, 2 cups of flour and 1 tablespoon oil and process until a ball of dough forms that begins to clean the sides of the bowl and rotate around the blades to knead. It may be necessary to add additional flour to form the dough ball. Process to knead for about 60 seconds.

Remove the dough and divide it into thirds. Flatten each portion and wrap in plastic wrap. Let the dough rest at room temperature until you are ready to process it through a pasta machine (page 291).

To cook, heat 2 quarts of water per pound of pasta to a boil. Add 1 tablespoon oil and a teaspoon of salt to pasta. Drain as soon as the pasta is tender to the bite, 30 seconds to 2 minutes.

If not serving immediately, rinse under cold water and toss with 1 to 2 tablespoons oil. Cover with plastic wrap and keep at room temperature until ready to use. To reheat, first rinse off the oil. Put the pasta in a colander and pour boiling water over it. Heat the pasta directly in the sauce or cream or in boiling water for about 30 seconds.

NOTE.   If you are using a pasta extruder, adjust your recipe, keeping the proportion of 3 chili pods to each 2¼ cups flour.

JALAPEÑO PASTA

1½ pounds

You will love this colorful, slightly spicy pasta. It is wonderful when fried for a snack or a garnish for soups or salads. Pasta made with all-purpose flour, rather than part semolina, puffs better when deep-fried. If you do not intend to fry the pasta, you could use semolina flour for a third of the total amount of flour.

4 ounces uncooked fresh spinach, rinsed
6 fresh jalapeño chilies, stemmed, seeded and with veins intact
1 teaspoon salt
2½ to 2¾ cups all-purpose flour
1 tablespoon vegetable oil
3 large eggs

Parsley also helps intensify the color of pasta flavored with fresh green chilies or cilantro as well as pesto sauces made from spicy green chilies and herbs.

Put the spinach in a blender or a food processor fitted with the metal blade and process until pureed. Scrape it into a towel or cheesecloth and squeeze to remove excess moisture. Then put the jalapeño chilies in the food processor bowl and process until minced. Add the salt, spinach, 2⅓ cups flour, oil and eggs and process until a ball of dough forms that will clean the sides of the bowl. If necessary, add ¼ cup more flour to form the dough ball. Knead in the processor at least 60 seconds.

Remove the dough and divide it into thirds. Flatten each portion and wrap it in plastic wrap. Let the dough rest at room temperature for 30 minutes or until ready to process in a pasta machine (page 291). Cook as directed in recipe for ancho-chili pasta.

NOTE.   If you are using a pasta extruder, adjust your recipe, using 6 jalapeño chilies and 4 ounces spinach to every 2½ cups flour.

MUSHROOM PASTA

1 pound

Many wild mushrooms have an intensity of flavor not found in cultivated mushrooms. They are not always available fresh but you can often find them dried. Chanterelles, boletus (cèpes or *porcini*) and oyster mushrooms are all excellent for making pasta. They grind easily and the flavor is pronounced. Mushroom pasta is excellent with game.

1 ounce dried mushrooms
3 large eggs
1 teaspoon salt
1 tablespoon safflower oil
1¾ to 2 cups all-purpose unbleached flour or ½ cup semolina flour and 1¼ to 1½ cups all-purpose flour

Put the mushrooms in a food processor fitted with the metal blade and process until finely minced. Add the eggs, salt, oil and 1¾ cups flour. Process until a ball of dough forms that begins to rotate around the bowl to knead. It may be necessary to add additional flour to form the dough ball. Begin with ¼ cup and process until a ball of dough cleans the sides of the processor bowl. Run the machine to knead the dough for at least 60 seconds.

Remove and divide into thirds. Flatten each portion and wrap in plastic wrap. Let the dough rest at room temperature until ready to process through a pasta machine (page 291). Cook as directed on page 291.

NOTE.   If you are using a pasta extruder, adjust your recipe, keeping the proportion of 1 ounce (1 cup) dried mushrooms to 2 cups flour.

Flans

Egg and cream flans are a delightful way to serve vegetables. You can make the flans as much as a day ahead, and then reheat them in a microwave oven or in a water bath, covered, in a hot oven. When watery vegetables such as mushrooms, summer squash, spinach or other greens are used, they need to be parboiled, then pressed through a strainer to remove excess moisture. Cabbage too can be baked in this way: it needs to be blanched and carefully drained. Eggplant is best when first baked or grilled and roughly chopped. Winter squash, bell peppers, corn, asparagus, broccoli and most other vegetables may simply be diced and parboiled for 1 or 2 minutes. Use the recipe for spinach flan, which follows, as a guide to the proportions of liquid, eggs and vegetables when creating your own vegetable flan.

SPINACH FLAN

6 servings

3 cups spinach, rinsed, stemmed and
   cut in strips
1 clove garlic, minced
1 cup heavy cream
⅞ cup milk
5 large or 6 medium egg yolks
½ teaspoon salt
2 teaspoons fresh thyme or tarragon
   leaves or ¼ teaspoon dried thyme
   or tarragon
⅛ teaspoon ground nutmeg
¼ teaspoon cayenne pepper
   (optional)
Butter for the molds

Preheat the oven to 375° F. Heat about 3 cups water in a large skillet to a boil. Add the spinach and press down as it wilts. Cook for 30 seconds, then drain. Press all the moisture from the spinach. Place in a mixing bowl and add the garlic, cream, milk, egg yolks, salt, thyme or tarragon, nutmeg and cayenne if using. Stir to mix. Butter 6 one-cup molds and divide custard mixture among them. Place in a baking pan half filled with water. Bake for 15 to 20 minutes or until barely set. Custard is done when a sharp knife inserted in the center comes out clean. Let the custards stand in the water bath for 5 minutes, then unmold and serve.

Variation
- Substitute 1½ to 2 cups parboiled diced vegetables, alone or in combination, for the spinach. Broccoli and asparagus are good choices for a flan.

CORN AND PEPPER FLAN

6 servings

Brightly colored corn and pepper flans liven up just about any meat, poultry or fish dish.

6 ears fresh corn, kernels cut from the cob
2 tablespoons minced onion
1 clove garlic, minced
1¾ cups whole milk
1 cup heavy cream
5 egg yolks
1 whole egg
1 teaspoon salt
1 jalapeño chili, stemmed, seeded and minced
¼ cup diced red bell pepper
¼ cup diced green chili or diced roasted and peeled poblano chili (page 20)
Butter

Preheat the oven to 350° F. Set 2 cups corn kernels aside. Put the remaining niblets in a saucepan with the onion, garlic and ¾ cup milk. Heat to a boil and then simmer, stirring occasionally, for 10 minutes. Pour the mixture into a blender jar and blend on high speed until smooth. Strain through a very coarse sieve into a mixing bowl. Add the remaining milk, cream, egg yolks, egg, salt, jalapeño chili, bell pepper and green chilies. Mix well.

Butter 6 six-ounce molds. Spoon the corn mixture into the molds and put them in a pan half full of water. Bake until the flans are set, about 35 minutes. Keep warm in the water bath for up to 15 minutes. Run a knife around the edge of each mold to loosen, then unmold on each serving plate.

ONION AND CHILI FLAN

6 servings

1 tablespoon butter
2 small white onions, thinly sliced
4 poblano chilies, roasted, peeled and cut in strips (page 20), or 1 can (7 ounces) whole green chilies, drained and cut in strips
1 tablespoon lemon juice
1 cup heavy cream
2 egg yolks
1 cup milk
1 cup grated mozzarella cheese
½ teaspoon salt
¼ teaspoon white pepper
Butter
2 cups thinly sliced corn tortillas, fried crisp (optional)

Preheat the oven to 350° F. Heat the butter in a medium skillet over medium heat. Add the onions and cook until soft and translucent, about 8 minutes. Stir in the chilies, lemon juice and cream and heat to a boil. Put the egg yolks and milk in a bowl and beat for 1 minute. Stir in the chili and onion mixture, grated cheese, salt and pepper. Butter 6 six-ounce molds and spoon the mixture in. Place in a pan half filled with water. Bake until set, about 35 minutes.

Run a knife around the edge of each mold to loosen, then unmold. If desired, arrange 6 to 8 crisp corn tortilla chips on each plate and unmold the flan on top.

SWEET-POTATO FLAN

6 servings

Roast turkey and a fresh cranberry relish and these pecan-topped flans will make your holiday dinner special.

1½ teaspoons vegetable oil
6 toasted pecan halves (page 50)
1 tablespoon maple syrup
2 tablespoons heavy cream

———

2 medium sweet potatoes (about 12 ounces)
4 eggs, beaten
1 cup half and half or heavy cream
1 tablespoon brown sugar
½ teaspoon salt
¼ teaspoon ground allspice
¼ teaspoon ground coriander
¼ teaspoon cayenne pepper
Butter

There are two kinds of sweet potato, one with a deep orange color and the other with a lighter, more yellow color. The yellow kind is less moist and therefore better for deep-frying. Use either one for a colorful potato salad to serve with barbecued meats.

Heat the oil in a small skillet over medium heat. Add pecans and sauté 1 minute. Add the maple syrup and cream. Simmer until the pecans are glazed, 1 to 2 minutes. Do not let the syrup caramelize. Transfer the pecans to waxed paper.

Preheat the oven to 400° F. Bake the potatoes for 40 minutes to 1 hour, until fork tender. Scoop the potato pulp into the bowl of a heavy-duty mixer. Add the eggs, half and half or cream, brown sugar, salt, allspice, coriander and cayenne. Beat until very smooth. Butter 6 six-ounce molds and pour the potato mixture in. Place the molds in a pan half filled with warm water. Reduce the oven temperature to 350° F. and bake the flans for 45 to 50 minutes or until set. Allow flans to cool 5 minutes, then unmold. Garnish each with a glazed pecan.

BREADS

Flour Tortillas
Raised Biscuits
Cheese and Chili Biscuits
Buttermilk Biscuits
Spiral Herb Rolls
Pimiento-Cheese Rolls
Poppy-Seed Onion Bread
Roast-Garlic Spoonbread
Corn Muffins with Cheese and Chilies
Hot-Water Cornbread
Cornsticks
Cornbread
Blue-Cornmeal Muffins
Grits Cakes
Jam Bran Muffins
Blackberry-Lemon Muffins
Lemon-Orange Muffins
Toasted-Pecan Muffins
Peppered Popovers
Corn and Chili Popovers
Cheese Straws
Cheese Wafers

Moist muffins with rich preserves, steaming and fragrant cornbread plump with corn kernels and thick homemade biscuits oozing with fresh butter and honey are all characteristic breads of the American West and Southwest. Flour tortillas, which always accompany *fajitas* and which act as a wrapper for the relishes and grilled onions or peppers that are usually served with those sizzling meats, are also a popular bread of the region.

Homemade muffins made with bran, nuts or juicy berries or with blue, yellow or white cornmeal and speckled with colorful, often spicy, red or green chilies can be the main attraction or an accompaniment to a salad or small meal. Soft yeast rolls made with aromatic herbs, onions or cheese, or with cinnamon and pecans bring back memories of those little neighborhood bakeries or, if you were one of the lucky ones, your grandmother's kitchen.

You will find many kinds of cornbread in this chapter, ranging in texture from a coarse-crumb muffin to a bread with a crisp crust to a moist polenta-like spoonbread. Sometimes cornbread is served as an accompaniment, sometimes as a savory shortcake topped with cheese and broiled. Sometimes it is split and served with seafood or with a game or beef ragout. Corn complements many of the fruits and vegetables of the Southwest and plays an important role in all the foods of the sun.

Soft spoonbread, fried or gratinéed after baking, or deep-fried hush puppies are often combined with corn muffins, sweet yeast rolls and biscuits in a basket on the lunch or dinner table as well as on the breakfast table. Flaky biscuits, which depend on a combination of skill, practice and low-gluten flour for success, are also served with all meals, often smothered in cream gravy.

Crisp, crusty French breads and whole-grain breads, too, are compatible with Southwestern food. They can be served right alongside the biscuits, rolls, popovers and muffins that are featured in the recipes that follow.

FLOUR TORTILLAS

12 to 14 tortillas

Flour tortillas go with all kinds of food of the Southwest. They can be a bit tricky to make as the dough is elastic and careful preparation is needed to make a tender tortilla. You may add finely minced hot chilies, minced herbs or crushed peppercorns to the dough if you like.

2 cups all-purpose flour
5 tablespoons vegetable shortening
2 teaspoons sugar
1½ teaspoons baking powder
1½ teaspoons salt
¾ cup hot water

Put the flour, shortening, sugar, baking powder and salt in a mixing bowl. Add the hot water and stir together to make a soft puffy dough. If necessary add more water by the tablespoonful. Cover the bowl with plastic wrap and let stand for 15 minutes.

Shape the dough into golf-ball-size balls and dip in flour. When all the balls are formed, begin with the first one and shape it with your fingers into a circle about 2 to 3 inches in diameter. Repeat with all the dough balls. Begin again with the first one, and using a very thin rolling pin—a piece of old broom handle is perfect—roll the tortilla firmly two times in one direction to make an oval, then turn and roll in the opposite direction to make a circle.

Heat a nonstick or seasoned griddle over medium-high heat. When drops of water sprinkled on the griddle sizzle, put a tortilla in the center. When bubbles rise, do not push them down to deflate, but turn the tortilla to brown lightly on the other side. Remove and repeat rolling and cooking the remaining tortillas. Stack between paper towels. When all are prepared, place in a covered tortilla dish or between two plates to keep warm.

NOTE.   Tortillas may be warmed in a microwave oven, in a 450° F. oven or directly over the heating element in a nonstick skillet.

Variation
* Substitute ¼ cup white or yellow cornmeal for ½ cup of the flour.

RAISED BISCUITS

16 to 18 biscuits

I use this as a basic recipe and vary it with fresh herbs. For example, if I am going to serve the biscuits with salmon, I'll add snipped fresh dill to the dough; if I am serving them with grilled or roasted chicken, then I'll add a combination of sage, parsley and thyme. The dough can be made in advance and kept in the refrigerator for up to 4 days. It needs to be punched down during the first 8 hours if you do this.

1 package dry yeast
1 teaspoon sugar
¼ cup warm water
1 teaspoon salt
1 teaspoon baking soda
3 cups bread flour
4 tablespoons solid shortening, melted
2 tablespoons butter, melted
1 cup buttermilk or yogurt, at room temperature

Stir the yeast and sugar into the water and let stand until foamy, about 5 minutes. Put the salt, baking soda and flour in a large bowl. Stir in the yeast, 3 tablespoons of the shortening, butter and buttermilk or yogurt. Stir until you have a soft, puffy dough. It may be necessary to add more buttermilk or more flour to achieve this consistency. Add flour or buttermilk if needed by the tablespoonful. Do not knead. Cover with plastic wrap and let stand in a warm place for 25 to 30 minutes. The dough may also be refrigerated for up to 4 days.

Preheat the oven to 375° F. Pat the dough out into a circle about ¾ inch thick. Cut out into 2-inch rounds and place on an ungreased cookie sheet. Let the biscuits rise a second time, covered with plastic wrap, for 30 minutes. Brush with the remaining melted shortening and bake until golden brown, 12 to 15 minutes.

Variation
• Add 1 tablespoon minced fresh herbs (dill, thyme, parsley, etc.) with the salt, baking soda and flour. Choose herbs that complement the dish you are serving the biscuits with.

CHEESE AND CHILI BISCUITS

8 biscuits

These biscuits may be served hot with soups such as corn and potato chowder (page 104) or with entree salads. They are also great buttered and toasted for breakfast or with poached eggs and tomato salsa. Strips made from scraps of dough are good to serve with salad.

1 cup all-purpose flour
2 tablespoons mayonnaise
2 teaspoons baking powder
Pinch sugar
½ teaspoon salt
1 tablespoon butter
1 tablespoon diced fresh onion
2 cloves garlic, minced
½ cup club soda, at room temperature
½ cup grated Cheddar cheese
2 fresh jalapeño chilies, stemmed and minced
1 tablespoon minced fresh parsley
Melted butter for brushing the biscuits

Preheat the oven to 400° F. Combine the flour, mayonnaise, baking powder, sugar and salt with a fork. Let stand for 15 minutes. Heat the butter in a small skillet over medium heat. Add the onion and garlic and sauté until soft, 1 to 2 minutes. Stir into the flour mixture. Add the club soda and stir to make a soft, puffy dough. You may need to add additional soda or flour if the dough is too stiff or too wet. Gently fold in the cheese, chilies and parsley.

Turn the dough out on a lightly floured surface and pat into an oval about ½ to ¾ inch thick. Cut the dough into 2-inch rounds and place on a lightly buttered baking sheet. Roll the scraps ¼ inch thick and cut into strips. Brush the tops with melted butter and bake for 20 minutes or until lightly browned. Serve immediately.

BUTTERMILK BISCUITS

16 to 18 biscuits

There is nothing quite like a light and tender homemade biscuit with rich, thick preserves. Biscuits have been prized for their white color and flaky texture. Southerners are fortunate to be able to buy flour that is low in gluten, so producing such biscuits is somewhat easier for them. After a few times you will develop a feel for the right amount of liquid. Adding an egg makes the biscuit lighter; however, the color will be yellower than when it is made just with buttermilk. It is important to use *chilled* shortening or butter: it is those cold little fat particles that make the biscuits flaky.

3 cups all-purpose flour
2 tablespoons sugar
4 teaspoons baking powder
1 teaspoon cream of tartar or
   1 teaspoon baking soda
1 teaspoon salt
¾ cup chilled vegetable shortening or
   6 tablespoons chilled unsalted
   butter and 6 tablespoons chilled
   shortening
1 cup buttermilk or ¾ cup buttermilk
   and 1 egg, lightly beaten

Preheat the oven to 450° F. Put the flour, sugar, baking powder, cream of tartar or baking soda and salt in a mixing bowl and stir to mix. Add the shortening and use a pastry blender or two forks to make a coarse crumbly texture. Add the buttermilk or buttermilk and egg and quickly stir to make a moderately soft dough that does not feel wet. Knead the dough, pressing and turning about 8 times.

Turn the dough out on a lightly floured surface and pat into an oval about ¾ to 1 inch thick. Use a floured 2-inch cutter to cut firmly into biscuits; do not twist the dough. Place biscuits on ungreased baking sheets. Bake for about 12 to 15 minutes, or until lightly browned. Cool on wire racks and serve as soon as possible.

To reheat the biscuits, preheat the oven to 400° F. Put a pan of water on the bottom rack. Wrap biscuits loosely in foil, place on top rack and heat for 10 to 12 minutes.

SPIRAL HERB ROLLS

18 rolls

These soft, tender rolls are flavored with herbs, preferably fresh, and Parmesan cheese. You may use dried herbs, though, if fresh ones are not available. Serve these rolls with grilled chicken, pasta dishes or roasted lamb or beef. Use the same dough but flavor it with cinnamon for a special brunch or Sunday family breakfast.

1½ packages dry yeast
1 teaspoon sugar
½ cup warm water
3 cups bread flour
1 teaspoon salt
2 tablespoons vegetable shortening, at
    room temperature
2 tablespoons unsalted butter
2 large eggs
½ cup warm milk
1 tablespoon minced fresh oregano or
    1½ teaspoons dried leaf oregano
1½ tablespoons minced fresh basil or
    1 tablespoon dried basil
1 tablespoon minced fresh marjoram
    or 1 teaspoon dried marjoram

———

1 egg white, beaten
2 ounces fresh goat cheese, at room
    temperature (optional)
½ cup grated Parmesan cheese
Butter for the pans
2 tablespoons butter, melted

*Use tiny herb blossoms or sprigs of fresh herbs
to garnish a bread and butter plate.*

Dissolve the yeast in sugar and warm water. Let stand until foamy, about 5 minutes. Combine the flour, salt, shortening and butter in a large mixing bowl. Blend together until the shortening and butter are incorporated. Add the eggs, milk, yeast mixture, and herbs and stir vigorously until you have a soft dough that holds together but is still somewhat sticky. It is not necessary to knead the dough. Cover the bowl with plastic wrap and put it in a warm place (80° F.) until the dough nearly doubles in bulk, about 1 hour.

Turn the dough out on a lightly floured surface. If it is still quite sticky, knead a little flour in by hand, but maintain a very soft dough. Roll the dough out into a rectangle about ½ inch thick. Brush with egg white, then spread with softened goat cheese if using and sprinkle evenly with ¼ cup Parmesan cheese. Roll up, jelly-roll fashion (see figure 1, opposite). Pinch the edges to seal. Cut the roll into 1-inch slices (figure 2). Place them cut side down in 2 lightly buttered cake pans. Cover with plastic wrap and put in a warm place to rise until soft and puffy, about 1 hour.

butter and sprinkle with the remaining Parmesan cheese. Bake until golden brown, 15 to 20 minutes.

NOTE. Baked rolls may be double wrapped and frozen for up to 2 months.

1. Rolling up the dough for Spiral Herb Rolls.

2. Cutting the dough into slices.

CINNAMON ROLLS

18 rolls

**Dough from recipe for spiral herb
rolls**

———

⅓ **cup light brown sugar**
¼ **cup granulated sugar**
½ **cup finely ground pecans**
1 teaspoon cinnamon
1 egg white, lightly beaten
Butter for the pans
2 tablespoons melted butter

GLAZE
2 cups confectioners sugar
4 to 6 tablespoons orange juice
1 teaspoon vanilla

Prepare the dough as described in the preceding recipe, omitting the herbs. Allow to rise until doubled.

Combine the brown sugar, granulated sugar, pecans and cinnamon in a small bowl. Turn the dough out on a lightly floured surface. If it is still sticky and too soft to work with, knead in several tablespoons of flour. Roll the dough out into a large rectangle about ¼ to ½ inch thick. Brush the surface with egg white, then sprinkle with the nut-sugar mixture. Roll up, jelly-roll fashion, and pinch the edges to seal. Cut the roll into 1-inch slices. Butter 2 round cake pans and place 9 rolls, cut side down, in each pan. Cover with plastic wrap and let rise in a warm place until light and springy to the touch, about 1 hour.

Preheat the oven to 375° F. Brush the rolls with melted butter and bake until lightly browned, 12 to 15 minutes.

Put the confectioners sugar, orange juice and vanilla in a small saucepan over medium-low heat. Stir vigorously to make a smooth glaze. Drizzle the warm glaze over the rolls.

Variation
- Add ½ cup seedless raisins or currants with the sugar-nut mixture.

PIMIENTO-CHEESE ROLLS

20 rolls

You are unlikely to find pimiento cheese outside of the Southwest; these soft rolls are one way to combine the two flavors.

1 package dry yeast
1 teaspoon sugar
¼ cup warm water

———

3 to 3½ cups bread flour
⅓ cup sugar
3 tablespoons butter, melted
2 tablespoons shortening, melted
1 teaspoon salt
1 tablespoon coarsely ground black or
    red peppercorns
5 eggs, at room temperature
3 tablespoons diced pimiento
4 ounces Cheddar cheese, grated
Melted butter

Dissolve the yeast and sugar in warm water and let stand until foamy, about 5 minutes. Put 2½ cups flour, ⅓ cup sugar, butter, shortening, salt and pepper in a large bowl. Add the yeast and stir to mix well. In another bowl, beat the eggs with an electric mixer for 5 minutes. Stir the eggs into the flour mixture and mix to make a smooth dough, 8 to 10 minutes. Stir in enough of the remaining flour to make a soft, spongy dough.

Butter both your hands and the work surface. Pat the dough out on the buttered surface into a rectangle that is about 5 × 12 inches (see figure 1). Evenly distribute the pimientos and cheese over the dough surface (figure 2), then fold the dough into thirds, like a business letter, to enclose all the cheese (figure 3). Roll the dough again into a 5 × 12-inch rectangle. Butter the top of the dough and then cut into 20 equal squares with a sharp knife (figure 4). Do not separate. Cover with oiled plastic wrap and let stand for 1½ hours, or until light and spongy to the touch.

Using a knife, remove each square and pinch the edges to enclose the cheese. Gently form squares into flat circles with your hands (figure 5). Place the circles on a lightly greased cookie sheet and let rise again, covered with plastic wrap, until light and spongy, about 45 minutes.

Preheat the oven to 375° F. Brush the rolls with melted butter and bake until lightly browned, about 15 minutes. Serve warm.

1. Patting dough for Pimiento Cheese Rolls into a rectangle.

2. Distributing cheese and pimiento over the dough.

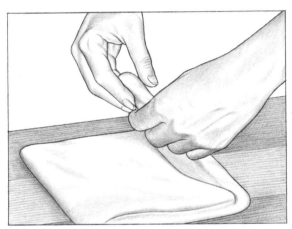

3. Folding the dough into thirds.

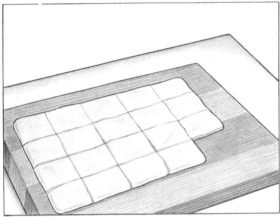

4. The dough cut into squares.

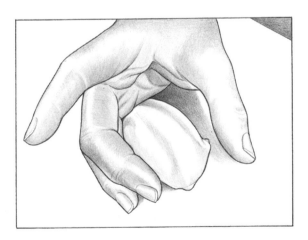

5. Pinching a square of dough to enclose the filling.

POPPY-SEED ONION BREAD

1 nine-inch loaf

Serve this warm or lightly toasted with a cheese spread or fresh butter.

1 package dry yeast
¼ cup warm water
1 teaspoon sugar
¼ cup vegetable shortening
¾ cup finely minced onion
⅓ cup honey
¼ cup (½ stick) butter, melted
3 large eggs, beaten
1 teaspoon salt
1¼ cups bread flour
1 to 1¼ cups all-purpose flour
1½ tablespoons poppy seeds
Butter for bread pan

Dissolve the yeast in warm water with sugar and let stand until a layer of foam coats the top, about 5 minutes. Heat the shortening in a small saucepan over medium heat. Add the onion and cook until soft and translucent, about 5 minutes. Stir in the honey and then set aside 2 tablespoons of the mixture to brush the top of the loaf before baking. Add the butter to the rest and stir to combine. Put the yeast, onion-honey-butter mixture, eggs and salt in a large bowl. Add the bread flour and stir vigorously. Stir in 1 cup all-purpose flour and the poppy seeds. Add additional flour if necessary to make a soft, elastic dough that pulls away from the sides of the bowl. (This dough does not have to be kneaded.) Cover with plastic wrap and let rise in a warm place for 2 hours. Punch the dough down, then cover again and refrigerate for at least 2 hours or overnight before using.

Preheat the oven to 375° F. Remove the dough from the refrigerator and place on a lightly floured surface. Shape into a loaf and place in a buttered 9-inch loaf pan. Cover with oiled plastic wrap and let rise until doubled in size and light and springy to the touch, about 1 hour.

Brush with the honey-onion mixture and bake 25 to 30 minutes. The bread is done when the bottom of the loaf sounds hollow when tapped. Cool in the pan on a wire rack.

ROAST-GARLIC SPOONBREAD

12 two-inch squares

This is a soufflé-like spoonbread that is moist when hot and surprisingly good cold. It has a very mild garlic flavor and crisp Parmesan crust. Use it as an accompaniment with beef or game when you have a sauce of natural juices, with black beans or with chile con carne (page 163). Spoonbread is also good for brunch with homemade sausages (pages 90–92) and fresh seasonal fruits.

6 large cloves garlic, not peeled
Olive or safflower oil
2 cups milk or water
1 cup white, yellow or blue cornmeal
1 cup buttermilk
6 tablespoons butter, at room
   temperature
4 eggs, separated
1 teaspoon baking powder
½ teaspoon baking soda
1½ teaspoons salt
1 tablespoon sugar
Pinch cayenne pepper
⅔ cup grated Parmesan cheese

Preheat the oven to 350° F. Soak unpeeled garlic cloves in oil for 15 minutes. Place in an oiled baking dish and bake until soft, about 25 minutes. Cut the core ends, squeeze out the soft garlic and mash with a fork.

Heat the milk or water to a boil. Put the cornmeal in a mixing bowl and stir in the hot milk. Stir to remove all the lumps, then add the garlic, buttermilk, 4 tablespoons butter, egg yolks, baking powder, baking soda, salt, sugar and cayenne. Stir vigorously to mix well. Beat the egg whites until stiff. Fold the whites and ⅓ cup Parmesan cheese into the batter. Generously butter an 8 × 11-inch casserole and sprinkle lightly with cheese, shaking out the excess. Pour batter into pan and sprinkle the remaining Parmesan cheese on top. Bake for 40 to 45 minutes or until the top is well browned and the inside set but still moist. Cool for 5 to 8 minutes, then cut into 2-inch squares and serve.

Variations
Before folding in the egg whites, stir one of the following vegetables into the batter:
- 1 cup shredded zucchini or yellow squash, drained
- 1 cup sliced spinach, blanched and drained
- 2 cups corn kernels

CORN MUFFINS WITH CHEESE AND CHILIES

12 to 14 small muffins or 28 miniature muffins

A basket of these colorful muffins will be the envy of your friends and something your guests will never forget. It is well worth buying some special pans to bake them in: I prefer madeleine molds.

Butter for the molds
1 cup yellow cornmeal
1 cup all-purpose flour
2 tablespoons sugar
1½ teaspoons salt
1 tablespoon baking powder
2 eggs, separated
¼ cup vegetable shortening, melted
2 cups heavy cream
4 ounces Monterey Jack or jalapeño
    cheese, grated (about 1 cup)
¾ cup corn kernels, drained
½ cup diced red bell pepper
¼ cup diced fresh jalapeño or mild
    green chilies

Preheat the oven to 425° F. Generously butter the molds and place them on top of the stove to warm them and melt the butter.

Combine the cornmeal, flour, sugar, salt, baking powder, egg yolks, melted shortening and cream in a mixing bowl. Stir in the cheese, corn, bell pepper and chilies. Beat the egg whites in a separate bowl until stiff. Fold the whites into the batter. Spoon into buttered molds. Bake the muffins for 12 to 15 minutes. Watch closely and do not allow the muffins to get too brown. The edges should be golden. Cool 5 minutes, then run a knife around the edges to loosen the muffins. Unmold on wire racks.

NOTE.   If using jalapeño cheese, omit the jalapeños or green chilies.

HOT-WATER CORNBREAD

16 two-inch squares

This is one of those regional dishes that vary from state to state in the South. This recipe is for a moist cornbread, a cross between Italian *polenta* and spoonbread. It has a crisp crust and must be served hot from the oven to be enjoyed at its very best. Serve it with any beef dish that has a sauce or gravy like Robert's game ragout (page 164) or as an unsplit shortbread biscuit with oysters (page 62). In Texas, hot-water cornbread is often deep-fried; to do so, omit buttermilk and eggs and drop cooked batter into hot fat to fry crisp.

3 tablespoons bacon drippings
1½ to 2 cups boiling water
1 cup white or yellow cornmeal
1 cup buttermilk
2 eggs, beaten
2 teaspoons baking powder
1 teaspoon baking soda
1 tablespoon butter
2 teaspoons salt

Preheat the oven to 425° F. Put about 2 tablespoons bacon drippings in an 8-inch-square pan or muffin tins and place in the oven to heat for 5 minutes. Pour the boiling water over the cornmeal, using the greater amount for a more custard-like result, and stir to remove all the lumps. Use an electric mixer to beat in the buttermilk, eggs, baking powder, baking soda, butter and salt. Pour into the heated pan and spread evenly. Brush the remaining bacon drippings over the top. Bake for 35 to 40 minutes or until browned on the outside but still moist on the inside. Cool for 5 to 8 minutes, then cut in squares and serve hot.

CORNSTICKS

12 cornsticks or 24 small muffins

This is a basic recipe for cornsticks or corn muffins. You will find several others in the book, each with a different texture or character. These freeze and reheat well. I prefer the shape of cornsticks or small madeleines over muffins for this recipe.

Butter for the pans
1 cup yellow cornmeal, preferably
    stone ground
1 cup all-purpose flour
2 tablespoons sugar
1½ teaspoons salt
1 tablespoon baking powder
6 tablespoons (¾ stick) unsalted
    butter, melted
2 cups heavy cream, at room
    temperature, or 1 cup buttermilk
    and 1 cup cream
2 eggs, separated, at room
    temperature

Preheat the oven to 425° F. Generously butter the muffin pans and place on top of the stove to warm. Stir the cornmeal, flour, sugar, salt and baking powder together in a mixing bowl. Add the melted butter, cream, and egg yolks and stir just enough to blend the ingredients. The mixture should be moderately stiff. Beat the egg whites in a separate bowl to soft peaks. Fold into the batter. Spoon into buttered cornstick or muffin pans or transfer to a pastry bag (no tip) and pipe into madeleine molds. Bake 12 to 15 minutes, until a toothpick inserted near the middle of a muffin comes out clean. Allow less time for small muffins. Immediately loosen the muffins with a knife and unmold onto cooling racks. Serve warm.

Variations
Add one or more of the following ingredients to the batter before folding in the egg whites. You will need to butter a few extra muffin cups where there is a larger amount of batter.
- 2 teaspoons fresh oregano or ½ teaspoon dried oregano
- 1 cup fresh corn kernels
- ½ cup chopped green chilies or 3 jalapeño chilies (red or green), seeded, stemmed and diced

CORNBREAD

16 two-inch squares

⅔ cup corn oil
2 eggs
1 cup sour cream
1 can (16 ounces) creamed corn
3 tablespoons minced onion
2 tablespoons minced green bell
    pepper
2 jalapeño chilies, stemmed, seeded,
    and minced
1½ cups cornmeal
2 teaspoons baking powder
1 teaspoon salt
Butter for baking dish

Preheat the oven to 350° F. Combine the oil, eggs, sour cream, and creamed corn in a mixing bowl and stir to mix well. Add the onions, bell pepper, jalapeño chilies, cornmeal, baking powder and salt. Generously butter an 8-inch-square baking dish. Pour the batter in and bake for 45 minutes or until a toothpick, when inserted, comes out clean. Cool for 5 to 8 minutes, then cut in squares.

BLUE-CORNMEAL MUFFINS

12 small muffins or 6 cornsticks

Blue cornmeal varies in texture and color depending on the source. These muffins have a rich blue color and wonderful flavor whether sweet or savory. They freeze and reheat quite successfully.

Butter for the molds
2 tablespoons vegetable shortening
2 tablespoons minced red onion
2 tablespoons butter
1 egg, separated
⅔ cup stone-ground blue cornmeal
⅓ cup all-purpose flour
2 tablespoons sugar
¼ teaspoon cayenne pepper
½ teaspoon salt
1½ teaspoons baking powder
1 cup heavy cream
½ cup cooked black beans, page 271
  (optional)
½ cup finely diced smoked ham
  (optional)

Preheat the oven to 425° F. Generously butter muffin molds and place on top of the stove to warm. Heat shortening in a small skillet. Add the onion and sauté 1 to 2 minutes, or until translucent. Remove from the heat. Add 2 tablespoons butter to the pan to melt. Scrape into a mixing bowl. Add the egg yolk, cornmeal, flour, sugar, cayenne pepper and salt. Dissolve the baking powder in the cream, then stir into the cornmeal mixture. Stir in the black beans or ham if using. Beat the egg white to soft peaks in a separate bowl, then fold into the batter. Spoon the batter into the prepared molds. Bake until a toothpick inserted near the center of a muffin comes out clean, 12 to 15 minutes, depending on size. Cool 2 to 3 minutes, then unmold on wire racks. Serve warm.

NOTE. Buttermilk may be substituted for half or all the cream; add ½ teaspoon baking soda if using buttermilk. When doubling or quadrupling the recipe, add 1 additional egg white each time you double the recipe, to keep the muffins light.

BLUE-CORNMEAL MUFFINS WITH BLUEBERRIES

8 large or 16 small muffins

Butter for the molds
¼ cup all-purpose flour
¼ cup confectioners sugar
1 cup fresh blueberries

———

2 tablespoons vegetable shortening,
  melted
2 tablespoons butter, melted
1 large egg, separated
⅔ cup stone-ground blue cornmeal
⅓ cup all-purpose flour
4 tablespoons granulated sugar
½ teaspoon salt
1½ teaspoons baking powder
1 cup heavy cream

Preheat the oven to 425° F. Generously butter muffin molds. Combine the flour and confectioners sugar in a bowl and then toss with the blueberries to coat evenly. Put the shortening, butter, egg yolk, cornmeal, flour, granulated sugar and salt in a mixing bowl. Dissolve the baking powder in the cream, then stir into the cornmeal mixture. Beat the egg white to soft peaks in a separate bowl, then fold into the batter. Gently fold in the blueberries. Spoon the batter into the buttered molds about ⅔ full. Bake until the toothpick test confirms muffins are done, 12 to 15 minutes, depending on size. Cool 2 to 3 minutes, then unmold on wire racks. Serve warm.

NOTE. See note at end of recipe for blue-cornmeal muffins if you want to use buttermilk or to double or quadruple the recipe.

GRITS CAKES

12 to 18 muffins

These moist little cakes could be fried on a hot griddle but I prefer to bake them in muffin tins or small molds. They are almost as moist as spoonbread. They can also be made even lighter if you separate the eggs, beat the whites and fold them into the batter at the last minute. Cakes may be savory, with pepper or cheese, or sweet, garnished with cinnamon sugar or served with maple syrup.

3 tablespoons melted butter or bacon
   fat
1 cup cooked grits, cooled
1 cup milk
1 cup plus 2 tablespoons sifted flour
4 teaspoons baking powder
2 eggs, beaten
2 tablespoons sugar
½ teaspoon salt

Preheat the oven to 425° F. Pour the butter or bacon fat into muffin tins and place in the oven. Remove the muffin tins after the fat is hot. Add any excess fat to the batter.

Put the grits in a large bowl. Stir in the milk, excess fat, flour, baking powder, eggs, sugar and salt and mix well. Fill heated muffin tins ⅔ full and bake for 30 minutes.

NOTE. For less moist grits cakes, add an additional ½ cup flour.

Variations
- Add 2 teaspoons each crushed pink and black peppercorns to the dough. Continue with recipe.
- Fill muffin tins ⅔ full. Sprinkle Parmesan cheese on top. Bake for 30 minutes.
- Fill muffin tins half full and sprinkle with cinnamon sugar. Fill ⅔ full and sprinkle muffin tops with additional cinnamon sugar. Bake for 30 minutes.

JAM BRAN MUFFINS

16 to 18 muffins

These breakfast muffins are adapted from a traditional Southern-Southwestern blackberry jam cake that was filled with whipped cream and caramel. The muffins are sweet and moist and reheat very well.

1½ cups all-purpose flour
¼ teaspoon salt
1 teaspoon ground cinnamon
1 teaspoon ground allspice
¾ cup brown sugar
½ cup (1 stick) unsalted butter, at room temperature
2 eggs, separated
1 teaspoon baking powder
½ teaspoon baking soda
½ cup buttermilk
¾ cup All-Bran cereal
1 cup blackberry, blueberry, raspberry or strawberry preserves, melted
¾ cup chopped raisins
¾ cup chopped toasted pecans (page 50)

Blackberries have a natural affinity for pecans and cinnamon. Frozen blackberries, sugared before thawing, are almost as good as the fresh.

Preheat the oven to 375° F. Combine the flour, salt, cinnamon and allspice in a 4-cup measure. Put the brown sugar, butter and egg yolks in a mixing bowl and cream with an electric mixer. Stir the baking powder, baking soda, buttermilk and bran into the melted preserves and let stand 5 minutes. Alternately stir the jam mixture and the flour into the eggs-sugar mixture. Stir in the raisins and nuts. Beat the egg whites until stiff, then fold into the batter. Fill paper-lined muffin tins ⅔ full and bake for 20 to 25 minutes. Cool on racks and serve warm.

Variation

- To make a jam cake, omit the All-Bran cereal and reduce the amount of buttermilk to ¼ cup. Follow the recipe directions but spoon the batter into a buttered 9 × 11-inch cake pan. Bake at 375° F. for 30 to 35 minutes. Serve with whipped cream or vanilla ice cream and caramel sauce (page 349).

BLACKBERRY-LEMON MUFFINS

12 muffins

When fresh blackberries are not in season, use frozen blackberries without thawing them or substitute blueberries.

1 cup fresh or unthawed frozen
   blackberries
1 tablespoon all-purpose flour
2 tablespoons confectioners sugar

———

1¾ cups all-purpose flour
½ cup granulated sugar
1 teaspoon lemon zest, finely minced
2½ teaspoons baking powder
¾ teaspoon salt
1 egg, at room temperature
6 tablespoons vegetable shortening,
   melted
¼ cup lemon juice
½ cup heavy cream
Butter for muffin tins (optional)

Gently toss the blackberries with flour and powdered sugar in a deep mixing bowl. Set aside. Preheat the oven to 375° F. Combine 1¾ cups flour, granulated sugar, lemon zest, baking powder and salt in a mixing bowl and stir to distribute the baking powder evenly. Stir in the egg, shortening, lemon juice and cream until all ingredients are moistened. Carefully fold in the coated blackberries, adding all the excess flour and sugar. Butter muffin tins or line them with paper muffin cups and fill them ¾ full. Bake until lightly browned, about 20 minutes.

LEMON-ORANGE MUFFINS

12 muffins

Peel from 1 orange, finely minced
Peel from 1 lemon, finely minced
⅔ cup sugar
½ cup (1 stick) butter, melted and
   cooled
2 eggs, separated
1 cup all-purpose flour
1 teaspoon baking powder
½ teaspoon salt
Butter for muffin tins

Preheat the oven to 375° F. Put the orange peel, lemon peel, sugar, butter and egg yolks in a mixing bowl and cream with an electric mixer. Sift together the flour, baking powder and salt, then mix into the batter. In a separate bowl, beat the egg whites until stiff but not dry. Fold them into the batter. Spoon the batter into buttered muffin tins, filling each cup ⅔ full. Bake until a toothpick inserted near the middle of a muffin comes out clean, about 15 minutes.

TOASTED-PECAN MUFFINS

12 to 14 muffins

These are rich with pecan flavor and slightly sweet. If you prefer a less sweet muffin, omit the sugar topping.

1½ cups toasted pecans (page 50)
¼ cup granulated sugar
½ cup light brown sugar, packed
½ teaspoon ground allspice
1¾ cups all-purpose flour
2½ teaspoons baking powder
¾ teaspoon salt
1 egg, beaten, at room temperature
5 tablespoons vegetable shortening, melted
1¼ cups heavy cream
Butter for muffin tins

Preheat the oven to 375° F. Put ½ cup pecans and the granulated sugar in a blender and blend on high speed until pecans are finely ground. Set about 3 tablespoons aside for the topping. Put the rest in a mixing bowl. Add the brown sugar, allspice, flour, baking powder and salt. Mix to distribute the baking powder. Add the egg, shortening and cream, gently stirring until the ingredients are moistened. Chop the rest of the pecans and fold them in. Spoon the batter into greased or paper-lined muffin tins ⅔ full. Sprinkle with pecan-sugar topping and bake until lightly browned, 15 to 20 minutes. Cool on wire racks.

Variations

- Coat 1 cup fresh or unthawed frozen cranberries with flour and confectioners sugar and fold them into the batter with the pecans.
- Substitute 1¼ cups almonds and ½ cup grated coconut for the pecans. Grind ¼ cup almonds and all the coconut with the sugar. Add blueberries or blackberries, coated with flour and powdered sugar, if you like.

PEPPERED POPOVERS

8 large popovers

These popovers are light and crisp on the outside; they are best served with steak or as a hot appetizer with cheese or dips.

4 large eggs, at room temperature
1¾ cups plus 2 tablespoons all-purpose flour
2 teaspoons salt
1 teaspoon coarsely ground black pepper
¼ teaspoon cayenne pepper
1 cup milk
Butter for the molds

Put the eggs, flour, salt, pepper, cayenne pepper, 1 cup water and milk in a blender jar. Blend on high speed until the consistency of heavy cream. Let the batter rest for at least 1 hour at room temperature or up to 8 hours refrigerated before baking.

Preheat the oven to 450° F. Generously butter custard cups or popover molds and then heat them for 4 to 5 minutes in the oven. Pour the batter into the cups ⅔ full. Bake for 15 minutes, then reduce the temperature to 375° F. and finish baking 10 to 15 minutes, or until puffed and crispy brown to the touch. Remove from cups and serve immediately.

Summer and winter savory, delicious with grilled chicken, give a unique twist to cornmeal muffins, crêpes and popovers.

CORN AND CHILI POPOVERS

8 popovers

These popovers have a sweet aroma and flavor which makes them a perfect candidate for a hint of chili spice. Eggs and flour both neutralize the bite of jalapeño chili peppers or crushed hot red peppers. These popovers are good with eggs and tomato relishes and omelets or as an accompaniment to grilled poultry or meat. Serve them hot from the oven; that is when they are at their best.

1½ cups corn kernels, about 3 ears corn
½ cup water
⅓ cup milk
2 eggs
1 teaspoon sugar
1 cup all-purpose flour
Pinch baking powder
½ teaspoon salt
¼ teaspoon white pepper
½ to 1 teaspoon crushed red pepper
1 jalapeño chili, stemmed and seeded (optional)
Butter for popover pans

Put the corn, water, and milk in a blender jar and blend on high speed until the corn is pureed. Strain and press to extract all the liquid from the kernels. You will have about 1¼ cups liquid. Put the strained liquid back in the blender jar and add the eggs, sugar, flour, baking powder, salt, white and red pepper and jalapeño chili if using. Blend on high speed until very smooth, the consistency of heavy cream. Let the batter rest 45 minutes to 1½ hours before baking.

Preheat the oven to 450° F. Generously butter popover pans and place them on top of the stove to melt the butter and heat the pans, 5 minutes. Fill the pans ¾ full and bake for 15 minutes. Reduce the heat to 375° F. and continue baking until puffed and lightly browned, 15 minutes. Remove from pans and serve immediately.

CHEESE STRAWS

2½ dozen

Goat cheese makes these both tender and flavorful. You can substitute another soft white cheese or even a spiced cheese like Boursin to attain the same tender result; however, the flavor will be stronger.

CRUMB MIXTURE
1 cup toasted, salted almonds, coarsely chopped (page 50)
2 tablespoons minced fresh parsley
¼ teaspoon cayenne pepper

PASTRY
½ cup (1 stick) unsalted butter, at room temperature
4 ounces mild goat cheese, at room temperature
3 tablespoons grated Parmesan cheese
1 cup all-purpose flour
¼ teaspoon white pepper
½ teaspoon salt

Preheat the oven to 375° F. Combine the almonds, parsley and cayenne pepper on a large plate or baking pan.

Cream the butter and goat cheese in a mixing bowl until very smooth. Add Parmesan cheese, flour, pepper and salt and mix until combined. The dough will be fairly stiff. Spoon the dough into a pastry bag with a number-5 star tip and pipe the dough in 3-inch strips directly onto the crumb mixture. Gently roll each strip to coat it with crumbs. Carefully transfer the strips to an ungreased cookie sheet and bake until the edges just begin to brown, about 8 minutes. Cool on wire racks. Store in an airtight container.

CHEESE WAFERS

8 dozen

The cereal gives these their crunch and nutty flavor. They make a perfect Christmas gift.

8 ounces sharp Cheddar cheese, grated
4 ounces fresh Parmesan cheese, grated
4 ounces (1 stick) butter, softened
3 tablespoons solid vegetable shortening
1½ cups all-purpose flour
¼ teaspoon cayenne pepper
½ cup Grape-Nuts cereal
1 egg white, beaten
Pecan halves, macadamia nuts and pistachio nuts for garnish

Put cheeses, butter, shortening, flour and cayenne pepper in a large bowl. Cream with a wooden spoon until well mixed, then add the Grape-Nuts. The dough may be shaped into wafers immediately or refrigerated for up to a month. Allow refrigerated dough to stand one hour at room temperature before shaping.

Use a miniature ice cream scoop to make uniform wafers. Flatten each ball of dough with the tines of a fork. Brush tops with beaten egg white. Put nuts on top, using each variety on a third of the wafers.

Preheat the oven to 350° F. Bake until lightly browned, about 18 to 20 minutes.

DESSERTS

Berry and Fruit Sauces
Raspberry-Serrano Ice
Blackberry Ice
Yellow Bell Pepper Ice
Plum and Cinnamon Ice
Cranberry Granita
Coffee Crunch Ice Cream Balls in a Pool of Hot Fudge
White Chocolate Ice Cream
Banana-Walnut Ice Cream
Caramel-Pecan Ice Cream
Maple Pecan Pie
Lime Chess Pie
Espresso-Hazelnut Brownies
Apple Spice Cake
Chocolate-Pecan Cake
Chocolate-Pecan Ice Cream Cookies
Coffee Toffee Crunch Cake
Cookie Tacos
Coconut Tostados
Bread Pudding
Banana Cream Pudding
Crème Brûlée
Brandy-Baked Peaches
Macadamia Cheese with Berry Sauce
Chocolate-Cinnamon Fritters
Fruit Fritters
Shortcake Biscuits
Warm Berry Shortcake
Blackberry Cobbler
Texas Peach Cobbler
Apple-Berry Cobbler
Berry Crunch
Blackberry Buckle
Custard Sauce
Warm Berry Sauce
Caramel Sauce
Caramel Cream
Liqueur Mix
Chocolate Fudge Sauce
Double Chocolate Jumbles
Maple-Glazed Pecans

Whether a dessert is simple, like a ripe peach with whipped cream, or refreshing, like a trio of fresh berry ices, or rich, like pecan pie, it should be able to stand on its own. I believe the desserts in this chapter have that star quality. They include ices, both sweet and savory, ice creams, cookies and dessert sauces as well as some wonderful cakes, pies and puddings.

The ices made with berries and chilies can be served between courses at a formal dinner as well as for dessert at the end of the meal. In fact, ices and ice cream are often a perfect conclusion to a Southwestern meal. But sometimes nothing other than the richness of crème brûlée or chocolate-pecan cake will do.

You will find those and some of my other favorite desserts here, like cookie tacos and tostados —crisp nut cookies served with a cream filling and fresh fruit and berries on a layer of sauce. Another favorite dessert of mine is an attractive arrangement of perfect berries, slices of mango or papaya, dessert cheeses that complement the fruit (one of them a rich triple cream cheese) and a few maple-glazed pecans on a large plate.

I am also very fond of cobblers and shortcakes made with fresh fruit and you will find several recipes for them in the pages that follow. In some cobblers the fruit or berries are topped with a pastry or biscuit crust; in others, with a cake batter. All can be baked in a single pan or in individual soufflé dishes. They are best served soon after baking since the fruit tends to get soft when reheated. Cobblers, incidentally, work well with frozen fruit, which you should use without thawing—a great boon in the winter months.

Shortcakes are like inverted cobblers: the fruit is on top of the biscuit instead of the other way round. My shortcake biscuits (page 342) have a rich, tender crust that quickly absorbs the juices from the fruit. If the biscuits are made ahead, they can be warmed without drying out. I like to serve shortcake on a large plate with freshly cut berries surrounding the biscuit and mashed berries in the middle. I sometimes line the plate with sauce first, white or dark chocolate sauce for raspberry shortcake or caramel sauce with blackberry; sometimes I use a custard sauce instead of the traditional whipped cream. Whatever combination you choose, I am sure it will please your family and friends.

BERRY AND FRUIT SAUCES

Desserts are anything but ordinary when complemented by a combination of dessert sauces. Colorful ribbons of fruit puree in a rich custard or white-chocolate sauce taste and look sinfully good. A rich caramel sauce swirled into a creamy custard base creates a beautiful background for fresh blackberries or raspberries. Cobblers, shortcakes and upside-down cakes move uptown with additional caramel or fruit sauce.

Fruit sauces are simple, nothing more than fresh or frozen fruit sweetened with maple syrup or sugar syrup. The thickness depends on how you plan to use the sauce; for piped designs, for example, sauces need to be rather thick or they will bleed into the base sauce.

SUGAR SYRUP
1½ cups water
¼ cup lime or lemon juice or ½ cup fresh orange juice
1 cup sugar

BERRY SAUCE
1 pint fresh berries or 1 package (16 ounces) frozen berries, preferably unsweetened
¼ to ½ cup sugar syrup or ¼ cup maple syrup and additional sugar syrup as needed
Fruit liqueur, such as Cassis, blackberry brandy or framboise (optional)

FRUIT SAUCE
About 2 cups fruit, peeled, pitted and cut up (see note)
¼ to ½ cup sugar syrup
Fruit liqueur (optional)

For sugar syrup, heat the water, juice and sugar to a boil and boil until clear. Set aside to cool.

For a berry sauce made with fresh berries, put the berries in a blender jar. Add ¼ cup sugar syrup or maple syrup and blend on high speed until pureed. Strain through a fine sieve and press to extract all the juice. Pour into a medium saucepan and heat to a boil. Reduce the heat and simmer until the sauce deepens in color and looks shiny. Add liqueur if using. Add additional sugar syrup to get the desired consistency and degree of sweetness. Refrigerate until ready to use. Most berry sauces will thicken upon standing, so you may need to thin the sauce with more sugar syrup just before using. (With frozen berries, it is not necessary to cook the sauce. Simply blend the berries and syrup, adjust to taste and strain.)

For fruit sauce, put the fruit in a blender jar. Add ¼ cup sugar syrup and liqueur, if using, and blend on high speed until pureed. Taste and adjust sweetness. Strain through a fine sieve and press to extract all the juice. It is not necessary to cook sauces made from peaches, nectarines, mangos or papayas. Plums and prickly pears need to be cooked briefly. Some fruits, peaches for example, tend to darken upon standing. If you find excessive darkening, lighten the color by adding 3 to 4 tablespoons heavy cream.

To serve a combination of several berry, fruit, custard, chocolate or caramel sauces at once, dip a ladle into each sauce and ladle them into the dish simultaneously. That way they keep separate. (You will need to recruit a second pair of hands if you want to combine more than 2 sauces in 1 dish.)

To create designs on a sauce, ladle the base sauce (custard, caramel or chocolate) in the center of a dessert plate. Lift the plate and tilt it so the sauce covers the entire plate surface. Put the sauce to be used for decoration in a squirt bottle. The design sauce must be thick enough to hold its shape without bleeding into the base sauce but thin enough to pass through the nozzle.

NOTE. For 2 cups of fruit, use 5 to 6 ripe peaches or nectarines, peeled and pitted, or 1 package (16 ounces) frozen peaches; 8 to 10 plums or prickly pears, peeled and pitted or seeded; 2 to 3 mangos, papayas or cherimoyas, peeled and pitted or seeded.

Serving Suggestions

Here are some attractive combinations. Custard sauces are on page 348.

- Fruit on custard sauce or white-chocolate custard sauce
- Chocolate fudge on white chocolate or cherimoya custard sauce
- Chocolate fudge and fruit on cherimoya custard sauce
- Caramel on custard sauce or white-chocolate custard sauce

RASPBERRY-SERRANO ICE

3½ cups

Chilies do not bring fire to ice. They add just a mild hint of spice and intensify berry flavors that often become muted when frozen.

2 cans (12 ounces each) mango nectar (see note)
2 serrano chilies, stemmed and cut in half
¼ cup sugar
1 package (10 ounces) frozen sweetened raspberries
¼ cup fresh orange juice

Heat mango nectar, chilies and sugar in a 1-quart saucepan to a boil. Reduce heat and cook for 2 minutes. In a blender, puree the raspberries with the orange juice, then combine with mango-chili mixture. Strain through a fine sieve or cheesecloth to remove chilies and seeds and press the solids to extract all the juices. Freeze in an ice-cream freezer according to manufacturer's instructions.

NOTE. If you prefer to use fresh mangos, puree the fruit and use 2 cups puree plus 1 cup water and ¼ cup sugar.

Variation

- Substitute frozen sweetened strawberries for the raspberries.

BLACKBERRY ICE

1½ quarts

Blackberries have grown in the South for a long time and are the center of many ices, cobblers and pies. Several new varieties are being developed.

5 to 6 cups fresh blackberries (about 2 pounds) or 2 packages (1 pound each) frozen blackberries
2 cups sugar
2 serrano chilies, stemmed, halved and seeded
About ¾ pound fresh watermelon, seeded and diced (2 cups)

Heat the blackberries, sugar, chilies and ½ cup water in a medium saucepan, stirring constantly until the mixture boils. Remove from heat, place in a food processor or blender and process until smooth. Strain and set aside to cool. Put the watermelon in the processor or blender and process until smooth. Combine with the strained blackberry mixture. Process in an ice-cream machine.

YELLOW BELL PEPPER ICE

1 pint

The color and texture of this savory ice are beautiful and silky smooth. It makes an unusual and refreshing sorbet course. If your guests have a sense of culinary adventure, serve a scoop of the sorbet in a shallow plate of tomato relish (not smoked or grilled) and garnish it with a crisp tortilla chip.

4 yellow bell peppers, stemmed, seeded and quartered
3 tablespoons sugar
½ cup white wine or water
Juice from 1 lemon, about 3 tablespoons
Salt
1 serrano chili, stemmed and halved

Heat the yellow bell peppers, sugar, 1½ cups water and the wine in a medium saucepan to a boil; boil until peppers are very soft, about 5 minutes. Place peppers and liquid in a blender jar. Add lemon juice and salt and blend on high speed until smooth. Add serrano chili and let the puree stand, undisturbed, for 5 minutes to absorb the flavor from the chili. Strain and cool. The recipe may be prepared up to this point several days in advance and refrigerated until ready to process in an ice-cream freezer. Process the ice in an ice-cream freezer the day you plan to serve it. Serve small scoops in cordial glasses.

PLUM AND CINNAMON ICE

1 pint

The combination of ripe plums, port wine and a whisper of cinnamon creates a subtle ice that could be served between courses or as a light dessert.

1 pound (about 8 to 10) whole Italian plums
½ cup tawny port wine
½ cup sugar
½ teaspoon ground cinnamon

Heat the plums, port wine, ½ cup water, sugar and cinnamon in a medium saucepan to a boil. Boil about 30 seconds, or until the skins split. Remove the pits and place plums and all the liquid in a blender. Blend on high speed until pureed. Cool, then process in an ice-cream freezer.

Italian plums, which are actually fresh prunes, are also delicious pureed and used in a sauce for poultry, duck, game or pork. Season, if desired, with hot, dried red chilies or chili paste (page 23). Plums can be added to barbecue sauce or diced and included in fresh berry chutney.

CRANBERRY GRANITA

1 quart

Granitas are like sorbets that have not been processed in an ice-cream freezer. They are refreshing palate cleansers, well suited to some of the spicy menus of the Southwest, and very easy to prepare.

1 package (12 ounces) fresh cranberries, rinsed
½ cup apple juice
1 cup sugar
8 sprigs fresh mint
1 bottle (750 ml) white wine such as Chenin Blanc or Riesling
Fresh mint sprigs for garnish

Heat cranberries, 4 cups water, apple juice and sugar to a boil. Boil until the cranberries pop, 5 to 8 minutes. Remove from heat and add mint; let it steep. Strain when cool.

Combine the cranberry mixture with the wine and pour into shallow pans to freeze. Stir ice every 30 minutes once it is partially frozen to ensure proper texture. The mixture is slushy at first but it eventually begins to harden and crystallize. Stop stirring at this point and freeze for 24 hours.

When ready to serve, stir through again to break up the solidified frozen mixture. The texture should resemble that of a frozen Margarita. Spoon into champagne or wine glasses to serve. Garnish each one with a fresh mint sprig.

COFFEE CRUNCH ICE CREAM BALLS
IN A POOL OF HOT FUDGE

4 to 6 servings, 1 cup crushed brittle

This is one of the easiest and most popular quick desserts among my friends. You can shape and coat the ice-cream balls in advance and then mound them in a silver serving bowl to serve at the table, or you could place them in chilled goblets, or you could serve them on a plate in a pool of hot fudge.

PEANUT BRITTLE
⅔ cup granulated sugar
1 tablespoon light corn syrup
2 tablespoons butter
½ cup skinned Spanish or unsalted
    peanuts, roasted (page 50)
½ teaspoon baking soda
Butter for the cooling surface

———

1 quart coffee ice cream
Sweetened whipped cream
Chocolate fudge sauce (page 350),
    heated to warm

Heat sugar, 2 tablespoons water, corn syrup and butter in a 5-quart saucepan to a boil. Boil for 1 minute, then cook over medium-high heat for 5 to 7 minutes until golden in color and the syrup spins a thread when dropped from a wooden spoon. Stir in the peanuts and baking soda and remove from heat. (The mixture will foam alarmingly.) Pour the brittle onto a heatproof, lightly buttered surface. When cool, break the brittle into coarse crumbs and spread out on a shallow plate.

Form small- to medium-size scoops of ice cream and put them on a chilled cookie sheet. Freeze for 1 hour or until very firm. Roll each frozen scoop in the brittle to coat completely. Freeze again for up to 3 hours.

To serve, pool the hot fudge in 8- or 9-inch plates and swirl to coat. Place 3 small scoops on each plate. Or mound the coated ice-cream balls in a silver bowl and serve them at the table with sweetened whipped cream or chocolate fudge sauce.

NOTE. Be sure to use a large saucepan for the brittle as it will foam when the baking soda is added.

WHITE CHOCOLATE ICE CREAM

1 quart

The subtle, rich flavor of white chocolate permeates this delicious ice cream. Serve it with fresh berries and chocolate brownies.

4 cups half and half or 2 cups milk
    and 2 cups heavy cream
8 ounces white chocolate, coarsely
    chopped
1 cup sugar
2 teaspoons vanilla
2 eggs, beaten

Heat the half and half in a medium saucepan to a boil. Add the chocolate and stir occasionally over medium heat until all the chocolate is melted, about 5 to 6 minutes. Whisk in the sugar and vanilla and cook for 5 more minutes, stirring occasionally. Cool. Add the eggs and process the custard in an ice-cream freezer according to manufacturer's directions.

Variation
• Add ½ cup chunky or smooth peanut butter.

BANANA-WALNUT ICE CREAM

1½ quarts

This wonderful ice cream is served at nearly every roadside cafe in Texas; at its best, it has a subtle but rich banana flavor. You can serve it plain or in a pool of caramel sauce (page 349) or chocolate fudge sauce (page 350).

3 eggs, beaten
1 cup sugar
1 quart whole milk
1 teaspoon vanilla
2 cups half and half or heavy cream
Pinch of salt
2 medium-ripe bananas, peeled and
    cut in pieces
1½ tablespoons lemon juice
2 tablespoons unsalted butter
2 tablespoons sugar
¾ cup toasted walnut pieces
    (page 50)

Put the eggs, sugar and milk in a large saucepan over medium heat. Cook, whisking constantly, until the custard thickens and coats the spoon, about 10 to 15 minutes. Stir in vanilla and heavy cream. Set aside 1 cup and cool the rest over ice water.

Put the bananas and lemon juice in a blender jar. Add the cup of reserved custard and blend on high speed until smooth. Stir into the cooled custard and then process in an ice-cream freezer according to manufacturer's directions.

Heat the butter in a small skillet. Stir in sugar and nuts and cook, stirring constantly, for 5 minutes. Cool on paper towel, then chop coarse and fold into the finished ice cream.

CARAMEL-PECAN ICE CREAM

1 quart

Caramel and pecans are used in many Southwestern desserts, though rarely are they combined in ice cream. This is particularly good on cobblers or apple spice cake (page 330).

1½ cups sugar
2 cups half and half
2 cups milk
1 cup toasted pecans, finely chopped
    (page 50)
1 stick cinnamon (optional)
1 egg, beaten
2 teaspoons vanilla

Heat ½ cup sugar in a medium saucepan over medium-high heat, watching closely, until it begins to turn amber. Stir until all the sugar has melted and turned amber. Add ¼ cup water and remove from the heat. The sugar will harden but it will melt again as the custard cooks. After the pan has cooled for a few minutes, add the half and half and milk and return the pan to medium heat. Add the pecans and cinnamon, if using, and cook, stirring constantly, until the caramelized sugar has dissolved. Whisk in the remaining sugar and egg, cook for 3 minutes, then remove from the heat and let the mixture stand, refrigerated, for at least 3 hours or overnight.

Strain, and press the pecans firmly against the sieve to extract all the flavor. Discard the cinnamon stick and pecans. Stir in the vanilla and process in an ice-cream freezer.

MAPLE PECAN PIE

1 nine-inch pie

The maple syrup and custard-like consistency of this pie elevate a traditional favorite to new heights. You can bake the filling in a buttered baking dish, without the crust, if you like, and serve it like a custard with vanilla ice cream.

1 pie shell (9 inches), unbaked

————

1 cup sugar
3 eggs
½ cup pure maple syrup
½ cup light corn syrup
½ cup chopped pecans
6 tablespoons melted butter
3 tablespoons cake flour
1 teaspoon vanilla
½ teaspoon salt
1 cup pecan halves, intact

GLAZE
2 tablespoons maple syrup
1 tablespoon melted butter

————

Sweetened whipped cream flavored with praline liqueur or brandy for garnish

Preheat the oven to 375° F. Prick the crust in several places and bake until lightly browned, 12 to 15 minutes.

Put the sugar and eggs in a mixing bowl and beat with an electric mixer until thick. Add the maple syrup, corn syrup, chopped pecans, butter, flour, vanilla and salt and mix thoroughly. Pour the filling into the baked crust. Arrange the pecan halves on top in a circular pattern.

Place in oven and bake for 10 to 12 minutes. Reduce the heat again to 325° F. and continue baking until the filling is puffed and set, about 20 minutes. Cool 5 minutes.

Heat the maple syrup and butter to a boil in a small skillet. Brush this glaze on the pecans. Cool the pie at least 2 hours. Serve with sweetened whipped cream.

Variation
• For chocolate pecan pie, substitute unsweetened cocoa powder for the flour and continue as directed.

LIME CHESS PIE

This pie is very light with an intense citrus flavor—a refreshing finish for any meal. You may use lemon in place of lime or Seville oranges when they are in season.

1 cup finely ground coconut
8 plain sugar cookies, crushed (about
    ¾ cup)
3 tablespoons melted butter

FILLING
5 egg yolks
1 cup plus 2 tablespoons granulated
    sugar
1½ tablespoons white cornmeal
½ cup lime juice
5 tablespoons butter
3 egg whites
Pinch of salt

————

Confectioners sugar
Sweetened whipped cream

Preheat the oven to 375° F. Combine the coconut with crushed cookies and melted butter. Stir to moisten all the crumbs. Gently press the crumbs in a 9-inch pie pan, at least 1½ inches deep. Bake for 5 to 6 minutes, just long enough to set the crust. Do not brown.

Put the egg yolks, 6 tablespoons sugar, cornmeal and lime juice in the top of a double boiler, over medium heat. Add the butter and stir constantly until thick, about 6 minutes. Set aside and let cool. Put the egg whites and salt in a clean mixing bowl. Beat until the egg whites hold soft peaks, then gradually add the remaining sugar, continuing to beat to stiff peaks. Fold the lime mixture into the egg whites and pour into the prepared pie shell. Bake until soft-set, but firm. Cool 15 minutes, then refrigerate for 24 hours.

Just before serving, sprinkle the pie with confectioners sugar. Serve with sweetened whipped cream.

Variation
- If using Seville oranges, substitute orange juice for lime juice and garnish the pie with fresh orange sections. Flavor the whipping cream with 2 tablespoons Triple Sec.

ESPRESSO-HAZELNUT BROWNIES

4 dozen

These are about as rich as a brownie can get. For a wonderful dessert, serve the brownies with white chocolate custard sauce (page 348).

Butter for the baking dish
¾ cup (1½ sticks) unsalted butter, melted
2 cups sugar
4 eggs
½ cup unsweetened cocoa powder
¼ cup espresso coffee or 2 tablepoons instant (not freeze-dried) coffee
1 tablespoon vanilla extract
⅓ cup all-purpose flour
½ teaspoon salt
6 ounces imported semisweet chocolate, coarsely chopped
½ cup hazelnuts, toasted, skinned and chopped (page 50)

Preheat the oven to 325° F. Lightly butter a 3-quart oblong glass baking dish. Put the butter, sugar, eggs, cocoa, coffee and vanilla in a mixing bowl and beat with an electric mixer until thoroughly combined. Stir in the flour, salt, chocolate and nuts. Spread the batter in the prepared pan. Bake until a tester inserted in the center confirms that the batter is still moist but no longer liquid, about 25 to 30 minutes. Cool the brownies in the dish on a rack. Cut into 1½-inch squares.

NOTE.   An equal amount of pecans, walnuts or almonds may be substituted for the hazelnuts.

APPLE SPICE CAKE

1 oblong 11 x 14-inch cake

This is an old Southern tearoom favorite; the cake has an intoxicating aroma of cinnamon and fresh apples. Try it warm, topped with whipped cream or vanilla ice cream or caramel-pecan ice cream (page 327) or caramel sauce (page 349).

2 cups all-purpose flour
2 cups dark brown sugar, firmly packed
½ cup (1 stick) unsalted butter
1 cup toasted pecans, coarsely chopped (page 50)
2 teaspoons ground cinnamon
1 teaspoon baking soda
½ teaspoon salt
½ cup seedless raisins
1 cup sour cream
2 teaspoons vanilla
1 large egg, beaten
2 cups peeled, chopped apples (about 2 medium apples)
Confectioners sugar

Preheat the oven to 350° F. Combine the flour, brown sugar and butter in a large mixing bowl and blend until you have a coarse, crumbly texture. Stir in the pecans and divide the mixture, measuring out 2½ cups for the crust. Press the 2½ cups into an ungreased, 2½- or 3-quart oblong glass baking dish.

Add the cinnamon, baking soda, salt, raisins, sour cream, vanilla and egg to the remaining crumb mixture and mix well. Fold in the apples and pour on top of the crust. Bake until a toothpick comes clean, 50 to 55 minutes. Cool 10 minutes, then sprinkle with confectioners sugar.

Variation
• Substitute 2 cups chopped peeled pears for the apples.

CHOCOLATE-PECAN CAKE

1 eight-inch cake

This is a light, delicate cake with a rich semisweet chocolate flavor. Serve it with ice cream or white-chocolate and mint sauce (page 348). For a special dinner you might want to try the cherimoya-custard sauce (page 348); garnish the cake plate then with fresh raspberries.

Butter for the pan
2 ounces unsweetened chocolate
2 ounces semisweet chocolate
½ cup butter
3 egg yolks
½ cup plus 2 tablespoons granulated
  sugar
2 tablespoons cherry liqueur
4 egg whites
Pinch of salt
1 cup toasted pecans, coarsely
  chopped (page 50)
Confectioners sugar

Preheat the oven to 350° F. Generously butter an 8-inch spring-form pan. Melt the chocolate and butter in the top of a double boiler over simmering water on medium-high heat. Beat the egg yolks, ½ cup sugar and liqueur in a small bowl until light in color, about 5 minutes. Stir in the warm chocolate mixture and set aside.

Beat the egg whites with salt in another bowl until they form soft peaks. Gradually add the remaining sugar and continue to beat until stiff peaks form. Fold 2 to 3 spoonfuls of the whites into the chocolate mixture, then fold the lightened chocolate and pecans into the whites. Pour the batter into the springform pan. Bake until the cake is firm, 35 to 40 minutes. Cool 5 minutes. Run a knife around the edge of the pan to loosen, then cool on a wire rack.

To serve, cut in wedges. Dust the cake with powdered sugar and serve with ice cream or one of the suggested sauces.

CHOCOLATE-PECAN ICE CREAM COOKIES

2½ dozen

One of my favorite desserts is a scoop of very rich ice cream served with these light meringue cookies.

⅛ teaspoon cream of tartar
2 egg whites
1½ cups confectioners sugar, sifted
1 tablespoon cornstarch
4 tablespoons unsweetened cocoa
  powder
1¾ cups chopped pecans or walnuts
  or sliced almonds, toasted
  (page 50)
1 teaspoon vanilla

Preheat the oven to 350° F. Beat the cream of tartar and egg whites in a clean mixing bowl until stiff peaks form. Gradually add the sugar and cornstarch and beat to shiny, stiff peaks. Break up any lumps in the cocoa and sprinkle it over the top, beating to incorporate. Fold in the nuts and vanilla and drop by the teaspoonful onto nonstick cookie sheets. Bake until crisp, about 25 minutes. Cool on wire racks.

COFFEE TOFFEE CRUNCH CAKE

1 ten-inch tube cake

A winner for entertaining...the bonus is that it *must* be prepared at least 24 hours or up to 36 hours in advance so the cream can soften the toffee and cake layers.

1 angel food tube cake, 1 day old

TOFFEE CRUNCH
1½ cups sugar
¼ cup espresso or strong coffee
¼ cup light corn syrup
1 tablespoon baking soda, free from lumps
Butter for the cooling surface

————

3 cups heavy cream
3 tablespoons confectioners sugar
2 teaspoons vanilla

————

Coffee ice cream
Liqueur mix (page 350)

Cut the cake horizontally into three layers. Set aside.

To prepare the toffee, heat the sugar, coffee, and corn syrup in a large saucepan or Dutch oven to a boil. Stir once to mix, then boil over medium-high heat until the sugar spins a fine thread, 290° F. Remove from heat and stir in baking soda. Do not stir the foam down. Quickly pour the mixture directly onto a lightly buttered surface and let cool 2 hours. Break the toffee into coarse, nut-size chunks.

Whip the cream in a deep, chilled bowl until thick and stiff. Add the sugar and vanilla and beat until very thick. Spread each cake layer with cream, then sprinkle with toffee. Frost the sides and top of the cake with whipped cream. Reserve enough toffee to garnish the cake later. Refrigerate for at least 24 hours or up to 36 hours.

About 2 hours before serving, evenly distribute the reserved toffee on the sides and top of the cake.

To serve, slice the cake and lay each slice on its side on a plate. Place a small scoop of ice cream on each slice and drizzle with the liqueur mix.

COOKIE TACOS

18 to 24 tacos; filling for 8 tacos

Cookie taco shells give a sugary-nut crunch to a creamy filling and fresh berries. All the preparations may be done in advance but the tacos do need to be assembled just before serving. The fruit sauce is light; a chocolate or caramel sauce would be spectacularly rich.

TACOS
1 cup granulated sugar
¾ cup skinned almonds or ¼ cup pine nuts and ½ cup skinned almonds

SAUCE
1 pint fresh raspberries or another seasonal berry
4 large mangos, peeled
¼ cup lime juice
⅓ cup granulated sugar

FILLING
1¾ cups heavy cream
½ cup ricotta cheese
¼ cup confectioners sugar

———

¼ cup grated white chocolate for garnish

Handle all berries gently. To store ripe, delicate berries, sort through and discard all spoiled ones. Store in a single layer, loosely covered. Place strawberries hull side down, and hull just prior to using. Mist blackberries, strawberries and blueberries just prior to using. Raspberries usually do not need to be cleaned; they should not be rinsed.

Preheat the oven to 375° F. Using a blender or food processor fitted with the metal blade, grind granulated sugar and nuts very fine. Add ¼ cup water and mix well. Let stand for 15 minutes. Line cookie sheets with parchment paper. Put the dough in a pastry bag without a tip and pipe small nickel-size rounds onto the parchment paper. Press each round flat to make a circle. Leave 4 inches between cookies to allow for spreading. Bake until evenly browned, about 10 to 13 minutes.

Remove from oven. Use scissors to cut in between cookies. Gently fold the edges of each to make a taco shape leaving an opening large enough to fill. Place between two boxes of kitchen wrap placed 2 inches apart until set, about 15 seconds. Work quickly to shape all the cookies. Gently peel away the paper and store the cookies in a sealed container. Cookies stay crisp for about 1 week.

Sort through the raspberries and separate on a plate to keep firm and undamaged. Cut 1 mango into a ¼-inch dice and set aside.

Cut away the flesh of the remaining mangos and put it into a blender jar. Squeeze all juices from around the large stone into the blender jar. Heat ½ cup water, lime juice and sugar to a boil in a small saucepan, then add to the blender jar. Blend on high speed until smooth. Add some cream if necessary to make a sauce the consistency of chilled heavy cream. Let cool.

Put 1½ cups cream in a chilled bowl and beat with an electric mixer until stiff. Fold in the ricotta cheese and confectioners sugar.

To assemble the tacos, first spread a thin layer of mango sauce on each plate. Carefully place several spoonfuls of the cream mixture in each taco and gently stand it on the sauce. Fill the taco with a combination of diced mango and fresh berries, allowing berries to spill over onto the plate. Garnish each taco with grated white chocolate.

Variations
- Substitute softened ice cream for the whipped cream and ricotta.
- Omit the mango sauce and use another dessert sauce such as caramel sauce (page 349), white-chocolate sauce (page 348) or a combination of white-chocolate and chocolate-fudge sauce (page 350).

COCONUT TOSTADOS

18 to 24 tostados; 8 servings

1 cup grated coconut, preferably
   unsweetened

TOSTADOS
1 cup sugar
¾ cup skinned almonds
⅓ cup grated coconut, preferably
   unsweetened

———————

3 cups mixed berries, such as
   raspberries, quartered strawberries,
   blueberries, blackberries
Custard sauce (page 348) or
   chocolate fudge sauce (page 350)

Preheat the oven to 350° F. Toast 1 cup coconut on a cookie sheet until golden brown, about 5 to 6 minutes.

Prepare tostados the same way as tacos in the recipe for cookie tacos (page 333), adding ⅓ cup untoasted coconut with ¼ cup water.

Raise the oven temperature to 375° F. Bake the cookies until evenly brown, 10 to 13 minutes. Cut them apart but do not fold. Peel off the paper.

To serve, spoon 3 mounds of berries on each cookie and top with toasted coconut. Serve with custard or chocolate sauce.

NOTE.   Serving size is 1 tostado per person. Save the rest of the cookies for another occasion.

Variation
- Place a scoop of ice cream or spread whipped cream on each cookie before topping with berries and toasted coconut.

BREAD PUDDING

8 servings

This unusual bread pudding has its roots in Mexican cooking but it reminds me of my grandmother's apple crisp—and she was from Minnesota!

¾ cup (1½ sticks) unsalted butter
16 slices (¼ inch thick) French bread, baguette size, crusts trimmed
1 cup toasted walnuts or pecans, coarsely chopped (page 50)
2 small apples, peeled and coarsely chopped (1½ to 2 cups)
½ cup seedless raisins or currants (optional)

SAUCE
1 cup light brown sugar, firmly packed
2 whole cloves
1 stick cinnamon
1 teaspoon anise seeds (optional)
2 to 4 tablespoons sherry or ruby port wine
2 egg yolks

TOPPING
2 egg whites
1 tablespoon granulated sugar
2 tablespoons light brown sugar
1 teaspoon ground cinnamon

Sweetened whipped cream or vanilla ice cream

Anise seeds are slightly sweet with a taste of licorice. Anise is often used to flavor breads, cookies and pastries, curries and cheese dishes. It can be used with fennel bulb and Mexican mint marigold to intensify the licorice perfume.

Heat 4 tablespoons butter in a medium skillet over medium heat. Add half the bread and sauté on both sides until golden. Add more butter and sauté the rest of the bread.

In the same skillet, melt remaining butter. Combine nuts, apples and raisins and add; sauté 2 minutes, until apples are tender.

Heat the sugar, 1½ cups water, cloves, cinnamon and anise seed, if using, to a boil in a medium saucepan; boil for 30 seconds. Remove and strain. Whisk in the wine and egg yolks and set aside.

Butter a 7 × 11-inch oval casserole dish. Arrange ⅓ of the bread in the casserole. Add half the apple-nut mixture, and about a third of the sauce. Repeat with half the remaining bread, the rest of the fruit, and half the remaining sauce. Cover with remaining bread and pour the rest of the sauce on top. Press the top layer down to be sure the bread is well soaked. The pudding can be refrigerated overnight at this point.

To bake, preheat the oven to 350° F. For the topping, beat the egg whites until stiff. Combine the sugar, brown sugar and cinnamon in a small bowl. Continue to beat the egg whites while gradually adding the sugar mixture. Spread on top of the pudding. Bake for 40 minutes. Turn the oven off and leave the pudding in the oven for 15 minutes, with the door ajar. Cut the pudding into squares and spoon excess juice on top of each serving. Serve warm with whipped cream or vanilla ice cream.

BANANA CREAM PUDDING

3½ cups

In this banana cream pudding the bananas are added just prior to serving so they are at their best. Spoon the pudding into a cookie taco or a pastry shell.

5 egg yolks
2½ cups whole milk or half and half
¾ cup sugar
2 tablespoons flour
1 tablespoon cornstarch
¼ teaspoon salt
3 tablespoons fresh orange juice
1 teaspoon vanilla extract
4 medium-ripe, unbruised bananas
8 cookie tacos (page 333)

Put the egg yolks, milk, sugar, flour, cornstarch, salt and orange juice in a medium saucepan and mix with an electric mixer until smooth. Cook over medium heat, stirring constantly, until the custard thickens. Stir in vanilla. Strain into a bowl and then put it into a larger bowl half filled with ice to cool quickly. Let stand until cool, stirring several times. Refrigerate until ready to serve.

Just before serving, slice the bananas and add to the custard. Spoon into the cookie shells.

Variations
- Add 1 mango, diced, with the bananas.
- Substitute 2 ripe cherimoyas, pureed, for the bananas.
- Substitute 2½ cups coconut milk for whole milk. To make coconut milk, heat 1 cup freshly grated coconut and 3 cups milk to a boil. Simmer for 20 minutes, then strain and cool. Refrigerate for up to 1 week.

CRÈME BRÛLÉE

8 servings

This is a favorite of mine and a recipe my friends constantly ask for. The custard is smooth and creamy and may be served in a variety of ways, including spooned over berries in a tortilla shell. A salamander or small propane blowtorch is the best tool to use to make the sugar coating crisp without heating the custard but you may also do it under the broiler.

2½ cups half and half
2 cups heavy cream
⅔ cup sugar
8 egg yolks
2 teaspoons vanilla
Pinch of salt
2 tablespoons liqueur (optional)
Sugar for the topping
Fresh fruit and berries

Most of the familiar berries (raspberries, blackberries, blueberries) were originally grown in the Northern and Midwestern states; however, many berries are now being developed to grow in warmer climates. All berries except strawberries must be picked ripe and used as soon as possible. Strawberries will continue to ripen for several days after being picked if kept in a cool place (not the refrigerator).

Preheat the oven to 325° F. Take a baking pan large enough to hold 8 eight-ounce custard cups and fill it half full of hot water to make a water bath.

Scald the half and half and cream. Beat the sugar and egg yolks in a mixing bowl with an electric mixer until thick and light yellow in color, 2 minutes. Add the hot half and half and cream, vanilla, salt and liqueur if using and mix well. Strain. Pour the custard into the custard cups and put them in the water bath. Bake 35 minutes. Remove from oven and let stand for 1 hour in the water bath. Custard will not appear completely set. Refrigerate for at least 8 hours or up to 2 days.

To make the sugar topping, sprinkle chilled custard lightly with sugar. Place cups in a baking pan and surround them with cracked ice. Preheat the broiler and place the pan under the broiling element with the door ajar until the tops are browned, about 2 minutes. Or light a small propane blowtorch and torch the sugar for a few seconds to caramelize it. You may also heat an old-fashioned salamander and apply it to the sugar. Refrigerate until ready to serve.

Serve with fresh seasonal fruits and berries.

Variation

- Deep-fry a flour tortilla until crisp. Hold the center down with tongs to make a cup shape. Dredge with granulated or confectioners sugar while still warm. Stand one tortilla cup on each plate and fill the center with seasonal berries. Spoon the custard on top. If you have a small propane blowtorch, sprinkle the custard with sugar and use the torch to caramelize it.

CHOCOLATE-CINNAMON FRITTERS

12 fritters

These are light, puffy and chocolatey with a hint of cinnamon. For chocolate fanatics, you may choose to serve these with white-chocolate ice cream (page 326) and chocolate-fudge sauce (page 350).

3 tablespoons butter
¼ cup granulated sugar
Pinch of salt
¼ teaspoon cinnamon
¼ cup unsweetened cocoa powder
1 cup all-purpose flour
2 teaspoons baking powder
1 teaspoon vanilla
3 eggs
1 quart peanut oil for frying
Confectioners sugar
Ice cream or white-chocolate sauce (page 348)
Fresh raspberries or strawberries for garnish

Heat 1 cup water, butter and granulated sugar in a saucepan to a boil. Add salt, cinnamon, cocoa and flour and stir vigorously over medium heat until the mixture masses around the spoon. Remove the pan from heat and put the dough in a food processor fitted with the metal blade. With the machine running, add the baking powder, vanilla and eggs, and process to incorporate and make a smooth dough. (You may also beat in the vanilla and the eggs by hand, one at a time.)

Heat the oil in a deep-fat-fryer or deep saucepan to 375° F. Form small rounds of dough 1 inch in diameter and drop 3 at a time in the hot oil. Fry 1½ to 2 minutes, then turn and fry on the other side for 1 to 1½ minutes. Spoon hot oil over the fritters as they fry to encourage puffing and even cooking. Remove and place on paper towels. Sprinkle with confectioners sugar while still warm. Continue until all are done.

To serve, arrange 3 fritters on each plate. Add 1 or 2 small scoops of ice cream and garnish with fresh berries. If using the sauce, spread some on the plate, place the fritters on top and garnish with fresh berries.

FRUIT FRITTERS

12 fritters

The combination of fruit fritters, ice cream and sauce makes a memorable dessert.

1½ tablespoons baking powder
1½ cups all-purpose flour
¾ cup riced potatoes, at room
    temperature
½ cup sugar
⅓ cup warm buttermilk
1 egg
1 teaspoon vanilla
1 cup diced fruit
¼ teaspoon ground cinnamon
    (optional)
½ cup toasted pecans, chopped, page
    50 (optional)

Peanut oil for frying
Confectioners sugar

Cut pineapple stores better than whole, unpeeled pineapple. Keep refrigerated, unsweetened, in a covered container. The peel may be boiled with water and sugar to make a syrup to use in ices or sangría or to sweeten lemonade.

Combine the baking powder and flour, stirring to distribute baking powder throughout the flour. Add potatoes, sugar, buttermilk, egg and vanilla and stir to make a soft puffy dough. Fold in fruit and the cinnamon and pecans, if using, and let the batter rest at room temperature for 15 minutes before frying.

Heat enough oil to deep-fry the fritters in a pan or deep-fat-fryer to 375° F. Drop batter by the tablespoonful into hot fat; do not crowd. Turn to brown all sides, for a total of 3 to 4 minutes. Drain on paper towels. Dust with confectioners sugar while still warm.

Serve fritters with ice cream and a sauce.

Serving Suggestions
- Papaya or mango fritters with vanilla ice cream and raspberry sauce (page 322)
- Peach fritters with almond ice cream and raspberry sauce (page 322)
- Pineapple fritters with coconut ice cream and raspberry sauce (page 322)
- Pear fritters with vanilla ice cream and chocolate fudge sauce (page 350)
- Banana fritters with caramel-pecan ice cream (page 327) and caramel sauce (page 349)

BRANDY-BAKED PEACHES

8 servings

A perfectly ripened peach at the height of the season needs few frills, but this easy recipe shows off the peach for an elegant dinner party. For an even more indulgent dessert, serve the peaches with caramel sauce (page 349) or caramel cream (page 350).

CREAM
¾ cup sour cream
¼ cup buttermilk
¾ cup heavy cream
2 tablespoons granulated sugar
1 teaspoon vanilla

———

8 large, unblemished peaches
Juice of 1 lemon
¼ cup cream sherry or peach brandy
2 tablespoons granulated sugar

———

5 tablespoons light brown sugar
Fresh raspberries for garnish

The best peaches are always those that have ripened on a tree nearby. Peaches are usually available from May to August. A seam on one side of the peach will tell you it's been tree-ripened; the process will continue at room temperature. Refrigerate ripe peaches for 3 to 5 days in a plastic bag.

Stir the sour cream, buttermilk, cream, sugar and vanilla together in a glass bowl and let stand at room temperature for 1 hour. Refrigerate for at least 2 hours before serving.

Bring 1½ quarts water to a boil in a medium saucepan. Dip each peach in the water for 30 seconds, then remove and peel with a sharp knife. Cut in half from top to bottom, remove the stone and enlarge the cavity with a spoon. Remove a thin slice from the bottom so each peach half will sit straight. As you finish preparing each peach half, drop it into a bowl of water and lemon juice to prevent browning. When all are done, transfer them to a shallow baking dish. Sprinkle with sherry and granulated sugar and refrigerate.

About 2 hours before you plan to serve the peaches, spoon some chilled cream into each cavity and freeze the peaches until the cream is frozen and the peaches partially frozen, from 1 to 2 hours. Do not allow the peaches to freeze completely.

Just before serving, preheat the broiler. Sprinkle the peaches with brown sugar and place them 4 to 6 inches from the broiling element. Broil until the sugar sizzles, about 2 minutes. Put two peach halves on each plate and surround with fresh raspberries.

MACADAMIA CHEESE WITH BERRY SAUCE

8 servings

Both the crumb mixture and the sauce may be prepared a day in advance. The key is to be sure the crumbs are soft and coarsely crumbled. Feel free to experiment with different sauces and fruit garnishes with a very mild, sweet cheese.

1 pound mild, young goat cheese

COATING
4 ounces macadamia nuts, lightly toasted and coarsely chopped
1 cup coarse cake crumbs (white, yellow or sponge cake), lightly toasted
2 tablespoons sugar
1 egg
4 to 5 tablespoons butter, melted

SAUCE
1 pint fresh raspberries or 1 package (12 ounces) frozen raspberries, thawed
¼ cup hot maple syrup

———

2 fresh mangos or papayas, sliced, for garnish
Seasonal berries for garnish

Preheat the oven to 375° F. Shape the cheese into 16 one-inch disks. Combine the nuts, cake crumbs and sugar on a shallow plate. Beat the egg and 2 tablespoons butter together in a small bowl. Dip each piece of goat cheese first in the egg, then place it in the crumbs and sprinkle crumbs on top to coat lightly. Do not press the crumbs into the cheese or cover it completely. Transfer the coated cheese to a cookie sheet and drizzle with remaining butter.

Put the raspberries and maple syrup in a blender jar and blend on high speed to puree. Pour fresh-raspberry puree into a small saucepan and cook over medium-high heat until the color deepens, about 5 minutes. (Frozen-raspberry puree does not need to be cooked.) Strain and refrigerate for up to 4 days.

Bake the cheese until warmed and lightly browned, 5 to 6 minutes. Spoon the sauce on the serving plate and place two pieces of cheese in the center. Garnish with fresh fruit slices or berries.

Variation
- Another fruit sauce may be substituted for the berry sauce. Try blackberry or peach or mango sauce (page 322).

SHORTCAKE BISCUITS

16 biscuits

Shortcake biscuits are best when served warm; if you have made them in advance, split them, butter lightly and sprinkle with confectioners sugar. Heat in a 500° F. oven until soft and warm, about 5 minutes.

1 cup all-purpose flour
1½ cups cake flour
1 tablespoon granulated sugar
1 tablespoon baking powder
1 teaspoon baking soda
1 teaspoon salt
7 tablespoons vegetable shortening, chilled
½ cup heavy cream
½ cup buttermilk

_____

Flour for dusting work surface
Confectioners sugar for dusting work surface
Butter for baking sheet
2 tablespoons melted butter
Granulated sugar for sprinkling

Preheat the oven to 450° F. Put the flours, sugar, baking powder, baking soda, salt and shortening in a mixing bowl. Blend with a pastry blender or two forks to make a coarse crumbly mixture. Add the cream and buttermilk and stir to make a moderately stiff but pliable dough. Turn the dough out onto a surface lightly dusted with equal amounts of flour and confectioners sugar. Pat the dough into an oval about ½ to ¾ inch thick. Press firmly to cut into rounds (do not twist the cutter) and put on a lightly buttered baking sheet. Brush the top of each biscuit with melted butter, then sprinkle with sugar. Bake until very light brown, 12 to 15 minutes.

WARM BERRY SHORTCAKE

8 servings

Try this when berries are at their peak. Gently warming the blueberries and blackberries with Cassis brings out their rich berry flavor.

Half the recipe for shortcake biscuits, above
4 tablespoons unsalted butter
1 pint blueberries
½ cup sugar
¼ cup Cassis
1 pint blackberries
½ pint raspberries
Sweetened whipped cream or vanilla ice cream

Prepare the biscuits and set aside.

Heat 2 tablespoons butter in a medium skillet over medium heat. Add the blueberries, sugar and Cassis and cook about 1 minute. Gently stir in the blackberries and remove from heat.

Split warm biscuits and put a half on each plate. Spoon the warm berries over each half, allowing berries to spill onto the plate. Put the other half of the biscuit on top. Heat the remaining sauce to a boil, then reduce the heat and whisk in the rest of the butter. Cool 5 minutes.

Put the raspberries around the shortcake. Spoon the warm sauce over each shortcake and place a dollop of sweetened whipped cream on top or a scoop of ice cream on the side.

BLACKBERRY COBBLER

8 servings

If you have eight-ounce custard cups, they can be used to make attractive individual servings. The crust in this recipe is a tender sugar-coated biscuit, very well suited to fresh berries. When berries are in season, I often combine three or four different kinds in one cobbler.

3 tablespoons butter
1½ pints fresh blackberries or 1 package (16 ounces) frozen blackberries
½ cup sugar
2 tablespoons blackberry brandy (optional)

BISCUIT TOPPING
1¼ cups all-purpose flour
½ cup sugar
1 teaspoon baking powder
½ teaspoon baking soda
¼ cup vegetable shortening
1 cup warm buttermilk
Sugar for sprinkling

———————

Sweetened whipped cream or caramel-pecan ice cream (page 327) or warm berry sauce (page 327)

Preheat the oven to 400° F. Heat the butter to melt in a small skillet. Divide among 8 eight-ounce custard cups or soufflé dishes. Combine the berries with sugar and brandy, if using, in a small bowl. Divide among the soufflé dishes.

Combine the flour, sugar, baking powder and baking soda in a mixing bowl. Add the shortening and mix until well blended. Stir in the buttermilk, just to combine. The dough should be soft and puffy. Drop the dough by the tablespoonful on top of the berries. Sprinkle generously with sugar and bake for 10 minutes. Reduce the heat to 350° F. and continue baking until the biscuits are lightly browned and a toothpick comes out clean, about 15 minutes. Remove from oven and let stand 5 minutes. Serve with whipped cream, ice cream or berry sauce.

TEXAS PEACH COBBLER

8 servings

The light, muffin-like batter bakes partly into the peaches. If you are using frozen peaches, do not thaw them; they will thaw as they cook.

12 fresh peaches, peeled, pitted and chopped, or 1 package (16 ounces) frozen peaches, partially thawed and chopped
1 tablespoon lemon juice
4 tablespoons sugar

MUFFIN TOPPING
3 tablespoons butter
3 tablespoons vegetable shortening
1 cup all-purpose flour
1 cup sugar
1½ teaspoons baking powder
1 teaspoon baking soda
¾ cup heavy cream
2 teaspoons apple cider vinegar
Pinch of salt
¾ cup chopped toasted pecans, page 50 (optional)

———

Vanilla ice cream or whipped cream

It is not necessary to peel fresh peaches before pureeing them for ices or preserves. Peeled, sliced peaches may be sprinkled with lemon juice and frozen.

Put the peaches in a shallow pan, add the lemon juice and 2 tablespoons sugar. Toss to combine and taste for sweetness. Add more sugar if necessary.

Preheat the oven to 400° F. Put the butter and shortening in a 9-inch-square pan and place in the oven to melt. Put the flour, sugar, baking powder and baking soda in a bowl and stir to distribute evenly. Add the cream, vinegar, salt and all but 2 tablespoons of the melted butter and shortening from the baking pan. Mix well.

Pour the peaches and all their juices into the baking pan and spoon the batter evenly on top. Sprinkle pecans on top. Bake 10 minutes. Reduce the heat to 375° F. and continue baking until the crust is cooked and browned, 20 to 30 minutes.

Serve warm with vanilla ice cream or whipped cream.

Variation
- Substitute fresh pineapple and Granny Smith apples for the peaches. Combine 3 cups chopped pineapple (1 small pineapple) and 1 cup chopped apple (1 large Granny Smith). Toss with lemon juice and 3 to 4 tablespoons sugar.

APPLE-BERRY COBBLER

8 servings

Some cobblers, like this one, have a cake-like crust, which is particularly well suited to the apple-berry filling. During the cranberry season I substitute a cup of whole-cranberry relish for the raspberries and sprinkle the top with cinnamon sugar

3 large Granny Smith or crisp Red
    Delicious apples or a combination
    of seasonal apples, peeled and
    cored
3 tablespoons unsalted butter
1 tablespoon lemon juice
⅓ cup granulated sugar
1 cup fresh raspberries or blueberries
    or 1½ cups chopped fresh
    strawberries

CAKE TOPPING
5 tablespoons unsalted butter
1 cup all-purpose flour
⅔ cup granulated sugar
½ teaspoon salt
1½ teaspoons baking powder
1 cup heavy cream
1 egg yolk

———

Confectioners sugar
Caramel cream (page 350) or
    almond-amaretto ice cream

Add delicious flavor to apple cakes, pies, cobblers and crisps by using several different varieties of apple instead of just one. Tart apples are wonderful with smoked chicken, duck or in poultry and ham salads. Use the fresh juice in meat sauces or in a butter sauce for tuna or salmon.

Cut the apples into bite-size pieces. Heat butter in a large skillet. Add the apples, lemon juice and sugar; cook over medium heat until softened, 5 to 6 minutes. Let cool for 5 minutes, then combine gently with the berries.

Preheat the oven to 350° F. Place butter in a 9-inch-square pan and put it in the oven to melt. Combine the flour, sugar, salt and baking powder in a mixing bowl. Add the cream and egg yolk and mix well. Remove the baking pan from the oven and pour all but enough butter to coat the pan into the batter. Spoon the apples and berries into the baking pan and pour the batter on top.

Place in the oven and check after 30 minutes: if the top is browning rapidly, cover the pan loosely with aluminum foil. Bake until a toothpick inserted near the middle comes out clean, confirming the cake is done, 35 to 40 minutes. Cool 30 minutes, then dust with confectioners sugar.

Serve warm with caramel cream or almond-amaretto ice cream.

BERRY CRUNCH

6 servings

When you spoon this berry crunch onto the plate, the natural juices make a mouth-watering sauce with the nutty crisp topping. You can use any combination of berries; I particularly like blackberries and raspberries together.

4 cups blackberries and raspberries, mixed, or a combination of blueberries, strawberries, blackberries and raspberries or all blueberries

½ cup granulated sugar

1 tablespoon orange juice or 2 tablespoons Cassis

CRISP NUT TOPPING
¾ cup oatmeal
⅔ cup all-purpose flour
½ cup light brown sugar, firmly packed
10 tablespoons unsalted butter, at room temperature
1 cup chopped pecans
2 tablespoons cinnamon sugar (optional)

———

Vanilla-bean ice cream

Stem and rinse the berries and combine them in an 8-inch-square baking dish. Sprinkle them with sugar and toss with orange juice or Cassis.

Preheat the oven to 400° F. Put the oatmeal, flour, brown sugar, butter and pecans in a mixing bowl. Mix with your hands to make a coarse, crumbly texture. Spread evenly over the berries, then sprinkle cinnamon sugar, if using, over the top. Bake for 15 minutes, then reduce the heat to 350° F. and bake an additional 15 to 20 minutes or until the topping is cooked. Serve warm with ice cream.

BLACKBERRY BUCKLE

8 servings

In this version of a cobbler, the berries are nestled between a cake bottom and a crunchy crust. I like it best served warm with vanilla ice cream.

1 quart fresh blackberries, rinsed
½ cup granulated sugar
1 tablespoon melted butter

CAKE BASE
1 cup all-purpose flour
2 teaspoons baking powder
½ teaspoon salt
¼ cup vegetable shortening
½ cup sugar
⅓ cup buttermilk
1 egg

CRISP TOPPING
½ cup light brown sugar, firmly packed
½ cup all-purpose flour
½ teaspoon cinnamon
¼ cup (½ stick) unsalted butter, at room temperature
½ cup chopped toasted pecans, page 50 (optional)

———

Vanilla ice cream

Put the berries in a mixing bowl and gently mix in as much sugar as needed to sweeten the berries.

Preheat the oven to 375° F. Generously butter a 9-inch-square pan. Combine the flour, baking powder, salt, shortening and sugar in a mixing bowl and mix well. Heat the buttermilk in a small skillet to warm, then stir into the dry ingredients. Stir in the egg. Spread the batter evenly in the pan. Spread the berries on top.

Combine brown sugar, flour, cinnamon, butter and pecans if using. Rub together to make a crumbly texture and sprinkle on top of the berries. Bake until the top is crisp and browned and the cake tests done, about 45 to 55 minutes. Serve warm with vanilla ice cream.

CUSTARD SAUCE

4 cups

This is a rich custard sauce that is perfectly smooth and foolproof. Cooling the custard over ice is a vital step that ensures success. The sauce is thick enough to hold a ribbon of fruit puree for decoration. If you prefer a thinner sauce, omit the cornstarch.

6 egg yolks
2 teaspoons cornstarch
2 cups heavy cream
½ cup sugar
2 cups half and half
2 teaspoons vanilla extract

Press a single impatiens blossom onto a custard sauce or around a dessert for a simple, attractive garnish.

Combine the egg yolks with cornstarch, cream and sugar in a mixing bowl. Heat the half and half to a boil in a 3-quart sauce-pan. Reduce heat to low and cook 5 minutes. Remove from heat.

Whisk ½ cup of the hot half and half into the egg yolks, then slowly stir the mixture into the remaining hot half and half. Cook over medium-low heat, stirring constantly, until the custard is thickened and coats a spoon, about 8 minutes. Strain the custard into a bowl. Stir in the vanilla. Fill a larger bowl with cracked ice and set the custard bowl in it. Let cool 1 hour, stirring several times.

Variations

- Kahlúa custard sauce. Stir 1 tablespoon Kahlúa into finished sauce and cook an additional 2 minutes.
- Caramel custard sauce. Reduce the amount of sugar to ¼ cup. Whisk ¼ cup caramel sauce (page 349) into the finished custard sauce. Use on cobblers and bread pudding (page 335).
- White-chocolate custard sauce. Melt 4 ounces white chocolate with ½ cup of the cream in a double boiler. Whisk this chocolate cream into the custard mixture while it is cooking.
- White-chocolate custard sauce with mint. Add 6 sprigs fresh mint to the half and half. When it is warm, stir in 5 ounces white chocolate. Continue as directed, removing mint when straining the custard.

CHERIMOYA CUSTARD SAUCE

2½ cups

Cherimoyas have a tropical-fruit flavor that is a perfect foil for chocolate. This sauce is delicious with a chocolate soufflé or chocolate-pecan cake (page 331). It is important to use uncooked fresh puree for the best flavor.

Half the recipe for custard sauce
2 ripe cherimoyas, 1 pound each

Prepare the custard sauce as described above and cool thoroughly.

Cut the cherimoyas in half and remove as many seeds as possible. Scoop out the flesh, discarding all seeds, and put it in a blender jar. Blend on high speed, until smooth. If the pulp is not smooth, strain it.

When the custard is completely cool, whisk in the cherimoya puree.

WARM BERRY SAUCE

4 cups

The only thing better than fresh-picked berries is a warm berry and Cassis sauce made from several kinds of berries. Use it on pancakes, waffles, ice cream, angel food cake or your favorite cobbler or shortcake.

2 tablespoons unsalted butter
½ cup sugar
¼ cup Cassis or blackberry brandy
1 pint fresh blueberries, rinsed
1 pint fresh strawberries, hulled, rinsed and cut in half
½ pint fresh blackberries
½ pint fresh raspberries

Melt the butter in a large skillet. Add the sugar and Cassis and cook over medium heat until the sugar is dissolved, about 1 to 2 minutes. Add the blueberries and cook until the berries are softened, about 2 minutes. Stir in the strawberries, blackberries and raspberries. Leave the berries in the skillet just until they are warm, gently tossing to combine and heat evenly. Serve immediately.

CARAMEL SAUCE

2 cups

The sweetness of caramel is very pleasant after a meal that has spicy flavors. The traditional Mexican *cajeta* caramel sauce is made by cooking milk and sugar for hours, until it reduces to a thick caramel, much the consistency of melted caramel candies. This version is quicker to prepare but just as delicious.

1 cup sugar
½ cup water
3 cups heavy cream
¼ teaspoon baking soda
4 tablespoons butter (optional)
1½ teaspoons vanilla

Place the sugar in a 5-quart saucepan over medium-high heat. Cook, watching carefully, until it begins to melt and turn golden. Stir if necessary if the sugar colors unevenly. When nearly all the sugar is a light golden color (before it turns dark amber), remove the pan from the heat. Add water and stir. The sugar will harden; however, it will melt again as it cooks. Return to medium heat, and add cream and baking soda. The mixture will foam alarmingly at first but it settles down quickly. Simmer over medium heat, stirring occasionally, for 30 to 35 minutes until the sauce is moderately thick with a rich color. Whisk in the butter if using and cook 5 more minutes, then stir in vanilla. Cool, stirring once or twice. Refrigerate until ready to use.

NOTE.   The sauce sometimes becomes quite firm when refrigerated. If so, use a double boiler to warm before serving and thin with cream if necessary.

CARAMEL CREAM

2½ cups

This sauce is especially good on warm cobblers or with poached pears or baked apples.

3 cups heavy cream
½ cup light brown sugar, firmly
   packed
¼ cup unsalted butter
1 teaspoon vanilla

Heat cream, brown sugar and butter in a medium saucepan to a boil. Reduce the heat and simmer, stirring occasionally, until mixture thickens, about 8 minutes. Remove from heat and stir in vanilla. Fill a large bowl with ice. Put the saucepan on the ice to cool for 1 hour. If the sauce is not smooth, put it in the blender on high speed for a few seconds. Refrigerate until ready to serve.

LIQUEUR MIX

1¾ cups

Use this mix to flavor coffee drinks or pour it over ice cream. It is also good on whipped cream cakes.

¼ cup plus 2 tablespoons Kahlúa
⅓ cup Triple Sec
2 tablespoons Amaretto
¾ cup plus 2 tablespoons Crème de
   Cacao

Combine the liqueurs and pour into a decanter. Store at room temperature until ready to use.

CHOCOLATE FUDGE SAUCE

2 cups

1 cup heavy cream
¼ cup (½ stick) unsalted butter
3 tablespoons light corn syrup
½ cup sugar
8 ounces imported bittersweet or
   semisweet chocolate, broken into
   small pieces
2 ounces unsweetened chocolate,
   broken into small pieces
2 teaspoons vanilla

Heat the cream, ½ cup water, butter, corn syrup and sugar to a boil in a small saucepan. Stir in the chocolate, then reduce the heat and cook, stirring constantly, until the chocolate is melted and the sauce is smooth and satiny. Stir in the vanilla. Serve immediately or store in the refrigerator. The sauce will become quite firm then and will need to be warmed in a double boiler before serving.

DOUBLE CHOCOLATE JUMBLES

3 to 4 dozen

Be prepared to give this recipe to all your friends. The candy has a refreshing taste, not too sweet, and is unbelievably simple to prepare.

1¼ pounds white chocolate, cut into chunks
1 package (6 ounces) semisweet chocolate morsels
2 cups coarsely crushed peppermint candy
Corn-oil cooking spray

Preheat the oven to 275° F. Put the white chocolate in an ovenproof bowl and heat until melted, about 15 minutes. Stir until smooth. Fold in the chocolate morsels and peppermint candy. Spray a cookie sheet lightly with corn-oil cooking spray and pour the candy on it. Carefully spread to about ½ inch thick. If the chocolate is not streaked, use a knife to make a marble effect. Cool until set, about 2½ to 3 hours, then cut into irregular chunks. Store refrigerated in a sealed container.

MAPLE-GLAZED PECANS

1 pound

You can serve these on a fruit and cheese plate, for snacks or with after-dinner coffee. They make a wonderful Christmas gift.

1 pound pecan halves
½ cup maple syrup
1½ tablespoons heavy cream
1½ tablespoons Grand Marnier
¼ teaspoon salt
¼ teaspoon cinnamon

Preheat the oven to 350° F. Put the pecans on a cookie sheet and bake for 12 to 15 minutes. Heat the maple syrup, cream and Grand Marnier in a large skillet to a boil. Boil for 2 minutes, then add salt, cinnamon and pecans. Stir constantly until pecans are completely coated with sauce. Put pecans back on the cookie sheet and bake for 10 minutes. Remove from the oven and cool. Break apart if necessary. Store in an airtight container.

ENTERTAINING AND MENUS

Having friends to your home for a special dinner is one of the most personal ways to let them know they are important to you. Anyone who cooks often for family and friends is aware of the extreme differences in personal food preferences. After years of teaching, cooking and consulting, I am convinced that the stress of menu planning and cooking does not come from the complexity of the dishes but from choosing ones that everyone will like. Once this feat is accomplished, the rest is easy.

The key is to keep the meal simple. This does not mean the food cannot be dazzling; it does mean doing some advance planning and organization and setting priorities. Think ahead when you organize; play through the evening in your mind so all will go smoothly. Remind yourself to put the emphasis on the people and the food. Sparkling sinks and polished floors will not make up for a frazzled, preoccupied or distracted hostess. Appealing food, served in an inviting, comfortable atmosphere with a relaxed host and hostess—this is what entertaining is all about. A few well placed plants, dim lights, fresh flowers and soft music as well as appealing, delicious food are what make for a memorable evening.

It is very difficult to make poor food from top-notch ingredients. When planning your menu, choose vegetables and fruits that are in season so that you need do little but enhance their natural fresh taste. Once you have decided on the mood (casual or formal), and the setting (indoors or outdoors), choose the main course and then build from there. If what you make best is meatloaf and mashed potatoes, serve that and give the meal a special touch with homemade muffins and preserves or garden-fresh vegetables in a colorful presentation.

Prepare only one thing that takes a lot of effort and time. If you plan to barbecue or spit-roast, which takes several hours, time the food so it is ready to come off the grill 15 to 20 minutes after your guests arrive. (All roasts benefit from a rest of 20 to 30 minutes before being sliced and served, which gives you time to put the rest of the meal together.) Serve cocktails outside, then start with a cold soup made earlier in the day or a salad for which everything was previously rinsed and chilled so that it is ready to toss. Fill a large bowl with liqueur-infused strawberries and blackberries and place it prominently in the room or fill several bowls to the brim with seasonal berries. Turn your energy to hot cornbread or muffins and a couple of seasonal vegetables. Your finale could be those berries topped with sweetened whipped cream and served with espresso-hazelnut brownies and a special coffee. Simple—but unforgettable!

If you decide on a more complicated main course, such as one that requires a relish or a butter sauce or both, choose a simple salad that can be put on plates in advance, like my Southwest fruit salad, and rely on a good bakery for fresh bread or rolls. Choose a dessert that can be made one or two days ahead. Whether the atmosphere is casual or rather formal, plan to invite your guests to help. Someone could tend to the wine; someone else might enjoy tossing the salad. When the mood is informal and the party includes friends, let it begin in the kitchen where there are plenty of opportunities for enthusiastic helpers to lend a hand.

Whatever the menu and whatever the mood, advance preparation is essential. If you use a lot of roasted peppers or chilies, always have some frozen and ready to use. Homemade stocks, pesto sauces, salad dressings and dessert sauces can all be made well in advance; many can be frozen. Vegetables can be blanched several hours ahead of time and quickly reheated. Ingredients for last-minute preparations can be cut or sliced, measured and grouped for quick assembly. The more organized you are, the simpler it is.

A well organized kitchen can save hours of time and frustration in menu planning and preparation. Among the ways to make life easier for yourself are the following:

- Invest in time-saving, high-quality kitchen equipment.
- Organize the kitchen to group ingredients and equipment by use: baking ingredients should be in one area; salad dressing ingredients in another.
- Group spices and all ingredients used for hot foods near the range and oven (keep the spices in a cool, dark place).
- For things you make often, for example homemade cornbread, measure out double the ingredients when you make a batch and you will be ahead of the game next time.
- Maintain a well stocked pantry of staples and hard-to-find foods like sundried tomatoes, grainy mustards, chutneys and a variety of nuts and spices. These items combined with seasonal foods often make a menu unique and manageable.

Find good suppliers, like a bakery that carries bread you like or will bake it to order and a pasta shop. Such little shops often have a wide variety of fresh pasta in bright colors and interesting flavors. One of the easiest parties to put together in a hurry is based on pasta: simply arrange three or four varieties of pasta, several sauces, some blanched vegetables and an assortment of fish or meat on a buffet table and let your guests create their own pasta dishes.

Once the menu is planned, work on creating the mood for your party. The room and table settings you select should be in harmony with the food you serve. A round table or several small tables create a climate for intimacy and encourage conversation; large ones lend a more serious, formal touch. Flowers, perhaps from your own garden, seem to make people feel more comfortable. Remember that it is always easier to serve formal food in informal surroundings than vice versa. Table linens, plates and cutlery in contemporary designs create a sophisticated atmosphere that puts people in the mood to risk new taste experiences. A country-cottage table with Laura Ashley linens creates a friendly atmosphere that suits home-baked foods, homemade jam, relishes and cobblers hot from the oven topped with a melting scoop of homemade ice cream. The classic look of silver candlesticks, bone china and heavy silverware is the perfect backdrop for grilled foods with an American accent, thick grilled lamb chops on a bed of greens, for example, with a creamy hot-water cornbread.

The choice of a room can also add to the mood. Intimate dinners at small tables in a cozy den or by the fireplace are wonderful for cold winter evenings. Informal dinners can begin with appetizers in the kitchen. A seated formal dinner can be followed by dessert and coffee in a more relaxed setting where people feel like lingering.

Plate Arrangement

How you put the food on a plate or serving platter is the final step of your cooking efforts. Whether you labored all day or simply picked something up on the way home, a little attention to detail can make an enormous difference. Plate arrangement should never take priority over the food: an overdecorated, sculptured look misses the vital essence of the foods of the Southwest. American regional food is characterized by the cornucopia look, which shows food at its peak or just-cooked best. Many dishes, like barbecued meats, whole birds or thick chops, have an inherently rustic nature, often countered by crisp relishes or spicy ingredients tamed into delicate sauces. Tamales, often considered peasant food, can be remarkably attractive, even elegant in their fringed husks. Slices of barbecued brisket, arranged on lightly dressed greens drizzled with a sauce of natural juices and served with wedges of hot polenta-like cornbread and a colorful tomato relish, look as good as they taste. Veal or lamb chops, arranged with the bone toward the center of the plate around a mound of salt-roasted potatoes and red, yellow and green roasted bell peppers, become visually enticing.

Intense, clear flavors, often many on the same plate, characterize the food of the Southwest. Chilies are prized and not just for their heat: they enhance the flavor of the foods they accent. The food is lively and colorful, best displayed on plain large plates. Appetizers should be served on luncheon- or dinner-size plates, especially when they are accompanied by one or more relishes. Simple grilled fish or tender morsels of duck on a bed of multicolored greens with crisp vegetables and slices of mango or avocado has the casual yet elegant look that characterizes the foods of the Southwest.

Garnishes should always be an edible part of the meal or at least be related to the other ingredients. A relish with tomatillo in it might be spooned into the papery husk. Fresh herbs, edible flowers or chive blossoms or fresh crisp greens are straightforward but decorative as well. A platter of grilled chicken atop some watercress or a thick beef tenderloin in its natural juices, surrounded by a fresh tomato and chili relish, this is the kind of presentation that puts the food at the center of attention. Avoid dull monochromatic plates of brown meat, white rice and yellow vegetables. Use relishes not only as a substitute for sauce but to add color and texture to the plate.

A buffet dinner is an easy way to entertain but you risk seeing your creations mixed and mounded in ways you might never have imagined. You might prefer to serve your guests yourself. Sometimes it is easier to serve three courses than to try to put everything out at the same time. The mood also benefits when there is a relaxed and gracious setting.

Even when the meal is simple, try to create the illusion of luxurious abundance. For example, you could choose a menu consisting of green gazpacho with corn muffins, followed by salmon fillet served on apple-mint butter sauce, with fresh peas. Rather than spooning the peas in a little pile, you could scatter them over the salmon and around the plate for a free, generous look with great appeal. Dessert could be fresh berries with ice cream and Cassis, served at the table. Pile the berries in bowls, scoop and freeze ice cream balls in advance and place them in a silver bowl. Serve the Cassis in small individual pitchers. It will make your guests feel much more pampered than if they think everything has been counted and measured out. That is the secret of Southwestern hospitality.

"Keep it simple. I like well-tailored food . . . and I like to see the plate."—James Beard

Menus for Entertaining

Brunch

Fresh fruit (melons, mango and berries)
Poached eggs on Gulf shrimp hash
Blue-cornmeal muffins

An off-dry white wine with good fruit flavor, such as Chenin Blanc

———

Tequila grapefruit and strawberries or raspberries
Roast-garlic spoonbread
Pepper bacon
Fresh seasonal vegetable (asparagus, broccoli, green beans or thinly sliced zucchini)

Spicy Gewurztraminer

———

Crabcakes with poached eggs and Veracruz butter sauce or cilantro hollandaise
Sliced oranges and strawberries
Fruit fritters

White wine sangría or a Chenin Blanc or Sauvignon Blanc wine

———

Papaya filled with raspberries
Grits soufflé with red roast bell pepper sauce or roasted pepper catsup
Zucchini and basil salad

Fruity Sauvignon Blanc

———

Fresh corn crêpes filled with mild cheeses, and three tomato salsa or a tomato relish
Sausage patties
Fresh fruit

A dry Chenin Blanc or medium-dry White Zinfandel wine

———

Vegetable and pasta Soufflé
Buttermilk buscuits
Poached eggs with a tomato relish
Crème brûlée with fresh berries

A medium to full-bodied Chardonnay wine

Scrambled eggs with chilies, cilantro and tortilla strips
Black beans
Tomato relish (*pico de gallo*)
Peppered popovers
Pastries and fresh fruit

Sparkling wine

Green gazpacho
Scallops in hollandaise
Lemon-orange muffins

Johannisberg Riesling wine

Crabmeat strata
Salad of mixed greens
Cinnamon rolls

Fruity, crisp Gewurztraminer

Panfried eggplant with poached eggs
Sausages
Hot-water cornbread gratinéed with cheese and herbs

Light Beaujolais or Gamay

Luncheons

Fresh melons
Shrimp tamales with corn sauce

A light Chardonnay

Fresh corncakes with smoked turkey
Cheese and pepper sauce
Apple pecan salad

Chardonnay

Fire shrimp with blue and yellow cornmeal muffins in tequila-orange butter sauce
Fresh corn niblets
Fruit salad
White chocolate ice cream and fresh raspberries

Crisp, medium-bodied Chardonnay

———

Roasted-red-pepper soup with corn
Chicken and wild rice salad
Cornsticks
Vanilla ice cream with warm berry sauce

Full- or medium-bodied Sauvignon Blanc

———

Chilled cucumber–Granny Smith apple soup with green gazpacho
Santa Fe tortillas with chili sauce and Gulf crabmeat
Apple spice cake with caramel sauce

Fruity Gamay wine

———

Chilled salmon with three tomato salsa
Cheese and onion *quesadillas* or lemon-orange muffins
Lime chess pie

Beaujolais or light Pinot Noir

———

Grilled chicken wings with avocado relish and tomato relish (*pico de gallo*)
Yellow and blue cornmeal muffins
Coconut tostados with fresh fruit

Fruity Sauvignon Blanc

———

Warm turkey salad
Jam-bran muffins and toasted-pecan muffins
Crème brûlée with maple-glazed pecans

Crisp, full-bodied Chardonnay

Late Sunday Winter Lunch or Informal Dinner

Chili con carne with black beans and accompaniments
Roast-garlic spoonbread or hot-water cornbread
Green salad with buttermilk ranch dressing
Espresso-hazelnut brownies with vanilla ice cream

Regional beers or a full-bodied, spicy Zinfandel

————

Tortilla pizzas
Black beans with a tomato relish
Texas tapas with red roasted-pepper catsup
Assorted ices and cookies

Full-bodied Chardonnay or Gamay Beaujolais

Informal Dinner

Grilled scallions with red roasted-pepper catsup and *quesadillas*
Rosemary-smoked chicken with grilled or panfried eggplant and a tomato relish
Cheese platter
French bread or rolls
Banana cream pudding in cookie shells

A crisp, medium-bodied Semillon-Sauvignon Blanc blend

Formal Dinner

Peppery, balanced Zinfandel wine
Watercress salad with cheese, grapes and toasted walnuts
Grilled or broiled veal chop with spinach flan and grilled-tomato relish
Cookie tacos with fresh berries and caramel sauce

Nicely balanced Merlot

————

Warm quail salad
Roast tenderloin with triple-mustard sauce or veal in lime and serrano chili butter sauce and creamy
scalloped potatoes
Fresh garden vegetables
White-chocolate custard sauce with three berries and fresh mint

Medium-bodied Pinot Noir

Mushroom pasta with lemon basil and sorrel garnish
Halibut with saffron sauce and tomato salsa
Sugar Snap peas
Mixed green salad with champagne grapes, roasted pecans and balsamic vinaigrette
Chocolate-pecan cake with white-chocolate and mint custard sauce and fresh berries

Crisp, full-bodied Sauvignon (Fumé) Blanc

———

Crabcakes with triple-mustard sauce
Panfried pepper steaks with three-tomato salsa
Mixed green salad with mango and toasted pecans
Apple-berry cobbler

With the crabcakes, a full-bodied Chardonnay; with the steaks a full-bodied Cabernet Sauvignon

Winter Dinner

Corn-and-potato chowder
Chilies with duck *picadillo* filling and crème fraîche
Mixed green salad
Bread pudding

Gamay Beaujolais or Merlot

Outdoor Grill Dinner

Grilled *quesadillas*
Grilled salmon with three-tomato salsa and corn-and-pepper flans
Ice cream with blackberry buckle

Rich, full-bodied Chardonnay

Hill Country Barbecue

Grilled chicken wings with buttermilk ranch dressing
Texas barbecued brisket
Creamy cole slaw
Corn muffins with cheese and chilies
Banana-walnut ice cream with caramel sauce

White Zinfandel, Gamay Beaujolais, or beer

Border Grill

Green gazpacho
Chicken and beef *fajitas* with avocado relish and three tomato salsa
Texas peach cobbler with Texas plum and cinnamon ice

Burgundy or a light Pinot Noir

———

Cream of cilantro soup with scallops
Rosemary-smoked chicken with roasted peppers or chicken with pomegranates
Coffee toffee crunch cake

Full-bodied, crisp Sauvignon Blanc

———

Double endive and radicchio salad with blue cheese
Grilled veal chop with papaya-and-red-pepper relish
Hot-water cornbread
Coffee ice cream with chocolate shavings and white-chocolate custard sauce

Rich, well-balanced Cabernet Sauvignon or a light, crisp Chardonnay

Suggested Combinations

The recipes in this book provide a foundation for mixing and matching and creating many new combinations. A number of suggestions follow: they are intended only as a guide. Recipes in the book are marked with an asterisk (*).

Foil-grilled red snapper with corn sauce.*

Boneless chicken breast, stuffed with an herb pesto and ricotta and served with a tomato relish or with corn sauce.*

Foil-grilled fillet of sole, rolled and stuffed with crab meat, and tomato-and-green chili relish* or three-tomato salsa* and served in a cilantro butter sauce.

Mixed grill of salmon fillets and swordfish with tomatillo relish,* grilled-corn-and-pepper relish* or tomato relish (*pico de gallo*).*

Mixed grill of game sausage, beef or game steaks and small double lamb chops with black beans and roast-garlic spoonbread.*

Red-bell-pepper pasta with slices of chicken, turkey or pheasant, with toasted walnuts and slivered spinach in a goat-cheese sauce.*

Smoked salmon, chilled and served with pistachio-flavored vinaigrette* and a relish of apple, jícama, zucchini, and fresh mint.

Panfried catfish* with a tomato relish, served with a smoked-pepper butter sauce.

Pork shoulder marinated in an ancho-chili marinade, grilled, sliced and served with apple pecan salad and cornsticks.

Brisket in its natural juices with barbecue sauce,* hot-water cornbread* and creamy cole slaw.*

Grilled warm tuna salad on a bed of greens, diced mango, and jícama with poblano-chili dressing.*

Warm scallop salad with tangerine vinaigrette,* served with greens and tangerine sections.

Appetizer plate of relish accompaniments and warm goat cheese served with roast-garlic spoonbread* or blue-cornmeal muffins.*

Ancho-chili pasta with smoked game birds or chicken, goat-cheese sauce,* fresh cilantro and tomatillo relish.*

Grilled salmon* with corn-and-pepper flan* and three-tomato salsa.*

Red snapper poached in yellow tomato relish* and served with Sugar Snap peas.

Wild-rice crêpes* stuffed with seafood and pimientos and served with cheese-and-pepper sauce.*

Fresh corn crêpes* or Chili crêpes* with Robert's game ragout* and a tomato relish.*

Ragout of seafood in Veracruz butter sauce* served on hot-water cornbread* with pepper-Jack cheese baked in the center.

Fresh corn crêpes* stuffed with soft cheeses and served with ancho-chili sauce with corn and tomatillos.*

Poached or steamed lobster with blue-corn tamales and corn sauce.*

Rosemary-smoked chicken* served on a bed of fresh rosemary sprigs with roasted red, yellow, and green bell peppers and herb-roasted potatoes.*

Grilled butterflied leg of lamb* with tomato-mint chutney* and grilled eggplant and zucchini or Dean's tobacco onions.*

Grilled pork roast with barbecue rub,* sliced and served with creamy cole slaw* and black beans.

Mixed shellfish, steam-grilled in foil with a basil or herb pesto, served on pasta in cream sauce with a tomato relish.*

Fresh corn crêpes* layered on a large plate with grilled pork loin in a barbecue sauce and surrounded with a combination of sautéed corn niblets, diced zucchini and red bell peppers and minced serrano chilies.

Panfried pepper steaks* with fire fries.*

Grilled or panfried veal chop* with garlic flan and grilled eggplant.*

An appetizer of grilled onions with a tomato relish.*

Fried sage leaves,* grilled eggplant and squash sections, with buttermilk ranch dressing* or roasted-pepper catsup.*

Crisp corn tostado with guacamole, fire shrimp,* and three-tomato salsa.*

A pepper jelly* and cream cheese with toasted croutons, mango slices, and game sausages.

Chicken-fried veal or chicken medallions with riccotta-ranch compote* and fresh watercress with diced yellow and red tomatoes.

Blue-cornmeal muffins* with lobster and crab with a butter sauce of smoked pepper or tomatoes and herbs.

Roast-garlic spoonbread* with wild-game picadillo, crème fraîche* and fresh raspberries.

Grilled chicken or fish basted with herb pesto and served with yellow roast-bell-pepper Sauce* and a tomato relish.*

MAIL ORDER SOURCES

GAME	Texas Wild Game Cooperative P.O. Box 530 Ingram, Texas 78025
MOZZARELLA CHEESE GOAT CHEESE SOUTHWEST CHEESES	Mozzarella Company 2944 Elm Street Dallas, Texas 75226
CAVIAR (BELUGA)	California Sunshine Foods, Inc. 144 King Street San Francisco, California 94107
BLUE CORNMEAL	Blue Heaven (Blue Corn Connection) 8812 4th Street N.W. Alameda, New Mexico 87114
	Josie's Best Tortilla Factory 1130 Agua Fria Street P.O. Box 5525 Santa Fe, New Mexico 87501
CHILI POWDERS ANNATTO SEEDS CHILI PODS	Casados Farms Box 1269 San Juan Pueblo, New Mexico 87566
	Albuquerque Traders P.O. Box 10170 Albuquerque, New Mexico 87114
NUTS	Midwestern Pecan Co. Business Highway 71 North Nevada, Missouri 64772

WILD RICE	Dick Stelzner
	Stelzner Vineyards
	P.O. Box C
	Youngville, California 94569

Guinness McFadden
McFadden Farm
Potter Valley, California 94569

Landreth Farms
Box 59
Black Duck, Minnesota 56630

SPECIALTY PRODUCE

Carol Bowman-Williams
Frieda's Finest Produce Specialties
P.O. Box 58488
Los Angeles, California 90058

Apple Source
Tom Vorbeck
Route 1
Chapin, Illinois 62628

DRIED WILD MUSHROOMS

Sally Brown
c/o Madame Mushroom
3420 West Malaga Road
Malaga, Washington 98828

William Clark
Woodland Pantry
P.O. Box 373
River Forest, Illinois 60305

FRESH FOIE GRAS
POUSSIN

W. G. White, Inc.
333 Henry Street
Stamford, Connecticut 06902

Wild Game, Inc.
1941 West Division
Chicago, Illinois 60622

Sey-Co Products Co.
7651 Densmore Avenue
Van Nuys, California 91406

D'Artagnan, Inc.
399 St. Paul Avenue
Jersey City, New Jersey 07306

FRESH DUCK LIVER	Commonwealth Enterprises Ltd. Mongaup Valley, New York 12762
SUNDRIED TOMATOES	The Chef's Catalog P.O. Box 1614 Northbrook, Illinois 60065
OLD-FASHIONED PORK SAUSAGE	Early's Honey Stand P.O. Box K Spring Hill, Tennessee 37174
VIDALIA SWEET ONIONS	Southern Cross Farms P.O. Box 627 Vidalia, Georgia 30474

INDEX